Proverbs, Ecclesiastes, and the Song of Songs

Westminster Bible Companion

Series Editors

Patrick D. Miller
David L. Bartlett

Proverbs, Ecclesiastes, and the Song of Songs

ELLEN F. DAVIS

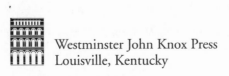

Westminster John Knox Press
Louisville, Kentucky

Except where noted, the scripture quotations contained herein are from the New Revised Standard Version of the Bible, copyright © 1989 by the Division of Christian Education of the National Council of the Churches of Christ in the U.S.A., and are used by permission.

Acknowledgments will be found on page viii.

Book design by Publishers' WorkGroup
Cover design by Drew Stevens

First edition

Published by Westminster John Knox Press
Louisville, Kentucky

This book is printed on acid-free paper that meets the American National Standards Institute Z39.48 standard. ∞

PRINTED IN THE UNITED STATES OF AMERICA

02 03 04 05 06 07 08 09 — 10 9 8 7 6 5 4 3 2

Library of Congress Cataloging-in-Publication Data

A catalog record for this book is available from the Library of Congress.

ISBN 0-664-25522-1

Contents

Acknowledgments

Grateful acknowledgment is made to the following for permission to reprint copyrighted materials.

Harcourt, Brace & Co., and Faber & Faber Limited, from T. S. Eliot, "Burnt Norton" and "East Coker," in *Four Quartets*, from *Collected Poems 1909–1962* (New York: Harcourt Brace & Company, 1952).

Alfred A. Knopf, Inc., from Chaim Potok, *My Name Is Asher Lev* (New York: Alfred A. Knopf, 1972).

New Directions Publishing Corporation, from Ezra Pound, "Canto LXXXI," *The Cantos of Ezra Pound*, copyright © 1948 by Ezra Pound. Reprinted by permission.

Princeton University Press, from James E. Pritchard, editor, *Ancient Near Eastern Texts Relating to the Old Testament*, copyright © renewed 1978 by Princeton University Press.

Series Foreword

This series of study guides to the Bible is offered to the church and more specifically to the laity. In daily devotions, in church school classes, and in listening to the preached word, individual Christians turn to the Bible for a sustaining word, a challenging word, and a sense of direction. The word that scripture brings may be highly personal as one deals with the demands and surprises, the joys and sorrows, of daily life. It also may have broader dimensions as people wrestle with moral and theological issues that involve us all. In every congregation and denomination, controversies arise that send ministry and laity alike back to the Word of God to find direction for dealing with difficult matters that confront us.

A significant number of lay women and men in the church also find themselves called to the service of teaching. Most of the time they will be teaching the Bible. In many churches, the primary sustained attention to the Bible and the discovery of its riches for our lives have come from the ongoing teaching of the Bible by persons who have not engaged in formal theological education. They have been willing, and often eager, to study the Bible in order to help others drink from its living water.

This volume is part of a series of books, the Westminster Bible Companion, intended to help the laity of the church read the Bible more clearly and intelligently. Whether such reading is for personal direction or for the teaching of others, the reader cannot avoid the difficulties of trying to understand these words from long ago. The scriptures are clear and clearly available to everyone as they call us to faith in the God who is revealed in Jesus Christ and as they offer to every human being the word of salvation. No companion volumes are necessary in order to hear such words truly. Yet every reader of scripture who pauses to ponder and think further about any text has questions that are not immediately answerable simply by reading the text of scripture. Such questions may be about historical and geographical details or about words that are obscure or so loaded with meaning that one cannot tell at a glance what is at stake. They may be about the fundamental meaning of a passage or about what connection a particular text might have to our contemporary world. Or a teacher preparing for a church school class may simply want to know: What should I say about this biblical passage when I have to teach it next Sunday? It is our hope that these volumes, written by teachers and pastors with long experience studying and teaching the Bible in the Church, will help members of the church who want and need to study the Bible with their questions.

The New Revised Standard Version of the Bible is the basis for the interpretive comments that each author provides. The NRSV text is presented at the beginning of the discussion so that the reader may have at hand in a single volume both the scripture passage and the exposition of its meaning. In some instances, where inclusion of the entire passage is not necessary for understanding either the text or the interpreter's discussion, the presentation of the NRSV text may be abbreviated. Usually, the whole of the biblical text is given.

We hope this series will serve the community of faith, opening the Word of God to all the people, so that they may be sustained and guided by it.

General Introduction: These Three Books

Legend has it that Solomon is the author of the three books treated in this volume: the Song of Songs in lusty youth, Proverbs in sober middle age, and Ecclesiastes in disillusioned (and disgruntled?) old age. Modern scholars now think it unlikely that much, if any, of these books comes from Solomon's own hand (see the introduction to each book on the questions of dating and authorship). Nonetheless, it makes sense to study these three books together, for they do have something essential in common. Namely, they all treat, in their very different tones, the phenomenon of what it means to live wisely before God. So these are the books (along with Job) in the Old Testament that are sometimes designated "wisdom literature."

The word "wisdom" sounds slightly old-fashioned. We all know many smart people. Most of us admire people who have a good education; we are eager that our children (if not ourselves) should be among them. But stop for a moment and think: how many people do you know whom you would describe as wise? How many people can you say, without qualification, live their lives day by day, even moment by moment, in a way that honors and glorifies God? For that is what "wisdom" meant to the biblical writers: living in the world in such a way that God, and God's intentions for the world, are acknowledged in all that we do. It sounds like a lofty goal, perhaps too lofty for ordinary people living busy lives. Such a goal of wisdom seems attainable only for great saints; maybe a hermit or a monastic could achieve it. Yet this is not the understanding of the biblical writers. It is important to recognize at the outset that they consider wisdom within the grasp of every person who desires it wholeheartedly. Wisdom does not require any special intellectual gifts. The fruit of wisdom, a well-ordered life and a peaceful mind, results not from a high IQ but from a disposition of the heart that the sages (wisdom teachers) of Israel most often call "fear of the LORD" (see the comment at Prov. 1:7).

So what is wisdom literature? It is spiritual guidance for ordinary people. Moreover, it comes from ordinary people, and this in itself makes the wisdom literature different from most of the rest of the Bible. Most of the biblical books represent God speaking through Moses or the other prophets. But the sages make no claim to having received special revelation from God. In contrast to Torah ("Teaching") from Sinai, much of the instruction they offer is inherited from their fathers and mothers, both biological parents and ancestors in the faith. In the case of the eccentric sage Koheleth (Ecclesiastes), inherited wisdom is submitted to critique and supplemented by his own learning in "the school of hard knocks." The Song of Songs speaks with the wisdom of the heart ravished by love—wisdom that is in its own way equally hard-won.

The journey through these three books takes the heart seeking wisdom through the full range of human emotion and experience. The books vary greatly in temperament. Proverbs has a tone of steady confidence as it sets forth instruction for "wise dealing" (Prov. 1:3). The extremes on either side are marked first by Koheleth's world-weariness and relentless shattering of illusions, then by the exuberance of the Song of Songs, all staccato notes, expressing the ecstasy and some of the inevitable anguish of love.

For all the differences among them, one thing that links these books is that all of them are poetry. That is, they seek to open the world to us through the artful use of words. They invite us to be patient and curious about the word choices they make. They speak to us at multiple levels, in suggestive ways, rather than through rational explanations. For all these reasons they must be read slowly, and this is a fact of great importance for the approach taken in this commentary. My aim here is to show how the biblical writers use words to generate deep, imaginative reflection on the realities they treat, which are the most ordinary and the most far-reaching experiences of life: birth and death, poverty and wealth, education and work, grief and joy, human love and love of God. As Bacon said, "Some books are to be tasted, others to be swallowed, and some few to be chewed and digested." Each of these biblical books demands that we read it a little bit at a time, even verse-by-verse, paying close attention to the particular words and the form of the poem, and at the same time letting our minds move freely to follow the associations they suggest. Especially important, as I try to show, is pondering the significance of echoes we hear from other parts of the Bible. This kind of meditative reading does not come naturally to most of us. Modern schools, textbooks, manuals, and novels all teach us to read quickly, to get the facts, or to find out what happened. Ours is among the high cultures of history perhaps the one least patient with carefully crafted words, written or spoken. But the sages of ancient Israel are teaching us to read for a kind of heart knowledge that cannot be quickly gained. The good news is that, once we acquire the habit of that kind of reading, we discover that our hearts yearn for it. To put it plainly, chewing the words of scripture is addictive.

In the ancient Near East, wisdom literature was considered a high achievement of a culture. Archaeology has enabled us to discover wisdom writings from Israel's powerful and sophisticated neighbors in Mesopotamia and Egypt. But in the modern world, this sort of poetic yet practical reflection on the nature of reality is rare. In Western society, we have followed the Greek preference for analytical prose writing, that is, for philosophy and, above all in the last three centuries, science.

The worldview represented in the wisdom literature is fundamentally opposed to a modern scientific approach, as it is pursued in most universities and research institutions. There, specialized knowledge is valued over a broad understanding of the world and the human place in it; abstract, theoretical thinking is valued over concrete ethical reflection; invention and discovery are valued over received tradition. The clash between a wisdom perspective and the modern outlook has become even more acute in recent years, with the changes in working and thinking that have accompanied the rise of computer culture. We are now a society that "processes" words rather than one that ponders them. In the "artificial intelligence" industry, middle-aged workers are pushed out in favor of fresh college graduates, who are willing to work longer hours for lower pay and, moreover, are skilled in the newest technology. It is obvious that this kind of industrial climate is hostile to the traditional idea that learning from our elders and our ancestors is essential to living a decent and contented life. On the contrary, traditional views are often suspect; they are regarded as out of touch with human needs, even oppressive. In a culture that has flattered itself into believing that we are inventing a new way of living, a new way of being human, the idea of trusting our predecessors to provide guidance can only seem foolish.

Yet even in our culture, it is possible to detect a longing for something that will serve the function of wisdom literature—that is, for guidance in making right choices in the midst of the bewildering flux of immediate experience. It is acutely ironic that the advertising industry has perceived this need and capitalized on it, as evidenced by the cleverest television commercials. Consider this ad copy for AcuVue contact lenses:

> I have seen the longest of winters;
> I have seen compassion conquer despair;
> I have seen that hope is a flame
> that can't be extinguished.

Or this copy for a high-priced automobile (Lexus):

> Follow no one.
> Because the only path to our purpose
> is the one never taken before.
>
> We determine our fate;
> it has to come from within.
> Yet this course demands sacrifice:
> forsaking the certainty of the familiar to risk
> confrontation with the inevitable.

These are shrewd parodies of wisdom sayings. Like the biblical sages, the advertisers assert that reward comes only to those willing to exercise demanding personal discipline and practice difficult virtues: compassion, hope, willingness to sacrifice for the sake of a high goal. But the nature of the goal marks the fundamental difference between these sayings and the biblical wisdom literature. The biblical sages are aiming at peace—peace of heart and peace with God and neighbor—and they understand that wisdom is the path (see Prov. 3:17) to that goal. By contrast, the goal to which advertisers urge us to devote ourselves is something material: a (supposedly) better appearance, a luxury car. Yet the one indispensable thing for obtaining the advertisers' goal is not in fact sound personal character (as the commercials imply) but rather money. From a biblically informed perspective, these "wise sayings" are more than dishonest; they are a way of mocking God!

The task of this commentary is to show how the biblical wisdom literature may serve as a resource for the theological work of ordinary Christians. Doing theology does not primarily mean defining and explaining doctrines, although that is what some professional theologians do. Much more fundamentally (and importantly), theology is the work done by every Christian who strives to respond to "the first and great commandment," to love God with all our *mind* (Matt. 22:37–38). Understood in this sense, doing theology is simply reflecting on our experience in the context of our relationship with God. In the modern church these three books are one of the most theologically underused parts of the Bible. Rarely are they read in worship, chosen as a preaching text, or taught in Sunday school. Yet a careful (slow!) reading reveals that they provide an invaluable model for how we ourselves may reflect upon the religious significance of the full range of human experiences—including and even especially things we do not normally think of as being "religious." It is a deep conviction of the Israelite sages that the sacred and the secular are not separate realms of experience and concern. Therefore the wisdom literature may speak with particular power to the spiritual needs of our highly secularized age. I mention three aspects of these books that are especially important in this regard.

First, in a time of acute ecological crisis, the biblical wisdom literature may help us to develop a creation theology adequate to our problems. The economist and modern sage E. F. Schumacher comments incisively: "We are now far too clever to be able to survive without wisdom" (*Guide for the Perplexed*, 55–56). The ecological crisis can be seen precisely as a crisis of knowledge without wisdom. In this century, powerful technological knowledge has proliferated, yet it is not sufficiently tempered and disciplined by a discerning understanding of how God has ordered the world. If technology is to be helpful and not destructive, then we—not only as scientists and technicians but also as ordinary consumers of technology—must learn to *contemplate* the world and ask what is God's intention for it, and how that sets limits on our own tinkering with the world. These three books can teach us to contemplate, for in different ways they highlight the marvelous order of creation, and especially the splendor and intricacy of nonhuman creation. Divine wisdom undergirds God's work in creation and is everywhere manifest in it. Correspondingly, human wisdom consists in observing the created order, learning from it, living in ways that do not violate—indeed, that contribute—to the well-being of the whole created order. As we shall see, each book shows that the biblical writers have reflected deeply on the early chapters of Genesis; they are seeking to understand our present experience in connection with creation and the early history of humanity.

This focus on the creation may actually have contributed to the undervaluing of the wisdom literature by previous generations of theologians, who noted the absence of references to the great events of "salvation history": the patriarchs and matriarchs, the exodus and the Promised Land, the kings and prophets, the exile and return to the land. Indeed, there is no mention of Israel at all! This, along with the obvious influence of Egyptian wisdom upon the biblical writers, led some to see this literature as a foreign body within the Old Testament—that is, as thinly disguised paganism. Surely it is time to redress the balance and appreciate the truth that "God spoke to our ancestors in many and various ways" (Heb. 1:1). Rather than being a detriment, the universalizing style of this literature may provide a model for the church in entering into dialogue with non-Christians who are nonetheless potential allies in caring for what one liturgy calls "this fragile earth, our island home" (*Book of Common Prayer*, 370). The very fact that the biblical wisdom literature shows non-Israelite influence indicates that the sages were willing to let their own religious understanding be informed by those who did not share their faith. Similarly, the secular wisdom of scientists, ecologists, naturalists, and philosophers may greatly enhance our appreciation of and our sense of responsibility toward the world that God has made. A contemporary biblical scholar wisely observes: "In the present state of human affairs, in which primary concerns are the survival of humanity and the planet, it is indeed feasible to ask whether it is again possible for philosophy and wisdom to converge—a type of philosophy that finds its way back to an understanding of creation as a whole, informs discourse that can be understood by all, and does not isolate itself in some elitist fashion" (Westermann, *Roots*, 137).

A second element of the wisdom literature that may be helpful to us is its profound exploration of the human place in the world. In Israelite wisdom, theology provides a solid base for anthropology. The search for wisdom is a search for the proper human place in the divinely established order. Much of the Old Testament is concerned largely with the whole people of God, the political, moral, and cultic (worship) life of the people Israel. But the wisdom literature focuses attention on the individual and therefore may speak to the many people in our society who do not have any strong sense of identification with a community, let alone a faith community. The underlying conviction is that life is something more than "a bunch of stuff that happens." At the same time, there is a refreshing honesty to the wisdom tradition. The sages are not afraid to voice radical doubts about whether in fact the cosmic order does benefit human beings, or whether we are merely "fish taken in a cruel net" (Eccl. 9:12), whether personal virtue makes any difference after all (this is the source of Job's anguish).

A third element of the wisdom literature that makes it a valuable resource for modern theology is the prominence of women in Proverbs and the Song of Songs. Indeed, when in the book of Proverbs wisdom is personified, it is as a lovely woman. This is initially surprising, for women had little public presence in ancient Israel; probably all official religious leaders were men. Yet there is precedent, of a sort, for this representation.

In ancient Near Eastern mythologies, a goddess often presides over the realms of wisdom and education (perhaps because a child's first teacher is usually a woman, mother or nursemaid). The biblical writers resolutely resist making God's attribute of wisdom (see Prov. 3:19) into an independent deity. Nonetheless, the association between wisdom and the feminine—real women and symbolical female figures—clearly implies that the character and work of women is a matter of profound religious significance for the life of all God's people.

But the portrayal of wisdom as a beautiful and alluring woman suggests something more. It suggests that wisdom is more than useful; it is desirable, in the strongest sense. Remembering that the sages' original audience was composed largely of young males, the student population of ancient Israel, we can see that the wisdom teachers are creating poems, some of them frankly erotic (the Songs of Songs), with the aim of cultivating healthy and life-giving desire. "Wisdom is a tree of life to those who lay hold of her" (Prov. 3:18). Great works of art stir us because they awaken in us a longing for what is essential for our humanity. The poet-sages of ancient Israel enable us to see "Lady Wisdom's" beauty, that we may love her, lay hold of her, live, and live well.

Proverbs

Introduction to Proverbs

The book of Proverbs is not high on the reading list of many modern Christians. As a source of spiritual inspiration and guidance, it is almost lost to us, at least to those in mainline churches, Protestant or Catholic. We rarely hear it read in church, let alone at home. Probably few of us would be able to identify a verse from Proverbs, let alone recite one. Yet it may be helpful to begin study with the recognition that over the centuries, this book has been to both Jews and Christians one of the most valued parts of the Bible. When the ancient and medieval rabbis wanted to talk in concrete terms about the practice of righteousness, they very frequently turned to the book of Proverbs; it is therefore not surprising that the apostle Paul, with his solid rabbinic training, quotes from the text (Rom. 12:20). In the seventeenth century, English Puritans treasured the book as the most reliable guide to the holy life. Digests of biblical proverbs were produced, and much used, to facilitate memorization. Even as late as the nineteenth century, the sophisticated essayist and art critic John Ruskin would say that the four chapters of Proverbs his mother had him memorize as a small child were "the one essential part of all my education" (cited by Smith, *Modern Criticism*, 300).

What the ancient rabbis, the Puritans, and Ruskin had in common is that they knew at least some of the biblical proverbs by heart. And this is the key to appreciating them fully. For the proverbs are little poems, each about the length of a haiku or a Zen koan. Like these Asian literary forms, the biblical proverbs are highly concentrated, and sometimes riddling, reflections on common elements of human experience. Read straight through, they are tedious and they run together in the mind, for there is no plot, no consistent development of a logical argument or a moral theme. But it is a quite different thing when one encounters them as they are meant to be *heard* (and not, in the first instance, read). Proverbs are meant to be pondered, one at a time. Medieval monks spoke of "chewing" the words of scripture, like grains of spice, until they yield their full savor. That is how the proverbs should be learned. Memorize a single saying; you can do it while taking a shower, waiting at the bus stop, or chopping the vegetables for dinner. Let it sit in what the ancient Egyptian sages (teachers, writers, and collectors of wise sayings) called "the casket of your belly" for a day or a week or more, returning to examine it from the different vantage points of varied experience. If you give the book of Proverbs that kind of time, then it will yield to you its wisdom. You will begin to sense the peculiar force with which the passages address the hearer who positions herself to listen well.

Proverbs are essentially oral literature; they circulate by word of mouth. Although some may be ascribed to a particular historical figure (the ascription of the biblical proverbs to Solomon will be discussed below), in a real sense their author is the community as a whole, which keeps them alive in its daily speech. It is, then, the authority of the community that speaks through them—and very significantly, not just of the present generation. These sayings have been passed on, first orally and later in writing, by countless "mothers" and "fathers" (see Prov. 1:8) in Israel offering their hard-won wisdom, the fruit of all their experience, to a new generation of faith. What makes it possible for the proverbs to come alive even today among people of biblical faith is that they shed light on things all of us worry about, for ourselves and for our children, the things people regularly consult their pastors about: how to avoid bitter domestic quarrels, what to tell your children about sex and about God, what to do when somebody asks to borrow money, how to choose the right friends and be a good friend, how to make a living that is decent, both ethically and financially. In short, the proverbs are instruction in the art of living well.

From ancient times, people have wondered if these popular sayings really have a place in the Bible. They do not seem to derive from revelation, a direct word of God. Rather, they reflect, quite literally, "common sense," the sense the faith community has made of its cumulative experience. If this is wisdom, then it is wisdom of the homeliest sort. But that is exactly the point. The proverbs are spiritual guides for ordinary people, on an ordinary day, when water does not pour forth from rocks and angels do not come to lunch. And maybe just that is their value to us in the present generation. In a secular age, when many people, and especially the young, cannot accept the claims of revelation, pondering the proverbs may open a path—to use the sages' own frequent image—into the life of biblical faith. Therefore they can serve as a starting point for Christian teaching, not only with the young but also with the disaffected.

Teaching people to "chew" these sayings and thus internalize them is an invitation into a distinctive way of looking at the world, an invitation into the community of faith. For, as we have learned from cultural anthropologists, the use of proverbs is one important way that a traditional people identifies itself as a community. You might say that the community is the group of people who share a particular set of perceptions about the ordinary experiences of life, perceptions that are condensed into their proverbial speech. Therefore native Hawaiians, recognizing that they are in danger of complete assimilation into mainstream American culture, are currently making an effort to revive the proverbs that are distinctive to their own culture, in order to preserve their identity and their unique worldview. An example: "When the *hala* is in bloom, the *wana* is fat." This saying is meaningless to someone outside the culture. But to "insiders"—specifically, those who can identify the blooming *hala* plant and know where the sea animal *wana* can be found—it conveys crucial information about the right season to go diving for seafood!

A LITERATURE FOR CRISIS: THE SOCIAL BACKGROUND OF PROVERBS

Proverbs express the basic values and perceptions that characterize a community through many generations. They are a key to the community's stable identity, and precisely this makes them valuable in times of transition and crisis. For example, West Indians hold proverb-telling sessions at wakes. The idea that proverbs can help in time of crisis may come as a surprise to us who do not belong to a traditional culture. We tend to think of proverbs as worn-out clichés. But ancient Israel, like modern traditional cultures, recognized proverbs as what they are: time-tested wisdom that can provide a point of orientation for those bewildered by change and the complexity of new experience. Because they take the long-range perspective, proverbs offer a way out of the maze of the present. The person who has mastered proverbs stands above the maze, where she can begin to discern the pattern and see a solution to the current impasse. An African saying runs: "The person who understands proverbs soon sets matters right." Yet the calm, measured tone that characterizes proverbial speech should not deceive us into thinking that the sages are merely offering pat solutions to the intractable difficulties of life. The precise language and regular rhythms may be compared to the assured demeanor of a person who has not only weathered many crises, but also matured through them.

An example of how a proverb may provide an anchor in a time of social upheaval is found in the biblical account of the early kingship in Israel. When Samuel sets out to anoint one of Jesse's sons as king, he first fixes on the tall and handsome Eliab, David's older brother. The Lord corrects Samuel: "Do not look on his appearance or on the height of his stature, because I have rejected him." The rebuke is followed immediately by a typical proverb: "The LORD does not see as mortals see; they look on the outward appearance, but the LORD looks on the heart" (1 Sam. 16:7). The proverb usage is significant. This was a key juncture in Israel's history. The anointing of a king, and the shift away from leaders who received direct empowerment from God's spirit, was met with mixed fear and hope, as the biblical account shows. In that situation of transition, the saying is a stabilizing force. It sounds the depths of the religious tradition and retrieves the truth that external matters—personal appearance and even political structures—are finally irrelevant to what God most desires, a faithful heart.

It is probably more than coincidence that the proverb occurs in the history of the monarchy, because there are good indications that the institution of kingship in Israel was in fact important for the consolidation of proverbial speech in Israel. Most obviously, this book is entitled "the Proverbs of Solomon" (1:1; see also 10:1). We are told that Solomon "composed three thousand proverbs" and that "people came from all the nations to hear the wisdom of Solomon" (1 Kings 4:32, 34). Does that mean that he wrote all the proverbs? This is unlikely for at least two reasons. First is the very nature of proverbs; they are essentially popular literature. Proverbs do not belong to an author so much as to a whole people. Sayings become proverbial when they have passed indiscriminately through many mouths. New "wisdom sayings" arise from time to time, sometimes created or fixed in everyday lore by famous public figures. A modern example is John Kennedy's "Ask not what your country can do for you but what you can do for your country." Such a saying survives not as a conscious quotation, but because it enters the language and is repeated over and over. We gradually forget who said it, just because it has come to represent the best intentions and aspirations of a whole people.

A second reason to doubt that Solomon wrote most of the biblical proverbs is that, more than any other major section of the Bible, this book represents the perspective of the "grass roots," in contrast to the views of clearly identifiable opinion leaders such as prophets, priests, or king. It is unlikely that Solomon, who built up his administrative and defense systems by imposing heavy taxes on the peasant population (see 1 Kings 12:4), would call attention to his unpopular action by creating a saying such as this one:

By justice a king gives stability to the land,
but one who makes heavy exactions ruins it.
(29:4)

Far from presenting a royal perspective, many of the proverbs uphold the values of peasant culture—that is, of the agrarian, kinship based, locally governed society that Israel was before the rise of the monarchy. Many sayings emphasize good care of the tillable soil (see the comment at Prov. 24:30–34). Conversely, there are sayings that express the peasants' experience of losing their land to the royal tax collectors:

The field of the poor may yield much food,
but it is swept away through injustice.
(13:23)

There are those whose teeth are swords,
whose teeth are knives,
to devour the poor from off the earth,
the needy from among mortals.
(30:14)

Proverbs such as these are a form of protest literature. It is likely that the rise of kingship in Israel gave impetus to the collection of proverbs in part to preserve a way of life that was endangered. It is important to remember that early Israel originated as a peasant culture that defined itself *over against* the kingdoms of Egypt and Canaan. Now that Israel had itself become "like other nations" (1 Sam. 8:5) in this respect, it was urgent to affirm the essential values that kept the community intact and faithful to its God: social and legal justice; mutual loyalty between parents and children, husband and wives, friends; diligence in work; honorable poverty; and above all, fear of the Lord. As we shall see, all these themes appear over and over throughout the book.

Even if the ascription to Solomon is not to be taken literally, it may well have a historical base. It was common for ancient Near Eastern kings to sponsor the collection of wise sayings; this enhanced the prestige of their reigns. Indeed, within the book of Proverbs, the collection ascribed to King Hezekiah begins with the observation, "The glory of kings is to search things out" (25:2). Solomon's relatively peaceful reign and the wealth of his court promoted international commerce; probably the trade was intellectual as well as material. Sages of different countries exchanged sayings, and the biblical proverbs show pronounced Egyptian influence (see the comment at 22:17–24:22). Despite the grassroots orientation of the book as a whole, it is evident that court sages have had some hand in shaping the book. Some sayings are openly flattering of kings (16:10; 21:1); others prescribe court etiquette. Imagine a gruff old courtier addressing a young aspirant with advice such as this:

> When you sit down to eat with a ruler,
> observe carefully what/who is before you,
> and put a knife to your throat
> if you have a big appetite.
>
> (23:1–2)

> Do not put yourself forward in the king's presence
> or stand in the place of the great;
> for it is better to be told, "Come up here,"
> than to be put lower in the presence of a noble.
>
> (25:6–7)

Jesus will turn the latter piece of advice into a parable of the kingdom of heaven (see Luke 14:7–11).

It is likely that the short sayings in chapters 10 to 29 are the oldest part of the book, and that many of these date to the period of the monarchy. More extended poetic sections, in chapters 1 through 9 and 30 through 31, provide a frame around the short sayings, the "proverbs proper." Most scholars believe that this framing material is later, and that the book assumed final form in the postexilic period, after the collapse of the nation-state before the Babylonian army (587 B.C.E.) and the exile of a significant portion of the population. This dating for the book makes sense in light of the notion that proverbs become especially important to a culture in crisis. In other words, if the crisis of the *rise* of kingship prompted the first proverb collections in Israel, then it is likely that the second crisis of the monarchy's *collapse* led to consolidation of this literary tradition, the formation of the book of Proverbs. When the nation-state Israel was no more, then it was the tradition of sacred literature that provided social cohesion and an understanding of what it meant to belong to the people Israel. Consolidation of the scriptural tradition—most of the Old Testament was written or assumed final form in this period—prevented Israel from disappearing from history, as did all the other defeated nations of the ancient world. Israel became at this point "the people of the Book."

Moreover, the social change that accompanied that second crisis accounts for the most pronounced feature of these framing chapters, namely, the prominence of women—or more accurately, of female figures, including and especially Wisdom personified. She is the star of a cast of female characters, each of whom is memorable in her own way: the smooth-talking adulteress (7:5–27), the bustling figure of personified Folly (9:13–18), the wife of youth to whom fidelity is due (5:15–20), and the quiet figure of the mother whose teaching, implicit and explicit, is represented throughout the book (1:8; 10:1; 15:20; 30:17, etc.). The final chapter focuses attention on two women, the mother of (the otherwise unknown) King Lemuel, whose instruction is cited here (31:1–9), and the wholly admirable "valorous woman" (AT, 31:10; in the NRSV, "a capable wife"), who sums up in her own person the teachings of the sages: she fears God; she serves her family and community with industry, dignity, and consummate skill.

This emphasis on the character and activity of women, both real and symbolical (Wisdom and Folly), is too marked to be coincidental. Moreover, it stands in contrast to most of the rest of the Old Testament, which commonly foregrounds the importance of men. But the structure of this book conveys a different message. The positioning of passages that feature women at the beginning and the end of the book suggests that for all practical purposes, how one reckons with these women is the measure of whether one has achieved wisdom. "In the book of Proverbs, one stands or falls in the eyes of God and community based on one's relationship to various women" (Camp, *Wisdom*, 256).

The drastic social change that underlies this unprecedented emphasis on women is this: with the collapse of the nation-state, the household became, for the first time in five hundred years, the focus of Israelite identity. The old centers of power—king, Temple, and priesthood—were gone or much reduced in significance. Even the great age of prophecy drew to a close with the exile. The infrastructure had disappeared, and the old symbol system had eroded. In this situation, the extended family became the means by which Israelite identity and faith were maintained and passed on to the next generation. It is obvious that in this situation, the character and activity of the woman of the household became much more than a personal matter. It is commonly observed that ancient Israel was a patriarchal society, where most important *public* roles were played by men. So the Israelite man would sit in the public council and administer "justice at the gate." But at the same time, the woman was active in a variety of roles that influenced the common life of Israel, even if most of her work was done at home. She was a counselor to her husband, so her wisdom also figured in deliberations "at the gate" (see Prov. 31:31). She and her husband were the primary teachers for their children, in religious as well as "practical" matters (although the book of Proverbs as a whole brings that distinction seriously into question). As domestic manager, she was an important economic producer in a society where the household was the primary unit of production. A wise and just woman would not only provide for her own family and servants but also extend her hand to the poor (Prov. 31:20). In sum, the woman was to a great extent responsible for maintaining faithful living in Israel. She had assumed many of the mediating, instructional, and guiding functions once performed by the important national figures of priest, prophet, and king. No wonder, then, that when Wisdom came to be personified, it was as a woman, builder and sustainer of the household.

TEACHING WITH POETRY

> Apples of gold in a setting of silver—
> a word fitly spoken.
>   (25:11, AT)

> Legs dangle limp from the lame;
> likewise a proverb in the mouth of fools.
>   (26:7, AT)

> A thornbranch brandished in the hand of a drunkard—
> likewise a proverb in the mouth of fools.
>   (26:9, AT)

In order to create proverbs such as these, the Israelite sages must have been intensely proud of their art. The first saying expresses the high value of fitting speech, as well as its extreme rarity; the second, the sages' contempt for those who pretend to a mastery they do not have; the third, their awareness that a proverb mishandled constitutes a threat. It is hard for us to understand the value they attach to fitting speech, for we in modern Western society make no distinction between artful proverbs on the one hand, and worn clichés and advertising slogans on the other. Many livelihoods depend on devising persuasive speeches; this is the basis of sales and politics, which between them determine the character of most of our public discourse. Getting *my* idea across convincingly, selling myself and the product I am currently backing, is a simple matter at which many have some skill. What it requires is a measure of self-confidence, which is relatively easy to come by. But "a word fitly spoken" is a far more difficult goal to achieve. It demands discernment of the peculiar fit between language and the human heart. In other words, while persuasive speech may derive purely from mere self-opinion, mastery of fitting speech requires moral exactitude, a penetrating understanding into both the present situation and the disposition of the heart.

The demand for moral exactitude explains why the teaching of the sages comes to us in the form of poetry. For poetry is the kind of language best suited to probing the inexhaustible mystery of the human situation *in its entirety*, and that is exactly what wisdom seeks to explore. Prose is the tool of analysis, of explanation, of scientific and academic research. But poetry looks at phenomena whole. By "poetry," I do not mean only rhythmic or rhyming language, but rather language that is primarily designed to engage the imagination.

Too often we consider the imagination to be frivolous, a nice "extra," but hardly a necessary part of the human endowment. But in fact the very opposite is the case. For, as virtually all the biblical writers know, the imagination is the chief faculty of moral discernment. It is by means of the imagination that we project ourselves into a situation that is not completely clear (and that is our situation most of the time) and choose a course of action. It is by means of the imagination that we enter into relationship with people who are not fully known to us—and that is virtually everyone we encounter, including our intimates. Almost every interaction that lasts for more than a few seconds demands that we imagine how the other person might feel, what might be her genuine needs, how my words and actions might affect him for good or for ill. The sages understand that living the moral life requires that we continually strive to exercise a *truthful* imagination—for the imagination can, of course, be perverted and devoted to the service of lies. Put most succinctly, that is what the book of Proverbs aims to help us cultivate in our various roles of parent, friend, teacher, neighbor, worker, boss, citizen.

In contemporary culture, poetry, like other forms of imaginative engagement, is often thought of as highly personal, even idiosyncratic. Poetry is often experimental, exploring new areas of consciousness. We greatly value spontaneity, and the most popular form for modern poetry, "blank verse," implies that this poem is an unpremeditated response to immediate circumstance, a unique moment. But traditional poets, including the sages of ancient Israel, conceived of their work in a very different way. Rather than highlighting uniqueness, they saw themselves responding to the recurrent situations of life, and they were striving for moral preparedness. C. S. Lewis, a twentieth-century theologian and critic of poetry, expresses the traditional poets' sensibility thus: "All that we describe as constancy in love or friendship, as loyalty in political life, or in general, as perseverance—all solid virtue and stable pleasure—depends on organizing chosen attitudes and maintaining them against the eternal flux (or 'direct free play') of mere immediate experience" (Lewis, *Preface*, 53–54).

The notion that one can and must "organize" for goodness lends an obviousness to many proverbs that, some think, disqualifies them as spiritual literature. This view dates back to ancient times, when some rabbis objected to the inclusion of Proverbs in the canon: "After all, they are just proverbs." To be sure, there is nothing exceptional in the sages' view that adultery, bad company, and careless talk are to be avoided, that excessive anger or drinking is destructive. But the sages make no claim to originality. On the contrary, their wisdom is validated by its anonymity; it has been discovered over and over again, tested and proven in countless lives. And they are quite right in recognizing that there is little of genuine originality in human life, far less than in our vanity we suppose. It is significant that one of the sages' favorite metaphors is the "path" one chooses to walk in life (see the comment on Proverbs 2); a path is characterized precisely by the fact that, crooked or straight, many feet have made it.

What makes for misery or satisfaction, wickedness or goodness, is simple and endures from one generation to another. But life is complicated; the sheer multiplicity of events makes it easy to lose sight of the basic principles. Sometimes the pervasive difficulty of life makes it hard to believe in them. Yet certain forms of conviction are not dispensable to our humanity. So moral decency requires that we learn what C. S. Lewis calls "stock responses" to the recurrent challenges of life, and learn them so deeply that the effort of right moral response becomes unconscious. It has traditionally been one of the functions of poetry to engage us in the contemplation of moral truths in a way that is compelling, but not preachy.

> The older poetry, by continually insisting on certain Stock themes—as that love is sweet, death bitter, virtue lovely, and children or gardens delightful— was performing a service not only of moral and civil, but even of biological, importance. . . . Since poetry has abandoned that office the world has not bettered. . . . We need most urgently to recover the lost poetic art of enriching a response without making it eccentric, and of being normal without being vulgar. (Lewis, *Preface*, 56)

The poetic art of proverbs is characteristically spare; with only a few words they give us access to a great deal of human experience. Proverbial speech is, in Marshall McLuhan's terms, a "hot medium"; proverbs have the potential to engage us deeply, in part because they require considerable effort on our part. The effort required of us is to find the wise saying that fits the present situation. For proverbs are of all literary forms the most context-sensitive. A given saying is wise only "in season" (15:23), when the speaker has correctly understood both the moment and the people involved. A saying (mis)applied in pat fashion is useless, if not dangerous, as the proverbs at the head of this section express.

It is perhaps this extreme context-sensitivity that explains the organization of the book, which at first consideration appears to be a frustrating lack of organization. One might expect all the proverbs on one subject— wealth and poverty, discipline of children, sexual relations—to be gathered in one place, as in a modern reference book. But instead they are scattered widely, across many chapters; it is impossible to "look up the answer" to the problem at hand. The only way to learn from the Proverbs is by living with the book for a long time, dipping in and out with regularity, or (ideally) working through it, proverb by proverb, even over years. Then one discovers that progress through the book is movement along a spiral. The same relatively few themes recur, but each time we are looking at them from a different angle. The difference is both textual and personal: How does this proverb occur in light of those around it? what has happened in my life since the last time I thought about this?

In other words, the structure of Proverbs blocks the desire, so much encouraged by modern education, to look for solutions in the abstract. Rather we are constrained to cultivate a flexible moral insight into concrete situations, which are always fraught with ambiguity and tension, sometimes to an acute degree. For example, the sages often cite the advantages of firm discipline for children (13:1; 29:15, 17). On the other hand, they advocate educating a child in "his own way" (see my translation and comment at 22:6), which implies a good deal of respect and freedom. These two educational ideals of discipline and freedom are in tension, and in any given instance one may be paramount. Yet wisdom ultimately transcends the tension: both are necessary for a child's health.

The artful composition of individual sayings also tends to work against abstraction. Metaphors and comparisons often lend sharpness to the sages' thumbnail characterizations. The effect is a sort of verbal cartoon that strikes to the heart of a situation:

> Like a bad tooth or a lame foot
> is trust in a faithless person in time of trouble.
> (25:19)

Unexpectedly, the most ordinary and necessary activities become excruciatingly painful.

The peculiar genius of proverbial speech is its ability to prompt moral reflection on basic truths without harangue. In other words, these teachings are not *moralistic*. Sometimes there is no explicit moral instruction at all. Rather the sages rely on poetic images to make their point—or perhaps more than one point. Here is an example of a saying that consists simply in a striking image that lingers in the mind and gradually yields understanding:

> Just as water reflects the face,
> so one human heart reflects another.
>   (27:19)

The proverb speaks to human experience at several levels. A pool of water is the mirror of the poor. Therefore this proverb says something about how I may come to see myself clearly: precisely by looking into the heart of the other. It is a strong statement on human empathy; it suggests that, for all of our individual differences, we are more alike than we are different. At the same time, the image of water implies the possibility that vision will be obstructed. For if the water is turbulent, or muddied, then there is no reflection. Am I a clear pool to further the self-understanding of others?

The sages avoid simplistic generalizations about classes of people: for example, the rich are greedy or the poor lazy, women are quarrelsome (the speaker's perspective for most of the proverbs is male). They prefer to sketch brief scenes of people in action, to show behaviors and their effects:

> A continual dripping on a rainy day
> and a contentious wife are alike;
> to restrain her is to restrain the wind
> or to grasp oil in the right hand.
>   (27:15–16)

It is evident to anyone experienced in dealing with a contentious male that the observation is accurate and not gender-specific.

Another way the sages prompt moral reflection is by setting close together sayings that together enrich our understanding more than might each alone:

> The rich rules over the poor,
> and the borrower is the slave of the lender.
>   (22:7)

> Those who are generous are blessed,
> for they share their bread with the poor.
> (22:9)

The near-juxtaposition of these two proverbs implies a truth that the New Testament confirms in several places: wealth, though not an absolute evil, must be recognized as the social and spiritual danger it is; generosity is the only alternative to oppression. Moreover, the difference between rich and poor is shown to be relative by a third proverb, which sets the others in perspective:

> Rich and poor are met together;
> the LORD is maker of them all.
> (22:2, AT)

A healthy person who looks hard at human behavior must find something funny in it. So there are humorous proverbs:

> Even fools who keep silent are considered wise;
> when they close their lips, they are deemed intelligent.
> (17:28)

Compare the wry observation of Abraham Lincoln: "It is better to keep silent and be thought a fool than to speak and remove all doubt." A slice-of-life vignette portrays a typical scene in a Near Eastern market, ancient or modern:

> "Bad, bad," says the buyer,
> then goes away and boasts.
> (20:14)

No instruction is conveyed, but the simple observation is a reminder that our actions and motives are not invisible to others.

A careful reading of Proverbs reveals a paradox. The sages speak out of a tradition of wisdom, and they seek to enlist new learners in that tradition. They make no claim to original discoveries. The interest in new behavioral theories that is so much a part of the modern mindset would seem to them odd. Yet, as the following commentary intends to show, reckoning with their sayings challenges every serious reader to fresh moral reflection. In some cases the new thinking required is so profound as to warrant the New Testament term *metánoia*, literally, "change of mind"; the common translation is "repentance" (Matt. 3:8; Rom. 2:4; 2 Cor. 7:10, etc.). The paradox: age-old wisdom occasions radically new thought in each generation. Yet, of course this must be so. For we human beings are learners, not creatures of instinct. Living a morally responsible life requires that we participate in a lifelong process of deep learning, and further, that we share in the most important task of each generation of adults: namely, guiding the young in the path of "wisdom," of profound reflection on what is good. The sages of ancient Israel are of inestimable help to us in meeting that responsibility.

A word on the style of the commentary that follows: I offer fairly full commentary on the long poems in chapters 1 through 9 and 30 through 31, which frame the "proverbs proper," the short sayings in chapters 10 through 29. With respect to the latter, I have made no attempt to be exhaustive. Rather, in a series of meditations I have tried to model the process of "chewing" the proverbs. These meditations are meant to stimulate your own theological reflection, not substitute for it.

1. Poetic Preface

THE GOAL OF LEARNING
Proverbs 1:1–6

1:1 **The proverbs of Solomon son of David, king of Israel:**

2 **For learning about wisdom and instruction,**
for understanding words of insight,
3 **for gaining instruction in wise dealing,**
righteousness, justice, and equity;
4 **to teach shrewdness to the simple,**
knowledge and prudence to the young—
5 **let the wise also hear and gain in learning,**
and the discerning acquire skill,
6 **to understand a proverb and a figure,**
the words of the wise and their riddles.

Here the sages set forth what we might gain from studying "Solomon's" proverbs. The first line (following the title) is better translated: "For knowing wisdom and *discipline*." The Hebrew word *mûsar* (here and in vv. 3a,7b, 8a) always denotes an authoritative instruction or correction from God or God's agent, personified Wisdom, or from a teacher or a parent. It is telling that the published translation avoids the word "discipline," which for us evokes pictures of grim-faced teachers rapping knuckles with their rulers. (Elsewhere NRSV translates *mûsar* variously as "correction," "discipline," "instruction," "lesson": Jer. 2:30; 5:3; 7:28; 17:23; 32:33; 35:13; Zeph. 3:2, 7.) Yet for the sages, discipline is an entirely positive concept. They speak of "loving discipline," which is tantamount to loving knowledge itself (12:1a). Furthermore, they state the alternative with remarkable frankness: "The one who hates reproof is dumb as an ox!" (12:1b, AT). Indeed, they put it even more strongly: hating discipline is a form of self-hatred (see the comment at 15:32a).

The sages can speak about loving discipline because they understand that it is not primarily something externally imposed, in order to make us do things we don't want to do. They maintain that the teacher's "rod of discipline" may help drive away the young boy's inherent folly (22:15). However, if discipline is to have a permanent and positive effect on character, it must be internalized by the student, as the Latin word *discipulus*, "student," implies. Therefore, those who would be wise must not only "receive *mûsar*" (8:10; 24:32) but also actively seek it out. The sages urge strongly, "Keep hold of *mûsar*; do not let go!" (4:13). "Buy *mûsar*" (23:23)—along with truth, wisdom, understanding. The price of a wise adulthood must be paid "up front," in a disciplined childhood: "Hear, my child, your father's *mûsar*" (1:8).

The use of the word *mûsar* twice in the first two verses is an early warning that the acquisition of wisdom is difficult and demands commitment. But, like good teachers of every age, the sages do not assume that their students necessarily begin with the necessary commitment. So indirectly they answer the question that is probably lurking in some minds, "Why should I care? What's in it for me?" The answer they offer is at once stirring and unsettling, as the Bible's answers often are. The sages' initial answer is "wise dealing," a morally neutral term that might mean nothing more than good business sense, "success." But then they immediately specify that term further, with language that comes straight from the biblical prophets: "righteousness, justice, and equity" (v. 3). So at the outset we see that the sages are aiming at the same goal as the prophets. They are not just preparing their students for personal success. "Righteousness, justice, and equity"— these are all relational virtues; they are the elements of healthy community life. They are also, as the prophets consistently teach, the qualities of character and common life that make the community of the faithful hospitable to God's holy presence. This is education for the kingdom of God.

The sages' statement of their educational aims is unsettling because it challenges our own deeply rooted, if unconscious, assumptions about education. For us, knowledge is a form of power. The idea that my power depends on what I know *and someone else does not* is fundamental to our increasingly information-oriented and professionally structured society. The mystique of specialized knowledge informs everything from Scotch ads to spy novels to college promotional materials; the whole military-industrial complex rests on the idea that knowledge is the highest form of power. We encourage our children to go to graduate school so they will know more than somebody else and (God willing) get a good job. Of course, this is a very old idea. Egyptian and Mesopotamian scribes tell their students: study hard, learn to write, there is a future for a good scribe. In ancient cultures, writing was a powerful form of technological expertise; those who had mastered cuneiform or hieroglyphics were the rocket scientists of their age. Considered in that context, it is apparent how countercultural was the educational perspective of the Israelite sages. Pursuit of "righteousness, justice, and equity" does not guarantee personal advancement, and no one schooled in biblical tradition could suffer from that delusion. Nonetheless, the sages of Israel teach that those who would be wise must aim, not at power, but at goodness.

As one who has spent most of her life in and around academic institutions, I can testify that that sounds weird. Scholars and professors—modern sages—have a great deal of specialized knowledge, but most would think it odd to speak of what they know as tending toward righteousness. That would be a category mistake. We are trained and hired to think rigorously and innovatively, not to be righteous and just—nor to instill those virtues in our students. But that shows how far we are from the perspective of the Israelite sages. It can be stated categorically: the Bible is not interested in abstract knowledge—that is, in knowledge abstracted from goodness. It is not interested in knowledge abstracted from the concrete problem of how to live well with our neighbors, in the presence of God.

Although what follows is often presented as parental instruction addressed to a child (see, for example, vv. 8–9), the introduction emphasizes that it is addressed to simple and sophisticated alike (vv. 4–6). "Simple" denotes, not lack of intelligence, but the natural condition of the young and untutored. The style of the biblical proverbs is extremely plain; most instructions are only two lines long, and the language is straightforward. They can be understood by a child, yet there is a depth of meaning that rewards long reflection. The best way to study proverbs is to "chew them" (as the medieval monks said of the words of scripture), one at a time, until they yield their full sweetness and nourishment. As this prologue indicates, the book of Proverbs is intended to be used in a program of lifelong learning.

The list of literary terms in verse 6 points to the sages' justifiable pride in their own skillful use of language. Thus they boasted of their wordcraft: "Apples of gold in settings of silver—a word fitly spoken" (25:11, AT). As we shall see, many of the proverbs employ turns of phrase and metaphors that are more than ornamentation; the word pictures can be probed to yield surprising shades of meaning. Moreover, the beautifully balanced language lends itself to memorization. Many or all of these proverbs originally circulated as oral literature, and in some traditional religious communities, many of them are still known by heart. After I had lectured on Proverbs to a group of seminarians, one of my African American students commented, "So that's where my grandmother got all those great lines!" It is the active memory of people of faith that gives these written words life.

THE FEAR OF THE LORD
Proverbs 1:7

> 1:7 **The fear of the LORD is the beginning of knowledge;
> fools despise wisdom and instruction.**

This, the first instruction in the book, is rightly set off by itself in the NRSV, for it is the cardinal teaching in all the biblical wisdom literature. Various sayings throughout the book repeat and amplify the idea that "the fear of the LORD" is the essence of wisdom (see 9:10; 15:33). Paradoxically, fear of the Lord is the only form of security that life holds (19:23; see also 10:27; 14:27). Modern scholars often observe that "fear" in this context means reverence rather than terror. Thus one translator renders the verse: "The first principle of knowledge is to hold the LORD in awe" (R. B. Y. Scott). It is true that in biblical usage, the phrase denotes a positive religious attitude. This is the most common term for what we would call "being religious" or "having faith." Nevertheless the distinction between fear of the Lord and ordinary fright should not be drawn too sharply. Indeed, to experience the full measure of God's power and *not* to feel some stirring of fear would indicate a profound state of spiritual numbness, if not acute mental illness. A sickly lack of fear in the face of God's power is exactly the condition described in the book of Exodus as Pharaoh's "hardheartedness"(see Exod. 8:15, 32; 9:7, and elsewhere). He doggedly endures ten plagues because he is too inert to respond to clear evidence that he is living in opposition to the real Power in the universe. Thus Moses diagnoses the spiritual condition that ultimately brings ruin on the whole land of Egypt: "But as for you and your officials, I know that you do not yet fear the LORD God" (Exod. 9:30; compare Exod. 14:31).

Yet fear of the Lord is something more than an emotional response to God's power. It implies also recognition of God's moral authority, recognition that shapes the believer's moral character and ultimately leads to a pervasive commitment of one's life. Therefore the sages speak of "the fear of the LORD" as something one *chooses* (1:29). Although Christian tradition affirms that faith is in part a gift from God, making it an effective force in our lives involves moral choice. More accurately, it involves developing the habit of making choices that do not merely reflect our own self-interest or the mood of the moment. Acting in accordance with our proper fear of the Lord means putting God's preferences before our own. Such a reversal of our natural priorities is what the Bible calls "humility," which is linked in several proverbs with fear of the Lord (15:33; 22:4; see comment at 15:33). Those with long and deep experience in the spiritual life habitually choose what God prefers, not because they are goody-goodies or without a will of their own, but because, unlike Pharaoh, they have the grace (literally) to see that the consequences of choosing otherwise are inevitably bad. Therefore fear of the Lord, linked on one side with humility, is linked on the other with hatred of evil (8:13; 14:16; 16:6; 23:17).

A sermon by the seventeenth-century poet John Donne offers one of the most moving meditations in the Christian tradition on "the fear of the LORD," which Donne calls "the art of arts, the root, and fruit, of all true wisdom" (*Sermons*, 6:96). Drawing his language and thought from the scriptures, he shows that this fear is, paradoxically, "the most noble, the most courageous, the most magnanimous, not affection [mere feeling], but virtue, in the world" (6:95)—the most noble and courageous, because it drives out all lesser fears, which diminish rather than build up our character. He offers a brilliant analogy for how this works: "As he that is fallen into the king's hand for debt to him, is safe from all other creditors, so is he, that fears the Lord, from other fears. He that loves the Lord, loves him with all his love; he that fears the Lord, loves him with all his fear too; God takes no half affections" (6:109). The final lines of the sermon bring together these two great religious emotions in an instruction that may open to us the depth dimension of the sages' teaching on fear of the Lord: "For this fear is inchoative [beginning] love, and this love is consummative fear. The love of God begins in fear, and the fear of God ends in love; and that love can never end, for God is love" (6:113).

BAD COMPANY
Proverbs 1:8–19

> 1:8 **Hear, my child, your father's instruction,**
> **and do not reject your mother's teaching;**
> 9 **for they are a fair garland for your head,**
> **and pendants for your neck.**
> 10 **My child, if sinners entice you,**
> **do not consent.**

11 If they say, "Come with us, let us lie in wait for blood;
   let us wantonly ambush the innocent;
12 like Sheol let us swallow them alive
   and whole, like those who go down to the Pit.
13 We shall find all kinds of costly things;
   we shall fill our houses with booty.
14 Throw in your lot among us;
   we will all have one purse"—
15 my child, do not walk in their way,
   keep your foot from their paths;
16 for their feet run to evil,
   and they hurry to shed blood.
17 For in vain is the net baited
   while the bird is looking on;
18 yet they lie in wait—to kill themselves!
   and set an ambush—for their own lives!
19 Such is the end of all who are greedy for gain;
   it takes away the life of its possessors.

The sages consider that bad company is—along with foolish speaking, anger, and laziness—one of the chief sources of personal disaster. This is the first of many warnings against it (see 4:14–19; 13:20; 22:24–25; 24:1 and the comment at 13:20). It is striking that the ancient editors who put the book in its final form chose to sketch as the "first scene" a crime in the making. Evidently the problem of violent crime in their society was serious enough to warrant this general warning to youth (in ancient Israel, it would have been addressed specifically to young men).

It is likely that the setting for this warning is the city. Israelite cities were tiny in comparison to modern cities or even to the great cities of Mesopotamia. Even after the expansion of Jerusalem in Josiah's reign (late seventh century B.C.E.), the population was probably no more than twenty-five thousand inhabitants, and other cities would have been much smaller. Nonetheless the prophets represented the capital cities of Jerusalem and Samaria as scandalously corrupt, places of idolatry and oppression (Ezek. 22:1–16; Amos 3:9; Micah 1:5).

The problems of the ancient cities were not very different from those that plague modern cities, although far less advanced. Beginning with Solomon's reign in the tenth century and accelerating greatly in the eighth to sixth centuries, the old tribal structure gradually eroded under the dual pressures of foreign wars and new economic opportunities opened up by foreign trade. Generations of youth entered into public life outside the protective kinship-based structure of community life in villages and were thereby exposed to many social and religious dangers.

In our own highly urbanized society, the warning against the temptation to make easy money by joining a gang of thieves rings a strikingly contemporary note. "Throw in your lot among us; we will all have one purse" (v. 14)—here the false comradeship of the streets is offered to the young person, who longs to be accepted by others. Imagine these words being spoken to a child in the inner city, where a ten-year-old must make a decision whether or not to deal drugs, where thirteen-year-olds are convicted sex offenders and sometimes murderers.

The whole passage is informed by an acute sense of irony. The gang members assume the identity of Sheol, in biblical cosmology the place of the dead, also known "the Pit." The sages know that speech is never wholly idle, and here the criminals' self-identification with Sheol foreshadows their future. The only certain effect of their crime as represented here is to bring their own lives to a violent and, it seems, swift end (vv. 18–19). Many proverbs affirm that God's judgment is both just and timely—a claim that the eccentric sages Koheleth (Ecclesiastes) and Job will call radically into question.

Verse 17 subtly draws our attention to the justice of God. This appears to be a traditional proverb put to unconventional use. The obvious meaning of the proverb is to expose the vanity of plotting against someone who has already figured out what the plotter is up to and therefore is able to escape "the net." But in the present context, it seems more likely that the one looking on is not the intended victim but God, who then brings a swift recompense. The sages give us a clue to this by using a poetic expression, "lord of the wing," here too simply rendered "bird." In fact, they are probably playing on two well-known metaphors for God: as the one whose watchful eye is always upon the faithful of Israel (Psalm 121:4), and also as the one whose "wing" is for the faithful a place of protection and joy (Psalm 63:7 [Hebrew v. 8]).

WISDOM'S CHALLENGE
Proverbs 1:20–33

> 1:20 Wisdom cries out in the street;
>   in the squares she raises her voice.
>   21 At the busiest corner she cries out;
>   at the entrance of the city gates she speaks:
>   22 "How long, O simple ones, will you love being simple?

How long will scoffers delight in their scoffing
and fools hate knowledge?
23 Give heed to my reproof;
I will pour out my thoughts to you;
I will make my words known to you.
24 Because I have called and you refused,
have stretched out my hand and no one heeded,
25 and because you have ignored all my counsel
and would have none of my reproof,
26 I also will laugh at your calamity;
I will mock when panic strikes you,
27 when panic strikes you like a storm,
and your calamity comes like a whirlwind,
when distress and anguish come upon you.
28 Then they will call upon me, but I will not answer;
they will seek me diligently, but will not find me.
29 Because they hated knowledge
and did not choose the fear of the LORD,
30 would have none of my counsel,
and despised all my reproof,
31 therefore they shall eat the fruit of their way
and be sated with their own devices.
32 For waywardness kills the simple,
and the complacency of fools destroys them;
33 but those who listen to me will be secure
and will live at ease, without dread of disaster."

Competing with the voices of the tempters is another voice, that of Wisdom "herself," who forcefully echoes the instruction of father and mother. This, the first of her three major addresses (see also 8:1–36 and 9:1–6), is a carefully constructed poem of self-introduction; virtually every line contains a term of self-reference: "I," "my," "me." The larger-than-life figure of Wisdom is astonishing. She has her counterparts in Mesopotamia and Egypt, where goddesses were thought to oversee education and the production of wisdom literature. But how could a figure reminiscent of pagan goddesses have passed muster in rigorously monotheistic Israel? "Lady Wisdom" is not a full-blown goddess, and there is no indication that a goddess of wisdom was ever worshiped in Israel. It seems that the sages are here inventing a bold literary device that compels attention and lends seriousness to their message, as when Wagner used Scandinavian mythology to create a setting for nineteenth-century German opera. Their audience stands at sufficient cultural and religious distance from the home base of that mythology to render it *theologically* neutral, even though it retains imaginative force.

The vivid representations of Wisdom in these opening chapters emphasize that "she" is much more than even the noblest ideal. Wisdom is closely associated with such intellectual and moral qualities as knowledge, prudence, righteousness, justice (1:3–4), but finally "she" is more than any of them. Wisdom is more like a person than a single quality—a total being who encounters us in the everydayness of the world, whom we may come to know intimately, whose summons we ignore to our peril. Wisdom resembles a compelling and (sometimes) alluring woman. Like the biblical prophets (whom she seems to imitate in this speech), she speaks to the heart, which in biblical physiology is the seat of the affections and the imagination as well as the rational mind.

The fact that the Hebrew noun *hokhmah*, "wisdom," is of feminine gender might have given initial inspiration for the femininization of wisdom. But "Lady Wisdom" does not match the common Near Eastern ideal, both ancient and modern, of the woman who is demure in public, however assertive she may be in the private sphere (for example, Sarah, Rebecca, Naomi, and Ruth). Wisdom sets out to establish herself as a public figure; she chooses the most prominent place in town to deliver her speech: the open space within the city gates (v. 21) where commercial, legal, and civic affairs were conducted.

She addresses herself directly to the "naïve" or "uncommitted" (v. 22). The uncommitted condition of those whom Wisdom addresses is initially morally neutral, though highly vulnerable. "Being simple" is the condition natural to the young, whose inherited commitments—to a religious tradition, a family, and a community, and to the values they seek to inculcate—have not yet been tried and firmed by experience. But cultivated "simplicity" is a vice. The sages are moral realists and know that lack of commitment, willfully prolonged beyond early youth, becomes a culpable and ultimately deadly vulnerability to sin: "waywardness kills the simple" (v. 32).

So in a ringing tone (the verb in v. 20 indicates a fervent, piercing cry—here of exhortation, elsewhere of joy or distress), Wisdom tells the "simple ones" that they must either grow up or grow down in moral stature. Ideally, the young are susceptible to sound instruction, and thus the simple person grows into one who "walks in integrity" (2:7; 10:9; 19:1; 20:7; 28:6). But there is also the possibility that they will refuse to take Wisdom's hand (v. 24) and commit themselves to "the path of [God's] faithful ones" (2:8). Verse 22 identifies the two levels of moral erosion to which the perpetually uncommitted person sooner or later descends: first to cynicism, "scoffing," and then to the open hatred of knowledge which is the condition of the fool. The scoffer and the fool are stock characters of the wisdom literature; the proverbs that follow (chapters 10–29) develop their profiles in detail. This introductory speech shows us their fate in the starkest terms (v. 32).

The representation of Wisdom as a woman shouting loudly in the public square is deliberately chosen to arrest attention. (As we shall see, chapter 7 offers another portrait of an aggressive woman who speaks persuasively, and there are even some similarities in the way Wisdom and "the strange woman" speak!) Her opening address here bears a striking resemblance to judgment speeches of the prophets, and doubtless the sages expect their audience to catch the echoes. The prophetic judgment speech (for example, Micah 3:1–4) announces God's decree of doom and gives the reasons why that decree is justified. As that passage shows, these speeches often open with a specific address to the audience: "O you heads of Jacob and rulers of the house of Israel"; compare here "O simple ones" (v. 22). Then they detail—often using graphic images—the reasons for judgment: "Because I have called and you refused . . . " (v. 24; compare Micah 3:2–3). Finally the form of judgment is announced, and that is identical in both passages: "Then they will call upon me, but I will not answer" (v. 28; compare Micah 3:4). The best explanation, then, for Wisdom's aggressiveness is that she is meant to sound like the prophets. Like them, she speaks transparently for God, and like them she risks public contempt in order to reach those—perhaps only the few—who can hear her message and "choose the fear of the LORD" (v. 29). The next chapter sets forth more fully the choice between the ways of life and death.

THE CHOICE BETWEEN TWO PATHS
Proverbs 2:1–22

The Search for Understanding (Proverbs 2:1–15)

2:1　My child, if you accept my words
　　　and treasure up my commandments within you,
2　　making your ear attentive to wisdom
　　　and inclining your heart to understanding;
3　　if you indeed cry out for insight,
　　　and raise your voice for understanding;
4　　if you seek it like silver,
　　　and search for it as for hidden treasures—

5 then you will understand the fear of the LORD
   and find the knowledge of God.
6 For the LORD gives wisdom;
   from his mouth come knowledge and understanding;
7 he stores up sound wisdom for the upright;
   he is a shield to those who walk blamelessly,
8 guarding the paths of justice
   and preserving the way of his faithful ones.
9 Then you will understand righteousness and justice
   and equity, every good path;
10 for wisdom will come into your heart,
   and knowledge will be pleasant to your soul;
11 prudence will watch over you;
   and understanding will guard you.
12 It will save you from the way of evil,
   and from those who speak perversely,
13 who forsake the paths of uprightness
   to walk in the ways of darkness,
14 who rejoice in doing evil
   and delight in the perverseness of evil;
15 those whose paths are crooked,
   and who are devious in their ways.

It has been aptly observed that "allegiance precedes understanding, not the other way around" (Newsom, "Woman and the Discourse," 147). Accordingly, the speaker asks first for the "child's" trust: "accept my words, inclining your heart to understanding" (vv. 1–2). The identity of the speaker is ambiguous, probably deliberately so. On the one hand, since no new speaker is introduced, we may take this as the continuation of Lady Wisdom's speech from the previous chapter. On the other hand, since wisdom is here referred to in the third person, the instructor may be a parent (see 1:8–19) or another teacher. The address "my child" or "my children" punctuates these opening chapters. It occurs once in what is specifically identified as "a father's instruction" (4:1) and once on the lips of Wisdom herself (8:32). But most of the speeches in which it occurs could be assigned equally to Wisdom, to a parent, or to a schoolteacher. The effect is that the instruction of divine Wisdom flows almost imperceptibly into the speech of her human representatives.

The figurative language suggests that acquiring wisdom is more like an adventure, a quest, than a homework assignment. First, you have to want understanding, and want it badly. "If you cry out . . . and raise your voice . . . "—these are the same verbs used of Wisdom's urgent call in 1:20–21.

The image of the treasure hunt suggests both strong motivation and also the rigors of the search. "If you seek it like silver"—in the ancient world, miners were lowered by ropes into deep narrow shafts; it was an occupation that few would choose! Yet, perhaps anticipating that many will fall away at the outset, the sages of Proverbs assure us that sure knowledge of God is possible (v. 5)—not because we are so smart, but because, in response to our earnest desire, "the LORD gives wisdom" (v. 6).

The rest of the passage is dominated by the image of two different kinds of "path" (several synonyms with this meaning occur here a total of thirteen times). The contrast is stark: between the path of life and justice and the way of evil, darkness, and death. The absoluteness of the contrast is hard for us to grasp. We are so accustomed to thinking in shades of gray, with an eye always to the extenuating circumstance. But the biblical writers frequently bring us up short. They remind us that in the things that touch our character and therefore our life with God, we must make a clear and conscious choice. In terms similar to those used by the sages, Moses in his final address confronts the Israelites: "See, I have set before you today life and prosperity, death and adversity" (Deut. 30:15).

The image of the path itself suggests something of what it means to seek wisdom. First, the decision to seek it is not made once and for all. A path may guide our movement but does not determine it. We may set our feet on "the paths of uprightness" and then go astray (v. 13). Wisdom and understanding come only to those who persist in walking that way, step by step, day after day. Second, no one walks the way that leads to wisdom entirely alone. A path is a public walkway. Many feet clear it, over a period of time; repeated use keeps it open. The biblical writers relieve us of the burden and delusion of radical individuality, which is such a strong element of our contemporary ideology. If we would find wisdom, then we must look to those who have walked that way before us. This is what it means to belong to a tradition, something of which the sages themselves are highly conscious. The notion of tradition is much underrated in our modern world, and therefore our sense of isolation is greatly increased. This is especially so for those who choose the path of wisdom, which is never in any age the main thoroughfare for travel. If we change our lives so that there is time to search for "knowledge of God," the immediate result may be a deeper sense of loneliness. Moreover, it may be difficult to find sound guidance; for sadly, few of us know a lot of people—or even one!—wise in the ways of God. Therefore it is well to remember that we may get encouragement, guidance, and deep spiritual companionship from the dead as well as the living, within what the Apostles' Creed calls "the communion of saints." Spiritual reading—from the Bible but also from books whose wisdom has been tested by time—gives us access to the wisdom that God "stores up for the upright" (v. 7).

The Strange Woman (Proverbs 2:16–22)

2:16 **You will be saved from the loose woman,**
   from the adulteress with her smooth words,
 17 **who forsakes the partner of her youth**
   and forgets her sacred covenant;
 18 **for her way leads down to death,**
   and her paths to the shades;
 19 **those who go to her never come back,**
   nor do they regain the paths of life.
 20 **Therefore walk in the way of the good,**
   and keep to the paths of the just.
 21 **For the upright will abide in the land,**
   and the innocent will remain in it;
 22 **but the wicked will be cut off from the land,**
   and the treacherous will be rooted out of it.

This final section focuses on the threat presented by "the strange woman" (the NRSV translation "loose woman" is inadequate, as explained below). The sages frequently caution the young men who would have been their original audience (since only in rare instances would women in ancient Israel have received formal education) against sexual indiscretion. Yet it is important to recognize that their concern is not simply (as often is the case in the modern church) with private morality and its consequences for "personal salvation." There is in fact an integral connection between the warning against infidelity and the promise that "the upright will abide in the land" (v. 21). That connection may be understood in light of the fact that the sages are upholding the traditional social structure of Israel, namely as a kinship-based society where the extended family was the primary socioeconomic unit. In other words, the multigenerational household traditionally known as "the father's house" was bound together not only by ties of blood, marriage, and affection, but also by strong economic bonds. Its primary activities were small-scale agriculture, tending flocks and herds, and processing raw materials into food and clothing. Much of the biblical legislation (e.g., the debt slavery laws in Exod. 21:2–11; Lev. 25:23–55; Deut. 15:1–18) aims at keeping the infrastructure of the society intact by enabling families to work as "free peasants" on their own land.

Yet the biblical emphasis on keeping families intact and on the land is motivated by more than political and economic wisdom. For the family was also the primary unit of religious life, and therefore the link between family and land also has central theological significance. On the one hand, the *Promised Land* of Israel is the earnest, the tangible evidence of God's commitment to the *people* Israel. On the other hand, it was in the everyday life of the family that God's commitment was most consistently felt and Israel's reciprocal commitment nurtured through religious education and observance. There is strong evidence that inclusion in a family structure was necessary for full participation in the religious life of Israel, which is one reason why the Old Testament frequently calls attention to the plight of those whose family structure has been weakened or destroyed: widows and orphans, sojourners and slaves.

The religious importance of family life grew in the period after the Babylonian exile, when the Temple and the monarchy had been destroyed. In the absence of the former priestly and royal mediators between God and Israel, the family assumed much greater responsibility for upholding and perpetuating the covenantal faith. There is good evidence that the religious role of women became correspondingly more important, precisely because they bore so much responsibility for home-based religious practices such as Sabbath observance and for cultivation of a moral environment in which children might grow into a healthy understanding of what it means to be "a good Israelite," faithful to Israel's God. Accordingly, the book of Proverbs, which assumed final form in the period after the exile, asserts: "Women's wisdom builds her house" (14:1, AT). It is noteworthy that *all* the memorable figures in this book, including Lady Wisdom herself, are women. Significantly, the final portrait of the "woman of valor" (31:10–31) gives us more insight than any other biblical passage into the work of ordinary women. At the same time, that female homebuilder is the sages' most fully developed example of someone who embodies "fear of the LORD" (31:30).

The negative attention that Proverbs gives to the adulterous woman (see also 6:24–35; 7:1–27) is the flip side of the positive highlighting of "women's wisdom." In light of the central social and religious role of women, "the strange woman" who makes light of the marital covenant is more than a source of grief to her husband and immediate family. She threatens the whole community at the core of its life—that is, in its relationship to God. The Hebrew text of this passage gives us several hints of the religious dimension of the threat, which have been lost in the NRSV translation. First, verse 17b literally reads, " . . . and she forgets the covenant of her God." The phrasing suggests that she has ignored not only her marriage vows but also the covenant promises by which God established himself as Israel's God and established the people Israel on their own land. Second, in biblical usage, the word "strange" frequently has the connotation of idolatrous worship ("strange gods"). Third, the references to death and the shades (v. 18) give a mythic dimension to the threat of extinction that results from her behavior. But more than personal death is implied. "The wicked will be cut off from the land" (v. 22); the undoing of the family unit through sexual irresponsibility leads to the undoing of God's blessing of Israel through the gift of the Promised Land. Far from being a pious cliché, the threat expresses the sages' keen social and religious perception that irresponsible sexual behavior is ultimately connected with the horrors of social collapse and religious disenfranchisement of the weak, especially children.

BEYOND THE LIMITS OF HUMAN UNDERSTANDING
Proverbs 3:1–12

3:1 My child, do not forget my teaching,
   but let your heart keep my commandments;
² for length of days and years of life
   and abundant welfare they will give you.
³ Do not let loyalty and faithfulness forsake you;
   bind them around your neck,
   write them on the tablet of your heart.
⁴ So you will find favor and good repute
   in the sight of God and of people.
⁵ Trust in the LORD with all your heart,
   and do not rely on your own insight.
⁶ In all your ways acknowledge him,
   and he will make straight your paths.
⁷ Do not be wise in your own eyes;
   fear the LORD, and turn away from evil.
⁸ It will be a healing for your flesh
   and a refreshment for your body.
⁹ Honor the LORD with your substance
   and with the first fruits of all your produce;
¹⁰ then your barns will be filled with plenty,
   and your vats will be bursting with wine.
¹¹ My child, do not despise the LORD's discipline
   or be weary of his reproof,

[12] **for the LORD reproves the one he loves,**
    as a father the son in whom he delights.

This instruction gives important insight into what might be called the educational theory of the sages. Wisdom does not come simply from study (although this is valued) nor from even the keenest native intelligence. Its foundation is not finally within ourselves at all but rather in the relationship we have with God. That relationship is one of practical trust—that is, trust so complete that it is evidenced in all we do (vv. 5–6). So the sages encourage us to put ourselves in the posture of a child (vv. 1, 11, 12)—even a newborn! This point is made by the striking imagery in verse 8 but not adequately conveyed by the English translation. The Hebrew reads, "It will be healing for your *navel* and *moisture* for your *bones*." Since this phrasing is no less curious in Hebrew than in English, it is likely that we are meant to ponder the image. This is formative instruction for spiritual neonates; in Paul's terms, it is milk for those who are not yet ready for solid food (1 Cor. 3:2).

The pronounced physicality of the image indicates that the biblical writers perceive no split between body and soul. Greek philosophy aims to "rise above" the body and its needs. By contrast, Israelite wisdom imbues the whole person: body, mind, and spirit (see 14:30; 17:22). Augustine expresses the biblical conception of wisdom when he says, "I want to be healed completely, because I am a complete whole" (Sermon 30.4).

No age limit applies to the call to look toward God with the trust of a child (see Jesus' similar call to receive the kingdom of heaven as a child, Mark 10:15 and parallels). The sages habitually address the reader as "my child." This is not demeaning but rather invites us to be free of the anxiety that may be the defining characteristic of what we generally—but unwisely!—call "adult life." Moreover, by sounding the keynote of trust, the sages counter the sickening fear that dominates the educational experience of so many, from elementary school classrooms to graduate school and on-the-job training, even to the extreme consequences of nervous breakdown and suicide at exam time. This instruction points obliquely to the cause of that fear: namely, exclusive reliance on our own understanding, the feeling (which, sadly, is often encouraged by teachers) that I need to "get on top of this"—this information, this subject, this situation, every possible situation—by sheer force of intellect. Yet sooner or later, that proves to be impossible. The sages know that the desire to learn is God-given and glorious: "It is the glory of God to conceal things, but the glory of kings is to search things out" (Prov. 25:2). But if that very desire is not finally to bring us to despair, then sooner or later each of us must give up reliance on our own intellect.

Paradoxically, the alternative to self-reliance and the unhealthy fear that attends it is fear of the Lord (v. 7). Trust and health-giving fear (see the comment on 1:7) are simply two different aspects of a comprehensive commitment of our lives into God's hands. Putting it another way, they are two elements of the deeply sane recognition that I am not God, and when I pretend to be God, I only destroy myself. When I truly recognize that, then the desire to honor the One who is God arises spontaneously in my heart.

But it can also work the other way around; concrete practices of honoring God may help me to get an accurate perspective on myself. So the sages remind their students to observe the regular practice of making an offering of first fruits (v. 9). This is the only injunction to formal religious practice in the book. The sages are normally silent on such matters, although one can point to an occasional jibe at insincere sacrifice (15:6). On the whole, they simply assume the sphere of public religious activity, while directing their attention to the cultivation of personal character and discipline. But there is no reason to suppose that the sages belong to an intellectual tradition that separates them from or makes them hostile to the more narrowly prescriptive and prohibitive teachings of Torah: Exodus, Leviticus, and Deuteronomy. Rather, the two kinds of teaching are complementary. Both wisdom and Torah are concerned with the sanctification of daily life in community. Both recognize that holy living ultimately comes down to matters of concrete and often minute practice in all the ordinary things of life. The "legal" prescription to offer the first fruits (compare Exod. 23:19; Lev. 23:10–14; Deut. 26:1–11, and elsewhere) with the accompanying promise of abundance (v. 10) can be seen as one way of making concrete the typical wisdom saying in verse 6 (compare 16:3). The assurance here expresses the generally optimistic outlook of the sages that the world is well-ordered under God's rule, and the faithful will prosper (a conviction that Job, the contrary sage, furiously refutes).

The sages of Proverbs are optimistic yet not naïve, as indicated by final mention of "the LORD's discipline." "Discipline" (Hebrew, *mûsar*) is always a positive concept for the sages (see the discussion at 1:1–6). Receiving discipline is good and necessary; nonetheless, it is not exactly fun. God, who gives to us unstintingly, also disciplines us as regularly and lovingly as a parent disciplines a child. There is no contradiction between the promise of plenty and the reminder of discipline. God is entirely generous toward us, yet part of the loving attention that God lavishes on us is disciplinary—

and there is good reason to believe that we never outgrow our need for either bounty or discipline!

LAYING HOLD OF HAPPINESS
Proverbs 3:13–26

3:13 Happy are those who find wisdom,
and those who get understanding,
14 for her income is better than silver,
and her revenue better than gold.
15 She is more precious than jewels,
and nothing you desire can compare with her.
16 Long life is in her right hand;
in her left hand are riches and honor.
17 Her ways are ways of pleasantness,
and all her paths are peace.
18 She is a tree of life to those who lay hold of her;
those who hold her fast are called happy.
19 The LORD by wisdom founded the earth;
by understanding he established the heavens;
20 by his knowledge the deeps broke open,
and the clouds drop down the dew.
21 My child, do not let these escape from your sight:
keep sound wisdom and prudence,
22 and they will be life for your soul
and adornment for your neck.
23 Then you will walk on your way securely
and your foot will not stumble.
24 If you sit down, you will not be afraid;
when you lie down, your sleep will be sweet.
25 Do not be afraid of sudden panic,
or of the storm that strikes the wicked;
26 for the LORD will be your confidence
and will keep your foot from being caught.

"You know, happiness is a high-tech thing." My father was speaking, sitting at the breakfast table with a quizzical look on his face. That morning, we were comrades in the task of trying to negotiate the difficulties of life. I was a quite-young adult at the time, and he was entering old age. At that point, happiness was eluding us both. Here I imagine the sages speaking to people like us, seeking to give us both encouragement and in-course correction. "There is only one thing that yields real happiness," they tell us. "It's really very simple—though that doesn't mean that happiness comes easily to anybody. You have to go down to bedrock to find it. You have to get to what is most real. That is wisdom, and it's with 'her' that happiness is to be found."

In this passage the sages take us down to the bedrock of reality. In mythological language—and the passage is laced throughout with mythological language—they take us back to the foundations of the world in order to show that laying hold of wisdom means nothing less than getting in touch with the structure of the universe, and shaping our own lives in accordance with that.

They begin with an image drawn from the mythology of Egypt, the ancestral home of the wisdom literature traditions. The verbal portrait of wisdom bearing long life in one hand and riches in the other is drawn from the visual representations of the goddess Ma'at, who personifies social order and justice. Many images show her holding in one hand a scepter, symbolizing wealth and power, and in the other the ancient Egyptian symbol of life.

Then the sages move home, to their own ancient tradition, with the reference to the tree of life (v. 18). The image stands out; because, outside the first chapters of Genesis, this is the only direct reference to that famous tree, from which our first disobedience separated us (see Gen. 3:24). The sages seem to suggest that laying hold of wisdom reverses our original exile and brings us back into Eden. Those who find wisdom experience something of the joy of paradise: "All her ways are ways of pleasantness" (v. 17). The sages here use a technique that is common among the biblical writers. In just a few words they evoke the story of Adam and Eve in the Garden of Eden, the foundational story for humanity's history with God. That story then remains in the background as a foil against which the sages' understanding of wisdom appears in sharp outline.

One might sum up all the teachings of Proverbs by saying that wisdom means holding two things always together: discerning knowledge of the world plus obedience to God. As we shall see, the tragedy that occurred in Eden was the separation of those two essential elements of wisdom. It is the sages' task to reconnect them. First, knowledge of the world: we were made to be curious about the world, to direct our minds to exploring its wonders and its difficulties, to feel its beauties and its horrors. In the language of Genesis, we were indeed meant to have "knowledge of good and evil" (Gen. 2:9). The sages of Proverbs use such words as "insight," "prudence," "wise dealing," "skill" (Prov. 1:2–5, etc.) to denote our capacity for discerning knowledge of the world. But we were meant to acquire that knowledge in the context of obedient relationship with God. That is what the sages mean when they say that wisdom begins with fear of the Lord (1:7) and advances only through trust (3:5). They urge us to heed wisdom's "counsel" (1:25) and "commandments" (2:1; 3:1).

The highly imaginative language of Genesis likewise implies that we were meant to learn of the world through a relationship of trusting intimacy. It seems that God came for an evening stroll in the garden, hoping to enjoy the company of the human beings (Gen. 3:8–9). Imagine how much they might have discovered about their new world through those evening walks with the Lord who founded the earth "by wisdom" (Prov. 3:19)! But the first human sin was to take the search for knowledge *outside* that relationship of trust. Eve saw the tree and its fruit as a means to become wise on her own (Gen. 3:6). The bitter irony is that the very opposite happened: the humans acquired only the cheapest scrap of knowledge, which in fact demeaned them in their own eyes: "They knew that they were naked" (3:7). It is no coincidence that the fallout from this first disobedience was the erosion of trust and harmony at every level of creation; blame comes between man and woman; enmity arises between woman's seed and snake's seed; the curse on the soil ends the pleasant work of gardening; the humans are excluded from God's garden; and death enters the world. We are still feeling those losses.

The sages strike directly at the root of the problem: "Do not be wise in your own eyes" (Prov. 3:7). If we would know the world without doing damage to it and ourselves, then we must raise our sights above our own cleverness and fix them on God, the creator of earth and heaven (vv. 19–20). Knowing the world without doing damage to it and ourselves—that is "prudence," a word the sages use frequently (3:21; see also 1:4; 2:11; 5:2, etc.). It is an old-fashioned word, but our ancestors in both philosophical and religious traditions have regarded it as one of the four "cardinal virtues" without which human life inevitably becomes degraded and destructive. Prudence is living in accordance with what *is*—that is, accepting the world as wisely made and preserved by God (vv. 19–20) and choosing a course of action that accords with that God-given reality. Prudence is nothing other than "acknowledging [God] in all your ways" (3:6, AT).

Maybe the concept of prudence sounds out-of-date because in the past century and a half we have come to believe that human technological progress frees us from the obligation to observe "what is." The rhetoric of industrial economics suggests that we have the power to create new realities, and so we act as though that were the case. We use an amount of oil in one day that it took the combination of systems we call "nature" ten thousand days to produce. We cut down the world's forests at the rate of one percent per year and watch the global temperature steadily rise, hoping the consequences will not catch up with us. We go on producing atomic waste that will be deadly for a geological age to come, assuming that somehow our "foot will not be caught" (v. 26). If we are reading the Bible as we should—with an informed eye to the world around us, praying that what we read will let us see the world with something of God's perspective—then we can hear the judgment of Proverbs on our imprudent actions. We are very far from the security to which this teacher would direct us (v. 23). Because we as a culture are "wise in our own eyes," we are dangerously out of touch with the wisdom by which God "founded the earth" (v. 19).

The biblical wisdom literature is of great value to Christians as we seek to deepen our theological understanding of creation and thus respond *out of our faith* to the ecological crisis that currently threatens its well-being. One of the pronounced features of this literature is its focus on creation as the realm where God's will and action is to be discerned. Unlike the rest of the Old Testament, the wisdom literature makes no specific reference to the "salvation history" of Israel, that is, the great events of the exodus, Sinai, the establishment of the Davidic monarchy, or the return from exile. Whereas the rest of the Old Testament tells the story of Israel, the wisdom literature speaks more directly about the human condition as a whole. As we have seen, the sages return us to the first chapters of Genesis. The fact that creation is the horizon for their thought leads them to show detailed interest in the daily workings of the nonhuman world (the sages were observant "naturalists"; see 6:6–8) and also of the human social order.

"The LORD *by wisdom* founded the earth": This brief statement sets forth the central truth underlying all biblical statements about God as creator. Unlike the creation myths of Mesopotamia and Greece, Israel's scriptures are not interested in the physical origins of the world—a point that has been missed in the ongoing debate between creationists and evolutionists. Rather, the truth that is upheld is about the nature of the world, namely, that it is a product of God's wisdom ("understanding . . . , knowledge") and exquisite care. It follows, then, that human wisdom necessarily has an "ecological" dimension, that is, it involves directing our own careful attention to learning about and preserving the world that God has made. The wisdom literature is an important part of the Bible's "creation story," for it illumines (more clearly than Genesis itself) the perspective of *creatio continua*, "ongoing creation," which acknowledges that creation and preservation of the world are inseparable aspects of a single work of God in which we are invited to be grateful and active participants.

THE SCORNERS
Proverbs 3:27–35

3:27 Do not withhold good from those to whom it is due,
      when it is in your power to do it.
  28 Do not say to your neighbor, "Go, and come again,
      tomorrow I will give it"—when you have it with you.
  29 Do not plan harm against your neighbor
      who lives trustingly beside you.
  30 Do not quarrel with anyone without cause,
      when no harm has been done to you.
  31 Do not envy the violent
      and do not choose any of their ways;
  32 for the perverse are an abomination to the LORD,
      but the upright are in his confidence.
  33 The LORD's curse is on the house of the wicked,
      but he blesses the abode of the righteous.
  34 Toward the scorners he is scornful,
      but to the humble he shows favor.
  35 The wise will inherit honor,
      but stubborn fools, disgrace.

This is the first concrete illustration of the behavior of the "scorners" mentioned in Wisdom's first speech (see the comment on 1:22, where the same word is translated "scoffers"). "Scorners" are those who have no sense of duty toward their neighbor. Duty is not a popular concept today, but the sages place very high value on apparently simple acts of maintaining faithfulness to commitments, even when one might get away with ignoring or reneging on them. They understand that honoring obligations to those to whom we are bound even by the involuntary ties of blood or neighborhood is essential to healthy community life and also to our own humanity.

The prohibitions in verses 27–28 could cover a variety of situations: delaying payment for goods and services (out of carelessness, or in order that we may invest the money in more "profitable" ways), hesitating to make a loan to a neighbor in need (an English proverb says aptly, "Whoever gives quickly, gives twice"). This instruction provides a balance to the warnings against standing surety for a neighbor's debt (see the comment on 6:1–5). Taking them together, we might understand the sages' advice as follows: give "when it is in your power to do it," generously but not to the point of genuine self-endangerment.

Verses 29–32 extend the prohibitions to cover various forms of aggression. "Do not plan harm against your neighbor who lives trustingly beside you"—the key word here is "trustingly." The same Hebrew word appears in verse 23, where it is translated "securely." The repetition points to the connection in thought between the two passages. As we have seen, the rest of the chapter aims at convincing us that the source of our security lies in trusting God and living in accordance with God's wisdom. This section complements that instruction by cautioning us that we may remain secure only if we extend that God-given security to our neighbors.

"Do not plan harm to your neighbor who lives trustingly beside you": We may easily apply that to personal situations. But equally, does it not set limits on public behavior? It condemns "the scorners" (v. 34), who construct nuclear power plants and solid waste incinerators with hollow assurances of safety; "the violent" (v. 31), industries whose practices have produced the various "cancer alleys" that dot North America; "the perverse" (v. 32), corporations who have moved their manufacturing operations to countries where the desperate need for cash continues to keep pollution controls low. Does it also condemn us, who enjoy their services and products at relatively low cost, without considering the price extracted from the "humble" (v. 34)?

LOVING WISDOM
Proverbs 4:1–9

4:1 Listen, children, to a father's instruction,
    and be attentive, that you may gain insight;
 2 for I give you good precepts:
    do not forsake my teaching.
 3 When I was a son with my father,
    tender, and my mother's favorite,
 4 he taught me, and said to me,
    "Let your heart hold fast my words;
    keep my commandments, and live.
 5 Get wisdom; get insight: do not forget, nor turn away
    from the words of my mouth.
 6 Do not forsake her, and she will keep you;
    love her, and she will guard you.
 7 The beginning of wisdom is this: Get wisdom,
    and whatever else you get, get insight.
 8 Prize her highly, and she will exalt you;
    she will honor you if you embrace her.

⁹ **She will place on your head a fair garland;**
she will bestow on you a beautiful crown."

The teaching is marked specifically as "a father's discipline" (Hebrew, *mûsar*; see also 1:8 and the comment there), something he learned as a child from his own father. The sages speak with the weight of generations behind them. They rarely appeal to their own authority or even their personal experience. They are not celebrities offering their philosophies of life, but rather anonymous "sons," passing on the lessons their own devoted parents taught them. In a traditional society such as ancient Israel, the time-tested understandings of the past are far more valuable than the fresh opinions of today's headliner. The transgenerational perspective is deeply comforting to people in transition or crisis, as the young often are. It implies that the present situation, though perhaps new and frightening to the person who confronts it, is analogous to others that have occurred many times in the past. Based on that long and broad experience, one may draw some conclusions about how best to proceed in this instance.

The personification of wisdom here suggests that "she" is something like the patron goddesses known in Mesopotamia and Egypt: "She will honor you if you embrace her. She will place on your head a fair garland" (vv. 8–9). The image comes from a pagan banquet. It is amazing that such risqué language survived editorial censorship, in light of the firm exclusion of other gods from Israel's official religion. Moreover, we know that goddess worship was sometimes (at least) part of the popular religion of Israel, despite strong prophetic condemnation (see Jer. 7:18; 44:15–19). So why do the sages take the risk of representing wisdom as something-like-a-goddess? A remark of C. S. Lewis affords the best explanation: "when the old poets made some virtue their theme they were not teaching but adoring, and . . . what we take for the didactic is often the enchanted" (*Preface*, p. v.). The poet-sages of ancient Israel were enchanted with wisdom. They used imagination and skill—and took a risk—so to evoke "her" that we might be enchanted, too.

THE ANATOMY OF WISDOM
Proverbs 4:20–27

4:20 **My child, be attentive to my words;**
incline your ear to my sayings.
²¹ **Do not let them escape from your sight;**
keep them within your heart.

²² **For they are life to those who find them,**
   and healing to all their flesh.
²³ **Keep your heart with all vigilance,**
   for from it flow the springs of life.
²⁴ **Put away from you crooked speech,**
   and put devious talk far from you.
²⁵ **Let your eyes look directly forward,**
   and your gaze be straight before you.
²⁶ **Keep straight the path of your feet,**
   and all your ways will be sure.
²⁷ **Do not swerve to the right or to the left;**
   turn your foot away from evil.

This is the conclusion of a larger section (vv. 10–27) that contrasts "the path of the wicked" (v. 14) and "the path of the righteous" (v. 18). It focuses our attention for the first time on the *person* of the one who follows the latter path and reveals that wisdom is, among other things, a physical disposition of the self. The passage is an anatomical inventory, which represents the attentive student in terms of a series of seven body parts: ears, eyes, heart, flesh, mouth and lips, feet. Seven is in biblical symbolism the number signifying completeness (e.g., the seven days of creation); the person as a physical totality is envisioned.

This sort of highly specific physical representation reaches its fullest development in the erotic poems of the Song of Songs, but here also it makes a strong impression. The effect is to illustrate the complexity of the self that must commit itself to the right path. Every part of the body is capable of being either a vehicle of faithfulness or the instrument of our destruction, and succeeding chapters will furnish multiple examples. Further, their enumeration underscores the fundamental unity between inner disposition and external behavior. What is within the heart inevitably flows outward (v. 21); and as Jesus teaches, it is what comes from within that has the potential to defile us (Mark 7:20–23).

Although we know nothing about ancient meditative practice, the poem might be used as the basis for a personal meditation. Each part of the self may be offered for God's service, and in turn we may ask that it be strengthened and guided in God's service. Compare the words of the modern hymn:

> Take my life, and let it be consecrated, Lord, to thee;
> take my moments and my days, let them flow in ceaseless praise.
> Take my hands, and let them move at the impulse of thy love;
> take my heart, it is thine own; it shall be thy royal throne.

Take my voice, and let me sing always, only, for my King;
take my intellect, and use every power as thou shalt choose.
Take my will, and make it thine; it shall be no longer mine.
Take myself, and I will be ever, only, all for thee.

Frances Ridley Havergal

The description of a physical orientation toward wisdom offered in these verses is an effective prelude to the instructions on sexual behavior in the following three chapters. Note that this portrayal of the one disposed toward wisdom has its counterpoint in two short poems in Proverbs 6: the graphic description of "a scoundrel and a villain" (vv. 12–15) and another anatomical inventory, the list of "six things that the LORD hates" (vv. 16–19).

FRANK TALK ABOUT SEX
Proverbs 5:1–23

5:1 My child, be attentive to my wisdom;
incline your ear to my understanding,
² so that you may hold on to prudence,
and your lips may guard knowledge.
³ For the lips of a loose woman drip honey,
and her speech is smoother than oil;
⁴ but in the end she is bitter as wormwood,
sharp as a two-edged sword.
⁵ Her feet go down to death;
her steps follow the path to Sheol.
⁶ She does not keep straight to the path of life;
her ways wander, and she does not know it.

⁷ And now, my child, listen to me,
and do not depart from the words of my mouth.
⁸ Keep your way far from her,
and do not go near the door of her house;
⁹ or you will give your honor to others,
and your years to the merciless,
¹⁰ and strangers will take their fill of your wealth,
and your labors will go to the house of an alien;
¹¹ and at the end of your life you will groan,
when your flesh and body are consumed,
¹² and you say, "Oh, how I hated discipline,
and my heart despised reproof!

13 I did not listen to the voice of my teachers
   or incline my ear to my instructors.
14 Now I am at the point of utter ruin
   in the public assembly."
15 Drink water from your own cistern,
   flowing water from your own well.
16 Should your springs be scattered abroad,
   streams of water in the streets?
17 Let them be for yourself alone,
   and not for sharing with strangers.
18 Let your fountain be blessed,
   and rejoice in the wife of your youth,
19 a lovely deer, a graceful doe.
   May her breasts satisfy you at all times;
   may you be intoxicated always by her love.
20 Why should you be intoxicated, my son, by another woman
   and embrace the bosom of an adulteress?
21 For human ways are under the eyes of the LORD,
   and he examines all their paths.
22 The iniquities of the wicked ensnare them,
   and they are caught in the toils of their sin.
23 They die for lack of discipline,
   and because of their great folly they are lost.

We generally assume that the biblical writers are prudish or perhaps simply uninformed about sex. The lack of embarrassment— indeed, the boldness—with which Proverbs offers instruction about sexual behavior may therefore come as a surprise. This instruction is largely concentrated here and in the following two chapters. This chapter sets forth the sharp contrast between a healthy eroticism, stimulated by the fresh-flowing waters of "the wife of your youth" (v. 18), and a perverse attraction to the honeyed lips of "a strange woman" (vv. 3, 20a; on this translation, see the comment at 2:16). Whereas the similar teaching in Proverbs 7 is conveyed by means of a story, here what is prominent is the vivid and highly suggestive imagery. The other poetic technique used throughout this chapter is repetition of key words, which serves to clarify the choice that must be made between the two alternatives. The frequency of repetition across the entire chapter indicates that this is a unified composition by a single poet.

The first repetition and contrast occurs in verses 2 and 3: between the "child's" lips, which are to guard knowledge, and the lips of the strange woman, which drip honey. It should be noted that the Hebrew of verse 3b is considerably bolder than the English translation indicates; literally, "her *palate* is smoother than oil," an image which suggests that her deep kisses are no less sweet and entrapping than her words. The contrast is reinforced by the echo between the *knowledge* that is to be guarded (v. 2)—presumably through steady repetition of the teacher's instructions—and the observation that the woman does not *know* her own steps have wandered (v. 6).

This instance of verbal repetition causes us to look backward from verse 6 to verse 2 and see the fundamental difference between the young man and the woman he should avoid. At the same time, the technique of repetition directs our attention forward to the end of the poem, where we see the consequences of their embrace. Two instances of repetitions connect verses 5–6 with verses 21–22, although neither is evident in translation. First, in reference to the "strange woman," verse 5b reads: "her steps *hold fast* [*tamak*] to Sheol"; the word suggests tenacity. It occurs again in verse 22: "in the bonds of his sin he is *held fast*." (The NRSV incorrectly translates the last three verses with plural pronouns: "their," "them," "they." The Hebrew in each case is masculine singular, thus establishing a connection between this summary statement and the preceding warning to the young man.) Drawing the connection between verses 5 and 22, we see that in the moment of embracing the strange woman, the man chooses the path of downward mobility, to Sheol, the place of the dead.

The second instance of repetition also concentrates on choice of the right path. Of the strange woman, we are told: "The path of life she does not *follow*" (v. 6a). She is heedless of where she is going (v. 6b), but God is not: " . . . and all [a person]'s tracks he *follows*" (v. 21, AT). Repetition of the rare Hebrew verb underscores the contrast between God's attentiveness and her disregard, and that is worth pondering. It is lack of attention that destroys our souls. Probably little of the behavior and attitude that the Bible terms "wicked" (v. 22) originates as malice, active enmity toward God and neighbor. It begins with the simple failure to take ourselves as seriously as does God, who gives exquisite attention to all our ways. Conversely, godliness begins by taking ourselves seriously—which is not the same thing as being self-important! The most godly people I know are pained by failings in themselves that seem to an outsider almost trivial. Things I would not even pause to notice (in myself!), or would dismiss as quirks, they see as signs that they have strayed from "the path of the righteous" (4:18a). At the same time, the godly are relatively heedless of the shortcomings of others. Their "eyes look directly forward" (4:25), and thus they are able to keep to the path "which shines brighter and brighter until full day" (4:18b).

All sexual relationships are deep. Adulterous love is deep and deadly; the strange woman and her lover are bound for Sheol, the death Pit. By contrast, "the wife of your youth" is a cistern, a well, a fountain (vv. 15, 18). The extended water imagery that represents the well-known and trusted woman is uniquely powerful; water is the most precious natural resource in semi-arid Israel, and it can never be taken for granted. As the Bible repeatedly reminds us, in a land where there is not nearly enough fresh running water, the rainwater that is stored in cisterns and replenishes deep underground wells is a sign both of God's graciousness and of Israel's continual dependence on God. Could not something similar be said of a faithful marriage? It is a sign of God's favor and a source of strength. Yet at the same time, we must remember that, like all living things, a marriage is frail and stands in continual need of God's grace and protection, as well as of human nurture.

"Let your fountain be blessed" (v. 18): The sages frequently use the fountain image to characterize wisdom and its sources. Wisdom (16:22), the fear of the Lord (14:27), the mouth or teaching of the righteous (10:11; 13:14)—all of these are "a fountain of life." So probably it can be said that marriage is likewise a source of wisdom, or it should be. The choice of a life partner determines to a very great extent how as adults we look at and continue to learn about the world. Marriage is a long "study": in cooperation, service, forbearance, love, forgiveness. Daily interaction with another mind also shapes our intellectual dispositions more than we generally realize. Maybe more young people need to hear that from their teachers. I vividly remember my pastoral theology professor's "wisdom teaching": "How you know what you know—that depends upon whom you marry!"

The imagery of flowing liquids is most extravagant in verse 19, where a more accurate translation would be "may her breasts *drench* you at all times." With that erotic ideal in mind, the sages drive home the utter folly of choosing a "stranger" by means of the threefold repetition of the word *shagah*, "besotted, intoxicated, infatuated" (vv. 19, 20, 23). It is no coincidence that this is the final word of the poem, although the NRSV misses its centrality. The final verse literally reads, "He dies for lack of discipline, and in his great folly he is *besotted*." A terse comment from the medieval rabbis captures the idea of moral choice developed through the whole chapter: "He did not wish to be infatuated with moral discipline [compare v. 12], so now infatuated by his great folly, he shall die" (see Visotzky, *Midrash*, 35).

It is possible that there is a second level of meaning to this poem, in addition to the warning against adultery. The original audience may also have heard here a warning against marriage to literal "strangers," that is,

foreigners. It is likely that this poem comes from the period after the Babylonian exile. Therefore it may be influenced by the "God-given wisdom"
(Ezra 7:25) of Ezra, a leader of the community of Jews returned from exile,
who insisted on the dissolution of all marriages between Israelite men and
non-Israelite women. Ezra's aim was to restore the religious integrity of
the Israelite community, where, in the absence of king, state, and temple,
the family had once again become the mediator of both social stability and
religious identity. The argument for this second level of meaning rests on
the prominence of references to strangers. The dangerous woman herself
is called both a "stranger" (*zarah*, vv. 3, 20a) and an "alien" (v. 20b; NRSV's
"adulteress" is inaccurate). The further threat that the property of the
heedless will pass to strangers and aliens (vv. 10, 17) suggests that the sages
may be concerned that foreign marriage will diminish the economic
resources of an already fragile community.

STANDING SURETY
Proverbs 6:1–5

> 6:1   My child, if you have given your pledge to your neighbor,
>   if you have bound yourself to another,
>   2   you are snared by the utterance of your lips,
>   caught by the words of your mouth.
>   3   So do this, my child, and save yourself,
>   for you have come into your neighbor's power:
>   go, hurry, and plead with your neighbor.
>   4   Give your eyes no sleep
>   and your eyelids no slumber;
>   5   save yourself like a gazelle from the hunter,
>   like a bird from the hand of the fowler.

The sages comment emphatically and often on the folly of standing surety
for a debtor, that is, offering one's own property as collateral for the debt
(compare 11:15; 17:18; 20:16; 22:26; 27:13). This attitude is initially surprising, since a number of passages encourage kindness toward the poor
(e.g., 14:21, 31; 17:5; compare 19:7). But the sages envision a situation in
which a generous impulse causes the inexperienced ("my child," v. 3) to
commit themselves beyond what they can afford to lose, if the debtor forfeits or dies. In that case the guarantor risks abject poverty or even debt
slavery (cf. 2 Kings 4:1), especially if the creditor is a non-Israelite (reading the word "another" [v. 1: literally, "stranger"] in the strongest sense.)

Nonetheless, the sages were not uniformly opposed to the practice. The last biblical sage, Jesus ben Sirach, asserts: "A good person will be surety for his neighbor" (Sir. 29:14); but he adds: "Assist your neighbor to the best of your ability, but be careful not to fall yourself" (v. 20). (See further at 22:22–29.)

PARABLE OF THE ANT
Proverbs 6:6–11

6:6 Go to the ant, you lazybones;
consider its ways, and be wise.
  7 Without having any chief or officer or ruler,
  8 it prepares its food in summer,
and gathers its sustenance in harvest.
  9 How long will you lie there, O lazybones?
When will you rise from your sleep?
 10 A little sleep, a little slumber,
a little folding of the hands to rest,
 11 and poverty will come upon you like a robber,
and want, like an armed warrior.

This parable may be taken at several levels. First and most obviously, the example of the ant offers practical encouragement to industriousness and foresight. Many of us in modern industrialized societies do not need to be told to work harder; between family and jobs, our lives are already frenetically busy. But one can be busy and yet be guilty of a disastrous lack of foresight. One instance of this is the heavy dependency on credit that afflicts "corporate America" and brings many individuals and families to grief. At a national level, our vast and growing indebtedness threatens to cripple the next generation. The ant "gathers its sustenance in harvest" (v. 8). Despite rapid cash flow and apparent economic sophistication, we do not teach our children adequately about saving. Indeed, the opposite is the case. Every new college graduate is immediately bombarded with multiple offers of a huge credit line and the opportunity to become a card-carrying, financially compromised adult.

Second, the parable may be seen as offering spiritual instruction. It warns of the danger of "sloth," traditionally identified as one of the seven deadly sins. Sloth is more than laziness, an aversion to work. One may have considerable achievements and still be slothful. The spiritually deadly sin is the refusal to be alert to the *new* opportunities that continually come to us from God, opportunities that require us to keep our hearts open, our minds fresh and restless in God's service. "A little folding of the hands to rest": Slothfulness may mean resting on our own past achievements, including our spiritual achievements. The slothful person says, "I've done enough." But can we imagine that we are ever done growing, stretching, spending ourselves in God's service, repenting where we were wrong, trying again where we failed? It is against such misguided self-satisfaction that Jesus warns his disciples: "When you have done all that you were ordered to do, say, 'We are worthless slaves; we have done only what we ought to have done!' " (Luke 27:10).

The parable of the ant functions at a third level of interpretation. This is a kind of "nature wisdom," acquired through close observation of the non-human world. Such observation has long been recognized as having religious significance. Solomon was reputedly skilled in sayings about plants and animals (1 Kings 4:33). Moreover, medieval Christianity claimed that one might learn of God's nature and will not only through the scriptures and prayer, but also through "the book of the creatures," that is, by contemplation of the natural world. The perception that the natural world can in fact instruct us about God and our place in God's world is found in the Bible itself, most notably in the beautiful poem of Job:

> But ask the animals, and they will teach you;
> the birds of the air, and they will tell you;
> or speak to the earth, and it will teach you,
> and the fish of the sea will recount to you.
> Who among all these does not know,
> that the hand of the LORD has done this,
> in whose hand is the life of every living thing
> and the breath of all human flesh?
>   (Job 12:7–11)

It is regrettable that the church has in the last three centuries largely lost sight of the fact that "nature wisdom" is indispensable to an accurate estimation of the proper human role in God's creation. Perhaps the time has at last come for the revival of this branch of theology. The pressure of the ecological crisis has made us far more aware of our connection to the non-human world and also of the limits to the wisdom of *homo sapiens*. Here biology may serve to instruct theology. It is intriguing that two contemporary biologists have in fact "gone to the ant" for instruction. Ants are possibly the most successful life-form on the planet, judged in terms of abundance, social complexity, and survival over some forty to sixty million years!

They conclude their study with what might well be considered a wisdom teaching. They observe the difference in effect between two modes of biological dominance: that of human beings and that of ants:

> We are the first species to become a geophysical force, altering and demolishing ecosystems and perturbing the global climate itself. . . . If all humanity were to disappear, the remainder of life would spring back and flourish. The mass extinctions now under way would cease, the damaged ecosystems heal and expand outward. If all the ants somehow disappeared, the effect would be exactly the opposite, and catastrophic. Species extinction would increase even more over the present rate, and the land ecosystems would shrivel more rapidly as the considerable services provided by these insects were pulled away. . . . [L]et us not despise the lowly ants, but honor them. For a while longer at least, they will help to hold the world in balance to our liking, and they will serve as a reminder of what a wonderful place it was when we first arrived. (Hölldobler and Wilson, *Journey to the Ants*, 206)

Probably the most damaging form of sloth ever practiced by human beings is our current "folding of the hands" as the earth and future generations are increasingly impoverished (v. 11) and each passing year shrinks the hope of reversing the harm already done. It is past time to "go to the ant."

ADORNED WITH THE COMMANDMENTS
Proverbs 6:20–24

6:20 **My child, keep your father's commandment,**
   and do not forsake your mother's teaching.
 21 **Bind them upon your heart always;**
   tie them around your neck.
 22 **When you walk, they will lead you;**
   when you lie down, they will watch over you;
   and when you awake, they will talk with you.
 23 **For the commandment is a lamp and the teaching a light,**
   and the reproofs of discipline are the way of life,
 24 **to preserve you from the wife of another,**
   from the smooth tongue of the adulteress.

The language and imagery in these verses (and similarly in 7:1–3; compare also 1:9; 3:3, 22) is a free adaptation of Deuteronomy 6:4–9, the basic creed of Judaism, which Jesus knew as "the greatest and first commandment" (Matt. 22:38). The image of binding on the commandments connects the parental "teaching" (*tôrah*, v. 20b) with the fundamental Torah (commonly translated "law," but "teaching" is more accurate) given to Israel through Moses at Sinai, of which the Deuteronomy passage is the summation. Orthodox Jews to this day literally bind that summation of Moses' Torah to the body (see Deut. 6:8) in the form of an amulet worn during prayer. Likewise, this parental teaching is to be worn—probably metaphorically—as a necklace (v. 21), an object of beauty and public display.

A second intriguing image is introduced in verse 22: wisdom as guide and intimate companion. However, the NRSV translation blunts its full effect. What is not apparent is that the grammatical subject of the verbs in verse 22 is feminine singular. It matches the feminine nouns in verse 20, "commandment" and "teaching," and further, plays off the representations of Lady Wisdom in the preceding chapters. So a literal translation of the Hebrew reads:

> When you walk, *she* will lead you;
> when you lie down, *she* will watch over you;
> and when you awake, *she* will talk with you.

The picture that emerges from this reading is of Wisdom as a gentle mentor and guardian, a maternal figure. The last line goes even further; it is ambiguously erotic, suggesting that the student might enjoy "pillow talk" with Wisdom. Imagine how that might sound to the adolescent males who were students of the sages. That impression is strengthened by the fact that the image appears immediately before a lengthy section that warns explicitly against sexual misconduct (6:23–7:27). They are fighting fire with fire, countering the lure of illicit sex with the wholesome yet genuine thrill of intimate encounter with the truth.

FEMME FATALE
Proverbs 7:1–27

7:1 **My child, keep my words**
   and store up my commandments with you;
  2 **keep my commandments and live,**
   keep my teachings as the apple of your eye;
  3 **bind them on your fingers,**
   write them on the tablet of your heart.
  4 **Say to wisdom, "You are my sister,"**

and call insight your intimate friend,
5 that they may keep you from the loose woman,
   from the adulteress with her smooth words.

6 For at the window of my house
   I looked out through my lattice,
7 and I saw among the simple ones,
   I observed among the youths,
   a young man without sense,
8 passing along the street near her corner,
   taking the road to her house
9 in the twilight, in the evening,
   at the time of night and darkness.

10 Then a woman comes toward him,
    decked out like a prostitute, wily of heart.
11 She is loud and wayward;
    her feet do not stay at home;
12 now in the street, now in the squares,
    and at every street corner she lies in wait.
13 She seizes him and kisses him,
    and with impudent face she says to him:
14 "I had to offer sacrifices,
    and today I have paid my vows;
15 so now I have come out to meet you,
    to seek you eagerly, and I have found you!
16 I have decked my couch with coverings,
    colored spreads of Egyptian linen;
17 I have perfumed my bed with myrrh,
    aloes, and cinnamon.
18 Come, let us take our fill of love until morning;
    let us delight ourselves with love.
19 For my husband is not at home;
    he has gone on a long journey.
20 He took a bag of money with him;
    he will not come home until full moon."

21 With much seductive speech she persuades him;
    with her smooth talk she compels him.
22 Right away he follows her,
    and goes like an ox to the slaughter,
    or bounds like a stag toward the trap
23 until an arrow pierces its entrails.

> He is like a bird rushing into a snare,
> not knowing that it will cost him his life.
> 24 And now, my children, listen to me,
> and be attentive to the words of my mouth.
> 25 Do not let our hearts turn aside to her ways;
> do not stray into her paths.
> 26 For many are those she has laid low,
> and numerous are her victims.
> 27 Her house is the way to Sheol,
> going down to the chambers of death.

This chapter builds on the earlier instructions about sexual conduct, but here the sages move beyond generalities to a particular incident, actual or imagined. This poem expands the scene hinted at in Proverbs 2:16–19 (similarly, 22:14); it is, in fact, the most developed narrative poem in the Bible. The details are drawn with swift but sharp strokes; it is easy to visualize the woman "decked out like a prostitute, . . . loud and wayward," lurking on street corners, "lying in wait" (v. 12) for a victim. The last phrase in verse 10 gives the key to her character, although the Hebrew is more subtle than the translation suggests—and ultimately, more revealing. Her heart is not "wily" but rather "guarded, closed, blockaded"; the same verbal form is used elsewhere of a city under siege (Isa. 1:8). To all appearances, she is open in her affection (v. 13), which is wholly devoted to this one young man: "I have come out to meet *you*, to seek *you* eagerly, and I have found *you!*" (v. 15). But behind her passionate words and gestures lies a blockaded heart, and so there is no possibility of genuine relationship.

This is another instance of the false community of the streets against which we were warned in the very first chapter (1:10–19). The verb "lie in wait" (v. 12) links her behavior with the more obvious violence of hoodlums (1:18). In both cases, there appears to be a strong bond of intimacy. The thieves say, "We will all have one purse!" (1:14). She cajoles, "Let us drench ourselves in love until the morning!" (7:18, AT). They appeal to the longing for deep companionship that often makes the best young people so vulnerable. But when the company is bad, the consequence of accepting that invitation is death.

As is typical of biblical narrative, the most important content is conveyed by speech. In this story, the speech is entirely a monologue of the loquacious, "smooth-talking" woman (vv. 5, 21; also 2:16; 5:3; 6:24); the young man remains dumb as an ox led to slaughter (v. 22). This is no ordinary harlot but a woman of substantial means and, it seems, social position. Although her speech may seem at first like flirtatious chatter, in fact every element is calculated for maximum impact, beginning with her opening words. She immediately lets him know that she is just back from the altar, thus establishing herself as a woman who is careful about fulfilling her religious obligations; she stays on God's good side. Although it is not evident in the translation, the Hebrew specifies the kind of sacrifice: "offerings of well-being." This was a meat offering in which (as prescribed in Lev. 7:11–18) the fat was burnt and the worshiper was permitted to consume most of the animal—and was required to consume it all on the day of sacrifice. She is thus letting him know that there is fresh meat for dinner, a considerable luxury in the ancient world. Moreover, in helping her eat it up, he is fulfilling a holy obligation.

No less careful is the description of her bed. Rich with Egyptian linens and spices from Arabia and India, it is a miniature of the ancient commercial world. The impressionable youth could easily regard time spent there as both adventure and privilege. Moreover, there is no need to fear discovery. "The man is not at his house" (contrary to the NRSV, the woman does not actually name him as her husband) and will not return until full moon (v. 20). That must still be some weeks away, since we are told in v. 9 that it is pitch dark; evidently no moon is visible. The note that he has taken his money bag with him is more than casual. First, it reinforces the impression that his business trip is extended. More significantly, it indicates that the woman is feeling some financial pinch—so she has gone looking for a young and well-to-do man to "tide her over," with both caresses and cash.

Her speech is framed on either side by the teacher's instruction. The frame serves to connect this vignette with several of the sages' recurrent themes. First and most importantly, in light of the continual emphasis on the need to discern between wise and foolish speaking, there is an implied competition between the teacher's "words" (vv. 1, 24) and those of the "strange woman" (v. 5). Life for the sages is a marketplace of discourse, where many persuasive speakers compete for our attention and allegiance. If you want to "buy wisdom" (4:7), then you must learn to turn a deaf ear to much else that is hawked on the streets. Second, the narrative lends vividness to the time-worn phrase, "the way of the wicked" (Prov. 4:19; see also Psalm 1:6). It suddenly becomes real in our imaginations through the description of the woman's house as "the way to Sheol" (v. 27); her basement has a trap door to the Underworld! Third, the image of the house with the absent man as a place for infidelity and disaster inverts the traditional Israelite ideal of the "father's house" as the center of social and economic stability (see the comment at Prov. 2:16–22). The perspective of the book is not biased against women, as shown clearly in the feminine representations of wisdom. On the contrary, the corrective to this negative picture is provided by the powerful concluding portrait of "the woman of valor" in Proverbs 31:10–31. The fact that the later passage picks up some of the imagery of this chapter indicates that the corrective is highly deliberate. In view of the frequent charge that the Bible's perspective is "patriarchal," it is very interesting that the answer to the danger posed by the *femme fatale* is not a reassertion of male domination. Rather, it is a strong woman who speaks in a wise and faithful manner (31:26), who runs "her house" (31:15, 21, 27) in a way that models what it means to live according to "fear of the LORD" (31:30).

WISDOM'S SPEECH FROM THE HEIGHTS
Proverbs 8:1–36

This is the second speech of "Lady Wisdom." Previously (Prov. 1:20–33), she adopted the tone of the castigating prophet. Here she makes a more positive appeal and speaks "noble things" (8:6). The style of self-praise which she adopts here was a common speech form in ancient Near Eastern literature, and especially in the speech of goddesses. Wisdom here never claims divinity for herself; like the sages themselves, she enjoins "the fear of the LORD." Nonetheless, Wisdom presents herself as the source of wealth and political power, intimately involved in the workings of creation. Immediately following the story of the fatal seductress in chapter 7, this lengthy speech offers a powerfully attractive alternative to her deadly charms.

The Universal Call (Proverbs 8:1–21)

8:1 **Does not wisdom call,**
       and does not understanding raise her voice?
  2   **On the heights, beside the way,**
       at the crossroads she takes her stand;
  3   **beside the gates in front of the town,**
       at the entrance of the portals she cries out:
  4   **"To you, O people, I call,**
       and my cry is to all that live.
  5   **O simple ones, learn prudence;**
       acquire intelligence, you who lack it.
  6   **Hear, for I will speak noble things,**
       and from my lips will come what is right;

⁷ for my mouth will utter truth;
   wickedness is an abomination to my lips.
⁸ All the words of my mouth are righteous;
   there is nothing twisted or crooked in them.
⁹ They are all straight to one who understands
   and right to those who find knowledge.
¹⁰ Take my instruction instead of silver,
   and knowledge rather than choice gold;
¹¹ for wisdom is better than jewels,
   and all that you may desire cannot compare with her.
¹² I, wisdom, live with prudence.
   and I attain knowledge and discretion.
¹³ The fear of the LORD is hatred of evil.
   Pride and arrogance and the way of evil
   and perverted speech I hate.
¹⁴ I have good advice and sound wisdom;
   I have insight, I have strength.
¹⁵ By me kings reign,
   and rulers decree what is just;
¹⁶ by me rulers rule,
   and nobles, all who govern rightly.
¹⁷ I love those who love me,
   and those who seek me diligently find me.
¹⁸ Riches and honor are with me,
   enduring wealth and prosperity.
¹⁹ My fruit is better than gold, even fine gold,
   and my yield than choice silver.
²⁰ I walk in the way of righteousness,
   along the paths of justice,
²¹ endowing with wealth those who love me,
   and filling their treasuries.

In the previous chapter we saw the woman lurking on a dark street corner, offering herself for a secret assignation to a young man selected because he can (presumably) afford the price tag. Here, by contrast, Wisdom stands at the most public place in the city and shouts, "My cry is to all humankind" (v. 4b; compare NRSV, "all that live"). There is no trace of elitism here, but the specific mention of humanity is important, for the desire for wisdom is a peculiarly human characteristic. Indeed, the very capacity to desire wisdom and ultimately to acquire it—or better, as the biblical imagery suggests, to enter into lifelong relationship with "her"—is perhaps what most distinctively marks us as human, as the term *homo sapiens* (compare Latin *sapientia*, "wisdom") suggests.

Although Wisdom associates herself with power and wealth (vv. 14–18), we must be careful not to read this speech as a guarantee of temporal success. As the following proverbs will show, the sages do not naïvely assume that all wise people are rich and well-positioned. Nonetheless, in their corner of the world, they have seen enough cases of virtue being rewarded to encourage them to believe that wisdom *may* bring temporal honor. They also dare to think that by the mediation of Wisdom the will of the one true God might still be reflected even in pagan political structures. There is a remarkable universality and optimism to the statement that *all* rulers reign by the Wisdom revealed to Israel, especially in view of the fact that by the time these sages wrote, Israel's own kingship had been eclipsed by Persian and Hellenistic rulers. Here we see the sages accommodating their theological thought to the new political realities that followed the collapse of Israel as a nation-state.

The connection between wisdom and wealth is occasional; what is invariable is the link between wisdom and righteousness (v. 20). In other words, wisdom is not a commodity or a technique that can be manipulated to whatever ends we choose; it has an essential connection with goodness. In this it differs fundamentally from technical expertise, so highly acclaimed in our modern world. Such expertise, gained through academic and laboratory study, is morally neutral. Twentieth-century horrors—Nazi extermination camps, the atomic bomb, the tattered ozone layer—attest to the terrible fact that technical genius can be easily directed to mistaken or inhumane ends. Augustine makes an observation that is worth pondering deeply: "True wisdom is such that no evil use can ever be made of it." In our century, technical expertise has greatly outpaced wisdom. In this situation, our humanity and even our survival may well depend on reasserting the preeminence of wisdom over the promiscuous cultivation of knowledge that is not disciplined by fear of the Lord.

Moreover, identifying wisdom with technological achievement or material reward ignores an important inference to be drawn from the fact that this book personalizes wisdom to such a high degree. Although the sages sometimes speak of seeking wisdom like treasure (2:4; compare 8:10), it is evident that for them, wisdom is more like a "she" than an "it." Wisdom can be sought and found only as a relationship is "found"—when we prepare our hearts for receiving the gift of the other, when we attend carefully to the responsibilities that relationship entails. Verse 17 parallels the assurance given to Israel through Moses: " . . . you will seek the LORD your God, and you will find him if you search after him with all your heart and soul" (Deut. 4:29). A passage in a late book of Israelite wisdom, the Wisdom of Solomon (which belongs to the Apocrypha), expresses with particular beauty the nature of that relationship. It is, in fact, one of mutual seeking:

> One who rises early to seek her will have no difficulty,
> for she will be found sitting at the gate.
> To fix one's thought on her is perfect understanding,
> and one who is vigilant on her account will soon be free from care,
> because she goes about seeking those worthy of her,
> and she graciously appears to them in their paths,
> and meets them in every thought.
>
> (Wisd. Sol. 6:14–16)

"She . . . meets them in every thought!" It is a stunning statement. This is in fact the assurance that underlies all the scriptures: that human beings can know God's mind, that God desires that we should know it. "The word is very near to you" (Deut. 30:14). This assurance that God actively seeks to communicate to us the wisdom by which the world was founded (Prov. 3:19–20) reaches its fullest expression in Paul's assertion that Christ is "the wisdom of God" (1 Cor. 1:24, 30). Through the gospel of Jesus Christ, the divine Word made flesh, we may come to understand what it truly means that the wisdom of God graciously appears to us in our paths, and meets us in every thought.

Wisdom speaks to "all humankind" (Prov. 8:4) and not only, as we might suppose, to the intellectually gifted. The phrase in verse 5 translated "intelligence" literally means "heart." The heart is in biblical physiology the organ by which we know the world altogether. Emotion, rational thinking, observation, imagination, desire—all these are activities of the heart. Wisdom speaks to our hearts. Nothing could be simpler or more "democratic"—after all, everyone has a heart. Yet that is the very reason we find it so difficult to hear her, because our hearts are otherwise occupied. The Hebrew phrase "to set one's heart" means "to pay attention." We have already set our hearts, our eager attention, in so many other directions.

According to Islamic tradition, Allah was moved by the sad condition of humanity and of the earth itself to send the archangel Gabriel on another mission to earth. Perhaps the Holy Book, the Koran, is too difficult, Allah thought. Gabriel can restate its wisdom in very simple terms, so that faith will be more effective, believers will live with more integrity, and the earth will be healed. So Gabriel set out; he traveled for a long time, all over the globe, using all the resources of heaven to speak the simple wisdom of

Allah. Finally he returned, utterly exhausted, his wings badly soiled. When Allah asked him if he had delivered the message, Gabriel replied: "Yes, certainly, but people did not have time to listen!"

The poignant story moves me to reflect on my work as a seminary professor. One might suppose that a Christian theological seminary would be a place especially receptive to the call of divine wisdom. Certainly we spend a considerable portion of each day in chapel and class, hearing and studying the scriptures and great literature of the Christian faith. Yet I believe few of my colleagues and students are convinced that we have truly "laid hold of [wisdom]" and found the peace that attends her (Prov. 3:17–18). Moreover, many of us would agree on the reason that wisdom eludes us—or, more accurately, we elude her! We have no time to linger on her "pleasant paths" (see Prov. 3:17). We are far too busy with the "good works" of preparing and attending lectures, writing and grading essays, committees, conferences, chapel duty, hospitality, field work. Like other professional Americans, we suffer from acute over-busyness—and worse, we are proud of our busyness, at the same time that we suffer from it. That is symptomatic of addiction. Therefore, for us, "seeking [Wisdom] diligently" (Prov. 8:17b) means, paradoxically, doing *less*. Like any other kind of love, loving Wisdom (8:17a) involves discipline of the heart. Can we discipline ourselves to be far more discriminating about the things to which we give those precious and scarce resources, our time and attention? Can we trust God that if we stop doing so many good works and wait quietly, Wisdom will indeed let herself be found by us?

Wisdom at Play (Proverbs 8:22–31)

8:22 **The LORD created me at the beginning of his work,**
    the first of his acts of long ago.
23 **Ages ago I was set up,**
    at the first, before the beginning of the earth.
24 **When there were no depths I was brought forth,**
    when there were no springs abounding with water.
25 **Before the mountains had been shaped,**
    before the hills, I was brought forth—
26 **when he had not yet made earth and fields,**
    or the world's first bits of soil.
27 **When he established the heavens, I was there,**
    when he drew a circle on the face of the deep,
28 **when he made firm the skies above,**
    when he established the fountains of the deep,

²⁹ **when he assigned to the sea its limit,**
   so that the waters might not transgress his command,
   when he marked out the foundations of the earth,
³⁰ **then I was beside him, like a master worker,**
   and I was daily his delight,
   rejoicing before him always,
³¹ **rejoicing in his inhabited world**
   and delighting in the human race.

This poem of primeval Wisdom is one of the most boldly "mythological" images in the Bible. It is important to distinguish this kind of poetic image from fully developed pagan myth, in which Wisdom might be portrayed as a deity in a pantheon. No one could write a "biography" of Wisdom based upon the several images in Proverbs; a goddess of wisdom would be abhorrent to Israelite monotheism (contrast the detailed realistic narrative about Athena in Greek myth). Rather the poet-sages use language that impresses itself vividly on the imagination in order to say that our search for wisdom moves us into relationship—delighted, even playful relationship—with our Creator. Wisdom was with God "at the beginning of his work" (v. 22), "rejoicing in his inhabited world and delighting in the human race" (v. 31). In other words, God's creative intention for the world is fundamentally connected with the actual workings of the human mind and of human society.

This verbal portrait may well have given inspiration to Michelangelo's painting of the creation on the Sistine Chapel ceiling. In the famous scene where the spark of life passes from God's finger to Adam's, there appears at God's side a lovely young woman with eyes alert, her knee bent, poised for action. God's "non-creating" hand is thrown around her shoulders in a casual but intimate gesture. The woman is sometimes identified as Eve, but the contrast between her strong but delicate beauty and the coarse figure of Michelangelo's Eve is pronounced. It is far more likely that this, the most convincingly *feminine* portrait he ever painted (his other female figures seem to be male bodies with enlarged breasts), is Wisdom as she is represented in Proverbs 8. Strong and eager, this is Wisdom the "master worker" (the translation is debated; other possibilities are "darling, ward"), sharing God's excitement and delight in the fresh new world and its inhabitants.

The NRSV translation of verses 30b–31 is weak. The carefully constructed lines are more accurately rendered:

> And I was *delights* daily, *playing* before him continually,
> *playing* in his inhabited world,
> and my *delights* were with human beings.

The phrase "I was delights daily" may suggest either that Wisdom experienced delight or that she was the occasion for God's delight. In either case, the twofold verbal repetition puts strong emphasis on the element of play, which the NRSV suppresses.

The picture of Wisdom playing, even giddily, before God must be allowed to stand as the important theological statement it is. This scene both complements and amplifies the picture of creation in Genesis 1, with its more sober statement of divine approval: "And God saw that it was (very) good." The element of playfulness in creation is present also in the great hymn to creation, Psalm 104, where Leviathan, the beast of chaos from ancient Near Eastern myth, is portrayed as something like God's bathtub toy: "There go ships, and Leviathan which you made to play with" (v. 26, AT).

On the theological significance of these glimpses of a playful Creator, Hugo Rahner comments insightfully: "When . . . we speak of God the Creator 'playing,' there lies concealed in that phrase the metaphysical truth that the creation of the world and of man, though a divinely meaningful act, was by no means a necessary one so far as God himself was concerned" (*Man at Play*, 11). The idea that it was not necessary for God to create the world does not imply a lack of seriousness or deliberateness on God's part. In fact, the opposite is true. God's decision to create the world was a matter of absolutely free choice, in no way constricted by preexisting conditions (this is what is affirmed by the traditional doctrine of creation-out-of-nothing (*ex nihilo*). Yet a free choice is not an arbitrary one. God created the world, including and even especially humanity, for the sake of God's own pleasure, as the twofold mention of "delights" suggests. These two, freedom and delight, belong together, in divine play just as in children's play.

Two further theological implications should be drawn from the picture of divine Wisdom playing with human beings "in the inhabited world." First, this image excludes any theological view that the universe is a closed system operating according to fixed laws, of either nature or human destiny, which determine every occurrence. A common form of this belief is called deism, which imagines a sort of "Watchmaker God" who set the universe ticking and then turned to other things. The Wisdom playing with human beings carries the implication of divine immanence (direct presence and involvement in creation). This is a trajectory which reaches its end and fullest expression in the doctrine of the Trinity. Christians confess that God not only created the world but dwelt in it as a human being; and God now continues to be present in our midst through the Holy Spirit, one of whose seven "gifts" is the wisdom of God.

The image of divine Wisdom playing with humanity suggests that conversely, playfulness is part of the proper human response to God. This is an obvious (though not necessarily common) way of understanding the famous dictum of Jesus: "Truly I tell you, unless you change and become like children, you will never enter the kingdom of heaven" (Matt. 18:3 and parallels). Theology is often considered to be a very sober business, but the picture of a boisterous divine Wisdom playing with humans implies that God's intention is quite different. Intellectual playfulness in ultimate matters is not only allowable; it is necessary—and not just for professional theologians, but for all of us, who are commanded to love God not only with heart and soul, but also "all your mind" (Matt. 22:37). How can we ever imagine the joy of heaven, or testify of it convincingly to others, if we cannot now discover the fun of turning our minds toward the things of God?

Promise and Threat (Proverbs 8:32–36)

8:32 **And now, my children, listen to me:**
happy are those who keep my ways.
33 **Hear instruction and be wise,**
and do not neglect it.
34 **Happy is the one who listens to me,**
watching daily at my gates,
waiting beside my doors.
35 **For whoever finds me finds life**
and obtains favor from the LORD;
36 **but those who miss me injure themselves;**
all who hate me love death."

A promise of felicity to those who succeed in finding wisdom is a predictable end to Wisdom's speech. But the final verse abruptly changes the tone, summing up in a forceful epigram the threat implicit throughout these introductory chapters. A more literal translation of verse 36a shows how strong the language is: "The one who misses me *does violence to* his own self. . . . " The religious significance of missing wisdom is suggested by a play on words which cannot be directly conveyed in English: the word translated "miss" (which literally refers to "missing a target") also frequently means "sin."

The shock delivered by the language here is meant to shake Wisdom's listeners out of the very common assumption that wisdom is the prerogative of the chosen few, while most of us bumble along in more-or-less well-meaning folly, and no great harm is done. The message here is that, even

if only a few attain to wisdom, nonetheless there is nothing well-meaning
and certainly nothing harmless about missing "her." "All who hate me love
death"—the fool, the scorner, does not come to grief accidentally; that
kind of disaster is the result of a "courtship" no less active than the court-
ing of wisdom.

Love of death rather than life—this is the great perversity to which the
human heart is prone, a riddle the Bible repeatedly probes with puzzlement,
sorrow, anger. Indeed, this perception that humanity chooses death may be
seen as marking the gulf between Israel's religious perspective and that of
its neighbors. The question that underlies the great religious literature of
Mesopotamia, including the tragic Epic of Gilgamesh, is this: "Why have
the gods withheld eternal life from humanity?" Because Israel locates the
fundamental problem of existence in the human heart (see Jer. 17:9) rather
than in the perversity of the gods or "fate," it asks a different question:
"Why would you reject life?" And that question in turn implies a challenge
that frequently becomes explicit: "Seek the LORD and live!" (Amos 5:6).

TWO INVITATIONS
Proverbs 9:1–18

This chapter develops the contrast between wisdom and folly set forth in
Proverbs 14:1: "Women's wisdom builds her house, but the foolish one
tears it down with her hands" (see also 24:3–4). The personifications here
show both "women" to be persistent, potentially engaging hostesses; but
one is an invitation to life (v. 6) and the other, to death (v. 18).

The Seven-Pillared House (Proverbs 9:1–6)

9:1 **Wisdom has built her house,**
     she has hewn her seven pillars.
  2 **She has slaughtered her animals, she has mixed her wine,**
     she has also set her table.
  3 **She has sent out her servant girls, she calls**
     from the highest places in the town,
  4 **"You that are simple, turn in here!"**
     To those without sense she says,
  5 **"Come, eat of my bread**
     and drink of the wine I have mixed.
  6 **Lay aside immaturity, and live,**
     and walk in the way of insight."

Wisdom prepares a feast—a sort of housewarming—and sends out invitations to her characteristic audience, the "simple" (see the comment at 1:20–33). The significance of the seven-pillared house is debated; the interpretations fall into three categories: the cosmological, the cultic, and the domestic.

The cosmological interpretation, that the house represents the creation of the world, builds upon the statement in 3:19, "The Lord by wisdom founded the earth," as well as the cosmological poem in 8:22–31. Ancient and medieval rabbinic interpretation identifies the pillars with the seven heavens or the seven pillars that uphold the world. A beautiful midrash (an imaginative commentary upon scripture from the rabbinic tradition) that follows this interpretation can serve as an inspiration to all teachers of religion:

> *Wisdom has built her house, she has hewn her seven pillars:* This refers to the Torah [here, meaning religious instruction in general], which built the entire universe through her wisdom. *She has hewn her seven pillars*—she was hewn from the seven firmaments and was given to humanity. Another interpretation: *Wisdom has built her house*—God said: If one has earned the merit of teaching Torah to others, [I will account it to him] as though he had erected the entire universe. (Visotzky, *Midrash*, 49)

The second line of interpretation argues that Wisdom's house is a temple, and indeed, archaeologists have uncovered examples of seven-pillared temples at various sites throughout the Near East. Accordingly, some scholars have argued that Wisdom and Folly are meant to be seen as rival goddesses. But this claim overstates the evidence; certainly the passage does not point to a "cult of Wisdom"—or of Folly, for that matter. Nonetheless, with the image of servant girls sent out to invite the simple to the feast, the poet may be consciously parodying the cultic practice of the Canaanite love goddess Astarte, whose priests and priestesses functioned as sacred prostitutes with whom devotees participated in fertility rituals. The sharpness of the image, then, comes from the fact that "the young women of chapter 9 have an educational mission; they invite young men not to bed, but to school" (McKane, *Proverbs*, 360).

The third interpretive possibility is that Wisdom's house is just that—a house, albeit an unusually large one (the average Israelite house had four pillars supporting the portico that half-covered the inner courtyard). The number seven may be a conventional round number, similar to our use of "a dozen" (see Prov. 24:16; 26:16); the point is that this home has room for anyone who cares to come. But it should also be acknowledged that the invitation is not offered casually, nor can it be refused without penalty. In the ancient Mediterranean world, hospitality was accorded primary value in the social sphere. The Trojan War was fought over a violation of hospitality; further, the sin of Sodom is not only sexual depravity but abuse of those who "have come under the shelter of [Lot's] roof" (Gen. 19:8). Hospitality is the first duty toward other human beings, just as fearing God is the chief duty toward God. Because it is a central cultural virtue (as distinct from our own view of hospitality as etiquette), the imperative to offer hospitality is unconditional. It must be extended to all who are in need. On the other side, to refuse hospitality is a bitter offense, as modern travelers to Mediterranean countries often discover. The scene depicted here bears an analogy to Jesus' parable of the wedding banquet (Matt. 22:1–14), and in fact later wisdom literature refers to Wisdom as a bride (Wisd. Sol. 8:2). The New Testament parable makes explicit what is implied here: once the invitation has been issued, you refuse it at your own peril.

The fact that scholars remain divided over whether this scene is cosmological, cultic, or domestic suggests that it is difficult to settle on any one line of interpretation. Finally, a single interpretation is not necessary, since this is an imaginative scene and not a historical reconstruction. The ambiguity of the poem is in fact part of its genius, for each sphere of meaning contributes to its richness.

Wisdom's Instruction (Proverbs 9:7–12)

9:7 **Whoever corrects a scoffer wins abuse;**
     whoever rebukes the wicked gets hurt.
  8 **A scoffer who is rebuked will only hate you;**
     the wise, when rebuked, will love you.
  9 **Give instruction to the wise, and they will become wiser still;**
     teach the righteous and they will gain in learning.
 10 **The fear of the LORD is the beginning of wisdom,**
     and the knowledge of the Holy One is insight.
 11 **For by me your days will be multiplied,**
     and years will be added to your life.
 12 **If you are wise, you are wise for yourself;**
     if you scoff, you alone will bear it.

The invitation to Wisdom's feast is followed immediately by a sample of the "fare" she offers. At the center of this instruction (v. 10) is the motto that stands over the whole book (see 1:7). Thus these nine introductory chapters are literally framed by the fundamental teaching that wisdom begins with "the fear of the LORD." That literary frame sums up the essence of Wisdom's message and at the same time clearly excludes her opposite, Folly, whose counter-invitation follows.

Paradox is one of the consistent elements of the sages' riddling wit, and verse 12 offers a superb example. At first glance, the verse would seem to be an assertion that wisdom is a "nontransferrable asset." Although this might accord with the modern ideology of individualism, such a view would invalidate the whole enterprise of teaching wisdom. Nor does ordinary experience confirm the suggestion that the burden of scoffing is borne by the scoffer alone. Much as we might wish that the foolish paid the whole cost of their arrogance, it is painfully evident that often they do not even bear the brunt of it. The ancient Greek translators attempted to make obvious sense of the verse by completely inverting its meaning: "If you are wise for yourself, you will be wise also for your neighbors." But it is better to work with the paradox; an explanation may hint at its meaning, but not exhaust it.

What may be inferred from this verse is that pursuit of wisdom is not an altruistic activity. You are wise, in the first instance, *for yourself*; wisdom is its own reward. Of course, if wisdom is genuine, it does not lead to smugness but rather to some measure of contentment. Though life may be very hard, there is peace in the attempt to live it in steady pursuit of "righteousness, justice, and equity" (1:3). Further, a subtle difference in wording between the two halves of the verse (which may be captured in English as the difference between "for yourself" and "by yourself") implies that, while wisdom is inherently satisfying, scoffing on the other hand is inherently isolating. Scoffers may cause pain to others, but nonetheless they remain fundamentally alone in their contempt. Wisdom always generates a community, or aims at serving a community; scoffing proceeds from alienation and serves only to deepen it.

Loud Folly (Proverbs 9:13–18)

9:13 **The foolish woman is loud;**
      she is ignorant and knows nothing.
   14 **She sits at the door of her house,**
      on a seat at the high places of the town,
   15 **calling to those who pass by,**
      who are going straight on their way,
   16 **"You who are simple, turn in here!"**
      And to those without sense she says,
   17 **"Stolen water is sweet,**

and bread eaten in secret is pleasant."
[18] **But they do not know that the dead are there,**
that her guests are in the depths of Sheol.

The thumbnail sketch of Folly (v. 13) is brilliant in its few words of description: she is "boisterous, bustling, loud"; the same word is used of the whorish woman in 7:11. The second term is more complex than the translation "ignorant" normally conveys. It comes from the same root as the word generally translated "simple"; here it denotes not youthful naïveté but a perpetual and therefore culpable lack of commitment. She can indeed be called "ignorant," provided we recognize that from a biblical perspective, knowledge involves some kind of investment of the self (the familiar use of the verb "know" to denote sexual intercourse is an instance of this). Therefore knowing—or choosing not to know— inevitably has consequences for both the development of our characters and the quality of our relationships. The person who "knows nothing" may truly be said to care about nothing.

Like Wisdom, Folly stations herself "at the high places of the town"; and their invitations to the simple are identical (vv. 4 and 16). The "wisdom" she offers (v. 17) is probably a popular proverb, similar to the modern Arabic proverb, "Everything forbidden is sweet" (McKane, *Proverbs*, 366). But whereas the proverb is meant to be heard as an ironic observation, she perverts it into an allurement to the senseless. Some see Folly's water as inferior to Wisdom's spiced wine, but it is more likely that we are meant to hear a reference to the most essential element of life. Drinking water was precious enough to be purchased by Israel on the Exodus journey (Deut. 2:6). With ears sensitized by the water imagery of chapter 5, we may recognize that stealing water is a threat of the most deadly kind.

2. Proverbs Proper

CONSTRUCTIVE AND DESTRUCTIVE CRITICISM
Proverbs 10:10

> 10:10 **Whoever winks the eye causes trouble,**
> **but the one who rebukes boldly makes peace.**

Although the book of Proverbs is not generally organized according to subject matter, this chapter contains many sayings that contrast wise and foolish or wicked speech (vv. 6, 11, 13, 14, 18, 19, 20, 31, 32) or illustrate wise and foolish responses to instruction (vv. 8, 17, 21). This proverb draws a contrast between open criticism and a contemptuous gesture made behind a person's back. Repeatedly and in no uncertain terms the sages assert the positive value of reproof. For example:

> Better is open rebuke
> than hidden love.
> Well meant are the wounds a friend inflicts,
> but profuse are the kisses of an enemy.
> (27:5–6)

The Proverbs are not addressed to fragile egos who cannot accept correction. The stock character, the fool, is someone who will not seriously consider the possibility of being wrong. The wise person, on the other hand, takes reproof to heart:

> A rebuke strikes deeper into a discerning person
> than a hundred blows into a fool.
> (17:10; see also 10:17; 13:18; 15:5; etc.).

Even more strongly, the sages assert that an apt criticism, well received, has a "beautifying" effect!

> Like a gold ring or an ornament of gold
> is a wise rebuke to a listening ear.
>
> (25:12)

But the manner in which criticism is offered is itself a test of wisdom. "A wise rebuke" aims at peace, that is, at continued goodwill between the two parties, but also at the well-being of the larger community. It is probably fair to say that we are only fully in community with those to whom we dare to offer criticism and from whom we are willing to receive it. But such direct dealing with another person requires skill in speaking as well as time to work the problem through. Nothing good can come of a "hit and run" encounter: "Whoever belittles another lacks sense" (11:12). Moreover, a rebuke that aims at peace and the upbuilding of community requires that the person who offers it also be open to correction. It is rare that we ask ourselves, before criticizing a child, a student, an employee, a spouse: "What just criticism might she make of me in return?" The good critic is not just "one who rebukes boldly." Does she also have the courage to invite the response that may expose a fault in herself?

Therefore criticism that truly tends to peace is difficult and time-consuming. It costs something to the person who offers it. By contrast, the gesture that comes so easily—and how often do we wink or roll our eyes in amused irritation, merely to get some third party to laugh or sympathize with us?—is by its very nature alienating, destructive of community. For no one can benefit from criticisms made behind the back; the only possible consequence of such an action is to infect others with our contempt and increase the isolation of the person whose behavior gives offense.

There are times, however, when wisdom and kindness dictate silence, as the nearly adjacent proverb suggests:

10:12 **Hatred stirs up strife,**
       but love covers all offenses.

Love's cover is not the same as neglect; love may perceive a fault but choose not to confront it now. I may wait to speak until the other person is stronger and able to hear criticism. Or I may wait until I am sure that I love this person deeply enough to speak wisely, in a way that makes for peace. Sometimes love chooses to overlook a fault altogether (17:9; 19:11). The advice I received as an uncompromising teenager—from a friend my own age!—is simple but enduringly useful: "You can't be too much of a perfectionist in relationships."

But on occasion even a well-intended criticism will misfire. In that case we must pray that love's cover will work to mitigate the offense given by the "bold rebuke" itself. The letter to the Colossians sets the whole community-building process of offense, rebuke, and counteroffense in the context of mutual forgiveness: "Bear with one another, and if anyone has a complaint against another, *forgive each other*. . . . Above all, clothe yourselves with love. . . . And let the peace of Christ rule in your hearts, to which indeed you were called in the one body. And be thankful" (Col. 3:13–15). There is consummate wisdom in that final word. For it is ultimately gratitude that makes forbearance of one another—in our families and friendships, at school, work, and church—something more than an exercise in teeth-gritting. A priest listened to my confession of anger against members of my community and assigned me the following "penance": "Every day think of something good that each of them brings into your life." The assignment moved me from the comfortable position of self-righteousness to the more demanding and fruitful task of discovering my blessings—not all blessings are obvious!—and giving thanks for them.

JOY IN HOPE
Proverbs 10:28

> 10:28 **The hope of the righteous *ends in* gladness,**
> **but the expectation of the wicked comes to nothing.**

The Hebrew text lacks the italicized words; it asserts, boldly and provocatively: "The hope of the righteous *is* gladness"! The faithful waiting, the eager hope of the righteous is already a source of joy, even before they experience anything that could conventionally be called "satisfaction"—even, perhaps, if they *never* experience satisfaction in this life. This idea stands in some tension with another proverb with which we may agree more readily:

> Hope deferred makes the heart sick,
> but a desire fulfilled is a tree of life.
> (13:12)

Yet when the apostle Paul writes of hope, as he frequently does, he follows the more difficult model of the first proverb. Perhaps he even has it in mind, for Proverbs was a favorite text among the Pharisees who were

Paul's teachers and early colleagues (he quotes Proverbs directly in Rom. 12:20). Paul exhorts the new followers of Christ in Rome to "rejoice in hope" (Rom. 12:12; compare 1 Thess. 2:19), even while reminding them that "hope that is seen is not hope" (Rom. 8:24).

Paul, as usual, gets his finger on the pulse of the Christian life, where much of the real excitement comes from the effort to maintain a hope that is both joyful and realistic. Such a hope dares to face "the evidence" squarely—all the devastation that sin has wrought in our public and private lives—and yet dares further to reimagine the shape of everything, including ourselves, in light of the kingdom of God. The righteous are those who regularly exercise the imaginative boldness of children. Again, couldn't this be a legitimate interpretation of receiving the kingdom of God as a little child (Mark 10:15; see Matt. 18:3 and also the comment at 8:22–31)? Imagination is a moral activity. It matters greatly whether our imagination is truthful and generous or deluded and self-serving. The hope of the righteous proceeds, not from their private preferences, but rather from a discerning understanding of the world and of how God is working for good in this situation. Where the power of sin is so great that God's action is not visible, then hope proceeds from faith, conviction that God's will is for healing and wholeness. Hope issues in prayer: God's will be done. The hope of the righteous is indeed gladness for themselves and for others. It is they who imagine and pray our world toward the kingdom of God.

A good spiritual discipline is to name regularly in our prayers some of the signs of righteous hope that appear in new forms each day. In the news recently, for example, was the Homeless Garden Project, in which homeless people, small businesses, community groups, and neighbors in a small California city engage in a joint project whose motto is "growing hope." Collecting stories of righteous hope, swapping them, magnifying their witness—this is a work of faith that is desperately needed in order to combat the sense of depression and cynicism that afflict so many in our society, especially (and most tragically) the young.

(On this proverb, see further at 20:20–21.)

GOSSIP
Proverbs 11:11–13

11:11 **By the blessing of the upright a city is exalted,**
      but it is overthrown by the mouth of the wicked.

¹² **Whoever belittles another lacks sense,**
but an intelligent person remains silent.
¹³ **A gossip goes about telling secrets,**
but one who is trustworthy in spirit keeps a confidence.

A Jewish folktale speaks of a man who confessed to his rabbi that he was a gossip and asked to be cured. The rabbi replied strangely: "Go to the market and bring me back a plucked chicken. It must be absolutely clean—not one feather left. And I need it immediately. Hurry!" The man ran from to the rabbi's house to the butcher's stall, threw down the money for the chicken and ran back, yanking out the feathers as he ran. He handed the bare chicken to the rabbi and stood panting, awaiting his response. The rabbi inspected the bird carefully, turning it all around before he pronounced: "You've done a thorough job. Not one feather is left. Fine, now go back and gather up all the feathers you scattered."

Gossip is like feathers thrown carelessly into the wind. Even things we immediately regret having said cannot be taken back; they scatter and spread, beyond anyone's control. The gossip may seem to have penetrating insight into the lives and characters of others; a sharp tongue strips a person bare in short order. A gossip is often an initially attractive person, someone to whom it is easy both to talk and to listen. Many people listen eagerly to the whispered words of phony wisdom, consuming them "like delicious morsels" (18:8; 26:22). But this is junk food, in contrast to the real nourishment offered by the righteous:

> The lips of the righteous feed many,
> but fools die for lack of sense.
> (10:21)

The gossip's pseudo-wisdom is the dry-rot of community. Always it works to sow distrust, to separate friends (16:28). The extent to which gossip undermines the common life is suggested by the juxtaposition between the proverbs on gossip (vv. 12–13) and verse 11. "The mouth of the wicked," powerful enough to overthrow a city, need not be telling military secrets. More truly, it is every kind of vicious speech that destroys mutual respect and keeps attention riveted on what is trivial and evil. This includes the gossip that is broadcast as national news: the sexual transgressions and violent acts of politicians, athletes, entertainers, royalty. Verse 12 points indirectly to the truth that we ourselves are diminished by obsessive interest in the failings of others.

WOMEN'S BEAUTY, WOMEN'S POWER
Proverbs 11:22

11:22 **A gold ring in a pig's snout**
       is a beautiful woman without good sense.

This is one of the most arresting and potentially offensive proverbs. As always when gender is at issue, the sages speak from a male perspective; the physical appearance of men is never mentioned in Proverbs. The proverb is related to a group of sayings which aim at the young man's choice of a compatible wife (12:4; 18:22; 19:13–14; 21:9; 25:24; 27:15). One way of "neutralizing" the proverb for a modern audience would simply be to apply the same observation to handsome but senseless men. That would not depart from the spirit of the book; for, as we have already seen, the sages elsewhere talk frankly about male sexual discretion, setting forth in plain language the kind of temptations and decisions which their young students will face.

But maybe gender-neutralizing the proverb is not the best approach. As we have seen, Proverbs is a book that holds up, almost uniquely in the Bible, the power of the feminine, above all in its representation of wisdom. All its readers are finally judged in terms of their relationship with the unmistakably feminized figure of personified Wisdom. Moreover, the book shows an unusual degree of interest in the behavior of real women, as they embody and teach wisdom (see chapter 31) or fail to do so. The present proverb is itself an oblique acknowledgment of women's attractive power, which they can themselves abuse, and men can ruthlessly suppress. The woman imagined here is a deliberate abuser of her allure. A more accurate translation is: "a beautiful woman, turned away from good sense"; she is not dull-witted but rather flagrantly indiscreet. The proverb implies that beauty is wasted on a woman who forsakes her good sense; a gold ring in a pig's snout would quickly be covered by muck. But one could say even more: When beauty is not allied with good sense, it is destructive. Ultimately, the beautiful woman may herself be destroyed—for the function of a ring in a pig's snout is to lead the animal to slaughter.

A related proverb appears in verse 16:

> A gracious woman gets honor,
> but she who hates virtue is covered with shame.
> The timid become destitute,
> but the aggressive gain riches.

The published translation departs radically from the Hebrew text, which has only the first and last lines. (The middle lines were added already in ancient times—to the Greek translation of Proverbs—probably in an effort to make sense of a difficult saying.) It is possible to make sense of the Hebrew text as it stands, and what one discovers is a particularly challenging and even seditious message:

> A gracious woman gains honor,
> and/but aggressive [males] gain wealth.

The repetition of the verb "gain" draws attention to the comparison between one graceful woman and a group of male "aggressors" (the Hebrew word is masculine plural). Whatever modern readers may think about the advantages of aggression, this is not a complimentary characterization. "Aggressive" never appears elsewhere in the Old Testament in a positive sense; it commonly means "violent" or "ruthless."

The interesting question for interpretation is whether the "gracious" woman is *like* or *unlike* the males. The relation between the two lines may be either complementary or contrasting, because the Hebrew conjunction may be translated equally as "and" or "but." Suppose it means "and." So one possible reading of the proverb is as a cynical observation that a beautiful woman uses her charms in the exactly same way that men use aggression: namely, to get what they want. In this case, her "grace" is only skin deep (see Prov. 31:30, where the same word denotes deceptive charm). Those who honor her are not perceptive. In some situations, such a cynical observation is entirely apt, and no doubt the proverb was sometimes cited with this intention.

Now read the conjunction as "but." Thus the proverb evokes a sharp contrast: although men may get rich by violent means, a truly gracious woman is honored for her qualities of character. Further, the opposition is underscored by the poetic structure, which contrasts singular with plural, female with male: "a woman" (perhaps only a rare one) is honored, as over against the "violent men," however numerous they may be. This reading reveals a proverb with seditious potential. It may be read as exposing the violence that too commonly characterizes business practices in the public world dominated by men. Moreover, it offers the counter-model of a woman who, lacking all "clout," nonetheless gains public recognition of her worth that is infinitely more valuable than money. Within the Bible, one thinks of such figures as Ruth, Abigail, Esther, Judith—and of course the "valorous woman," whose "works praise her in the city gates" (Prov. 31:31).

THE ROOT OF THE RIGHTEOUS
Proverbs 12:3, 12

12:3 **No one finds security by wickedness,**
      but the root of the righteous will never be moved.

12:12 **The wicked covet the proceeds of wickedness,**
       but the root of the righteous bears fruit.

This chapter includes several teachings about the immovability or invulnerability of the righteous (see also 12:7, 19, 21, 28). The sages do not, of course, mean this literally; they know only too well that the innocent are sometimes driven off their land (30:14) or carried away to death (24:10–12). When they say that the righteous cannot be moved, they are speaking of an internal disposition of stability.

Yet even in this, there is room for misunderstanding. In our modern world, we tend to think of stability as a personal psychological state. This is true even in the church, where candidates for ministry must have their "stability" validated by a psychologist before they can be ordained. This is unquestionably a good idea, but the stability that the sages have in mind is deeper than any psychologist could validate. "The root of the righteous will never be moved," because the righteous are rooted in God. The first psalm, often called a "wisdom psalm" because it shares so much of the sages' thought and language, gives us a clear visual image of the deep-rooted righteous:

> . . . their delight is in the law of the LORD,
> and on his law they meditate day and night.
> They are like trees planted by streams of water,
> which yield their fruit in its season,
> and their leaves do not wither.
> (Psalm 1:2–3)

In Christian thought, the most profound explorations of the theological concept of stability come from the monastic tradition. "Stability" is one of three vows (along with obedience and "conversion of lifestyle") which form the basis of the sixth-century Rule of Benedict, the great architect of European monasticism. Today increasing numbers of nonmonastic Christians find in Benedict's Rule an enduring wisdom that guides their spiritual growth.

The principle of stability rests on the simple perception that "God is not elsewhere." As a monastic vow, it entails a commitment to serve God and neighbor from within *this* particular community, for some, even to the point of spending a lifetime within one set of walls. The choice of a permanent home and enduring relationships is meant to lead to an inner stability, which the monks call "single-mindedness." But the concept of stability has meaning for all Christians. As a principle of the spiritual life, it involves a decision to accept the present situation, with all its limitations, as providing the necessary conditions for faithful living. A stay at a Trappist monastery enabled Henri Nouwen—priest, professor, and world-renowned spiritual writer—to discover his own lack of single-mindedness. That lack was related to his very success. Thus he articulates his desire for rootedness: "Wherever I am, at home, in a hotel, in a train, plane, or airport, I would not feel irritated, restless, and desirous of being somewhere else or doing something else. I would know that here and now is what counts and is important because it is God himself who wants me at this time in this place" (cited by de Waal, *Seeking God,* 61). In short, stability means having the grace (literally) to *be* where I *am.*

The principle of stability challenges the well-trodden path of "upward mobility," which is littered with discarded ideals and causes, broken relationships, tumbleweed lives. Living in a culture that values personal choice above all else and is pathologically afraid of permanent commitments, we may be shocked to recognize that the Bible considers chronic rootlessness as the condition of the wicked: "They are like chaff that the wind drives about" (Psalm 1:4, AT). Exactly so our proverb observes: "No one can be fixed in wickedness" (Prov. 12:3, AT). Whether God always brings the wicked to a terrible end in this world is, from the perspective of both the biblical text and practical experience, an open question. What is certain is that they have guaranteed their eternal insignificance. They have no spiritual substance, and so, in the end, the way of the wicked simply "vanishes" (Psalm 1:6, AT).

As Benedict saw, inner stability is essential to all life in community, that is, to life lived in the genuine interest of others as well as oneself. "The root of the righteous bears fruit"; without stability, whatever good intentions we might have would be sterile. We cannot act justly toward others, we cannot do any substantial work for the common good, if we are continually running after some new fantasy image of ourselves. Achieving singlemindedness is always a matter of maintaining a firm inner resistance against false self-images. This is no less true for us in secular North American society than it was for the medieval monks, for many of our acts of injustice, both economic and personal, stem from the

vain pursuit of our "real self," which more money, a more exciting marriage, more prestigious friends will surely enable us to realize. "No one
can be fixed in wickedness" (Prov. 12:3), but only in God. Acknowledging that, the psalmist offers us a short vow of inner resistance and rootedness in God:

> My heart is fixed, O God, my heart is fixed.
> I will sing and make melody.
> > (Psalm 57:7, AT)

WORKING FOR OURSELVES
Proverbs 12:9

12:9 **Better to be despised and have a servant,**
     than to be self-important and lack food.

The proverb as translated here is almost unintelligible. Some commentators see an implied contrast between the person who lives carefully,
employing a single servant, and those who make a great show and over-
extend themselves. But such an interpretation requires reading more into
the first line than is there: it does not say *"only one* servant"—to say nothing of the fact that very few people in the ancient world had more than
one!

But the Hebrew words are susceptible to another translation that makes
perfect sense:

> Better to be looked down on and work for oneself
> > (literally: be servant to oneself)
> than pretend to be of great standing and lack bread.

The teaching upholds the virtue of economic self-sufficiency, being able
to provide for basic needs primarily out of one's own labor. Perhaps it originated in the Hellenistic period, when Israel's old economic base—subsistence farming and the home-based economy—was increasingly replaced
by a mercantile, monetary economy. Some Israelites prospered, but the
inevitable result of a shift away from a subsistence economy is a widening
gap between rich and poor. In light of such a shift, the saying appears as
one of a number of proverbs which reflect the values and experience of
common people, artisans, and landed peasantry. Some of these specifically
encourage hard work:

Those who till their land will have plenty of food,
but those who follow worthless pursuits have no sense.
(12:11; compare 28:19)

In all toil there is profit,
but mere talk leads only to poverty.
(14:23)

The appetite of workers works for them;
their hunger urges them on.
(16:26)

This proverb was undoubtedly meant as a challenge to the newly rich—
or those who were endangering themselves and their families by acting as
though they were rich. Likewise, asserting the value of self-sufficiency is a
challenge to our society, for in general we do not value being "servant to
ourselves." If few of us can afford a full-time servant at home, most working people have a functional equivalent. We depend upon others to provide for us a variety of domestic services—making our clothes and keeping
them clean, cooking our meals, caring for our children, cleaning our
houses, tending our gardens—so that we can do other "more interesting"
or more lucrative things. It is a lifestyle that keeps many, not in abject
poverty, but nonetheless in constant need of cash. Perhaps the majority
even of white-collar workers in our society lives from paycheck to paycheck. Moreover, the result of all these services is not in most cases a
higher "quality of life" (a term that itself reflects the industrial economy).
Certainly they do not give us more genuine relaxation. On the contrary,
stress is a dis-ease of epidemic proportions among us, commanding more
medical attention than any other. Many would assent to the plaintive and
genuinely bewildered remark of my friend, a highly placed professional
who has met her goals for family and career and nonetheless is exhausted
by her success: "Life should be sweeter than this!"

One must wonder if part of the problem is the kind of work we do. Are
we frantic because we have ignored the simple truth that it is inherently
satisfying to meet basic needs through our own labor? "Being servant to
ourselves"—gardening, cooking, sewing, and carpentry—far from being
demeaning, these forms of work are pleasurable and, moreover, they are
humanizing. They contribute to the stability of community life and even
the health of the economy. (Contrary to the popular wisdom, a massive
cash flow does not in itself make an economy healthy. People spending no
more than they can afford constitute a healthy economy.) Has anyone considered the long-term economic impact of bringing up—as we now have

done—a generation of children, the majority of whom do not know how to cook a meal, let alone grow a tomato, who must purchase virtually every single thing they use? What are the psychological effects of growing up in a home where no productive work is done, where the family gathers merely to consume what it has bought, or to plan what it will buy next?

In a sharply provocative tone reminiscent of our proverb, Wendell Berry comments:

> A person dependent on somebody else for everything from potatoes to opinions may declare that he is a free man, and his government may issue a certificate granting him his freedom, but he will not be free. . . . What is the First Amendment to him whose mouth is stuck to the tit of "the affluent society"? Men are free precisely to the extent that they are equal to their own needs. The most able are the most free. (*Continuous Harmony*, 130)

CHOOSING COMPANIONS
Proverbs 13:20

13:20 **Whoever walks with the wise becomes wise,**
     but the companion of fools suffers harm.

A very appealing aspect of Proverbs is its emphasis on the importance of friendship (see the comment at 18:22–24). The sages' piety is *essentially* communal. The sages understand that faith, though deeply personal, can never be private. We are inevitably "going to God" in the company of others. Indeed, godly friendship is one regular means by which we grow in faith and love of God. It is, to use an old Christian term, "a school of charity."

The medieval rabbis tell a memorable parable in connection with this proverb:

> To what may this be likened? To one who enters a perfumer's shop—even if the owner sells him nothing, nor does he buy anything from the owner, after he leaves his person and his clothing are scented, nor does the scent leave him all day long. It is of such a one Scripture says, "He who keeps company with the wise becomes wise." [Another parable:] To what may this be likened? to one who enters a tanner's shop—even if the owner sells him nothing, nor does he buy anything from the owner, after he leaves his person and his clothing are evil-smelling. Nor does the stench leave him all day long. It is of such a one that Scripture says, "But he who consorts with dullards comes to grief." (Visotzky, *Midrash*, 68)

The sages teach that bad company is one of the four ways we commonly bring disaster on ourselves (the other three being careless speech, immoderate anger, and laziness). Their repeated warnings against keeping bad company (Prov. 1:15; 4:14; 22:24–25; 24:1–2) may seem excessive, indeed "un-Christian." Jesus made a point of associating with "tax collectors and sinners" in great number (Mark 2:15), as well as the occasional woman of bad reputation. Nonetheless the apostle Paul forcefully echoes the sages on the dangers of bad company, even quoting a (nonbiblical) proverb: "Bad company ruins good morals" (1 Cor. 15:33; see also 1 Cor. 5:9–13; 2 Cor. 6:14–18).

Paul follows the sages in taking seriously the vulnerable condition of the "simple ones" to whom their teaching is addressed. The young—or even the not-so-young who are yet inexperienced in "walking in integrity" (Prov. 2:7, etc.)—are more likely to lose their own discipline than to persuade "fools" to share it. It is vain to pray, "Lead us not into temptation," while cultivating friendships that regularly lead us into it. Such double-mindedness makes our prayer a mocking of God, and Wisdom warns sternly of the consequence:

> . . . because you have ignored all my counsel . . .
> I will mock when panic strikes you.
>
> (Prov. 1:25–26)

DISCIPLINING CHILDREN
Proverbs 13:24

13:24 **Those who spare the rod hate their children,**
but those who love them are diligent to discipline them.

The sages follow the view, common in the ancient Near East, that corporal punishment is a necessary part of the discipline of children (see the similar proverbs at 22:15; 23:13–14 [and comment]; 29:15, 17). This is an instance in which modern wisdom casts serious doubt on the validity of the biblical saying. Contemporary psychology alerts us to the fact that the harsh discipline of young children frequently has violent repercussions when they become adults. In a remarkable study, Alice Miller (*For Your Own Good*) asserts that one factor that contributed to the Nazi Holocaust was the child-rearing theory that prevailed in Germany in the early part of this century: break a child's will before he is two, and he will never rebel against you. What the theory did not take into account is that the child's rage will be displaced and eventually vented violently on someone else.

The problem with which the proverb confronts us is how to judge between a clear biblical teaching and reliable evidence that seems to contradict it. This is a problem that the biblical wisdom literature anticipates and even highlights. Two of the most compelling witnesses to faith in Israel's God, Job and Koheleth (Ecclesiastes), are compelling precisely because they struggle with elements of the tradition they can no longer affirm. Tradition is neither immutable nor closed. On the contrary, it *must* grow and change in order to be "tradition," literally "(a process of) passing on" from mind to mind, and not merely an artifact preserved in a history book. Tradition is *the shared learning of the community over time.* Consequently, an important function of tradition is to make us aware of the extent to which our feelings and understandings are limited by our personal circumstances and location in time. Inevitably the consensus of the community shifts at various points, when social and historical changes confront us with instances in which the old wisdom does not work, or perhaps when social norms no longer require us to hide painful aspects of our experience. Then it is the work of new "sages" to investigate, reflect, teach, and write, and thus to foster the emergence of a new consensus.

Even if (as I would judge to be the case) it is no longer valid to uphold corporal punishment of children as a general principle, nonetheless we may learn much from this saying. The English-speaking reader immediately thinks of the proverb: "Spare the rod, spoil the child." That saying probably developed as a paraphrase of the biblical verse, and sadly, more people know the paraphrase than what the Bible actually says! And the differences are crucial. The all-important context for the Israelite sages' teaching is the parent's active love for the child (the singular form "child/son" appears in the Hebrew), or the disastrous lack of it. Indeed, as the introductory chapters to the book establish, the whole learning process that emanates in wisdom has the character of love (4:1–4). The stark opposition between love and hate in this verse and elsewhere in scripture (e.g., Gen. 29:31; Deut. 21:15; Mal. 1:2–3) points to the truth that in intimate relationships, anything less than love that actively seeks the good of the other is experienced as hatred.

This affective dimension is completely absent from the paraphrase, which has been stripped even of personal pronouns: "the rod . . . the child." By contrast, the Hebrew verse, which consists of only seven words altogether, is punctuated by four pronouns (of which only three are represented in the NRSV translation): "*his* rod," "*his* child," "loves *him*," "disciplines *him* early" (or "diligently"). These pronouns give a pronounced rhythm to the verse (all are pronounced "-ô"). More importantly, they drum into the hearer the element of personal involvement and the consequences for relationship that are involved in every decision about whether and how to discipline one's child.

A further implication that may be intended here is the importance of early discipline. The last of the four verbs has the connotation of diligent or early action; the final clause might be literally translated: "acts early toward him [for] discipline." At various points the sages show themselves to be astute child psychologists (see the discussion at 22:6). The internalization of discipline belongs to an early stage of child development, certainly within the first ten years. Another saying points to the crucial element of time in unambiguous and unforgettable terms:

> Discipline your children while there is hope;
> do not set your heart on their destruction.
> (Prov. 19:18)

The adolescent or young adult who has not been helped to acquire discipline for herself is marked for deep frustration, if not tragedy. In fact the child of indulgent parents often does come to feel a pervasive, unfocused rage—and might not disagree with the biblical judgment that she is indeed a "hated" child.

This proverb should be considered in the larger context of the sages' observations about children. The first verse of the chapter is no doubt set in deliberate balance to this one, affirming that children themselves are capable of moral discernment:

> A wise child loves discipline,
> but a scoffer does not listen to rebuke.
> (13:1; compare 12:1)

A further realistic note is added by 20:11:

> Even children make themselves known by their acts,
> by whether what they do is pure and right.

That observation complements our proverb in exposing a common delusion of indulgent parents that their children are exempt from public judgment. "Even children make themselves known by their acts," and the loving parent takes care that they make themselves known at an early age as having made the choice for wisdom.

(See further at 23:12–14.)

HONORING SOLITUDE
Proverbs 14:10

> 14:10 **The heart knows its own bitterness,**
> **and no stranger shares its joy.**

This poignant saying is surprising in a book that so strongly praises companionship in friendship and marriage (see the comments at 13:10 and 18:22–24). The saying is more than balanced by others that attest to the empathy and penetrating insight that may exist between companions:

> The human spirit is the lamp of the LORD,
> searching every inmost part.
>   (20:27)
>
> Just as water reflects the face,
> so one human heart reflects another.
>   (27:19)
>
> Perfume and incense make the heart glad,
> And the sweetness of a friend is better than one's own counsel.
>   (27:9; this translation follows the Hebrew text;
>   compare the NRSV translation and note)

Further, the sages affirm that the very simplest act of mercy—a good word—brings genuine comfort:

> Anxiety weighs down the human heart,
> but a good word cheers it up.
>   (12:25)

But is the preponderance of contradictory proverbs meant to invalidate this one? It is one of the paradoxes of human existence that we are impelled to share both our peak joys and our deepest sorrows; so weddings, baptisms, and funerals are public occasions. Yet at another level the intimate experiences they represent cannot be shared. Proverbs 14:10 could well serve as a byword for all those engaged in pastoral ministry—ideally, then, for all members of the church, in the care they show to their neighbors. As a reminder of the limits to our understanding, it should not discourage us from offering sympathy to those in grief but rather counsel humility and respect for the ultimate solitude of the other, which for all our good intentions we must not violate.

JOY AND SORROW
Proverbs 14:12–13

14:12 **There is a way that seems right to a person,**
         but its end is the way to death.
   13 **Even in laughter the heart is sad,**
         and the end of joy is grief.

Perhaps these two proverbs are juxtaposed because both of them take the long view of experience, pointing to the fact that we often judge an endeavor—especially, perhaps, an endeavor of love—very differently at the end than we did at the beginning.

The tone of verse 13 is somewhat at variance with the generally "upbeat" outlook of Proverbs. In the entire book there is no more haunting saying. The frank acknowledgment that joy is inseparable from grief anticipates the hard sayings of Koheleth (Ecclesiastes). Indeed, that unrelenting realist might have taken this verse as his motto.

Some commentators take pains to argue that the verb phrases would be better translated conditionally: "the heart *may be* sad, and the end . . . *may be* grief." But there is no grammatical distinction between this proverb and countless others that are commonly rendered as absolute statements (e.g., vv. 12, 14, 20). That argument misses the fact that many (if not most) proverbs treat aspects of human experience that are regular, though not invariable. Every laugh does not conceal active grief, but nonetheless it is true that any deep commitment of ourselves inevitably brings grief as well as the potential for joy. There is nothing "sub-Christian" about admitting this; love of a friend caused Jesus to weep at Lazarus' tomb; love of his own life caused him to weep in Gethsemane. Indeed, a convincing proclamation of the Easter faith depends on facing that reality squarely. Joy in the risen Christ is not the joy of escaping death, but rather the far more sober joy of those who know they will surely endure death and yet *in Christ* triumph over it.

A Presbyterian minister, widowed after only three years of marriage, said to me some time after her husband's death, "We need to be more frank with people when we are preparing them for marriage in the church. Every marriage will end either in death or in divorce. We need to help couples think about that from the beginning." An effective pastoral ministry should prepare Christians to face the grief that shows itself, perhaps only after many years, as the shadow side of love. A child whose birth seemed so full of promise dies prematurely, or is permanently stunted in the struggle to grow up in a world that offers many children so little security and encouragement. Economic cutbacks force out workers with decades of good service who are too young to retire and too old to find new work. Old age robs virtually all those who reach it of the powers in which they rejoiced and the friends they loved (see Eccl. 12:1–8). Few people escape personal experience of the truth that "the end of joy is grief."

Yet we need encouragement and wise counsel if we are to meet the recurrent griefs of life without falling away from God. Traditional Christian moral theology teaches about cultivating the virtue of patience. As an aspect of Christian practice, patience (which comes from the Latin word meaning "endurance") is the ability to stand fast against the corrosive forces of despair. Patience, in the phrase of the German abbess and mystic Hildegard of Bingen (1098–1179), is "the pillar that nothing can soften" (cited in Pieper, *Four Cardinal Virtues*, 129). We moderns may think of patience as a dreary quality—no one names their daughters for that virtue anymore! But a more accurate understanding suggests that patience enables us to participate in life in all its fullness, to hold together joy and grief without confusion of heart. The Gospel suggests that our eternal life depends upon it: "By your endurance you will gain your souls" (Luke 21:19).

CHILDREN'S INHERITANCE
Proverbs 14:18, 26

> 14:18 **The simple are adorned with folly,**
> **but the clever are crowned with knowledge.**

> 14:26 **In the fear of the LORD one has strong confidence,**
> **and one's children will have a refuge.**

The first proverb has been "corrected" in the NRSV translation, so its two lines are parallel in sense. But this has obscured the meaning of the first line, which is perfectly clear in Hebrew:

> The simple *inherit* folly.

In a very real sense, children are invariably heirs to their parent's folly. As we have seen, the sages are continually mindful of the "simplicity" of the young; they are susceptible to instruction both good and bad. We worry about the vice that our children may learn on the streets; are we as concerned about the foolish behavior they learn, earlier and far more effectively, in their own homes? Many adults labor lifelong under the burden of their inheritance of folly, or spend years painfully gathering strength and wisdom to renounce it.

The seventeenth-century poet and preacher John Donne graphically describes (in a wedding sermon!) parental neglect of children's moral inheritance. Although the language may sound quaint, his challenge to parents is still timely. More than three and a half centuries later, all of us know families who meet his sad description:

> Art thou afraid thy child should be stung with a snake, and wilt thou let him play with the old serpent [the devil], in opening himself to all tentations [temptations]? Art thou afraid to let him walk in an ill air [plague was common in Donne's day], and art thou content to let him stand in that pestilent air that is made of nothing but oaths and execrations of blasphemous mouths round about him? It is St. Chrysostom's complaint: "They buy perdition at a great price; they do not want to accept salvation as a gift." We pay dear for our children's damnation, by paying at first for all their childish vanities, and then for their sinful insolencies at any rate; and we might have them saved, and ourselves into the bargain . . . for much less than ours and their damnation stands us in [costs us]. (*Sermons*, 3:245–46)

Like the biblical sages, Donne makes us aware of how dangerous it is to sentimentalize the bond between parent and child. We delight in seeing that our children have our noses and our musical talent. In our prosperous age, as in Donne's, some parents are able to give their children luxuries they themselves once lacked. They delight in doing so, and later, they take pride in leaving behind a substantial estate for their heirs. Such pleasures are natural and in themselves harmless, even good. But they are dangerous if they blind us to the fact that the only thing of eternal significance we can give to our children is neither genes nor money, but character. The sages point us to the question of what we must do in order to secure our children's moral inheritance. Are we willing to subject our own lives to God's discipline, in order that our "children will have a refuge" (v. 26)?

THE RELIGIOUS SIGNIFICANCE OF THE POOR
Proverbs 14:20–21

14:21 **The poor are disliked even by their neighbors,**
but the rich have many friends

²² **Those who despise their neighbors are sinners,**
but happy are those who are kind to the poor.

These two verses look at the same phenomenon from different sides: those who are judged according to their financial condition, and those who do the judging. The first verse bluntly states a truth known to every school-child (though less likely to be acknowledged by adults), that the rich are likely to meet with social approval and the poor to be shunned (similarly, 19:4, 7). One of the great trials of poverty is the sense of shame that often attaches to it. But the second verse directs our attention to the source of real shame, namely, failure to treat the poor with respect. The person who overcomes contempt of poverty with shame is more than "happy," at least in the conventional understanding of that word. The Hebrew word (*'ashrê*) has a distinctly religious connotation; it is better translated "blessed." This verse is one of the Old Testament "beatitudes" (see also Prov. 3:13; 8:32; Psalm 1:1; 114:15, etc.). Like Jesus' Beatitudes (Matt. 5:3–12; Luke 6:20–23), it identifies those who are privileged in the eyes of God. That status is attained only through defiance of the value judgments commonly rendered in every society.

It is a curious and often neglected fact that the Old Testament gives far more attention than does the New Testament to the *religious* significance of the poor. The phrase "poor and needy" designates those who are right-eous and humble before God; their plight and their voice are often heard in the Psalms (Psalms 40:17; 70:5; 72:4, 12–14; 109:22, etc.). The sages, like the prophets, make it clear that God responds to us according to our response to the poor:

> If you close your ear to the cry of the poor,
> you will cry out and not be heard.
>
> (21:13)

In a painfully graphic way, Dutch theologian Kornelis Miskotte demon-strates the religious significance of the poor: "The poor man is the real neighbor; the way in which he stands, *or rather lies*, in his life has some-thing to do with the nature of the fear of God itself! . . . The poor man is above all the figure in whom the neighbor meets me, as it were, in classi-cal form, as a test case. The book of Proverbs bears witness to this" (*When the Gods Are Silent*, 249–50; italics mine). The neighborly act of the poor toward us who are rich by comparison is literally to lie in our way as we go about our business. I am still haunted by the memory of an encounter with my poor neighbors the day I went with my fiancé to "the Diamond District" of New York City to choose a wedding ring. In order to enter the building, we stepped over the semi-supine bodies of young people who, apart from their dirtiness and vacant facial expressions, very much resembled our students and children. Their presence transformed an experience that might otherwise have been merely sentimental. Through their neighborliness, we became conscious of the blessing and the judgment of God. First, we had to recognize the fairly modest gold band we bought as a sign of our wealth. Moreover, they reminded us that, viewed from the perspective of eternity, the value of Christian marriage depends on the degree to which it strengthens the partners to perceive and respond to the needs of others.

Other proverbs make the theological dimension even more explicit:

> Those who oppress the poor insult their Maker,
> but those who are kind to the needy honor him.
> (14:31)

> Those who mock the poor insult their Maker;
> those who are glad at calamity will not go unpunished.
> (17:5)

Ancient Egyptian wisdom also enjoins regard for the poor as a religious duty: "God desires respect for the poor more than the honoring of the exalted" (Amen-em-opet 28, cited in Pritchard, *Ancient Near Eastern Texts*, 424). But what is striking about Israelite wisdom is the highly personal way it connects the teaching about the poor to the doctrine of creation: "Those who oppress the poor insult their Maker." Through the poor, the creator of heaven and earth becomes vulnerable to our contempt! Likewise, in them God waits to be honored. The Gospel parable of "the sheep and the goats" (Matt. 25:31–46) develops this insight: "Just as you did it [or did not do it] to one of the least of these, you did it [or did not do it] to me." Thus we learn that righteousness is not a matter of conformity to some objective code of behavior. Rather, it is finally a matter of how we treat God, who is directly on the receiving end of our actions, both good and evil.

> The rich and the poor have this in common:
> the LORD is the Maker of them all.
> (22:2)

> The poor and the oppressor have this in common:
> the LORD gives light to the eyes of both.
> (29:13)

By means of simple observations, these proverbs establish the biblical doctrine of creation as the standard by which all economic relations must be
judged. Everyone and everything we have an opportunity to exploit or
respect, to treat kindly or ignore, is a creature whose very existence proceeds from God's intention. This is, of course, a fact of the greatest political significance. The Declaration of Independence states this as self-evident
truth: "that all Men are created equal, that they are endowed by their Creator with certain unalienable Rights. . . . " It is because biblical faith affirms
that we have political rights precisely *as the creatures of God* that totalitarian
governments must always suppress it. They can only be effective and secure
as long as they perpetuate the myth that no one and nothing is more than
a creature of the state, its tool and hopeful beneficiary.

The medieval theologian Thomas Aquinas taught that justice is precisely the responsibility that we owe one another as fellow creatures of the
One God. We live in a time when almost every social appeal is framed as
a justice issue: for women, minorities, the unborn, and the elderly. We now
speak of the rights of animals, even of rivers and rainforests. But in most
cases, questions of justice and rights have been sheared off from their root
in the doctrine of creation. The current ecological crisis makes it crucial
that the modern church be able to demonstrate the connection between
economic justice and creation. In our age, nature itself has been aptly
termed "the new poor" (S. McFague, *Body*, 164). That is, our earth has
joined the ranks of those whose physical needs are routinely overlooked,
whose well-being is treated as expendable in the pursuit of profit. By setting treatment of the poor in the context of God's work of creation, the
sages help us to see that human disregard of the earth is nothing less than
contempt of God. Conversely, respect for the earth is an essential element
of reverencing the God who is "the Maker of us all."

HEALING SPEECH
Proverbs 15:4

> 15:4 **A gentle tongue is a tree of life
> but perverseness in it breaks the spirit.**

The NRSV translation is misleading; the Hebrew reads "a healing tongue."
The sages were well aware that healing speech is not always gentle; a bold
confrontation is sometimes salutary (see comment on Prov. 10:10). Elsewhere the healing tongue is aptly contrasted with rash speech (12:18).

The proverb picks up the image from the Genesis story to suggest the restorative power of speech. The story of Eden is so familiar to us that we might have expected the tree of life to become a tired cliché for any desirable thing that is hard to obtain. But in fact, the image appears in the Old Testament only in Proverbs, where it characterizes wise speech and other marks of wisdom (Prov. 3:18; 11:30; 13:12). The inference would seem to be that wise speaking points the way back to Eden. More than any other sphere of human activity, speaking has the potential to effect healing at the deepest level. It is a tree of life; it restores us to the condition of harmony with God and our fellow creatures for which we were made.

With an edge of cynicism, we say, "Talk is cheap." To us, then, the sages' confidence in the power of speech may seem greatly exaggerated. Yet perhaps this proverb, by orienting us to the creation story, may move us to consider that the unique capacity for human speech is a mark of our creation in God's image. The first chapter of Genesis shows God creating and ordering the world by means of words. It is significant that the first independent human act is a verbal one: the naming of the animals (Gen. 2:19). It is, then, an exercise in what Christian spirituality calls *imitatio Dei*, "the imitation of God." Adam continues the work that God began, using language to order the world. And God validates that action, accepting these new human-created words—hippopotamus, elephant, camel—so that "whatever the human being called every living creature, that was its name."

But almost immediately, speech is perverted. With clever words the snake beguiles Eve; with evasive, alienating words Adam shifts the blame to Eve and Eve to the snake. Words "fell" in Eden, along with their speakers. The degradation of speech is now so complete that we simply take it for granted. A successful business executive says, "I don't need to hear ninety percent of what is being said, so I've learned to filter out the excess noise and pick up the ten percent I need." It is not only in the business world that speech is regarded as so much "noise." In many families, children routinely tune out their parents, and (perhaps with less excuse) parents tune out children; teachers and preachers expect most of what they say not to be heard; friends half-listen to one another, waiting for their turn to hold the floor.

Yet we have not completely lost the understanding that true speaking holds the power of life. This is the presupposition common to poets and psychotherapists, to those who pray and write love letters, to those who ask for forgiveness and wait hopefully to hear absolution pronounced by a minister or by a loved one.

Conversely, the second line of the proverb points to the destructiveness that inevitably follows from perverted speech. The poetic structure of the Hebrew is more open to different interpretations than the translation suggests. It consists of two noun phrases set side by side without a verb: "But perversion in it [the tongue]—a break in the spirit." At least three inferences may legitimately be drawn. Most obviously (as the NRSV translation indicates), perverse speech hurts others in deep ways. "Sticks and stones will break my bones, but words will never hurt me"—nothing could be farther from the sages' way of thinking or from the truth. Second, perverted speech inevitably springs from the speaker's own wounded spirit. Hard though this is to remember when we ourselves have been hurt, it is one of the keys to learning to pray for our enemies. Third, perverted speech works finally toward the speaker's self-destruction. Indulging in it can break an already weak spirit, as many proverbs recognize:

> Lying lips conceal hatred,
> and whoever utters slander is a fool.
>
> (10:18)

> The lips of the righteous feed many,
> but fools die for lack of sense.
>
> (10:21)

> The mouth of the righteous brings forth wisdom,
> but the perverse tongue will be cut off.
>
> (10:31)

(See also the comment at 18:20–21.)

GAINING A HEART
Proverbs 15:30–33

15:30 **The light of the eyes rejoices the heart,**
      and good news refreshes the body.
   31 **The ear that heeds wholesome admonition**
      will lodge among the wise.
   32 **Those who ignore instruction despise themselves,**
      but those who heed admonition gain understanding.
   33 **The fear of the LORD is instruction in wisdom,**
      and humility goes before honor.

This is one of the sages' core instructions; it teaches about the formation of the self. A literal translation of verse 32 reads thus:

> The one who casts off *discipline* despises *his own self*,
> but the one who *hears* reproof gains *a heart*.

In biblical language, "the heart" is the center of the personality. Not only feeling but also thought and faith originate in the heart. Accordingly, the Hebrew word *lev*, "heart," is often translated as "mind" (e.g., Prov. 16:1; 25:2). The sages' most important insight is that a truly human heart, full personhood, is not a natural endowment, given at birth. Like the tin woodsman in *The Wizard of Oz*, we who aspire to be wise must earnestly desire to *acquire* our hearts.

The further insight to which this saying leads is that the key to acquiring a heart is "an ear that hears life-giving reproof" (v. 31a, AT). That point is made by means of a series of verbal echoes. Each of the following words occurs twice: "hear" (vv. 31a, 32b), "heart" (vv. 30a, 32b), "admonition/reproof" (vv. 31a, 32b), "discipline" (translated in vv. 32a and 33a as "instruction"; see the comment at Prov. 1:1–6). Following the progression forces us to reevaluate the first part of the saying, which at first seem to be merely a truism:

> *A good thing heard* refreshes the bone.
> (v. 30b, AT)

In every line that follows, it becomes clear that the "good thing heard" that ultimately strengthens the self is not (contrary to the NRSV translation) what we generally call "good news." Often, it is something challenging and therefore easy to ignore.

Here the sages counter our inclination to ignore criticism with what is perhaps their most striking statement on the value of correction (v. 32). Ignoring discipline and the "reproof of life" (v. 31a) is an act of self-hatred! Our modern society has idealized the journey of self-discovery, often making it appear as a solo flight into the unknown. The sages do urge respect for the learner's own "way" (see the comment at Prov. 22:6). Yet at the same time they caution strongly that a stable self is achieved in large part by accepting correction from others who see us differently and often more accurately than we see ourselves. This is the principle that underlies the monastic tradition of spiritual direction. A Christian "self" is formed by seeking the guidance of someone who knows us better than we can know ourselves, because they know God, in whose image we are made. In recent years growing numbers of Christians—lay people as well as clergy—have rediscovered the wisdom of the ancient practice of seeking regular instruction and "in-course correction" from others in the community of faith who are further ahead on their way to God.

Verse 33 introduces another concept, humility, which belongs essentially to faith lived in community. Yet too often what we call "humility" is something that can hardly be considered a virtue. We mistakenly think that humility requires downplaying our own worth and denying our talents. But the sad result of such false humility is resentment of those around us who also fail to acknowledge them. Genuine humility is the very opposite of angry self-denial. It means accepting your talents as a gift from God, recognizing them as God's gift to the world through you, and preparing yourself to use them accordingly. In the letter to the Ephesians, the call to humility is followed directly by a list of the gifts with which God has "equip[ped] the saints for the work of ministry" (Eph. 4:1–16).

The proverb rightly connects discipline with humility, for genuine humility demands diligence in nurturing our talents. The medieval theologian Thomas Aquinas offers a definition that can hardly be improved: "Humility is nothing other than the patient pursuit of your own excellence." Humility means seeking *your own* excellence, the fullness of being that God particularly intends for you. Discerning our own excellence requires listening for the correction of those reliable teachers that God has given us. Equally, it requires that we *close our ears* to the abundant false counsel with which the "image makers" in our society bombard us, in words and pictures: "You must be slim. You must never look old. Never show you are afraid or uncertain about what to do. It is better to be beautiful and clever and rich than kind."

"Humility goes before honor"—the saying is ambiguous in Hebrew as in English, and probably intentionally so. Humility is to be preferred to honor; the wise person is active in the humble pursuit of excellence rather than honor. Yet it is also true that honor may follow and reward the practice of humility (see Prov. 22:4; 29:23), just because it aims at magnifying God's gifts rather than realizing our private ambitions. Thus humility inevitably contributes to the well-being of the community.

AUTONOMY AND OBEDIENCE
Proverbs 16:1–9

16:1 **The plans of the mind belong to mortals,**
     but the answer of the tongue is from the LORD.

2 All one's ways may be pure in one's own eyes,
   but the LORD weighs the spirit.
3 Commit your work to the LORD,
   and your plans will be established.
4 The LORD has made everything for its purpose,
   even the wicked for the day of trouble.
5 All those who are arrogant are an abomination to the LORD;
   be assured, they will not go unpunished.
6 By loyalty and faithfulness iniquity is atoned for,
   and by the fear of the LORD one avoids evil.
7 When the ways of people please the LORD,
   he causes even their enemies to be at peace with them.
8 Better is a little with righteousness
   than large income with injustice.
9 The human mind plans the way,
   but the LORD directs the steps.

This is the most overtly theological section of the book, and it is no coincidence that the ancient editors set it prominently in the middle of the book (16:17 is the exact middle, counting by verses). The equation of "fear of the LORD" with wisdom (15:33) is further developed in this cluster of proverbs treating the complex dynamic between human intention and divine initiative—in other words, the dynamic between human autonomy and obedience.

The first verse is sometimes interpreted as establishing a firm distinction between what comes from us and what comes from God. This seems to be the sense of the Egyptian proverb

> One thing are the words which people say,
> another is that which the god does.
>
> (Amen-em-opet 18, cited in Pritchard,
> *Ancient Near Eastern Texts*, 423)

Establishing that distinction is also the intent of Thomas à Kempis's famous maxim, "Man [*Homo*] proposes but God disposes." But here it is unlikely that such a distinction is intended, since "the plans of the mind (literally, 'heart')" and "the answer of the tongue" both involve human agency. The proverb is probably pointing to the fact that however carefully we may plan our remarks—for a marriage proposal, a job interview, a confrontation with a close friend or spouse, a sermon—what comes out in the heat of the moment is often a surprise. Indeed, our own unexpected remarks are one of the ways that God reveals us to ourselves. Sometimes the surprise is a happy one:

To make an apt answer is a joy to anyone,
and a word in season, how good it is!
(Prov. 15:23)

An apt answer is from the sages' perspective the consummate joy, not just because it makes us look good, but because it indicates that we are right with God.

But the wise person learns also from the words she wishes she had *not* said. Verses 2 and 5 point to the fact that self-suspicion is an essential element of wisdom. Self-suspicion is the only effective antidote to arrogance. In matters of speech, it expresses itself as the willingness to explore the feelings that lie behind a remark that "didn't come out right," to discover our own malice and confess it as a sin. Healthy self-suspicion derives from the recognition that our knowledge of ourselves is always woefully incomplete:

All our steps are ordered by the LORD;
how then can we understand our own ways?
(20:24)

The sages also struggle with the problem of external evil, the fact that the wicked have not been eliminated from God's order (v. 4). One might infer from the present translation that the wicked are divinely ordained to be wicked, but that is probably more than the proverb intends. The first line may also be rendered: "The LORD has made everything in relation to its counterpart." The idea here is close to that of the New Testament parable of the wheat and the tares (Matt. 13:24–20): the bad cannot be fully separated from the good until the day of judgment.

The passage ends with another strong affirmation that the mind directed toward God and the movement of God in human life are finally compatible (v. 9; see also v. 3). Far from denigrating the importance of human planning, this proverb suggests that choosing the right way is in fact our responsibility; then God shows us how to walk it. This is contrary to the common belief of pious people, that "the big design" of their lives comes from God, and they simply fill in the details.

A woman at a key juncture in her life exclaimed in frustration to her spiritual director, a nun of much experience and wisdom: "I'm forty years old, and I don't know whether I want to get married or be a nun!" The nun replied: "It doesn't matter." "What do you mean it doesn't matter? Doesn't God have an opinion?" "No. What God cares about is that you live faithfully and give yourself fully, whichever path you choose. You are free to decide, and *you* must decide. You must go through the pain of decision in order to give yourself fully."

It might be easier for us if God made our plans and decisions unnecessary, but evidently it would be less gratifying for God. For then there would be nothing that could meaningfully be called human autonomy and no possibility of our making to God the gift of a faithful life.

THE POWER AND THE JUSTICE OF KINGS
Proverbs 16:10–16

16:10 **Inspired decisions are on the lips of a king;**
　　　　his mouth does not sin in judgment.
　11　**Honest balances and scales are the LORD's;**
　　　　all the weights in the bag are his work.
　12　**It is an abomination to kings to do evil,**
　　　　for the throne is established by righteousness.
　13　**Righteous lips are the delight of a king,**
　　　　and he loves those who speak what is right.
　14　**A king's wrath is a messenger of death,**
　　　　and whoever is wise will appease it.
　15　**In the light of a king's face there is life,**
　　　　and his favor is like the clouds that bring the spring rain.
　16　**How much better to get wisdom than gold!**
　　　　To get understanding is to be chosen rather than silver.

The sages' frequent references to kings suggest that many of the early wise men belonged to court circles. It is likely that both Solomon (Prov. 1:1) and Hezekiah (25:1) sponsored the collection and promulgation of wise sayings, as did their royal neighbors (31:1). Royal courts housed the research academies of the ancient world. In Israel and elsewhere, a dynasty's prestige was enhanced not only through military victories, foreign trade, and monumental construction, but also through patronage of the arts and sciences:

> It is the glory of God to conceal things,
> but the glory of kings is to search things out.
> Like the heavens for height, like the earth for depth,
> so the mind of kings is unsearchable.
>
> (25:2–3)

The word translated as "inspired decisions" (v. 10) is surprising, for it is used elsewhere of divination, which was firmly outlawed in Israel. Its use here expresses the conviction that a king's wisdom is something more than the product of a good education; it is a gift from God. The history of Israel's kings illustrates this with the story of Solomon's dream at Gibeon (1 Kings 3:3–15). Solomon's virtue (despite many flaws, as it turns out!) is that he values "a listening heart" to govern wisely more than silver and gold (see v. 16 above). Thus he wins an enduring commitment from God. Verse 11 points to how divine justice operates through the king at the most mundane level, in the marketplace. Enforcing the use of standard weights and measures was a function of the royal house. Indirectly, every household was affected by the king's exercise of responsibility in this matter.

The sages are not naïve about the possibility of kings behaving tyrannically. Some sayings express considerable wariness:

> The dread anger of a king is like the growling of a lion;
> anyone who provokes him to anger forfeits life itself.
> (20:2)

> My child, fear the LORD and the king,
> and do not disobey either of them;
> for disaster comes from them suddenly,
> and who knows the ruin that both can bring?
> (24:21–22)

These warnings could come from inside or outside the palace, for people at any level of society are liable to discover that the king's power is absolute and his displeasure, whether expressed personally or impersonally (through the law), is deadly.

The sages are realistic about the abuse of power (see also 28:15, 16; 29:2), yet the tone of the book never sinks into cynicism. This is remarkable, because by the time Proverbs was edited, the Davidic monarchy had failed, both politically and morally, and Israel was ruled by foreign kings, not all of whom were benevolent. Nonetheless, the sages uphold the ideal that kings—even pagan kings—are possessed of wisdom: "By me kings reign" (Prov. 8:15). That statement, like the ones in verses 10 and 13 above, should be taken as an expression less of fact than of hope. It is intended to inspire a ruler with "a listening heart." For only if the king is a lover of wisdom is there any hope that justice will prevail in the public sphere and evil be repressed (20:8, 26).

Kings who act wickedly put themselves in jeopardy, and not foremost from political rebels; for they undermine the cosmic foundation of their rule. The king's throne is secure only when it is "established by righteousness" (v. 12); the same words are used of God's own throne (Psalms 9:8; 89:15; 97:2). In view of this connection between God's justice and the king's, it is likely that the language of life and death in this passage (vv. 14–15) is meant to go beyond political expediency and suggest that obedience to a just ruler is part of the obligation one owes to God, the author of life and death (see also 24:21).

The New Testament likewise asserts that governmental authority, even though flawed, exists by the appointment of God (Rom. 13:1–2; John 19:11). This view has few adherents in modern culture, and many regard the prayers for the president (or the queen) and others in authority that are a fixed element of many liturgies as merely quaint relics; some consider them heretical. Yet if such prayers were said sincerely, they would serve to remind us that peace and the well-being of any community depend not only on political organization but also on a sense of justice, which is ultimately a gift from God. Such prayers might also sensitize us to the particular virulence of the temptations that assail those in public office (see 1 Tim. 2:1–3), which others of us may give thanks to have been spared.

Finally, praying earnestly for our leaders might keep us from the sin of cynicism, the willful abandonment of hope. Several years ago, at a time when a political scandal was receiving much press coverage in the United States, a friend who is a citizen of another country commented: "You Americans are so naïve. At home we just assume that anyone who runs for public office is a scoundrel." That is a tragic assumption. It is a national tragedy if hordes of tourists can visit the Lincoln memorial each year and not be moved by the nobility of purpose expressed in the address inscribed on its walls:

> With malice toward none; with charity for all; with firmness in the right, as God gives us to see the right, let us strive on to finish the work we are in; to bind up the nation's wounds; to care for him who shall have borne the battle, and for his widow, and his orphan—to do all which may achieve and cherish a just and lasting peace, among ourselves, and with all nations. (Second Inaugural Address, March 4, 1865)

Perhaps our sincere prayers could contribute to the revival in the public mind of a sense of the inherent dignity of public office. Unless that sense grows among ordinary citizens, it is likely that most of those offering themselves for "public service" will merely be seeking their own private advantage.

TRUSTING GOD
Proverbs 16:20

> 16:20 **Those who are attentive to a matter will prosper,**
> **and happy are those who trust in the LORD.**

Both lines of the proverb speak of the practical and spiritual necessity of paying close attention. The benefit of attending to a practical matter is obvious, but less obvious is the fact that trust in God also involves focusing our attention. Although we commonly speak of "blind trust," genuine trust is never blind; for it is based on an assessment of the other person's character. Jewish theologian Martin Buber observes that trust is "the intimate reflection and outcome of another person's integrity" (*Israel: An Echo of Eternity*, 96). Therefore enduring trust, in God as in other people, is both a decision and a gift. It reflects a decision to probe God's character, by reading the scriptures in order to find out what God is really like (and the answers are often surprising and sometimes deeply puzzling), by meditating on our own personal histories and remembering what God has done for us, and by gaining some skill in spiritual discernment, in order that we may see God's faithfulness even in situations that did not turn out as we had hoped. But trust in God is also a gift, for it is made possible by God's prior integrity. It is only because God is indeed trustworthy that enduring faith and confidence in God are possible. Moreover, trust produces "happiness." (A better translation might be "blessed are those . . ." This is the same Hebrew word which lies behind Jesus' Beatitudes; see Matt. 5:3–12; Luke 6:20–23.) Trusting God, we feel both God's holiness—that is, God's wholeness, the perfect integrity of perfect love—and also God's presence with us. This is the inference that traditional Jewish thought has drawn from a verse similar to this one: "Blessed is the person who trusts in the LORD, whose trust is the LORD" (Jer. 17:7). The rabbis comment: "Trust in God *is* God" (*Deuteronomy Rabba* 1:12).

Trust in God, waiting on God, is receptivity, not passivity. Rather, the Bible represents trust in God as an active attitude that expresses itself in prayer. Urgent trust can even motivate God to act. The psalms of lament often bring the pressure of trust to bear on God:

> O my God, in you I trust;
> do not let me be put to shame;
> do not let my enemies exult over me.
> Do not let those who wait for you be put to shame;
> let them be ashamed who are wantonly treacherous. . . .

> Lead me in your truth, and teach me,
> for you are the God of my salvation;
> for you I wait all day long.
>
> (Psalm 25:2–3, 5)

(On trust in God, see also the comment at 3:1–12.)

TEMPERANCE
Proverbs 16:32 and 25:28

16:32 **One who is slow to anger is better than the mighty,**
and one whose temper is controlled than one who captures a city.

25:28 **Like a city breached, without walls,**
is one who lacks self-control.

These proverbs uphold the virtue of temperance, traditionally regarded by Christians as one of the four "cardinal virtues" (along with prudence, justice, and fortitude). The NRSV translation narrows the first proverb to speak of controlling anger, but a more accurate translation allows for a broader understanding:

> Patience is better than being a hero,
> and the one who has self-control than the one who takes a city.

Temperance is fundamentally a deep regard for the gifts God has given us, including our "ordinary" human powers and physical health. Therefore temperance forbids any form of self-degradation—through excessive anger, but also through too much food or too little, misuse of alcohol and drugs, squandering healthy sexual desire through indulgence of lust. In light of the sages' many teachings about the need for steady discipline in educating a child, we can see that temperance is nothing other than the full internalization of discipline. It means respecting ourselves enough to choose for ourselves the things our wisest and most caring teachers would choose for us. The twelfth-century monk Bernard of Clairvaux comments forcefully on the second proverb: "Every man is his own attacker. Every man throws himself down—indeed you need not fear any attack from outside, if you can keep your hands from yourself" (*On the Song of Songs*, vol. 4, 198).

The notion of temperance seems old-fashioned and even unhealthy to many of us, for ours is a culture that places high value on "being in touch with your feelings" and expressing them freely, recognizing desires and indulging them (think of all the advertisements whose theme is: "Go ahead, you deserve this"). But it is crucial for us to make the distinction between an unhealthy repression of desire and the necessary virtue of temperance. Repression is rooted in fear: what will happen if I do what I really want to do, if I reveal who I really am? Yet the practice of temperance, true self-control, is possible only for those who have a strong sense both of self and of vocation. As a Christian virtue, temperance is the ability to respond to God's call to us and to set aside the passing whims, the small but regular self-indulgences, even the strong passions that would divert us from answering that call. Temperance does not exclude the expression of passion, including anger, but it demands that we use our passions wisely rather than being tyrannized by them. Above all, temperance aims at keeping us free for God's service.

The apostle Paul—himself well tutored in the wisdom of Proverbs—teaches that without temperance, one cannot live the Christian life. When summoned by the Roman governor Felix to "speak concerning faith in Christ Jesus," he reduces the basic catechism to only these three elements: "justice, self-control (temperance), and the coming judgment" (Acts 24:24–25). This remarkable digest of the faith challenges the very common view that self-indulgence, though perhaps not admirable, doesn't really hurt. At least, we imagine, it doesn't hurt anyone or anything but ourselves. But Paul alerts us to the fact that self-control is in fact fundamentally linked with our capacity for justice. If we cannot show proper regard for ourselves, then how can we even recognize the basic needs of others, let alone show respect for their well-being? Certainly the ecological crisis presses modern Christians to draw the connection between justice and self-control in their own lives. We in the industrialized nations constitute about 20 percent of the world's population and use about 80 percent of its goods. Can we learn to look at our habitual overconsumption with new eyes, and see it for what it is: not a delightful abundance, but rather a violation of human dignity—the dignity of the poor and also of ourselves? Can we learn to see our gross overconsumption as a kind of spiritual obesity, for which we will be answerable in "the coming judgment"?

(On temperance, see also the comment at 30:7–9.)

CHOOSING THE GOOD
Proverbs 17:1

17:1 **Better is a dry morsel with quiet**
   than a house full of feasting with strife.

This is one of a number of sayings that follow the formula, "Better is X than Y":

Better is a little with the fear of the LORD
than great treasure and trouble with it.
Better is a dinner of vegetables where love is
than a fatted ox and hatred with it.
                    (15:16–17; see also 16:8, 16, 19;
                                      19:22; 21:3; 22:1; 28:6)

The sages seek always to orient us toward the good. Yet it is encouraging to find that they understand that one must often choose a good that is much less than perfect. With these "better than sayings" they acknowledge obliquely that fear of the Lord does not necessarily bring prosperity (contrast 3:9–10; 8:21; 10:22). Although it would be nice to have both love and the fatted ox (the ancients did not view vegetarianism as an ideal), these sayings show judgment informed by realism and humility. This is down-to-earth wisdom: concrete, unsentimental pictures of what is good, which the simplest can understand and safely follow.

No society can thrive or long endure without such pictures of the choices of value that ordinary people must regularly make. Yet our multi-billion-dollar advertising industry does exactly the opposite. The proverbs direct us to choose what is truly good—domestic peace, love, a living faith—over what is merely attractive. Madison Avenue plies us constantly with what might be seen as a parody of the "better than" proverbs: images of the "simple joys" in countless material forms, from designer athletic shoes and sweatsuits to diamond eternity rings. The prevalence of such advertisements suggests that mock simplicity sells well. The images may seem innocent enough, even healthy—but children in the ghetto murder other children for a pair of designer sneakers. Proverbs forces us to ask: by feeding our children and ourselves seductive images of the desirable, are we mocking God? For we are creating appetites that can never be satisfied with what is good, though not ideal.

Better is a little with righteousness
than large income with injustice.
                                    (16:8)

THE DANGER OF ISOLATION
Proverbs 18:1–2

18:1 **The one who lives alone is self-indulgent,**
     showing contempt for all who have sound judgment.

> ² **A fool takes no pleasure in understanding,**
> **but only in expressing personal opinion.**

The NRSV renders the first saying too narrowly. The Hebrew word here translated as "lives alone" refers more generally to isolation as a way of life, voluntary or involuntary. The same word appears in Proverbs 19:4: "The poor are left *friendless*." Verse 1 here is better translated:

> The one who isolates himself seeks his own pleasure;
> he breaks out against all sound judgment.

A German proverb expresses the same view in striking terms: Ein Mensch ist kein Mensch (One person is no person at all). The alternative to isolation points to the ultimate value of human community as the biblical writers understand it: "If people are united in one covenant, they behold the Presence of God" (cited by Cohen, *Proverbs*, 118).

The second line goes further to suggest that self-isolation constitutes a positive danger. The verb, "breaks out," implies a violent reaction against good sense; elsewhere it is used of the outbreak of a quarrel (Prov. 17:14). Self-isolation is an active rejection of the literally "common sense" of the community. The price of abandoning community is more than personal loneliness or lack of fulfillment. It is anarchy, personal chaos that eventually and perhaps inevitably becomes open hostility toward others.

It is important to recognize that the dangers of isolation are not confined to the behavior of individuals. Indeed, they are far greater when isolation is elevated to a cultural principle, as has happened in modern Western society, where the major social structures—industrial, educational, professional—are based on the form of isolation we call "specialization." Specialization is regarded as an advanced state of knowledge requisite for efficiency and professional credibility. Of course, specialization has its place. If you need brain surgery, then you want a doctor more experienced in such things than the old-fashioned family doctor. But for the *maintenance* of health, which should be the chief object of medical care, a well-informed general practitioner is more useful, precisely because her attention is focused less on this particular *disease* than on what constitutes health for this particular *person*.

We have vaunted specialization of knowledge naïvely and forgotten that it also constitutes a danger. The danger inherent in all forms of culturally endorsed isolation is the tendency to ignore the first fact with which the

Bible confronts us: namely, that everything is related to everything else, because it proceeds from the will of a single creator. "God saw *everything* that he had made, and indeed, it was very good" (Gen. 1:31). Each thing, considered by itself, is "good"; only the totality is pronounced "very good." The theological principle that everything is related to everything also fundamentally informs the proclamation of who Jesus Christ is: "the firstborn of all creation; for in him all things in heaven and on earth were created ... *and in him all things hold together*" (Col. 1:15–17).

Our culture's devotion to specialization is rooted in the modern university system, where the task of learning is divided among various specialized disciplines, each operating in nearly perfect isolation. The modern university is not one ivory tower but many, each one housing—or imprisoning?— an expert. Yet this is completely contrary to the vision that led to the founding of the European university by theologians in the Middle Ages. As its name indicates, the universe-ity was formed in accordance with the biblical understanding that there is an underlying unity to all reality. For everything that is proceeds from the intention and wisdom of the one God:

> The LORD by wisdom founded the earth;
> by understanding he established the heavens;
> by his knowledge the deeps broke open,
> and the clouds drop down the dew.
> > My child, do not let these escape from your sight ...
> > > (Prov. 3:19–21a)

The biblical wisdom tradition seeks that underlying unity of all that is. Viewed from that perspective, the loss of this unifying vision within the modern university is more than ironic. It is a cultural tragedy that affects all of us. For virtually all handling of advanced knowledge in our society is done by people trained to examine each aspect of the world as a pure—that is, isolated—phenomenon. Never in the history of the world have specialized researchers "controlled" so much data; never have they had such powerful tools for manipulation of the world, in both its physical and its social aspects. And never has there been so little disciplined inquiry into what all this knowledge is good for, or whether it is good at all.

We are not prepared to ask questions about the value of what we know; for as a whole, we lack a standard for measuring such value. We have no common vision of what is the goal of education in our society. Certainly we have no common agreement that education should be good for our souls. In a recent study, 75 percent of college freshmen surveyed stated that their foremost goal was to make money. Only 40 percent mentioned that they hoped a college education would contribute to formation of a sound "philosophy of life." In the sages' terms, the vast majority are using education in order to "seek their own pleasure." They are prime candidates for the isolating environment of the modern university.

The sages counter this isolating tendency by putting the question of value foremost. The collection of proverbs begins by stating the goal to which all our learning should tend: "righteousness, justice, and equity" (Prov. 1:3). They understand that the possession of knowledge always confers moral responsibility. Albert Einstein, when told of the dropping of the atomic bombs on Hiroshima and Nagasaki, is reported to have sat silent for a time, his head in his hands. Then he said, citing a proverb: "The old Chinese were right: you cannot do whatever you want." One might add, "or whatever you know how to do." It is no coincidence that he responded out of an ancient wisdom tradition. Even the most technically sophisticated handling of knowledge is nothing more than "the venting of personal opinion" (18:2), if it is not disciplined by the sound judgment of a morally sensitive community. Twentieth-century history offers more than enough evidence that the self-expression of "fools" is incomparably destructive.

DEADLY AND LIFE-GIVING SPEECH
Proverbs 18:20–21

> 18:20 **From the fruit of the mouth one's stomach is satisfied;**
> **the yield of the lips brings satisfaction.**
> 21 **Death and life are in the power of the tongue,**
> **and those who love it will eat its fruits.**

The first verse, taken by itself, could be read as a purely utilitarian statement: a good command of words puts food on the table. So I recently heard a patent attorney comment that his business is "selling words." Such a utilitarian view of speaking is very common among us; words are widely regarded as marketable commodities. Politicians and advertisers are eager to find words that will sell but rarely feel morally bound by what they have said. A presidential press secretary, confronted with a clear contradiction in his remarks, observed that the earlier statement was "inoperative." It is telling that he chose a word that comes from the world of machinery. One might say that we have become a culture of "word processors." We rapidly produce words and delete them, hoping they will disappear without a trace from human memory, as they do from a computer screen.

But the second verse shows how inadequate is that mechanistic understanding of speech. The fruit-bearing tongue is a living source of nourishment, delight, sustenance. "A healing tongue is a tree of life" (Prov. 15:4; see the comment there). But words can destroy as well as heal: "Death and life are in the power of the tongue." That proverb is at the opposite pole from our own: "Sticks and stones will break my bones, but words will never hurt me." On the contrary, the biblical perception is that words are powerful bearers of intention, for good and for ill. In speaking, we imitate God, who once spoke the world into being. Serving God requires that our words further the intentions first expressed in God's own purposeful word:

> . . . my word . . . that goes out of my mouth,
> it shall not return to me empty,
> but it shall accomplish that which I purpose,
> and succeed in the thing for which I sent it.
> (Isa. 55:11)

The widespread degradation of words in our culture points to the need to highlight the clear biblical witness in this matter, if the church is itself to be a center of godly speech that gives life to its members. Within the New Testament, the letter of James, whose thought at many points echoes that of the sages, names an undisciplined tongue as "a fire . . . a world of iniquity" (James 3:6). One contemporary theologian issues a profound and imaginative challenge to the church: to recognize itself as a "guild of philologians," literally "word-lovers." He challenges us, not to be better Scrabble players, but to engage in "that word-caring, that meticulous and conscientious concern for the quality of conversation and the truthfulness of memory, which is the first casualty of sin" (Lash, "Ministry of the Word," 476). Truthful words, backed up with our lives, are all that we offer God in worship. Caring words are often all that we have to offer one another, the best salve that we have for healing wounds, the best mortar we have for building up the whole body of the church.

GOOD COMPANIONS
Proverbs 18:22–24

18:22 **He who finds a wife finds a good thing,**
　　　and obtains favor from the LORD.
　23 **The poor use entreaties,**
　　　but the rich answer roughly.

²⁴ **Some friends play at friendship**
   but a true friend sticks closer than one's nearest kin.

Each of these proverbs deals with the need for reliable companions, in both marriage and friendship. One aspect of the affliction of the poor is the fact that they are often friendless (14:20; 19:4). But even the more fortunate should be prepared to discover that many friends are of the "fair weather" variety. Indeed, with a subtle turn of phrase the third proverb hints that this may be the majority. Note the contrast between the plural—"*friends* who play at friendship"—and the singular: literally, "but *one who loves.*"

The sages place high value on fidelity to friends (see 17:17). In a kinship-based society like ancient Israel, it is striking to find an affirmation of nonfamilial ties of affection such as the following:

> Better is a neighbor who is nearby
> than kindred who are far away.
> (27:10)

The fact that the sages of Proverbs attach special importance to friendship—more than in any other biblical book except Ruth—may reflect their awareness of a change in social structure (see the Introduction). Kinship bonds weakened as some Israelites chose or (probably more often) were forced to move off the family land, out of the ancestral village, and into the city or to neighboring areas to find work. Far from home, they now had to look to friends rather than family for support and help in time of trouble. With a degree of caution (see v. 24 above), the sages are accommodating to the new social reality.

Jesus likewise valued friendship highly; these were apparently the human bonds that were most important to him (John 15:15; Mark 3:31–35). The biblical emphasis on the importance and joy of friendship—as expressed also in the stories of Ruth and Naomi, Jonathan and David—is instructive for us. Though countless self-help books treat the health of sexual and familial relations, the pleasures and the art of friendship are largely ignored. People who lead rich lives filled with love nonetheless carry a vague sense of deprivation and incompleteness because they are not married. The church, too, often styles itself as a "family," deliberately (or not) conjuring up the image of a married couple with children. But this model excludes very many members or would-be members of the church. Millions of people in our mobile society derive most of their emotional sustenance from friends. Fostering and celebrating healthy friendships, then, no less than healthy marriages and good parenting, should be part of the pastoral ministry of the church. None of these primary emotional bonds can be separated from the life of faith; each of them is an avenue along which we can move deeply into life with God.

The nonexclusive love that characterizes friendship is an important value within the monastic life, and this is one of the many contributions that tradition can make to the church as a whole. A story is told of a young friar in the monastery of Saint Francis of Assisi who fell into a morbid depression. He idolized Francis, but he had got it into his head that his hero despised him. The young man became deeply withdrawn and secretive, until one day Francis spoke to him with disarming candor: "Do not be troubled, for you are dear to me, even one of those who are most dear. You know that you are worthy of my friendship and society; therefore come to me, in confidence, whenever you wish, and from friendship learn faith" (Chesterton, *St. Francis*, 154–155). Francis had a genius for being a neighbor. "From friendship learn faith"—this is the same low-profile, labor-intensive style of evangelizing which Jesus used. Can the church afford not to practice it?

CONTENTIOUSNESS
Proverbs 19:13

> 19:13 **A stupid child is ruin to a father,**
> **and a wife's quarreling is a continual dripping of rain.**

Modern readers chafe at the several references to a quarrelsome wife (21:9, 19; 25:24; 27:15–16). These attest to the fact that the authorial perspective of the book is male. We rightly note that petty faultfinding is not a sin confined to women. In fact, there are several proverbs that make a similar point in terms that include both sexes:

> One who forgives an offense seeks love,
> but one who harps on a matter alienates an intimate.
> (17:9; AT)

> Those with good sense are slow to anger,
> and it is their glory to overlook an offense.
> (19:11)

Gratuitous quarrels are of course contrary to true wisdom. But these proverbs warn also against being quick to anger even over a real offense.

They are valuable for the challenge they offer to the popular wisdom of our own culture, which places a high priority—for both sexes—on confrontation, on being right, on asserting "my rights" in every situation, on not letting anyone get away with anything. From our cultural perspective, it is surprising, even shocking, to hear that the ability *not* to react angrily redounds to a person's glory. Proverbs does not suggest that the wise are better at swallowing their anger. More likely, they do not even *notice* minor failings or transgressions that keep others in a permanent state of irritation!

Even when no personal affront is given, we often make faults an excuse for withholding expressions of love or venting anger. A child comes home with a report card of Bs and As—and hears only about the one C. My husband has dinner on the table when I come home from a trying meeting that ran overtime, and I cannot resist chiding him for forgetting to turn off the stove and burning the pan. The proverb warns me that gradual alienation is the price I will pay for indulging my petty irritations.

As a young seminarian, I made one of my first pastoral visits to an elderly widow who was largely housebound. I soon discovered that there was no need for me to bring her solace or stimulation. I was, however, welcome to enjoy the company of this woman who lived very contentedly in her modest house. To her it was not empty but rather filled with memories of a strong sixty-five-year marriage. Thus she summed up the secret of their happiness: "We figured out pretty early that it's not so important to be right." Not every fault needs to be dealt with exhaustively, even when one can be sure that the other is at fault! "It's not so important to be right"—there is much wisdom in that for those who "seek love" (17:9).

FAST MONEY
Proverbs 20:20–21

> 20:20 **If you curse father or mother,**
>   **your lamp will go out in utter darkness.**
>   21 **An estate quickly acquired in the beginning**
>   **will not be blessed in the end.**

In the ancient world, cursing was regarded as more than disrespectful. The invocation of superhuman forces against another person was treated as an act of violence. The crime of cursing father and mother carries the death penalty in the Torah (Exod. 21:17; Lev. 20:9). It is likely that an editor has juxtaposed these two sayings so that they may be read together. The word translated "estate" literally means "ancestral inheritance" (the same word appears in Prov. 19:14). When these two proverbs are read together, the second concretizes the first. What is condemned as "cursing" is any behavior by which a (presumably grown) child seeks to appropriate parents' property prematurely. The condemnation is no less apt today than in ancient Israel. The sages are alerting us to a kind of crime within the family about which no generation can afford to be naïve. In our own society, a large network of social workers and attorneys who specialize in protecting the rights of the elderly attests to the continuing relevance of the saying. It is a sad fact that elderly parents who give their children control of finances they can no longer manage, often lose their right of choice altogether. Shakespeare's *King Lear* is probably the greatest literary exploration of this persistent human tragedy.

However, verse 21 may also be read as an independent saying and probably originated as such. It is likely that it referred generally to any act of aggression against the institution of family land holdings that was the basis of the Israelite economy in the tribal period. With the rise of the monarchy and the creation of a landed aristocracy, the old system of free peasants working their own land was increasingly threatened (see the discussion at 22:22–29). The story of Naboth's vineyard is a powerful account of the Israelite king's illicit appropriation of his own subject's land. The peasant Naboth is literally "cursed" (1 Kings 21:9, 13) and murdered because Ahab covets his ancestral inheritance, his share of the blessing of land allotted to every Israelite.

Because the concept of ancestral inheritance carries so much religious and social significance, verse 21 is the sharpest of several sayings that condemn "get-rich-quick" schemes:

> Wealth hastily gotten will dwindle;
> but those who gather little by little will increase it.
> (13:11)

> One who augments wealth by exorbitant interest
> gathers it for another who is kind to the poor.
> (28:8)

> The miser is in a hurry to get rich (literally, "The person who is evil of eye
> is troubled for wealth")
> and does not know that loss is sure to come.
> (28:22)

Such sayings point to the inherent instability of fast money and also to the unstable character of the person who is eager to be rich. The phrase "troubled for wealth" (28:22) is telling. It suggests the fundamental lack of peace that characterizes the miser. The kind of patience that enables one to "gather little by little" (13:11) and live contentedly within one's means has not developed. Another proverb implies further that eagerness to be rich always entails some form of unrighteous behavior and therefore brings judgment from God:

> The faithful will abound with blessings,
> but one who is in a hurry to be rich will not go unpunished.
>
> (28:20)

A saying from another ancient wisdom tradition, that of Confucius, echoes the ideas found in these proverbs. It makes explicit the connection between unrighteous behavior and the instability of wealth: "If not obtained in the right way, [riches] do not last."

Both the Chinese and the Israelite proverbs point, explicitly or implicitly, to the necessity of the cardinal virtue of prudence. Prudence is the virtue that focuses us on the means we use to achieve desired ends. It is the very opposite of what Proverbs 28:22 graphically describes as being "evil of eye." Prudence means living each day out of a respectful regard for the world as God's own creation (see the comment at 3:13–26). It means looking for nonexploitative means to achieve our own well-being, recognizing that the well-being of every creature is ultimately bound up together. For Christians, the unity of the creation is ultimately to be found in Jesus Christ; for in him "all things in heaven and on earth were created . . . and in him all things hold together" (Col. 1:16–17).

Yet prudence is no longer a virtue highly admired among us. Parents don't name their daughters Prudence anymore. Rather, our society exalts the unwise substitute for true prudence: namely, "street smarts," which often means a cunning regard for our own private interests. The medieval theologian Thomas Aquinas wisely observes that all false prudence stems from covetousness; it promotes the indulgence of selfish desire.

Early in the modern era of economics, the highly influential economist John Maynard Keynes issued a remarkable exhortation to the practice of such false prudence. In 1930, during the worldwide depression, he speculated on the "economic possibilities for our grandchildren" and imagined a day when everyone would be rich. Then we shall "once more value ends above means and prefer the good to the useful." He continued with the following "caution," which reads as a mockery of biblical wisdom:

> But beware! The time for all this is not yet. For at least another hundred years we must pretend to ourselves and everyone that fair is foul and foul is fair; for

foul is useful and fair is not. Avarice and usury and precaution must be our gods for a little longer still. For only they can lead us out of the tunnel of economic necessity into daylight. (Quoted in Schumacher, *Small Is Beautiful*, 24)

No contemporary economist would dare be so frank. Yet reading Keynes's words today, one must acknowledge that the industrial economy has adopted Keynes's counsel as its philosophy. The result, however, is not "daylight" but widespread degradation of the created world. Avarice has been assiduously practiced, yet we are very far from the universal wealth that Keynes fantasized would come of this exercise of "precaution." For increasing numbers of the profoundly poor around the world, the hope of securing even what constitutes "economic necessity" is dying. Contrary to Keynes's advice, foul means have produced a foul end.

The sages of every culture, including ancient Israel's, orient us to prudence, for "Hope lives in the means, not the end" (Berry, *Continuous Harmony*, 131). There is profound insight here, in the recognition that hope and prudence are finally inseparable. All genuine hope—that is, hope that can be turned into prayer—must be grounded in unswerving obedience to righteous means. This connection between the hope and the action of the righteous is the key to the otherwise difficult saying about hope:

> The hope of the righteous is gladness,
> but the expectation of the wicked vanishes.
> (10:28, AT; see the comment there)

RADICAL PEDAGOGY
Proverbs 22:6

22:6 **Train children in the right way,**
and when they are old, they will not stray.

The NRSV renders the verse as a truism; no one would deliberately bring up a child in the wrong way. But in fact the Hebrew text reads very differently from the standard translation:

> Educate a child according to *his* way;
> even when he is old he will not depart from it.

The Hebrew is grammatically unambiguous and simple enough for an elementary language student to understand. The difficulty lies in the radicality of the sages' pedagogy, which the NRSV translation (and many others) chooses to avoid.

The child is not formless clay, to be shaped entirely according to the teacher's or parent's own pre-established views. Educating each child according to her own way means that we must relax our theories and pay attention to this particular child, adjust our methods to the way in which she may best learn, nurture her particular gifts, respect her interests. In short, it means teaching the child and not only "the material"—something that is far more demanding of a teacher's wisdom. The teacher or parent must also have a measure of humility before the child. The saying is an oblique acknowledgment that the child herself has some incipient wisdom. (By putting this saying first, the sages subtly qualify their assent to the contrary saying in v. 15: "Folly is bound up in the heart of a boy.")

A missionary family returned from work in India to a furlough camp in the States. Unexpectedly the homestay became permanent; the professor-father accepted a university teaching position. But the five-year-old son was distressed not to be returning to the only place *he* felt to be home. When his parents began looking for a house, he said firmly: "All right, I'll move one more time; but it has to have fields!" Surprisingly, his parents took him seriously. They bought an old farmhouse on five acres outside the city, land that was inexorably becoming suburban. Forty years later, the respect they showed for a child's desire reveals itself as wisdom. Their son has built up the exhausted soil and is now farming it as a community-supported garden, feeding thirty families from its produce and educating young people in the art of organic farming. Knowingly or not, he is adhering to ancient wisdom of many cultures, including Israel's, which asserts the primary importance of the soil:

> Prepare your work outside,
> get everything ready for you in the field;
> and after that build your house.
>   (Prov. 24:27)

Land that had been drained of much of its vitality is now productive for the first time in a century; a child who had to have fields is now a man who works them with pleasure and profit to himself and others.

THIRTY SAYINGS
Proverbs 22:17–24:22

Learning from Ancients

22:17 **Incline your ear and hear my words,**
       and apply your mind to my teaching;

18 for it will be pleasant if you keep them within you,
   if all of them are ready on your lips.
19 So that your trust may be in the LORD
   I have made them known to you today—yes, to you.
20 Have I not written for you thirty sayings
   of admonition and knowledge,
21 to show you what is right and true,
   so that you may give a true answer to those who sent you?

The collection of "thirty sayings" (v. 20) offers evidence that some Israelite sages drew on an international tradition of wisdom literature that was already ancient in their own day. The sayings in this section do not in fact number thirty. Probably that number reflects the influence of the thirty-chapter Egyptian *Instruction of Amenemopet*, to which it bears striking resemblance. Happily, *Amenemopet*, dated to approximately 1200 B.C.E., has been preserved up to modern times (see Pritchard, *Ancient Near Eastern Texts*, 421–24). The verbal echoes are too close to be coincidental. Perhaps the strong notes of humility and the deep reflectiveness that mark the Egyptian text attracted the interest of an Israelite sage, who then freely adapted it for an Israelite audience.

Protecting the Poor (Proverbs 22:22–29)

22:22 Do not rob the poor because they are poor,
      or crush the afflicted in the gate;
23 for the LORD pleads their cause
   and despoils of life those who despoil them.
24 Make no friends with those given to anger,
   and do not associate with hotheads,
25 or you may learn their ways
   and entangle yourself in a snare.
26 Do not be one of those who give pledges,
   who become surety for debts.
27 If you have nothing with which to pay,
   why should your bed be taken from under you?
28 Do not remove the ancient landmark
   that your ancestors set up.
29 Do you see those who are skillful in their work?
   they will serve kings;
   they will not serve common people.

These instructions begin with several warnings that find repeated echoes elsewhere in Proverbs: against taking advantage of the poor (vv. 22–23), against associating with those who are chronically angry (vv. 24–25;

compare 15:18 and 29:22), and against various practices involving the forfeiture of property. The placement of these warnings at the head of the "thirty sayings" suggests that these offenses are regarded as particularly serious.

These sayings are addressed to those who are well-placed in society: "When you sit down to eat with a ruler . . . " (23:1). Therefore it is probable that the robbery envisioned here is not ordinary theft but rather legally sanctioned forms of oppression, disguised as sound business practice. "Robbing the poor because they are poor" (v. 22): The practice is familiar to us. The same item from the same chain store often costs more in the inner city than in suburbia, where customers have a wider choice of stores, as well as automobiles to facilitate comparative shopping.

Complementary to the warning against abusing the poor is the warning against *self*-impoverishment through misguided generosity in standing surety for debtors (vv. 26–27; see the comment on 6:1–5). There is a strong note of realism in the direct question posed in verse 27. Since this is not a common rhetorical device in Proverbs, it has the effect of shaking up the listener and firmly discouraging naïveté about "the system." The next verses substantiate that warning.

Likewise, the prohibition against removing the ancient landmark (v. 28) almost certainly does not refer to a blatantly illegal act. Moving a boundary stone in the night could hardly have succeeded, since property lines persisted through generations and would have been well known by the whole community. Rather, this warns of the worst possible consequence of pledging one's land as collateral for a debt, one's own or a neighbor's. Equally, it could be a warning to creditors against accepting ancestral landholdings as collateral.

This proverb accords with numerous prophetic injunctions against enlarging the estates of the rich at the expense of the poor (e.g., Isa. 5:8; Hos. 5:10; Micah 2:2). The social background of this prohibition is the institution of the ancestral inheritance, which the Old Testament throughout upholds as the way land tenure must operate in Israel. The biblical concept of land allotments held through generations represents a radical alternative to the understanding of private property that was common in the ancient world, as it is in modern industrialized nations. Inheritance was a community-based, intergenerational system of ownership that aimed at giving all Israelites permanent access to the basic means of subsistence. Israel believed that it held its land by a sort of trust agreement with God. Each tribe and family had its allotted portion, and the land could not be sold outright or permanently transferred outside the family. Although land might be temporarily sold or leased to pay off debts, no family should remain landless in perpetuity. The Jubilee legislation (Leviticus 25) decrees that in every fiftieth year, all leased land must be restored to the original family allotment. It is accurate to say that Israel understood that the people belonged to the land as much or more than the land belonged to the people. Not only did their livelihood depend on the land. Even more fundamentally, the land was given to them as a pledge of God's faithfulness and as the place to demonstrate their own faithfulness. Dwelling in the land and maintenance of the system of land tenure was a matter of primary religious as well as economic significance.

The biblical insistence on keeping families on the land is certainly crucial for the church's response to the acute farm crisis now occurring in North America, as family farms are increasingly swallowed up by large-scale agribusiness, factory farms run by multinational corporations (see Berry, *The Unsettling of America*). In urban settings, one might argue that a partial analog to the Israelite inheritance system would be a national commitment to provide all people with the means for acquiring a good education and opportunities for decent work, the essential elements of economic security. But any such analog is incomplete if the religious element, which is central to virtually every mention of land in the Bible, is omitted. The magnitude of the ecological crisis is moving many Christians to think more carefully about the various linkages among social structures, care for the land, and God's will for the well-being (*shalom*) of the whole created world. Perhaps the greatest theological challenge that modern Western Christians face is to recognize the irreducibly religious dimension of our basic economic arrangements and further, to see that all those arrangements do affect—directly or indirectly, positively or negatively— the well-being of the land and the potential for people in this generation and the future to live on it.

Many commentators treat verse 29 as unconnected to what precedes, as praising the person who has a good head for business. In favor of the view that it is a positive statement, one may cite the similar statement in *Amenemopet:* "As to a scribe who is experienced in his office, he will find himself worthy to be a courtier" (27:16–17). But if the juxtaposition with verse 28 is deliberate, then the saying on "those who are skillful in their work" may in this context not be praise at all. Rather, it is part of the critique of legalized oppression noted in the previous verses of this section. Like verse 27, it is formulated as a direct question (it could also be translated as a statement: "You have seen . . . ") which calls upon the hearers to draw the inference based upon their own experience. Taken together, verses 26–29 create a picture of a systematic, royally sanctioned threat against the ancient land tenure system, which ideally guarantees to each member of the community the means of subsistence. "Those skillful (or swift) in their work" are the highly educated and highly placed professionals working through courts and other legal channels. There is a bitter irony to the comment that they serve kings and *not* the common people, since the king was divinely charged to protect the common people. Even now the Lord is serving as *pro bono* attorney for the poor (v. 23), pleading their cause in the city gate, where the council of elders held court! It is also ironic that these people, who have benefited the most from their society, are in fact using their skills to destroy the infrastructure on which the health and long-term survival of the society depends. Thus it is through their own action that their prosperous lives will ultimately be "despoiled" (v. 23).

(See the related saying at 23:10–11.)

The Fatherless (Proverbs 23:10–11)

23:10 **Do not remove an ancient landmark**
      or encroach on the fields of orphans,
   11 **for their redeemer is strong;**
      he will plead their cause against you.

Building upon the picture developed in 22:22–29, this saying refers specifically to the most vulnerable members of society, the fatherless. In a kinship-based society where property ownership and the legal status associated with it were the prerogative of adult males, widows and fatherless minors (this is what the biblical term "orphans" means) easily lost their land and with it their only secure economic base. Removal of the ancient landmark refers to the diminishment of the ancestral inheritance, probably because, in the absence of an adult male to work the land and thereby pay the heavy taxload, it is lost to creditors. The eighth-century prophet Micah graphically portrays their vulnerability: "The women of my people you drive out from their pleasant homes; from their young children you take away my glory forever" (2:9). The prophet understands that having a home, an ancestral inheritance in the land of Israel, means having a tangible share in God's blessing to the people Israel. When the link between land and people is broken, the social structure becomes unstable. But more than that, Micah sees that where many are deprived of the basic means of subsistence, God's powerful and benevolent presence cannot be fully felt.

The steady biblical emphasis on protecting orphans and widows should touch us, for in modern urban society the majority of the poor are women and children living in fatherless households. Yet the connection between economic and religious life is not easy for us to grasp, perhaps because we tend to regard religion as a matter of private (and therefore optional) interest. But a woman in modern India makes that connection readily: "When you are hungry, it is hard even to think about God." The hungry are deprived of God's glory.

The second part of the saying (v. 11) makes it clear that God will not passively endure their deprivation. The debt-slavery legislation specifies that the next-of-kin should redeem the family property (Lev. 25:25); the story of Ruth and Boaz builds imaginatively on this law. Nonetheless, here the "strong redeemer" almost certainly refers to God. God is frequently designated as Redeemer (Psalm 19:14, etc.). Proverbs 15:25 specifically states that "The LORD . . . maintains the widow's boundaries." Moreover, early in the "thirty sayings," God is specifically identified as the one who "pleads their cause"—and now we are told, "against you"! Here the sages come close to the prophets in directly charging the audience with an offense against God and neighbor. (See also 24:10–12 and the comment there.)

Corporal Discipline (Proverbs 23:12–14)

23:12 **Apply your mind to instruction**
and your ear to words of knowledge.
13 **Do not withhold discipline from your children;**
if you beat them with a rod, they will not die.
14 **If you beat them with the rod,**
you will save their lives from Sheol.

The second verse is grammatically ambiguous. The "if" clause, on its own, might be taken as concessive: "*Though* you beat them with a rod, they will not die"—that is, from the blows. But equally, it could state the necessary condition for the children's safety: "If [and only if] you beat them . . . , they will not die"—the implication being that strong discipline saves youth from their own deadly folly. The rest of the saying resolves the ambiguity. The Hebrew text of verse 14 is very emphatic. It literally reads: "You yourself— beat him with a rod, and you save his life from Sheol." The view that corporal punishment is mandatory is common in Egyptian and Mesopotamian wisdom literature. An almost identical saying is found in

The Words of Ahikar, a fifth-century B.C.E. wisdom text that perhaps originated in Assyrian court circles:

> Withhold not thy son from the rod,
> else thou wilt not be able to save [him from wickedness].
> If I smite thee, my son, thou wilt not die,
> but if I leave thee to thine own [heart thou wilt not live].
>   (Pritchard, *Ancient Near Eastern Texts*, 428;
>   brackets indicate reconstruction of a damaged text.)

The threat of death resulting from the failure to discipline the young is
also forcefully expressed in Proverbs 19:18, one of the few sayings that
address the hearer with a direct imperative:

> Discipline your children while there is hope,
> Do not set your heart on their destruction (or: on letting them die).

As noted before (see the comment at Prov. 13:24), the sages' advocacy
of physical punishment of young children may be challenged in light of
modern insights. But two cautions should be observed before a saying such
as this one is wholly dismissed. First, the key word here is "discipline" (v.
13), which for the sages denotes primarily an *internal* disposition, not an
application of force. They are wisely insistent that it is the parent's responsibility to help the child acquire discipline early in life ("while there is
hope"). Failure to do so is the most grievous form of child abuse:

> The rod and reproof give wisdom,
> but a mother is disgraced by a neglected (literally, "driven away") child.
>   (29:15; see also 29:17)

Second, the few verses that advocate physical discipline of children are
vastly outweighed by hundreds that are devoted to the subject of self-
discipline. The effect is that no saying concerning the discipline of children
is more than a few verses removed from another which cautions against
excessive anger (e.g., compare 19:18 and 19:19; 29:15, 17; and 29:11) or
urges attention to the wise, who are known by their self-restraint (e.g.,
compare 13:24 and 13:20; compare 19:18 and 19:20). In the saying treated
here, 23:12 calls the parent to *heed* discipline (*mûsar*; see the discussion of
this word at Prov. 1:1–6) before they seek to *apply* discipline (*mûsar*) to a
child (v. 13). This crucial connection is lost in the NRSV translation, which
translates the same word as "instruction" and "discipline." Similarly, the

sages may intend us to see a connection between the "beating" inflicted by a caring parent (vv. 13–14) and the "beating" of which the drunkard says: "I did not feel it. . . . I will seek another drink" (23:35). Perhaps they are suggesting that timely punishment, wisely administered, can save a child from the fruitless humiliation that always accompanies a wasted life.

Answering Evil (Proverbs 24:10–12, 17–18)

24:10 **If you faint in the day of adversity,**
      your strength being small;
   11 **if you hold back from rescuing those taken away to death,**
      those who go staggering to the slaughter;
   12 **if you say, "Look, we did not know this"—**
      does not he who weighs the heart perceive it?
      Does not he who keeps watch over your soul know it?
      And will he not repay all according to their deeds?

24:17 **Do not rejoice when your enemies fall,**
      and do not let your heart be glad when they stumble,
   18 **or else the LORD will see it and be displeased,**
      and turn away his anger from them.

A major theme of this chapter is separating oneself from evil. Verse 1 warns against envying the wicked their success (see also v. 19) and seeking their company; other verses specify their behavior (vv. 8–9, 15, 28) and their fate (vv. 16, 20). But the saying in verses 10–12 is unique in the book; only here do the sages urge direct opposition to evil. The rhetoric itself is unusual, although this is not clear from the translation. Verse 11 begins with an imperative: "Rescue . . . !" Thus it becomes unmistakably clear that one element of wisdom is moral courage, the virtue that is traditionally known as "fortitude." Reckoned as one of the four "cardinal virtues" essential to Christian character, the virtue of fortitude is readiness to face danger, to fight (though not necessarily with arms) and even die for the sake of God's truth. It should not be confused with recklessness. Fortitude is the *deliberate courage* of martyrs and those "who hunger and thirst for righteousness" and therefore suffer persecution (Matt. 5:6, 10). Nor is fortitude the same as being physically adventuresome. It is fundamentally *moral* courage, even though the consequences of opposing evil may be physical torture or even death. Stories of those who show courage in the face of evil indicate they are more likely to be shopkeepers, housewives, farmers, teachers than mountain climbers. Courage emerges out of the depths of faith—or in some cases, out of a profound sense of our common humanity.

The sages may have originally envisioned a situation of rescue in which prisoners had been unfairly convicted, or travelers had been attacked by robbers. But modern readers cannot fail to see here haunting reflections of recent history: the Nazi Holocaust, when both public officials and private citizens in Europe and North America chose "not to know" about the destruction of the Jews until it was too late; or the present widespread willingness to turn a blind eye to what promise to be the devastating effects of such phenomena as global warming and ozone destruction. The passage forces reevaluation of the kind of knowledge that is essential for wisdom. We must expand our definition to include awareness of political and scientific realities and the kind of action that is necessary to promote justice in the public arena.

The second saying (vv. 17–18) deals with the internal aspect of separating oneself from evil: namely, avoiding vengefulness. This cannot mean that one should not be glad when an evil scheme fails, but rather that one should not lose all compassion even for the wicked. I must not allow the evil of another person to diminish my humanity:

> Do not say, "I will do to him as he did to me;
> I'll get that guy back for what he did."
>
> (24:29, AT)

So far the advice accords with the gospel, but some commentators take offense at the sequel (v. 18). One commentator observes: "The absence of every trace of human feeling for the enemy who is down and out is uncanny and unpleasant. The attitude which is to be adopted towards him is measured with an eery, impersonal coldness" (McKane, *Proverbs*, 404). But this misses the fact that the appeal of the passage is precisely to human feeling, the very natural feeling of righteous indignation. The psalmists regularly call upon God to requite their enemies (Psalms 55; 109; 137; 143, etc.). But appealing to God for vengeance is a very different thing from seeking it oneself. In the midst of fierce rage, giving our anger to God is the first step in praying for our enemies. The sages and the psalmists are acute spiritual psychologists; they recognize that this is usually a step that must be taken *before* we are ready to move on to the work of forgiveness.

The subtle humor in the passage may be intended to facilitate the move to compassion. The sages do not override natural feeling with a moralistic harangue. Rather, they take our side and then with gentle irony confront us with one of our most persistent forms of idolatry: the egotistical conviction that God cares as little for our enemies as we do. The spirit of this saying is captured in a legend the ancient rabbis told of God's concern for Israel's enemies. When the Egyptians were overthrown in the Red Sea, the ministering angels began to sing a hymn of praise, and God hushed them, saying, "The work of my hands is drowning in the waters, and you would sing?!" (Cohen, *Proverbs*, 162). The proverb suggests that the first step to reconciliation with our enemies is overcoming our instinct to gloat. When we have done that, then perhaps we can begin to consider how God really feels about them.

(On answering evil, see further at 25:21–22).

THE COST OF LAZINESS
Proverbs 24:30–34

> 24:30 **I passed by the field of one who was lazy,**
> **by the vineyard of a stupid person;**
> 31 **and see, it was all overgrown with thorns;**
> **the ground was covered with nettles,**
> **and its stone wall was broken down.**
> 32 **Then I saw and considered it;**
> **I looked and received instruction.**
> 33 **A little sleep, a little slumber,**
> **a little folding of the hands to rest,**
> 34 **and poverty will come upon you like a robber,**
> **and want, like an armed warrior.**

The sages are hard on those they term "lazy" or—perhaps a better translation—"slothful" (see below). At times their representation of the lazy amounts to caricature:

> The lazy person says, "There is a lion in the road!"
> There is a lion in the streets!"
> As a door turns on its hinges,
> so does a lazy person in bed.
> The lazy person buries a hand in the dish,
> and is too tired to bring it back to the mouth.
> (Prov. 26:13–15)

Sloth is in their judgment one of the chief causes of disaster (along with immoderate anger, foolish speaking, and bad company). This passage points to one tragic consequence: the dereliction of land once well-tended.

The first-person narration in Proverbs 24:30–34 is almost unique in the book (see also 7:6ff.) and gives particular importance to the saying. All the proverbs are based on empirical evidence, but here we are called upon to witness the actual process whereby disaster comes to the unwary.

This is one of many sayings in Proverbs that preserve the insights and values of an agrarian culture, which places primary value on care of the land that sustains life:

> Prepare your work outside,
> get everything ready for you in the field;
> and after that build your house.
>
> (24:27)

The sages are fully in accord with the view of Genesis that the first and most important form of human work is "to work and to keep" (Gen. 2:15; one might also translate it, "to *serve* and to *preserve*"!) the fertile soil from which humankind was brought forth. The semi-arid and mountainous land of Israel is susceptible to serious drought and erosion. The ancients knew that maintaining the fertility of the land through generations depended on what one modern farmer calls "kindly use" of the land that God had given them. Positive alternatives to this picture of dereliction are found in the injunction to the practice of careful pastoralism in Proverbs 27:23–27 and the portrait of the "woman of valor" tending her land (31:10–31).

At first sight, the vignette here seems to hold little instruction for us. Ours is the most thoroughly urbanized culture in the history of the world; farmers constitute only 3 percent of the U.S. population. But even where farming is practiced, this picture of sleepy neglect hardly seems to apply to modern agriculture, which is increasingly a high-energy industry managed by multinational corporations. Tractors plow huge fields fence-row to fence-row; herbicides eradicate the thorns and nettles. The "miracle" of twentieth-century agriculture has since midcentury dramatically increased crop yields through the development of new hybrids, heavily irrigated and boosted by fertilizers.

Yet despite this energetic appearance, the biblical warning about poverty stalking the lazy farmer may not be far off the mark. There are strong warning signals that the modern world is teetering on the edge of an agricultural disaster that will indeed bring on us "want, like an armed warrior." Industrialized agriculture has provided abundant and cheap food for the present generation of Americans, but it now appears likely that the coming generations will contend with widespread food scarcity. The efficacy of fertilizer has reached a plateau and may be declining. We have overpumped fresh water from rivers and underground aquifers, so that water tables are now falling in food-producing regions all over the world and many rivers (including the Colorado) are drained dry before they reach the sea. Dependence on hybrid plants and monoculture has drastically reduced the genetic diversity of crops in industrialized nations, greatly increasing susceptibility to devastating blight and famine (as happened in the famous Irish Potato Famine of 1846–47). Worldwide, almost all the land that can be farmed on a large scale is currently under cultivation. But the fertility of that land has been reduced through massive erosion of topsoil as well as by "chemical dependency." Global grain production is for the time being holding steady but has not increased. Meanwhile, the human population grows apace.

In light of this highly volatile situation, the biblical text might prompt us to explore the paradox that our efficiency may disguise what is in fact a form of sloth. The Christian tradition identifies sloth as one of "the seven deadly sins." The kind of laziness that kills is not simply an easygoing preference to avoid hard work. Its essence is choosing the way that is easiest in the short run, *regardless of the long-term damage and cost.* The biblical passage illumines the precarious state of modern agriculture, because it rightly suggests that the land itself bears the cost of our sinful disregard for the ultimate cost of immediate convenience.

Farmer and essayist Wendell Berry comments on the false efficiency that guides our modern agricultural practice: "Instead of asking the farmer to practice the best husbandry, to be a good steward and trustee of his land and his art, it puts irresistible pressures on him to produce more and more food and fiber more and more cheaply, thereby destroying the health of the land, the best traditions of husbandry, and the farm population itself" (*Continuous Harmony*, 94). We are, he concludes, "hurrying to nowhere." Yet there is a powerful agricultural and food-processing industry that promotes the production of cheap farm products and insists that this is necessary to maintain our standard of living. On such short-sighted yet dominant business practice, the sages might comment:

> The lazy person is wiser in self-esteem
> than seven who can answer discreetly. (Prov. 26:16)

DELIVERING THE MESSAGE
Proverbs 25:11–13

25:11 **A word fitly spoken**
is like apples of gold in a setting of silver.

12 **Like a gold ring or an ornament of gold
is a wise rebuke to a listening ear.**
13 **Like the cold of snow in time of harvest
are faithful messengers to those who send them;
they refresh the spirit of their masters.**

In three striking metaphors, the sages point to the supreme value of "a word fitly spoken" (v. 11). At first sight verse 13 seems to be only another vivid metaphor, but in fact it makes a wry social observation. For harvesting is a *hot*-weather activity (see Isa. 18:4). In Israel, most of it is done between April and September. This is the dry season, when virtually no rain falls (see Prov. 26:1), let alone snow. Allowing for some poetic exaggeration, then, the implication is that a faithful messenger is an extreme rarity.

It is important to remember that, in a time before telephones, airplanes, regulated postal service, and mass media, messengers played a vital role in the public sphere. They mediated all but the most immediate communications, either oral or written. In the former case, messengers might easily yield to the temptation to alter the communication to serve their own interests, especially in view of the fact that bearers of ill tidings sometimes paid for bad news with their lives! But the sages warn that an unreliable messenger constitutes the greatest danger to the sender:

> It is like cutting off one's foot and drinking down violence,
> to send a message by a fool.
>
> (Prov. 26:6)

In our own time, the proverb might serve as a reminder that we habitually send and receive messages from those whom the sages would not hesitate to label as fools. We patronize mass media programming that aims largely at glamour and sensation rather than truthfulness and compassion. A highly successful young journalist who had advanced rapidly to become city editor of a major metropolitan newspaper recently quit her job. She had come to see the professional lust for sensation as ethically incompatible with her own growing religious commitment (to Judaism). "The public has a right to know," reporters are told, when they are sent to interview the families of murder victims within minutes of the discovery of the body.

The problem will not be solved merely by the proliferation of avowedly Christian programming, which itself often feeds a lust for sensation. It would be far more valuable for the church to cultivate a new understanding of the mass media in general, as bearing a sacred trust to "refresh the spirit" (v. 13). Thus it might educate its members to become critical consumers of media programs. Further, among youth with talents suited to media work, the church might encourage vocations that are genuinely religious, so that they may see themselves not as potential celebrities but as faithful messengers ministering to God and God's people.

DEFEATING EVIL
Proverbs 25:21–22

> 25:21 **If your enemies are hungry, give them bread to eat;**
> **and if they are thirsty, give them water to drink;**
> 22 **for you will heap coals of fire on their heads,**
> **and the LORD will reward you.**

This is the strongest statement in the Old Testament about actively opposing evil with good (see also Exod. 23:4–5; Lev. 19:18; Job 31:29–30; Prov. 24:17–18, 29). At first sight, the second verse seems to invalidate the first. This is a case where some knowledge of cultural background can correct a misinterpretation. The image of coals of fire probably stems from an Egyptian penitential rite, in which live coals were placed on the head of a penitent. This was probably no more than a metaphor to the sages; there is no indication that the rite itself was ever practiced in Israel. In several memorable sayings they make the point: whereas a harsh response only makes enmity more intense, kindness may instill shame and repentance. "A soft tongue can break bones" (25:15; see also 15:1).

Christian readers will immediately think of such New Testament passages as Romans 12:17–20 (where Paul quotes this saying) and the Sermon on the Mount (Matt. 5:38–48). However, it is noteworthy that the wisdom literature of Israel's neighbors includes similar passages. A Babylonian text, written no later than 700 B.C.E., comments:

> Unto your opponent do no evil;
> your evildoer recompense with good.
> (*Counsels of Wisdom*, cited in Pritchard,
> *Ancient Near Eastern Texts*, 426)

We tend to imagine that Jesus invented "from scratch" the whole message of the gospel of love. But here it becomes apparent that in calling on his followers to return good for evil and thus coopt the enemy, he was drawing on a tradition of wisdom that predated him by many centuries. He drew forth the most radical elements of that tradition. But what is far more important, his life and death on a cross are the full expression of this teaching of returning good for evil. The image of Jesus Christ crucified for our sins has supplanted the sages' image of coals of fire to express the power of divine kindness that brings us to repentance.

A FOOL'S ANGER
Proverbs 27:3

> 27:3 **A stone is heavy, and sand is weighty,**
> **but a fool's provocation is heavier than both.**

The metaphor of weight is highly suggestive. Healthy anger is supple: it arises in response to provocation and generally stimulates some necessary action—which should include careful self-examination in order to identify the cause accurately. But the fool's anger is immovable, intransigent. Its dead weight effects no positive change, though it is powerfully destructive of joy. Such anger is fundamentally a form of injustice; for the anger of fools presses especially hard on those who are weak—by reason of age, health, or social circumstances—and are thus unable to flee from it. The seventeenth-century poet and preacher John Donne develops the saying brilliantly, in a passage that offers astute social critique as well as theological insight. He takes up each element of the comparison with mounting effect:

> "Sand is heavy," says Solomon, and how many suffer so? under a sand-hill of crosses, daily, hourly afflictions, that are heavy by their number, if not by their single weight? And "a stone is heavy" (says he in the same place), and how many suffer so? How many, . . . even in the midst of prosperity and security, fall under some one stone, some grindstone, some millstone, some one insupportable cross that ruins them? But then (says Solomon there), "A fool's anger is heavier than both." And how many children, and servants, and wives suffer under the anger, and morosity, and peevishness, and jealousy of foolish masters, and parents, and husbands, though they must not say so? . . . And (God knows) all is weight, and burden, and heaviness, and oppression; and if there were not a weight of future glory to counterpoise it, we should all sink into nothing. (*Sermons*, 7:53–54)

ENVY
Proverbs 27:4

> 27:4 **Wrath is cruel, anger is overwhelming,**
> **but who is able to stand before jealousy?**

The Hebrew word (*qin'ah*) which is here rendered "jealousy" can refer to two distinct phenomena: jealousy, the essence of which is desire to occupy an exclusive place in a relationship, and envy, desire for what belongs to someone else. The two must be carefully distinguished, for envy, which is probably what is intended here, is always a sin; and jealousy is not. Indeed, jealousy in the proper sense is one of God's attributes (Exod. 20:5; 34:14; Deut. 4:24; 5:9; 6:15); it designates God's zeal to be Israel's only God. In human terms, jealousy is the natural response of the cuckolded husband (Prov. 6:34), and it draws no censure from the sages.

According to traditional Christian theology, envy is one of the seven deadly sins, and the language of the proverb indicates the reason for that judgment. Anger is characterized as something "overflowing"; the word is used elsewhere of rushing waters (Psalm 32:6; Job 38:25). Anger's flood is sweeping, intense; but nonetheless it passes on. If we manage to escape its initial violence, we are likely to be safe.

By contrast, envy is an abiding disposition. It is by nature insidious. If anger wreaks havoc like a flash flood, envy is potentially even more damaging, in that it often works its destruction secretly, over months or years. The subtle workings of envy are nowhere more brilliantly portrayed than in Shakespeare's *Othello*. The treacherous servant Iago, whose military-hero master, a black man, has just eloped with the Venetian aristocrat Desdemona, speaks with the very voice of envy:

> . . . make after him, poison his delight,
> Proclaim him in the streets; incense her kinsmen,
> And, though he in fertile climate dwell,
> Plague him with flies: though that his joy be joy,
> Yet throw such changes of vexation on't,
> As it may lose some colour.
>
> (1.1. 68–73)

The sole aim of envy is to wreck the delight of another, even if the envious person gains nothing thereby. Iago so poisons Othello's mind with false accusations of infidelity that the Moor kills both Desdemona and himself. At the extreme, envy demands the annihilation of the person whose good fortune is itself perceived as an affront. On the streets of American cities, gangs of young people attack and even kill for a pair of athletic shoes, a bicycle, a portable CD player. It is not enough to steal the desirable object; its owner must also be beaten or killed. "Who can stand before envy?" To the envious, another's happiness is an intolerable reminder of the emptiness within themselves. "Envy is emptiness in action" (Stafford, *Disordered Loves*, 95).

The very first act of violence in the Bible stems from envy. Cain murders his brother because Abel's sacrificial offering found particular favor with God, while Cain's did not; and it is telling that no reason is given for God's preference. Envy resents God's freewheeling generosity, in bestowing favor for no good reason at all. Why should that woman have a better job than I, or more "regular" features? Why should that couple be able to conceive a child when we cannot? "The sin of envy is a rebellion against finitude" (Stafford, *Disordered Loves*, 97). Each human life is a piece of art in the making, an opportunity to make something beautiful in God's eyes by working within the limits of our own particular gifts. After his first failure, Cain apparently gave no further thought to pleasing God; he simply eliminated the opposition.

The remedy for envy is, simply enough, to count our own blessings. But the fact that the cure is simple does not mean that it is obvious. It is the nature of envy to blind us to all the good things that we ourselves have received from God. The Latin word *invidia* (from which "envy" is derived) is related to *videre*, "see"; envy is a perverse kind of sight. The Romans called envy "the evil eye" and believed that it was possible to work harm on another with a look of penetrating malice. From a Christian perspective, envy is a problem in the realm of morality, not magic. Above all it is a problem between us and God, because it keeps us from seeing the particular form of God's generosity toward us. The only antidote to this "ill-seeing" is to give thanks daily and in concrete terms for some of the countless gifts I have already received as evidences of God's endlessly inventive love.

CHOOSING SILENCE
Proverbs 27:14

> 27:14 **Whoever blesses a neighbor with a loud voice,**
> **rising early in the morning,**
> **will be counted as cursing.**

This is practical wisdom, humorously offered, for anyone who lives in close proximity to others, be it in an Israelite village, a college dormitory, or a house with thin walls. Moreover, it has a depth dimension that goes beyond consideration for others' sleep, and that has to do with the special quality of the morning's silence.

Many religious communities practice a rule of silence through the first few hours of the day, so that the night's fasting—from words as well as from food—may not be too harshly broken. I came to understand the wisdom of this when studying at a theological seminary where breakfast was eaten in silence. The experience of being with others and not having to "make conversation" is strangely formative of community. Although eating in silence may seem like an isolating practice, it proved to be a lesson in *com-panion*ship (literally, "sharing bread"). We needed to pay closer attention to one another, since no one could ask aloud for the butter or the coffee! Moreover, there is an inclusivity to such silence: no comments are intended for one set of ears only; no one is more or less "interesting" than anyone else. I discovered that these meals were themselves part of our theological education, for becoming attuned to the unspeaking presence and unspoken needs of others is a crucial part of the work of ministry, both lay and ordained. Often companionship in silence is the only comfort we have to offer infants, the deeply depressed, the desperately sick, and the dying.

North Americans are generally uncomfortable with silence, and the American church is no exception. How would the cultivation of a greater tolerance for silence affect pastoral work, committee work, Bible studies, even sermons? As Christians, our individual and common life would be greatly enriched by more disciplined practice of what Belden Lane calls "the silence of choice" (in contrast to the numbed silence of great grief or terror): "a simple decision not to clutter one's conversation with an endless flow of chatter." Our conversation itself would be enriched, for silence that is chosen is never a mere blankness. Rather, "[i]t offers a generous, imaginative border around the few words that one chooses to speak. Silence, then, is . . . a different form of presence, a subtler expression of meaning" (*Landscapes*, 63).

The sages bluntly point to the folly, even the sinfulness, of too many words:

> When words are many, transgression is not lacking,
> but the prudent are restrained in speech.
> (Prov. 10:19)
>
> Do you see someone who is hasty in speech?
> There is more hope for the fool than for anyone like that.
> (29:20)

Dare we imagine—and take the risk of discovering—that less chatter would promote the increase of charity within the church?

3. Closing Frames

THE WORDS OF AGUR
Proverbs 30:1–33

This small collection of sayings is attributed to the otherwise unknown Agur son of Jakeh. The fact that these are not Hebrew names indicates that some of the sayings may have originated outside Israel. Moreover, the special name of God revealed to Israel ("the LORD," see Exod. 3:15) occurs only once in this chapter (v. 9), whereas it is common everywhere else in Proverbs. Since Agur's speech is entitled "an oracle," it is possible that he is a foreign prophet, like Balaam (see Num. 24:3–4). Nonetheless, in its present form the chapter has been given an Israelite cast. The opening verses are full of echoes from other parts of the Bible (see below, on vv. 1–6).

The collection has some distinctive features that mark it as a distinct literary unit. The whole shows much careful reflection on the natural world as well as the social world, which is summed up in sweeping statements: the numerical sayings (vv. 15–16, 18–19, 21–23, 24–28, 29–31), and the "classifying" observations of verses 1–14. Moreover, it is pervaded by a sense of wonder at creation and keen awareness of the limits to human understanding, as well as a sly sense of humor (vv. 32–33). The collection seems to have been placed here at the end to lend humility to the whole enterprise of gaining wisdom. Although the rest of the book speaks with confidence about the search for wisdom, Agur's words remind us that such confidence has no basis in ourselves. Rather, from the beginning, we are told that it rests upon trust in God (Prov. 3:5). Thus we have already within Proverbs a sharp challenge to the complacency of those who are "wise in [their] own eyes" (Isa. 5:21). Job and Ecclesiastes will develop that challenge further.

Agur's Complaint (Proverbs 30:1–6)

30:1 **Thus says the man: I am weary, O God,**
  I am weary, O God. How can I prevail?

² **Surely I am too stupid to be human;**
 I do not have human understanding.
³ **I have not learned wisdom,**
 nor have I knowledge of the holy ones.
⁴ **Who has ascended to heaven and come down?**
 Who has gathered the wind in the hollow of the hand?
 Who has wrapped up the waters in a garment?
 Who has established all the ends of the earth?
 What is the person's name?
 And what is the name of the person's child?
 Surely you know!

⁵ **Every word of God proves true;**
 he is a shield to those who take refuge in him.
⁶ **Do not add to his words,**
 or else he will rebuke you, and you will be found a liar.

The tone here departs completely from the somewhat detached perspective of most of the sayings in the preceding chapters. Here Agur begins by lamenting his lack of understanding and then poses—presumably to himself—a series of "impossible questions." The genre is most familiar from the divine speeches at the end of the book of Job (chapters 38–41); such questions are found also in Mesopotamian literature as early as 1200 B.C.E.:

> Who is so tall as to ascend to the heavens?
> Who is so broad as to compass the underworld?
> > (from *The Dialogue of Pessimism*, cited in
> > Perdue, *Wisdom and Creation*, 118)

The answer to these impossible questions is, obviously, "no one." In the Mesopotamian literature, they serve a wholly negative function: to discourage human trespassing on the divine realm, through the quest for immortality or even the quest for what is good.

But Agur's questions serve a somewhat different function. As in the Mesopotamian literature, the first question serves to debunk human aspirations to ascend above the limits of our condition. All the following questions, however, lead to a different answer and a positive one, namely "God." The questions are framed in terms familiar from hymns of praise to Israel's God, who "gathers the wind/breath [Hebrew: *ruah*]" (Psalm 104:29; see also Job 38:24; Psalm 135:7) and "wraps the waters" in garments of cloud (Job 26:8), whose dominion extends to "the ends of the earth" (Psalm 59:14). Involuntarily, it seems, Agur is led by his own questions to make an affirmation of faith in a God who is much more than a remote Creator.

The traditional language of Israel's faith provides the substance of Agur's affirmation. Verses 5–6 are almost in their entirety a tissue of quotes from other parts of scripture. They point to a speaking God whose word has proven trustworthy, to a God who is present to those seeking refuge (see Psalm 18:30). God's word must not be amplified (see Deut. 4:2; 12:32), that is, falsified through the vanities of human "wisdom." The stern warning in verse 6 recalls Job's challenge to the "worthless physicians" who come to lay theological truisms on his sores:

> Will you speak falsely for God,
> and speak deceitfully for him? . . .
> Will it be well with you when he searches you out?
> Or can you deceive him, as one person deceives another? . . .
> Your maxims are proverbs of ashes,
> your defenses are defenses of clay.
>
> (Job 13:7, 9, 12)

Thus, as the book of Proverbs draws to a close, the sages remind us that mouthing a lot of pious words does not make a person seem wise or holy. Indeed, real wisdom may counsel the very opposite: "Never be rash with your mouth, nor let your heart be quick to utter a word before God, for God is in heaven, and you upon earth; therefore let your words be few" (Eccl. 5:2).

The Value of "Enough" (Proverbs 30:7–9)

30:7 **Two things I ask of you;**
     do not deny them to me before I die:
  8 **Remove far from me falsehood and lying;**
     give me neither poverty nor riches;
     feed me with the food that I need,
  9 **or I shall be full, and deny you,**
     and say, "Who is the LORD?"
     or I shall be poor, and steal,
     and profane the name of my God.

As the only verses in the book explicitly formulated as prayer, these words carry particular force. The first petition—"Remove far from me falsehood and lying"—underscores the message of verse 6. It cautions that truthful speaking, on which the whole book puts so much emphasis, is not wholly within our control. Lying is something of which we are all too capable on our own; we need divine grace to put falsehood out of our reach! Moreover, the second petition—"give me neither poverty nor riches"—reveals that my income, no less than my speech, has a bearing on whether my relationship to reality is a true one.

A crucial insight here is that having more-than-enough is not just unnecessary; it is positively bad for the soul. The danger of more-than-enough is godless pride, just as the danger of less-than-enough is envy. The Christian tradition is unanimous in asserting that pride is the greater danger of the two. Pride is considered to be the root of all other sins because, as this prayer indicates, it makes us incapable of recognizing God at work. The supreme biblical example of the proud person who cannot recognize God is Pharaoh of the exodus story: "Who is the LORD, that I should heed him and let Israel go? I do not know the LORD, and I will not let Israel go" (Exod. 5:2). Pharaoh's proud refusal to recognize any power greater than his own leads to the destruction of his own land (10:7) and his death, along with his whole army, in the Red Sea. Satiety, too much wealth, makes us all little pharaohs.

The prayer also gives insight into the spiritual danger of the poor. The translation "profane" (v. 9b) is doubtful. The Hebrew word ordinarily means "lay hold of." It is likely that the sense here is metaphorical. Agur fears that were he to be caught for theft, he would in turn "lay hold of God," that is, blame God for having made him poor and thus forcing him to steal.

Agur's prayer has grave implications for a society such as ours, where most people have either far too much or too little. It would seem to follow that most of us, rich and poor alike, are therefore in acute spiritual danger, if we are not actively blasphemous. The best remedy for those of us who are comparatively rich is to pray that we may come to recognize and accept sufficiency, "enough." This is, of course, how Jesus taught his disciples to pray: "Give us this day our daily bread"; he may well have had in mind Agur's prayer for "the food that I need"—today.

The first clear biblical statement that God wills for us sufficiency, *not* superfluity, is the story of the manna in the wilderness. The Israelites were told to gather as much as they needed, but only for one day. "And Moses said, 'Let no one leave any of it over until morning.' But they did not listen to Moses; some left part of it until morning, and it bred worms and became foul" (Exod. 16:19–20).

Each day affords countless opportunities to offer Agur's prayer for sufficiency. For virtually everyone in our culture is daily under assault by a multi-billion-dollar advertising industry that presses on us ever-new images of ourselves, to be realized through new cars, new clothes, quantities of "stuff" to fill our already bursting homes, and sooner or later our landfills. This saying alerts us to the fact that not only our homes but also our souls are "over-stuffed," with the result that we habitually deny God (v. 9) and ascribe the ultimate power in our lives to "the economy." For the sake of our souls, then, Agur offers us this prayer of resistance. Traveling on the subway or the freeway, going through the mail or the mall, watching television, we are repeatedly challenged to practice inner resistance to false images of ourselves, pray for "the food that I need," and find contentment in that. The implication of Agur's words are that when we find contentment in sufficiency, we will also find God.

A Destructive Generation (Proverbs 30:11–17)

30:11 **There are those who curse their fathers**
and do not bless their mothers.
12 **There are those who are pure in their own eyes**
and yet are not cleansed of their filthiness.
13 **There are those—how lofty are their eyes**
how high their eyelids lift!—
14 **there are those whose teeth are swords,**
whose teeth are knives,
to devour the poor from off the earth,
the needy from among mortals.

15 **The leech has two daughters;***
"Give, give," they cry.
Three things are never satisfied;
four never say, "Enough":
16 **Sheol, the barren womb,**
the earth ever thirsty for water,
and the fire that never says, "Enough."

17 **The eye that mocks a father**
and scorns to obey a mother
will be pecked out by the ravens of the valley
and eaten by the vultures.

*The "daughters" are the suckers on either end of the leech.

This section is marked off as a literary unit by the two sayings about children who scorn their parents (vv. 11 and 17). In between are several say-

ings that continue from the previous section the related themes of pride
(v. 13) and greed, the inability to be satisfied with "enough" (vv. 14–16). In
order to understand the unit as a whole, it is necessary to ask if there is any
relation between the two main sins treated here: contempt of parents and
insatiable greed? This is the main question taken up below.

The tone of the passage is similar to that of the prophets, who identify
in urgent and, indeed, violent terms the sins of the present generation and
their punishment (v. 17). Each line of the fourfold saying (vv. 11–14) literally reads: "There is *a generation* that curses. . . . There is *a generation* that
is pure . . . ," etc. The NRSV translation, by eliminating the insistent repetition of "generation," sacrifices the element of temporality that is so
strong in prophetic speech. The prophets make us aware that people and
events are embedded in time, that we necessarily have a share in the sins
that characterize our own generation, and that the work of repentance is
always done under acute pressure of time.

The two kinds of sin treated here—contempt for elders and rapacious
greed—tear at the very fabric of society. The prophets likewise link the
sins of oppression and mistreatment of elders (see Isa. 3:5), but it is harder
for us to appreciate the seriousness of the latter. Our society is relatively
tolerant of rude and rebellious behavior toward parents, regarding it as
part of the growing-up process. The biblical text is probably not here concerned about the behavior of young children but rather of adults toward
their elderly parents, who now depend upon them for care and maintenance. In ancient Israel, parents of "a stubborn and rebellious son" were
within their rights to bring him to the town council, who would condemn
him to death by stoning (Deut. 21:18–21)! Israel reserved the death
penalty for those few crimes that threatened the well-being of the entire
community and its ability to host God's presence in its midst.

The two sins may be correlated thus. Father and mother are for most
of us our personal link to the past, to all the generations that preceded us.
Showing contempt for them means despising the past, taking ourselves as
the beginning of history. Those who "curse" (v. 11) their ancestors, disregard their predecessors, are unlikely to look kindly on their neighbors and
contemporaries. Indeed, the saying suggests they do not even lower their
eyes to see them (v. 13). Their own desires are all they can see, and any
means by which they secure them is "pure in their own eyes" (v. 12).

The poem has a striking contemporaneity. It forcefully describes the
mindset of the "generation" currently living in industrial societies, both
youth and adults. Our obsession with progress has made "cursing elders" a
norm for us. As a culture, we have generalized adolescent rudeness into a

general disregard for all that preceded us. There has probably never been a generation so isolated in its own immediate experience as ourselves, largely ignorant of the past and so accustomed to a bewildering rate of change that we are quite unable to imagine the future. Not to be connected to the past by grateful memory and trust, nor to be able to look toward the future with hope—that might be a fair representation of hell, and it is the experience of very many in these current generations, most especially of the young.

The intertwining in this passage of the two themes of disrespect and rapaciousness suggests that the present generation's utter failure to value both our elders and the past may be linked to our unprecedented greed and destructiveness. For we are bereft of the critical perspective that a knowledge of the past always brings to bear on the present. Certainly one of the functions of elders in every traditional society is to give *critical attention* to the young and thus to protect them from some of the problems that tend to characterize youth. These are the very problems the sages identify here: shortsightedness, extreme self-satisfaction, failure to observe proper limits on behavior and consumption. We are now living in the second generation of entrenched "youth culture," and it is evident what happens when those characteristics are allowed to dominate. Our consumption is guided not by genuine need or even enduring pleasure but rather by the fashion or compulsion of the moment. We, the inventors of planned obsolescence, of disposable everything, have a society—not of affluence, for many grow poorer—but of waste. Along with waste goes mounting violence, first against the poor (v. 14). But the fierce language of the passage indicates that all those who have acted like contemptuous juveniles will meet a violent end (v. 17).

Like Agur, the twentieth-century Jewish Christian writer Simone Weil implies a connection between violently destructive greed and contempt for the past. She asks a question that presses even more heavily fifty years after her death: "Where will a renewal come to us, to us who have spoiled and devastated the whole earthly globe?" and answers, "Only from the past, if we love it" (cited by Milosz, *Witness of Poetry*, 114). Forming a living, respectful connection with the past—this is one avenue of healing from greed. The next verses point to another: namely, wonder at creation.

Finding Healing in Wonder (Proverbs 30:18–23)

30:18 **Three things are too wonderful for me;**
      four I do not understand:
   19 **the way of an eagle in the sky,**

the way of a snake on a rock,
the way of a ship on the high seas,
and the way of a man with a girl.

20 This is the way of an adulteress:
she eats, and wipes her mouth,
and says, "I have done no wrong."

21 Under three things the earth trembles;
under four it cannot bear up:
22 a slave when he becomes king,
and a fool when glutted with food;
23 an unloved woman when she gets a husband,
and a maid when she succeeds her mistress.

There is less integrity among these various sayings than in the previous sections. The theme of greed is continued from the last two sections, for the image of the adulteress wiping her mouth suggests aptly that adultery is a form of greed. In the previous section we saw the logical link between contempt for elders and insatiable greed. Here again, one may ask if the juxtaposition of sayings implies an intrinsic connection between greed and another theme that occupies much of Agur's attention, namely, the wonders of the created world.

The ecological crisis of our own day urges us to consider that connection as having the most vital importance. A first step in drawing the connection between greed and God's work in creation is the apostle Paul's simple observation: "Of course, there is great gain in godliness combined with contentment, for we brought nothing into the world, so that we can take nothing out of it; but if we have food and clothing, we will be content with these" (1 Tim. 6:6–8). "Godliness combined with contentment"—this is the diametric opposite of greed. Greed is not only restless but also Godless. It is a refusal to embrace the security that is our natural condition—that is, the security that comes from accepting our God-given place in the created order. Greed is, then, fundamentally unnatural. Therefore it inevitably leads us into abusive relationship with others of God's creatures, both human and nonhuman. Philip Sherrard's definition of avarice (greed) is deeply perceptive: "[A]varice is a disposition of the soul which refuses to acknowledge and share in the destiny common to all things and which desires to possess and use all things for itself, as if these things existed only to satisfy our own individual or mass cupidity" (*Human Image*, 170). By indulging our greed we effectively set ourselves outside the created order.

Thus we debase our own being as well as rupturing the harmony in which God intended all creation to exist together: "And God saw *all* that he had made, and behold, it was very good!" (Gen. 1:31, AT).

There is a sad irony to our situation. To practice greed in its various forms, sexual as well as material, is to exempt ourselves from the created order. But this self-exemption is finally impossible. We can greatly disrupt the order that God ordained; the verb in verse 21a is used elsewhere to denote disruption on a cosmic scale, when God does battle against evil (Isa. 13:13; Amos 8:8; Job 9:6). But by no act of will can we change our nature and destiny as creatures, nor can we create another order according to our own preferences. Therefore the greed that works such devastating effects on the earth is inevitably self-destructive. If we are to survive, we must be healed of our greed, and Agur shows the way to our healing, by repeatedly pointing to the wonders of the created world and the nonhuman creatures.

The saying in verses 21–23 portrays the disruption of what is presented as the divinely ordained social order. Portrayal of "the world upside down" was a common literary technique common in the ancient Near East (see the similar saying at Prov. 19:10). The perspective represented here is that of the upper class; perhaps the saying originated in the royal court, where there is particular abhorrence of a slave becoming king and a maidservant succeeding her mistress (the latter term can also mean "queen-mother"). Yet one should be cautious of dismissing the poem as thoughtlessly conservative. Agur's small collection also includes a saying that obliquely recognizes God's regard for the rights of slaves:

> Do not slander a servant to a master,
> or the servant will curse you, and you will be held guilty.
>
> (v. 10)

There is some truth in each of the sayings. Why does the whole earth tremble when a slave becomes king? As we have seen, the sages take the responsibilities of government with the utmost seriousness. Although they are not naïve about the foibles of kings, nonetheless they understand just government as a noble task for which careful training is required. The evidence of history is that when revolution has elevated slaves to kings, the new rulers are rarely less tyrannical and often more violent than those they overthrew. (The French Revolution provides a modern example; the ancient world had its own.) The statement about the fool glutted with food is sharper than is apparent from the translation, for the Hebrew word *nabal* denotes more than a garden-variety fool. This is the person devoid of religious and ethical sensibility, who lacks all capacity to discern God's hand in events (Psalm 14:1; Deut. 32:6; 1 Sam. 25:25). When such a person is glutted, she turns the world upside down within herself, for she refuses to return thanks to God for what has come from God. "The worst moment for the fool is when he is really thankful and has nobody to thank" (Dante Gabriel Rossetti).

The condemnation of the good fortune of the "hated woman" (as the Hebrew literally reads) in verse 23 is somewhat more puzzling, since the Bible generally favors the underdog. We might think of Leah, Rachel's less beautiful sister, who becomes Jacob's first wife only through a trick. The biblical narrative frankly describes her as "hated" (Gen. 29:31, 33). But probably a different kind of situation is envisioned here, where the newly married woman is not only hated but hateful. Think of an instance, common in the modern world as in the ancient one, when one woman connives to displace another in her husband's affections. Israel tolerated polygamy, at least in some periods and circumstances, and the displaced wife might not lose her home. Nonetheless, for her the world is forever turned upside down.

Learning from the Creatures (Proverbs 30:24–31)

30:24 **Four things on earth are small,**
      yet they are exceedingly wise:
  25 **the ants are a people without strength,**
      yet they provide their food in the summer;
  26 **the badgers are a people without power,**
      yet they make their homes in the rocks;
  27 **the locusts have no king,**
      yet all of them march in rank;
  28 **the lizard can be grasped in the hand,**
      yet it is found in kings' palaces.
  29 **Three things are stately in their stride;**
      four are stately in their gait:
  30 **the lion, which is mightiest among wild animals**
      and does not turn back before any;
  31 **the strutting rooster, the he-goat,**
      and a king striding before his people.

Agur, who initially (30:2) complained of his own subhuman stupidity, now turns to the nonhuman world to learn wisdom. The shape of the chapter as a whole suggests that, though we may aspire to heavenly wisdom (30:4), we learn best from the creatures with whom God has set us on this earth. Indeed, if we can accept their teaching, the lowliest creatures may break through our presumptions and misconceptions about power and thus impart to us wisdom. A similar mood and message is found in Ezra Pound's Canto 81:

> The ant's a centaur in his dragon world.
> Pull down thy vanity, it is not man
> Made courage, or made order, or made grace,
>   Pull down thy vanity, I say pull down.
> Learn of the green world what can be thy place
> In scaled invention or true artistry.
>   Pull down thy vanity, . . .
> The green casque has outdone your elegance.

Attention to the creatures persuades us that many or most of the qualities on which we pride ourselves are not exclusively human qualities; power, grace, even wisdom and artistry may be more pronounced in other species. The lives of the smallest creatures are characterized by the nonheroic virtues of persistence, cooperation, stability—in stark contrast to our own frenetic involvement with cars and computers, our preoccupations with deals and deadlines. Yet the ant and the badger "succeed" against difficult odds. The lizard in the king's palace, the badgers in their rock fortresses, the lion and the rooster evenly matched in stateliness—these thumbnail sketches brilliantly illustrate the simple but sadly forgettable fact that all of these creatures of God have their own beauty. In the last analysis, they are more alike than they are different, for they owe every moment of their existence to their One Maker. Even the king looks remarkably like the strutting rooster, if you squint.

The fifth-century monk John Cassian (approximately 365–435) found in this picture of the badgers seeking shelter in the rocks a powerful image for the faithful at prayer. He says the meek soul is "a sort of hedgehog of the spirit hidden under that protective rock" of God's mercy (Conference 10.11, *Conferences*, 136–37)! Conscious of their own weakness, they constantly ask: "O God, make speed to save me; O Lord, make haste to help me" (Psalm 70:1, AT [Hebrew v. 2]). Cassian offers a wonderful example of the holy "poverty of spirit" that enables us to see all the world as the kingdom of God (see Matt. 5:3).

THE WISDOM OF WOMEN
Proverbs 31:1–31

The book of Proverbs, which begins with several portraits of the larger-than-life figure of Lady Wisdom, ends with two teachings of real women, one royal, the other an ordinary Israelite citizen. Together they provide strong support for the saying, "Wisdom of women builds her house" (14:1). The fact that we have instructions from both queen and commoner suggests that the "house" built by wise women may be equally a state or a family home.

The Teaching of Lemuel's Mother (Proverbs 31:1–9)

31:1 **The words of King Lemuel. An oracle that his mother taught him:**

2 **No, my son! No, son of my womb!**
   No, son of my vows!
3 **Do not give your strength to women,**
   your ways to those who destroy kings.
4 **It is not for kings, O Lemuel,**
   it is not for kings to drink wine,
   or for rulers to desire strong drink;
5 **or else they will drink and forget what has been decreed,**
   and will pervert the rights of all the afflicted.
6 **Give strong drink to one who is perishing,**
   and wine to those in bitter distress;
7 **let them drink and forget their poverty,**
   and remember their misery no more.
8 **Speak out for those who cannot speak,**
   for the rights of all the destitute.
9 **Speak out, judge righteously,**
   defend the rights of the poor and needy.

The genre of the royal instruction, addressed to the crown prince, is common in Egyptian literature. This passage is distinctive in that the advice comes from the queen mother, rather than the reigning king or his vizier. She calls the king "son of my vows" (v. 2), indicating that she made promises to God in exchange for the birth of this son (see the story of Hannah and Samuel, 1 Samuel 1). Mothers at all times and places warn their sons against dangerous women and drunkenness (compare also the incisive poem in 23:29–35), although the damaging effects are greater when the son is a king. But here the mention of a vow suggests also that his misbehavior might even cast a shadow over *her* integrity in the eyes of God.

King Lemuel and his mother are otherwise unknown. Rabbinic tradition associates the name with Solomon and relates the following story: Solomon married Pharaoh's daughter on the day that the Temple was dedicated, and she kept him awake all night with music. The next morning he overslept, and since the keys to the Temple gates were under his pillow, the morning sacrifice was delayed. When his mother heard of it, she hurried to offer this admonition. Although the story may have little historical value, it reflects the biblical conviction that the king must seek godly wisdom above his own pleasure—even the seemingly harmless pleasure of sleeping late the first day of marriage!

The Bible records as the first mark of Solomon's greatness the fact that he asked God, not for riches, but for "an understanding mind to govern your people" (1 Kings 3:9). Nowhere does the Bible celebrate royal power as admirable in itself. While the Queen of Sheba was evidently impressed with Solomon's well-appointed household, she rightly acclaims him for what is truly important: "Because the LORD loved Israel forever, he has made you king to execute justice and righteousness" (1 Kings 10:9). Likewise, Lemuel's mother affirms that the king's role is "to speak out for those who cannot speak" (v. 8). A king's majesty is ultimately judged by the same standard by which God's own greatness may be judged: namely, the demonstration of protective love for the weakest members of society.

A Valorous Woman (Proverbs 31:10–31)

31:10 **A capable wife who can find?**
She is far more precious than jewels.
¹¹ **The heart of her husband trusts in her,**
and he will have no lack of gain.
¹² **She does him good, and not harm,**
all the days of her life.
¹³ **She seeks wool and flax,**
and works with willing hands.
¹⁴ **She is like the ships of the merchant,**
she brings her food from far away.
¹⁵ **She rises while it is still night**
and provides food for her household
and tasks for her servant-girls.
¹⁶ **She considers a field and buys it;**
with the fruit of her hands she plants a vineyard.
¹⁷ **She girds herself with strength,**
and makes her arms strong.
¹⁸ **She perceives that her merchandise is profitable.**
Her lamp does not go out at night.
¹⁹ **She puts her hands to the distaff,**
and her hands hold the spindle.
²⁰ **She opens her hand to the poor,**
and reaches out her hands to the needy.

21 She is not afraid for her household when it snows,
   for all her household are clothed in crimson.
22 She makes herself coverings;
   her clothing is fine linen and purple.
23 Her husband is known in the city gates,
   taking his seat among the elders of the land.
24 She makes linen garments and sells them;
   she supplies the merchant with sashes.
25 Strength and dignity are her clothing,
   and she laughs at the time to come.
26 She opens her mouth with wisdom,
   and the teaching of kindness is on her tongue.
27 She looks well to the ways of her household,
   and does not eat the bread of idleness.
28 Her children rise up and call her happy;
   her husband too, and he praises her:
29 "Many women have done excellently,
   but you surpass them all."
30 Charm is deceitful, and beauty is vain,
   but a woman who fears the LORD is to be praised.
31 Give her a share in the fruit of her hands,
   and let her works praise her in the city gates.

Although the topic of good and bad women is common in Egyptian and Babylonian wisdom instructions, nothing in all ancient Near Eastern literature matches this tribute to a woman's strength, dignity, and social power. Moreover, within Hebrew scripture this is the most unambiguously flattering portrait of any individual, man or woman. As the final movement of the book of Proverbs, it builds on such proverbs as these:

> A woman of valor [see discussion below] is the crown of her husband,
> but she who brings shame is like rottenness in his bones.
>
> (12:4, AT)

> He who finds a wife finds a good thing,
> and obtains favor from the LORD.
>
> (18:22)

The poem is an alphabetic acrostic: the first verse begins with the first letter of the Hebrew alphabet, the second verse with the second letter, and so on. Therefore the logical order is somewhat loose; the point is to sing the lady's praises "from A to Z." Nonetheless, the language makes it clear that this woman is the human counterpart to Lady Wisdom. This is especially clear in the affirmation that her price is far beyond jewels (v. 10; compare 3:15; 8:11). When the woman opens her mouth, the voice of wisdom becomes audible (v. 26). Moreover, the ultimate aim of the poem is that the woman's praises should be publicly sung "in the gates" (v. 31; see also v. 23). This is just where Lady Wisdom takes her stand to speak of her own deeds (8:3).

The NSRV translation of the initial line is unsatisfactory on two counts. First and more importantly, "capable" is a colorless translation for the Hebrew word *hayil*, which elsewhere denotes physical strength (the same word is used of Lemuel in v. 3 above), valiant military action (Num. 24:18), strong moral character (Exod. 18:21; Ruth 3:11), even material wealth (Ruth 2:1). "Valorous" better captures the tone of the extravagant poem of praise that follows. This is a public tribute to a local hero! Second, the first line is better rendered as a statement than a question, since the latter suggests that such a wife is virtually impossible to find. The intended sense of the Hebrew is probably as follows: "Whoever finds a valorous wife [knows that] her price is beyond jewels."

Unfortunately, the NRSV translation has blunted several surprising phrases in the poem. Verse 11 literally reads: "her husband . . . does not lack *booty*"; the term is elsewhere always used of goods acquired through raiding or war. Use of the word implies that this gain is hard-won, through the woman's courage and ingenuity. Similarly, the word used for "food" in verse 15 generally denotes *prey* hunted down by wild animals! These words suggest that the woman is engaged in an adventure, pitting her prowess and resourcefulness against difficult odds, and succeeding in a remarkable way. Through her work in building up the household, she emerges as an important public figure. This is especially clear from the words chosen to designate her speech. "She provides . . . *tasks* for her servant girls" (v. 15)—the word normally designates acts of public authority, legal decrees, both divine or human. Moreover, she speaks with religious authority: "the *teaching [tôrah] of lovingkindness* is on her tongue" (v. 26). This is covenant language. "Lovingkindness" is the quality that binds covenant partners together in intense devotion, each to the well-being of the other. When she speaks, she offers torah, religious instruction of the highest order. In other words, the woman of valor carries on the teaching work of priests and prophets and thus builds up not only her household but also the entire community.

There are other echoes of specifically religious language. She is "girded with strength" (v. 17). Some suppose that her dress is cinched up for serious work (see 2 Kings 4:29). But the reader whose ears are attuned to the language of hymnody hears an echo of the psalmist's description of God's appearing: "the LORD is robed, he is girded with strength" (Psalm 93:1, AT). Likewise, she is "robed in strength and splendor" (v. 25, AT). The same phrase appears in Isaiah's call to redeemed Zion (Isa. 52:1) and God's challenge to Job (Job 40:10). This is how one "dresses" to meet God! The way religious language is subtly woven into the whole description, like fine gold threads, tells us something about the kind of life that exemplifies "fear of the LORD" (v. 30). It is striking that the sages hold up as a model of piety, not a "religious professional" (priest, prophet, scribe), but an ordinary citizen whose faith is pervasive and deeply practical.

The passage shows wife and husband functioning as a team, the two "faces" of the family, the former more private and the latter more public. Therefore it is noteworthy that the house is twice called "hers" (vv. 21, 27), not "his"—although legally this would have been the case—or "theirs." There is probably a deliberate parallel to the action of personified Wisdom, who "builds her house" (Prov. 14:1). Much emphasis is placed upon this real woman's industriousness in upbuilding the household with the work of her own hands. They are her outstanding physical feature. Five times the poet calls attention to their movement: working eagerly (v. 13), planting a vineyard (v. 16), taking hold of spindle and distaff (v. 19), extended to the poor (v. 20), receiving the material reward of her labors (v. 31). Her prosperity comes from the earth and her own skill and diligence in using its bounty. The picture of material abundance here recalls the portrait of the wealthy merchant's wife in chapter 7, but there is a striking contrast between the two women. The contrast is not simply one of character, between a woman whom a husband can trust (v. 11) and one whom he cannot. It is also a difference between a woman whose "place" is the city streets (7:12) and one who is identified by her relationship with household and fields. With that difference in locale comes a fundamental difference in their economic situations. In a word, it is the difference between a life spent in idleness and pure consumption and one spent producing the means of one's own subsistence.

One detail in particular links the two passages and provides a focal point for that contrast. In chapter 7, there is an elaborate description of the adulterous woman's bed, decked with expensive linen "coverings" (v. 16) from Egypt. The same word is used here and nowhere else in the Bible. The valorous woman weaves her own "coverings" (v. 22) and even spins the flax herself! Those bed coverings symbolize the difference between the two poles of the Israelite economy: the consumptive economy of the city versus the productive economy of the villages. We have seen that the sages uphold the values of the peasant economy, placing primary emphasis on maintaining the productivity of the soil (see the comment at Prov. 24:30–34). As the two contrasting portraits of Proverbs 7 and 31 imply, city and village accorded women different social and economic roles. Outside the cities, the household was the primary economic unit, where most real goods were produced. Within this economic system, not only was the labor of women essential, but also their social, managerial, and even diplomatic skills, as the story of Abigail (1 Samuel 25) exemplifies.

The present poem was probably created, not to honor one particularly praiseworthy woman, but rather to underscore the central significance of women's skilled work in a household-based economy. The fact that the poem ends on a strongly imperative note may suggest that women did not often receive public recognition for their role in maintaining the well-being of family and community. It is likely that the poem was composed in the period after the Babylonian exile, when, with the collapse of the great national centers of government and religion, the home became the central social and religious institution, the place where Israelite identity was established. It is noteworthy that the poem continues to be recited every Sabbath eve in traditional Jewish homes, for it is precisely there that Jewish faith still finds its bearings.

Nonetheless, it should be frankly admitted that for many modern Christians and Jews, "the valorous woman" is hard to appreciate. A (woman) student at a prestigious urban university observed, "This is not the kind of woman we've learned to admire!" It is indeed the case that women whose work is primarily at home are accorded little public admiration in our society. But the problem of appreciating this woman goes even deeper than that. It will not do to make facile comparisons between the biblical figure and the suburban housewife, or alternately between her and the modern career woman. The difficulty of appreciation lies in the profoundly different social structure and function of the home in modern technological culture, and it is a difference that encompasses men's lifestyles and work as much as women's. For virtually all of us, the home is primarily a place of consumption rather than production. Very few households in our highly industrialized culture aim at self-sufficiency or produce any significant portion of their own food or clothing.

To us, then, there is an acute challenge in the fact that this picture of self-sufficiency stands at the end of the book as an example of embodied wisdom. It challenges us to recognize our "consumer society" for what it is: a complete aberration, both in nature and in history. The consumer is one who uses something up, who destroys or discards and does not give back. This is completely contrary to the economy of nature, in which everything is continually used but never used up. Through death and decomposition all matter is returned to the ecological "common fund" from which it came. Moreover, throughout human history most people have lived fairly close to the level of subsistence; the phenomenon of mass overconsumption which industrialization has made possible in the past few generations is unprecedented and—as we now know—unsustainable.

Another wisdom tradition, represented by the *Great Digest* of Confucius, gives the formula for the production of wealth (meaning real goods, not money) thus: "That the producers be many and that the mere consumers be few; that the artisan mass be energetic and the consumers be temperate" (cited by Berry, *Continuous Harmony*, 105). The notion of temperate consumers is a Madison Avenue nightmare. But the Confucian formula accords fully with the view of the Israelite sages. The "valorous woman" is a model of energetic production. More importantly, she models the true happiness (v. 28) that the virtue of temperance bestows on those who practice it. The Christian tradition has regarded temperance as one of the four "cardinal virtues" essential to the well-being of individuals and the communities in which they live. The person who requires little beyond what she herself can produce is utterly free of anxiety about the uncertain future (v. 25). She is free to act generously toward others (v. 20); her own "happiness" is a sphere of active blessing. Significantly, it is her children who rise up to pronounce her happy. In taking only as she also gives back, she practices an economics of permanence that works to secure the future for coming generations.

Ecclesiastes

Introduction to Ecclesiastes

WHY IS THIS IN THE BIBLE?

> The beauty of Rebbe Barukh [of Medzebozh] is that he could speak of faith not as opposed to anguish but as being part of it. "Faith and the abyss are next to one another," he told his disciple. "I would even say: one within the other. True faith lies beyond questions; true faith comes after it has been challenged." (Elie Wiesel, *Four Hasidic Masters*, 59)

Reading on from Proverbs to Ecclesiastes means moving from mainstream Israelite wisdom to the most eccentric of Israel's sages. It means moving from a way of thinking that largely conforms to common sense, while at the same time showing theological depth, to one that highlights every absurdity in human experience, every contradiction in human thought. In his brilliant homilies on Ecclesiastes, Gregory of Nyssa (334–394) rightly observes, "just as those who have trained in wrestling in the gymnasium strip for greater exertions and efforts in the athletic contests, so it seems to me that the teaching of Proverbs is an exercise, which trains our souls and makes them supple for the struggle with Ecclesiastes" (*Homilies*, 33).

Ecclesiastes is in its entirety a book of incongruities, and chief among them is the fact that this radically critical book—some would say, "pessimistic, cynical"—is in the Bible at all. We know that the first-century rabbis debated its inclusion in the canon of scripture, and ever since there have been those who have denied that it has any revelatory value. Yet a Vietnam War chaplain attested that it was the only part of the Bible that his soldiers were willing to hear. One of my students, who suffers from recurrent bouts of depression, says that reading Ecclesiastes is "like slipping into a warm bath." It is comforting that even the experience of total alienation from life (2:17) is given voice within the biblical tradition. Alienation and despair are recognized as one moment, at least, in the journey toward faith.

Any exploration of this book must begin with its incongruities, which surely are not incidental to its religious value. For example, the author of Ecclesiastes is impatient with all pious talk (5:2) and debunks more than he affirms. Yet many have found that the book leads them to a more genuine faith. Martin Luther said we should read "this noble little book" every day, precisely because it so firmly rejects sentimental religiosity! Another incongruity: Ecclesiastes over and over urges enjoyment of life. Yet at the same time the author never forgets the inevitability—and to his mind, the finality—of death (9:10). Again, the book is a careful composition, the product of a keen and learned mind. Yet it debunks even the effort of writing and reading books: "Of making many books there is no end, and much study is a weariness of the flesh" (12:12). A final incongruity: "The Teacher" (1:1) laments the fact that "there is no enduring remembrance of the wise" (2:16). Yet he has written a book so intensely personal that, twenty-two centuries after his death, people still find not only wisdom in his words, but a soul mate in their own anguished doubt.

So who was this Ecclesiastes? The title is a Latin translation of the Hebrew word *koheleth*. It seems to be not a proper name but a job description: "One who convenes an assembly." So Ecclesiastes/Koheleth has often been rendered as "the Preacher" and now, in the NRSV, as "the Teacher." Although the first verse describes him as "the son of David, king in Jerusalem," the language of the book indicates that it comes from a period many centuries after Solomon. The fact that it bears a close resemblance to rabbinic Hebrew suggests that this is one of the latest books in the Old Testament. Moreover, as we shall see, Koheleth seems to have had contact with Hellenistic thought and culture. This implies that he lived after Alexander the Great had conquered the Eastern Mediterranean (333–323 B.C.E). His sayings presuppose a prosperous society enjoying domestic peace, a situation that did not occur before 300 B.C.E. On the other side, the author of the apocryphal book of Ecclesiasticus, which was composed before 180 B.C.E, is familiar with the book of Ecclesiastes. So our book must have been well established as an authoritative text by the early second century. It is likely, then, that Koheleth lived around the middle of the third century B.C.E., when Jerusalem had become a sophisticated international city. The book is addressed, at least in part, to young men with "good prospects" (see, e.g., 9:7–12; 11:9). Perhaps "the Teacher" was an instructor at the ancient equivalent of a prep school, where his students were the sons of businessmen, bankers, minor court officials—the next generation of "movers and shakers."

Koheleth's strategy with his students is to cut through their illusions.

Or perhaps more accurately, he outdoes his students in the skepticism characteristic of youth: "All things [or 'words'] are wearisome, more than one can express" (1:8). No adolescent could be more scathing of the delusions under which her successful and success-driven parents labor. For this reason, the book has a special appeal for youth of high school and college age, as well as for young adults struggling with the disappointments of "the real world." One by one, the Teacher exposes the vanity of our pretensions to uniqueness, our expectations of lasting fame or enduring achievement. Just because the challenge to our common delusions is so radical, the identity of this nay-sayer becomes important. Perhaps this explains the ascription to Solomon. Any lesser figure who dismissed the ultimate value of human wisdom, achievement, and wealth would be open to the charge of "sour grapes." Thus the ancient rabbis remarked: "People might say, 'This fellow, who never owned two cents, presumes to despise all the good things of the world!' " (see Gordis, *Koheleth*, 40). As it is, the book comes to us with the authority of someone who has seen it all, done it all, had it all, and has rendered a comprehensive judgment: "All is vanity and a chasing after wind" (1:14).

This Teacher is no mere cynic, content to strip us of illusions and leave us bare. Rather, his nay-saying is the means by which he conveys essential religious instruction and carves out his own niche within the canon of scripture. If the sages of Proverbs teach the nature of "righteousness, justice, and equity" (Prov. 1:3), Koheleth teaches, more concretely than any other biblical book, about humility. And the core of his teaching on humility is this: life can never be mastered or shaped in conformity with our desires. It can only be enjoyed, when pleasures great and small come our way, or, when enjoyment is not possible, it must be endured. What Koheleth aims to instill in his students is the ability to receive the pleasures of life as the gift they are and to recognize God as Giver, "for apart from him, who can eat or who can have enjoyment?" (2:25). The verb "give" occurs twenty-eight times in this short book, in fifteen instances referring to a divine act.

The word "humility" derives from the Latin word *humus*, "soil"; humility is the quality of being "profoundly earthed" (Esther de Waal). This is a wholly earthy book. Koheleth confines his vision to this world; he speaks of sorrows, frustrations, and joys experienced "under the sun." The fact that Ecclesiastes holds out no hope of an afterlife (9:5) is offensive to some readers. But it is a mistake to expect every book of the Bible to contain the fullness of revelation. Koheleth's insistence on taking pleasure expresses a genuinely religious form of humility, because it is God "who makes everything" (11:5) and therefore ultimately it is God who enables every form of enjoyment. Koheleth is not content with vague injunctions; he specifically urges us to realize three forms of pleasure in our lives: sensual (enjoying eating and drinking, sleep and sunlight), relational (enjoying friendship and conjugal love), and vocational (enjoying work). The fact that Koheleth breeds in his students love of the world, rather than fear or contempt, is another reason for his enduring appeal to the young. Thus Martin Luther comments on his sensitivity to the spiritual needs of the young: "Solomon is . . . the best of teachers of youth. . . . One must see and hear the world, so long as there is a good teacher present. . . . Joy is as necessary for youth as food and drink, for the body is invigorated by a happy spirit" (*Notes*, 177).

As a well-educated Hellenistic Jew, Koheleth probably had some familiarity with Greek philosophy. He himself may well be compared with what the philosophers call "the grave-merry person." The rigorous Stoic considers that gaiety and joy have no part in wisdom. But "the grave-merry person" has a lively sense of the absurd. Koheleth may well have drawn at least indirect inspiration from the fifth-century philospher Plato, who argues precisely what Koheleth implies: namely, that the wise person must be able to hold together in view things that seem to be opposites: "For it is not possible to learn serious things without the laughable, nor the converse of anything without its contrary, if a person is about to be intellectual" (*The Laws*, vii/19, p. 298). It is likely that the most acute spiritual vision belongs to the person who loves the world, recognizes that it proceeds from God, and yet can smile at its limits and especially at human limitations in understanding the world.

The peculiar mixture of gravity and merriment that constitutes Koheleth's humility is not purely a matter of personal temperament. Rather, it emerged within the cultural context of Hellenism and should be seen in part as a response to the anxiety that was the dominant mood of that culture. It was anxiety, one might say, on a cosmic scale: "world-anxiety." The traditional world of the Greek city-state had been drastically altered by Alexander's conquests. Suddenly Greeks were in regular contact with the East, with its different customs and especially its mysteriously powerful religions. Meanwhile, the traditional religion, the pantheon, had eroded completely under the steady criticism of philosophy. What was left was only a vague, impersonal notion of divinity; people spoke abstractly of "deity," "the gods," "fate." Several centuries after Koheleth, the apostle Paul encountered this same disoriented religiosity in Athens, evidenced by the altar "To an unknown god" (Acts 17:23). An intellectually privileged few were able to take refuge in philosophy. Most people simply suffered the uncomfortable awareness of a world complex beyond their understanding and control, governed by unidentifiable and indifferent "principalities and powers" (Rom. 8:38; Eph. 6:12; Col. 1:16). Human life seemed to be reduced to a vain search for material or moral security, for any kind of meaning—a search that ends only in the oblivion of death. Grave epitaphs of the Hellenistic period bespeak a sense of cosmic loneliness:

> But Hades carries men off without seeing whether they are good or virtuous.
>
> Rich and poor, wise and foolish are equal in death.
>
> Truly, the gods take no account of mortals; no, like animals we are pulled hither and thither by chance, in life as in death. (Cited by Hengel, *Judaism and Hellenism*, 1:123)

Koheleth's response to this world-anxiety is powerful precisely because he does not simply dismiss it as an aberration of the benighted pagans— though as a religious Jew, he might have done so. As an educated Hellenist, he might have adopted the Greek preference for tranquil intellectual and aesthetic pleasures over bodily ones; since philosophy allows for at least the illusion of self-control. But Koheleth chooses the hard route. He takes on the anxiety as his own; he feels its full toll on the human spirit. His witness of faith was preserved within the circles of Jewish and later Christian piety precisely because of its "dangerous" unconventionality, because he dares to look at radical doubt *from the inside* and thus speaks to those whom no ordinary assurances could satisfy. Koheleth is an important model for our own religious witness at the turn of the twenty-first century, in a culture where a sense of cosmic dislocation is widespread and conventional religious expressions are unconvincing to so many.

THE POETICS OF HUMILITY

"The Teacher sought to find pleasing words, and he wrote words of truth plainly" (12:10). Koheleth is a poet of great power; some of the most poignant passages in scripture come from his pen (e.g., 1:4–11; 3:1–8; 9:11–12; 12:1–8). Surely it is no coincidence that this enduringly youthful message often takes the form of poetry. For a poet is not a person with interesting ideas that happen to be well written. Ideas and style are not finally separable. We are all aware that political speeches tend to sound alike, for most are animated by no genuinely fresh insight, no vision that compels dedication even from the speaker. In a different vein, but for the same reason, scholarly writing is often tedious in the extreme. In contrast to both, Koheleth's words are invariably simple and concrete. His tone is earnest; the thought comes to us in breath units: "Again I saw that under the sun the race is not to the swift, nor the battle to the strong, nor bread to the wise, nor riches to the intelligent, nor favor to the skillful; but time and chance happen to them all" (9:11).

The form of the entire book reflects Koheleth's essential humility, the down-to-earth quality of his thought. Ecclesiastes appears to some as a collection of incoherent maxims. But this judgment seems to miss the way in which style and meaning are connected. Koheleth is reflecting on the great questions that occupy thinkers of every generation: the meaning of life, the unfairness of fate, the inevitability of death—but more, death's cruelty in stripping us of all dignity, distinctiveness, achievement. His mind is restless, subtle, unable to accept any answers, even his own. Ponderous philosophical discourses might have hidden that unease and created the illusion of "solutions." Instead, Koheleth chooses an unsettled style that imitates life itself. He raises questions that never receive a direct answer (1:3; 2:16; 6:12). He keeps returning to his basic themes—work, money, pleasure, power, wisdom, death, God—yet never gives a lengthy statement on any of them. Moreover, he seems not to mind if he contradicts himself in the process.

As with Proverbs, the spiraling structure serves as a guard against overgeneralization. But perhaps more significantly here, it serves as a guard against false certainty. "That which is, is far off, and deep, very deep; who can find it out?" (7:24). Koheleth initiates us into something of the circling movement, the perpetual uncertainty of his own progress in wisdom. The indirect communication of Koheleth might be compared to Jesus' speaking to the crowd in parables (Mark 4:33–34), his repeated warnings to his followers not to tell others the wonders they had seen (Mark 5:43; 7:36; 9:9). About the routine, the predictable, we can speak unambiguously. But ultimate truths can only be intimated, not directly expressed, even by the most talented wordsmith. This is so because God's truth so far transcends our intellect: "As the heavens are higher than the earth, so are my ways higher than your ways, and my thoughts than your thoughts" (Isa. 55:9) Therefore incomplete comprehension, misunderstanding, and offense belong to the very nature of God's self-revelation. According to Kierkegaard, this necessarily flawed communication constitutes the chief form of Christ's suffering. Yet he observes: "If the possibility of offense were lacking, direct communication would be in place, and thus the God-

Man would be an idol. Direct recognizableness is paganism" (cited by Ellul, *Reason for Being*, 119).

The overt contradictions in the book have perplexed readers since ancient times. The Talmud records the early rabbis' doubts about the sacred status of the book: "The sages sought to withdraw the book of Koheleth because its words are mutually contradictory. Why then did they not withdraw it? Because it begins with words of Torah and it ends with words of Torah" (Shabbat 30b). Though the rabbis found enough orthodox teachings in the book to neutralize the offensive contradictions, this has not solved the problem for later readers. One modern approach is to see them as a sign of serious disturbance in Koheleth's mind. Another is to suggest that conservative editors have introduced their own views to balance Koheleth's wilder statements, or that Koheleth is setting up "straw men," quoting the opposition only to refute it. A more traditional strategy is to harmonize conflicting statements by arguing that Koheleth is talking about different things. For example, "Anger lodges in the bosom of fools" (7:9) is said to refer to perpetual anger. By contrast, "Anger is better than laughter" (7:3, AT) might refer to the appropriate, transitory anger of the wise. (It is noteworthy that the NRSV "solves" the problem by translating the same Hebrew word in two different ways: "anger" and "sorrow," respectively!)

A more satisfactory approach than any of these is to consider the contradictions as the way Koheleth conveys that it is only when we confront irreconcilable contradictions that we know we are grappling with the real questions of life. The modern sage E. F. Schumacher (*A Guide for the Perplexed*, 120–36) identifies two kinds of problems that occupy us. "Convergent problems" are those that have a solution. When sufficient research has been devoted to them, the evidence points in a certain direction and the problem is solved: the steam engine is invented, the structure of DNA is understood, a polio vaccine or the source of the ceiling leak is found. But to the abiding problems of life, the problems that generate great literature, long conversations among friends, and hours of wordless prayer—to these there is never a full solution. They are "divergent problems," which will never yield to a single line of thought or definitive answer. Schumacher gives the example of how to educate children: Is discipline the key? Is freedom? As we have seen, the book of Proverbs offers both answers, and they contradict one another (e.g., Prov. 13:24 and 22:6). But Proverbs everywhere indicates that education must take place in an atmosphere of love and harmony. In such an environment, wisdom transcends the contradiction, which cannot be otherwise dissolved.

This is precisely the value of divergent questions for those who have the patience and courage to engage them: they push us beyond our accustomed ways of thinking, our prepared answers. By exposing our limitations, they push us into the uncomfortable position of growing in both our humanity and our faith, and thus gaining what the biblical sages call wisdom. Schumacher observes: "when things are most contradictory, absurd, difficult, and frustrating, then, *just then*, life really makes sense: as a mechanism provoking and almost forcing us to develop toward higher Levels of Being. The question is one of faith, of choosing our own 'grade of significance' " (*Guide for the Perplexed*, 134–35). The faith that such engagement requires, and at the same time deepens, is faith that there is a stable reality *beyond* this world of our immediate perceptions and experiences. Like the New Testament writers, Koheleth knows that we will never have full relief from puzzles, frustrations, and trouble (see John 16:33) as long as we are "under the sun." Koheleth never presumes to make positive statements about the nature of reality "beyond the sun," yet the admonition to "fear God" (5:7; 12:13) implies that that ultimate reality always conditions his thought. To regard this (as some do) as a pious editorial addition is to miss the essential function of the contradictions. "The sayings of the wise are like goads" (12:11); even as they perplex us, they prod us to choose a higher level of significance for our lives.

Koheleth's language is invariably simple; most of his vocabulary is known to a first-year Hebrew student. But because he has a poet's sensibility, he is aware that words have multiple levels of meaning, and he plays with them. Unfortunately, not all of these verbal ambiguities carry over in translation. Here the most significant translational loss is in the common rendering of Koheleth's very first (and often repeated) words: "Vanity of vanities." The Hebrew word is *hevel*, which literally means "mist, vapor, breath." Modern commentators consider that Koheleth is using the word metaphorically and variously explain its meaning as "absurdity," "meaninglessness," "emptiness." According to this view, *hevel* expresses the total disparity between what we plan for and what actually happens, a disparity that undermines the very notion of moral action and finally deprives our lives of significance.

There are instances in which Koheleth's use of the word does indeed imply moral incongruity: "There is a *hevel* that takes place on earth, that there are righteous people who are treated according to the conduct of the wicked, and there are wicked people who are treated according to the conduct of the righteous" (8:14). But it is wrong to conclude that Koheleth therefore sees life as entirely void of meaning. "Emptiness" is not the only connotation of the word *hevel*. Metaphorical meanings are not divorced from literal meanings, as a master craftsman of language like Koheleth (12:10) would surely know. In Hebrew as in English, "breath, vapor" (*hevel*) chiefly connotes ephemerality (e.g., Psalm 62:9; Job 7:16), not emptiness, and this is the sense it has most often for Koheleth. In rendering judgment on the human condition, Koheleth is struck not only by moral disorder but also, and even more poignantly, by the fragility of our selves and everything we value: "All is *hevel*" (1:2), passing like an early morning mist.

In this perception Koheleth is very close to the poet of Psalm 39, who may well have inspired him. Psalm 39 is an intensely personal statement of human vulnerability. The Psalmist struggles in prayer to come to an accurate self-understanding even in the midst of what she experiences as divine affliction (vv. 9–10):

> LORD, let me know my end,
> and what is the measure of my days;
> let me know how fleeting my life is.
>
> (v. 4)

There is already wisdom and spiritual courage in that prayer. It is easy enough to ask for reprieve and long life (and there is nothing unbiblical about that request!), but far more difficult to ask that God deepen our knowledge that our lives are always passing away. But the psalmist forces herself to look at that reality and its consequences for wise living. And three times the word she chooses to express it is *hevel*:

> Here, you have made my days a few handbreadths,
> my lifespan is as nothing before you.
> Ah, every human being stands, altogether vapor (*hevel*).
> Ah, everyone walks about as a mere shadow-figure;
> ah, for ephemerality (*hevel*) they make a fuss;
> they heap up and do not know who will gather it in.
> . . . With reproofs for sin you chastise everyone,
> and you consume like a moth what they hold dear.
> Ah, surely every human being is vapor (*hevel*)!
>
> (vv. 5, 6, 11 [Hebrew vv. 6, 7, 12], AT)

The psalmist is not saying, "Life is a cruel joke!" but rather, "Life is so short; let me not live it stupidly." Far from being a pronouncement of absurdity, the repeated declaration of *hevel* is part of an appeal for God's mercy. At the same time, it expresses the psalmist's resolve to orient herself wholly to the one source of value that does not pass away:

> And now, what do I wait for, Lord?
> My hope—it's in you! (v. 7 [Heb. v. 8], AT)

Similarly, Koheleth's own pronouncements of *hevel* serve as a wake-up call, to remind us that the very brevity of human life has implications for moral living. This is the understanding of Martin Luther, who brings together the two meanings of *hevel*, ephemerality and absurdity, thus: the very fact that life is passing quickly away exposes the absurdity of certain human behaviors—unfortunately, behaviors that are very common among us all. What is condemned in this book is

> the depraved affection and desire of us people, who are not content with the creatures [created things] of God that we have and with their use but are always anxious and concerned to accumulate riches, honors, glory, and fame, as though we were going to live here forever; and meanwhile we become bored with the things that are present and continually yearn for other things, and then still others. . . . But if someone compares the good things he has with the bad things he does not have, he will finally recognize what a treasure of good things he has. . . . He denounces the inconstancy and vanity of the human heart, which enjoys neither present nor future goods; it does not acknowledge or give thanks for the blessings it has received, and it vainly pursues the things it does not have. This is really being suspended between heaven and earth! (*Notes*, 8, 11)

The refrain of *hevel* evokes an echo from another biblical text, one that was surely in Koheleth's mind as he composed his book: namely, the first chapters of Genesis, where *hevel* appears as a proper noun; it is the Hebrew spelling for the name "Abel." (As this commentary will show, Koheleth has pondered deeply the early history of *adam*, "humankind"—a word he himself uses fifty times, more frequently than any other book of the Bible.) By contrast, Cain's name means "possession, acquisition." The names of the two brothers are heavy with portent: Permanence and Impermanence, Possession and Ephemerality. Koheleth sees that in a profound way the history of *adam*, humankind, mirrors the history of the younger brother Hevel/Abel, who enters the biblical narrative only to die. His death is nonsensical, as is every murder. But is his life then meaningless, entirely absurd? The one thing we know about Hevel/Abel is that he offered the best of his flock as a sacrifice that brought God pleasure (Gen. 4:4). And is not just that the point of human life, to give some pleasure to God, to make our work in this world holy by offering something of it to God?

From Koheleth's perspective, the short history of Hevel son of Adam is emblematic of human life altogether, for in this book everything is examined in light of our inescapable mortality. The Teacher does not try to persuade us of the sentimental and ultimately cruel view that every death—or any death—"makes sense." Rather, he reminds us that death is at every moment a possibility for all of us, and he would not have us live foolishly or die "suddenly and unprepared." Moreover, for all his reticence in religious matters, Koheleth asserts that God takes pleasure in human beings (2:26; 9:7). The *hevel*-life we all share is ephemeral but not empty of meaning.

With Ecclesiastes, then, we come to the most diffident book of the Bible, and the most "profoundly earthed." Koheleth is not much of a theologian, in the narrow sense; he tells us very little about God and nothing about the world to come. But he tells us a great deal about what it means to be human: to live in this world responsibly and joyfully, in the peculiar tension between limitation and freedom that is the human condition. In short, he teaches us to "be lowly wise," in John Milton's lovely phrase (see the meditation on 3:16–22, below). There has never been a time in the history of the world when such wisdom was more necessary than it is now, as "the whole creation groans and suffers agony" (Rom. 8:22, AT) because we humans have failed to live wisely within our limits. Moreover, it is because of the very earthiness of Koheleth's religious vision that his book serves an important function as a kind of preface to the New Testament, as some Christians have long seen. He keeps us from hearing the gospel as a fairy tale about a fantasy world where we might be free from the basic facts of life that constrain us in this present one. Reading Ecclesiastes regularly should motivate Christians to be rigorous in correlating the gospel's demand and promise with the realities of their daily experience, to treasure and give thanks for God's good gifts that we are continually receiving even in this cramped world.

INTRODUCING KOHELETH
Ecclesiastes 1:1

> 1:1 **The words of the Teacher [Hebrew *Koheleth*], the son of David, king in Jerusalem.**

It is fitting that the book begins with a puzzle, the author's peculiar name. "Koheleth" does not in fact seem to be a name at all but rather a job title.

It means the convener of an assembly (*kahal*), maybe something like "speaker of the house." The rendering "Ecclesiastes" derives from the ancient Greek translation; the Greek word *ekklesia* designates a public gathering (equivalent to the Hebrew *kahal*). Later, *ekklesia* came to mean "church," and so Koheleth is traditionally known as "the Preacher." The ironic humor that characterizes the whole book is present already in this title, for Koheleth's ruminative, contradictory, and highly personal style seems at the furthest pole from the discourse of public assemblies.

Martin Luther, who takes the ascription to Solomon to be historical, comments that it would be more correct to call this "the *Politics* or the *Economics* of Solomon" (*Notes*, 5). He comments perceptively that it offers help to the heads of state or households—or, one might add, people with any administrative responsibility, for it exposes the foibles of bureaucracies and offers help in remedying them. "Therefore this book should especially be read by new rulers, who have their heads swollen with opinions and want to rule the world according to their own plans and require everything to toe the mark. But such people should first learn to know the world, that is, to know that it is unjust, stubborn, disobedient, malicious, and, in short, ungrateful" (Luther, *Notes*, 140).

THE GREAT QUESTION
Ecclesiastes 1:2–3

> 1:2 **Vanity of vanities, says the Teacher [*Koheleth*],**
> **vanity of vanities! All is vanity.**
> 3 **What do people gain from all the toil**
> **at which they toil under the sun?**

(On the meaning of the initial phrase, see pp. 166–69 above.)

"What do people gain . . . ?" This is the question that prompts Koheleth's investigation into the nature of human experience. The term "gain" comes from the language of commerce; it means: "profit, the bottom line" (since the word is a noun, the line is better translated, "What is the gain for a person . . . ?"). Yet the fiction that Koheleth is king over Jerusalem implies that he already has every imaginable material asset. Thus we recognize that Koheleth is asking more than the common question of economic self-interest, "What will I get out of this?" His question is not utilitarian but existential: "What is the human value? Is there any meaning? Will it make me any more of a person?"

Koheleth begins with a question that many people stop asking early in life. This gives the book a tone of youthfulness, despite the vast experience it reflects. Koheleth never loses the restless spirit most often seen in adolescents. Like them, his company is stimulating and sometimes irritating to more settled souls. We often look to the Bible to soothe us. But there is such a thing as a holy restlessness, which Augustine's prayer expresses beautifully: "You made us for Yourself, and our heart is restless until it comes to rest in You" (*Confessions* 1.1).

INSTABILITY AND AMNESIA
Ecclesiastes 1:4–11

1:4 **A generation goes, and a generation comes,**
    but the earth remains forever.
  5 **The sun rises and the sun goes down,**
    and hurries to the place where it rises.
  6 **The wind blows to the south,**
    and goes around to the north;
    round and round goes the wind,
    and on its circuits the wind returns.
  7 **All streams run to the sea,**
    but the sea is not full;
    to the place where the streams flow,
    there they continue to flow.
  8 **All things are wearisome;**
    more than one can express;
    the eye is not satisfied with seeing,
    or the ear filled with hearing.
  9 **What has been is what will be,**
    and what has been done is what will be done;
    there is nothing new under the sun.
 10 **Is there a thing of which it is said, "See, this is new"?**
    It has already been, in the ages before us.
 11 **The people of long ago are not remembered,**
    nor will there be any remembrance
    of people yet to come
    by those who come after them.

Koheleth immediately contrasts human transience to the unchanging rhythms of nature. The initial image of the sun "*panting* to the place where it rises" (v. 5) stands in ironic contrast to the psalmist's elegant image of the sun springing forth invigorated as a bridegroom, "rejoicing like a strong man to run the course" (Psalm 19:5). Surely the fatigue here is in the eye of the beholder. Koheleth's ostensible judgment is, "All things are wearisome"; and that judgment makes sense with respect to much human activity. Indeed, becoming weary of the things that used to amuse us may indicate that we are growing in wisdom, if those things are trivial or confining to the human spirit. It is good, for example, to outgrow an adolescent fascination with gossip or shopping or hairdos. But it is absurd, and also sad, to become weary of sunrise and sunset, the circuit of the winds, streams renewing the seas. The psalmists see the physical order of the world as a proof of God's faithfulness (Psalms 33:6–9; 93:1; 104). In Job, it is a sign of God's majesty that transcends human comprehension (chapters 38–41). Therefore there is an implied judgment in the contrast between the natural world, rhythmic and reliable, and Koheleth's representation of the human disposition to boredom even as our lives are passing away. The contrast should lead us to recognize our own instability of spirit. The fourth-century theologian Gregory of Nyssa draws wise spiritual instruction from this opening poem: "Let your sobriety abide unshaken, your faith firm, your love constant, your stability in every good thing unmoved, so that *the earth* in you *may stand to eternity* (v. 4)."

Gregory sees that spiritual instability often manifests itself as greed, which he frankly identifies as a disease. This diagnosis is important for contemporary readers, for no society in history has had so much opportunity to indulge its greed as does the modern industrialized West. Gregory, instructed by Koheleth, sees that the perpetual desire for more does not derive from enjoyment of what we already have. Although Madison Avenue would flatter us into believing that our capacity for pleasure is infinite, the fact of the matter is that we are often bored by the good things of this world (v. 8). So Gregory proposes the paradox that we are not satisfied with what we have because we do not give enough away! In his sermon on this passage, Gregory urges anyone afflicted by greed to look at the real sea, which remains at the same volume, despite the streams entering it.

> [I]n the same way human nature too, restricted by specific limits in the enjoyment of what comes to it, cannot enlarge its appetite to match the extent of its acquisitions; *while the intake is endless, the capacity for enjoyment is kept within its set limit.* If therefore enjoyment cannot exceed the amount fixed by nature, for what reason do we attract in [draw in] the flood of acquisitions, never overflowing for the benefit of others from our additional income? (*Homilies*, 40–41; emphasis added)

The last verses of the poem (vv. 9–11) express a painful reflection on history—or, more accurately, the lack of it. In a sense, everything is history. Nothing that happens is more than a rerun of the past: "What has been done is what will be done" (v. 9). But in another truer sense, there is no meaningful history, because there is no living memory: "The people of long ago are not remembered" (v. 11). Koheleth here gives voice to the rootlessness felt by many in Hellenistic society, where new cultural practices were mixed indiscriminately with the old—and even new gods, as the exotic Eastern cults of Isis, Mithras, and Sarapis became popular among the Greeks.

Some Jews were drawn to what seemed to be vastly expanded cultural horizons. But others felt the threat acutely, for disconnectedness with the past is directly contrary to biblical thought. "Remember!" is the imperative that carries Israel's faith forward from one generation to another. Every Israelite is commanded: "Remember that you were Pharaoh's slave in the land of Egypt, and the LORD your God brought you out of there" (Deut. 5:15; see also 7:18; 8:2; etc.). Connecting with the experience and the faith of the ancestors gives Israel the power to endure the vicissitudes of the present. Remembering what God did for the ancestors strengthens Israel to look for "marvelous works" going unnoticed in their own lives. It is a deep biblical conviction that a keen, discerning memory is the only firm basis for a realistic hope. Therefore those who see history as one wearisome repetition (v. 9), and those who are infatuated with what is new (v. 10), are equally cut off from "the hope of the righteous," which is, in every generation, the source of true joy (see the comment at Prov. 10:28).

It is noteworthy that this wise teacher does not counter the amnesia of his age with a harangue, or even a vigorous exhortation. His own imperative "Remember!" is delayed until the book's conclusion (12:1). He begins instead with a lament. He undertakes to express the sadness of his generation. And perhaps it is not incidental that Koheleth begins his investigation of the human condition with a poem, for poetry is the language of intense observation. The very form of this opening lament is an antidote to the blasé disregard it expresses.

KOHELETH'S MEMOIR
Ecclesiastes 1:12–2:26

This section represents a new literary genre for the biblical writers, an autobiographical memoir. Koheleth himself did not invent it. He seems to be adapting an Egyptian literary form, the "grave biography," which in

Hellenistic times had already been in use for two thousand years. The grave biography was a posthumous statement written in the name of a ruler or some other prominent person and recorded on the walls of the tomb or the funerary monument. It had three elements, all of which are present in Koheleth's memoir: a recitation of accomplishments, a collection of ethical maxims that had guided the deceased through an exemplary life, and exhortations to visitors to reflect on their own death and live accordingly. The aim of these biographies was twofold: to perpetuate the memory of the dead among the living, and also to make a case (before the gods) for admission to a happy afterlife. Inscriptions from the Hellenistic period show the spread of skepticism: can the dead really be happy, as the Egyptians and Greeks had once believed? As faith in the afterlife faded, the importance of joy in this life became an insistent theme.

The book of Ecclesiastes carries throughout "the scent of the grave," yet there is an irony in Koheleth's use of this literary form. Whereas the Egyptian grave biographies testified (truly or falsely) to successful lives, Koheleth produces a poignant admission of failure. The fiction that this is a royal memoir underscores the remarkable humility with which Koheleth speaks. So Martin Luther observes that this "Politics of Solomon" stands as a hedge against moral arrogance that should be daily consulted by all who hold any degree of authority, at home or in business as well as in public office!

The Pain of Insight (Ecclesiastes 1:12–18)

1:12 I, the Teacher [Koheleth], when king over Israel in Jerusalem, 13applied my mind to seek and to search out by wisdom all that is done under heaven; it is an unhappy business that God has given to human beings to be busy with. 14I saw all the deeds that are done under the sun; and see, all is vanity and a chasing after wind.

15 What is crooked cannot be made straight,
　　and what is lacking cannot be counted.

16 I said to myself, "I have acquired great wisdom, surpassing all who were over Jerusalem before me; and my mind has had great experience of wisdom and knowledge." 17And I applied my mind to know wisdom and to know madness and folly. I perceived that this also is but a chasing after wind.

18 For in much wisdom is much vexation,
　　and those who increase knowledge increase sorrow.

Koheleth's memoir begins with his disillusionment. A proverb that probably originated as a comment on lazy students (v. 15) becomes a sweeping indictment of "all the deeds that are done under the sun." Agur son of Jakeh (Prov. 30:1–6) laments his inability truly to understand anything (see also Job 42:1–6). By contrast, Koheleth boasts that he has gained wisdom, and that itself is the source of his sorrow. More than any other sage, Koheleth testifies to the pain that often accompanies real understanding (v. 18). The saying inverts all ordinary views of the educational enterprise. We accept the fact that learning requires some tolerance for discomfort; "no pain, no gain," in the study as well as in the gym. But Koheleth says, not that pain is necessary to gain wisdom, but the reverse: wisdom *brings* pain to those who seek it. Here again, Koheleth distances himself from his philosophical contemporaries. Followers of the Greek philosopher Epicurus memorized his sayings, which were meant to wean them from love of money and material pleasures. Their ideal was to achieve freedom from pain and anxiety through the wisdom of self-control. But Koheleth, with far deeper insight, recognizes that "anyone who is very wise has many reasons to become angry, as one who daily sees many things that are wrong" (Luther, *Notes*, 28).

This insight sets Koheleth firmly within the biblical tradition, where "holy grief" is a steadily recurring theme. Jeremiah and the anonymous poet of Lamentations weep over the destruction of Jerusalem. "My tears have been my food day and night," cries the psalmist (Psalm 42:3), anguishing over God's apparent absence. Isaiah gives us the remarkable portrait of "a man of sorrows, and acquainted with grief" (Isa. 53:3), whom Christians have always identified with Jesus Christ. "Blessed are those who mourn" (Matt. 5:4).

The astonishing realism of the Bible is evident in this honest grieving. Life in this world is no easier for the faithful than for those who have fallen away from God. Indeed, it may be more difficult, for faith requires that the faithful enter into situations where evil seems to have triumphed. Through work and prayer, they must make God's presence known there. Christians are increasingly conscious that human stewardship of the earth is an area for deep mourning and for the kind of profound new thinking that the New Testament calls "repentance." The great ecologist Aldo Leopold notes, "One of the penalties of an ecological education is that one lives alone in a world of wounds" (*Sand County Almanac*, 197). Yet would we really choose not to grow in understanding, even if such growth is painful? Koheleth repudiates that option in what constitutes his first contradiction (contrast 1:18 and 2:13–14). To refuse wisdom would be to resign ourselves to "walking in darkness" (Eccl. 2:14), to working further heedless destruction in the world. Turning away from evil—the evil we see and the evil we do—to some pleasant distraction is an option only for those who do not yet believe.

Koheleth has faith enough to grieve over evil and further, to implicate God in the "unhappy business" (v. 13) in which all humans are necessarily engaged. In this he is like Job, the other great nay-sayer of the Bible. Neither of them can speak about human anguish without at the same time speaking about God, in some way holding God responsible. And this is precisely a sign of the strength of their faith. When suffering comes to people of weak faith, they may take it as a sign that there is no God after all. But that "out" is not available to those who know themselves to be bound indissolubly to God. The story is told of Jews at Auschwitz who convened a rabbinical court to try God for having abandoned the Jewish people. At the end of the day, a verdict of "guilty" was rendered—and then the rabbis said evening prayer!

The Great Experiment (Ecclesiastes 2:1–11)

2:1 I said to myself, "Come now, I will make a test of pleasure; enjoy yourself," But again, this also was vanity. ²I said of laughter, "It is mad," and of pleasure, "What use is it?" ³I searched with my mind how to cheer my body with wine—my mind still guiding me with wisdom—and how to lay hold on folly, until I might see what was good for mortals to do under heaven during the few days of their life. ⁴I made great works; I built houses and planted vineyards for myself; ⁵I made myself gardens and parks, and planted in them all kinds of fruit trees. ⁶I made myself pools from which to water the forest of growing trees. ⁷I bought male and female slaves, and had slaves who were born in my house; I also had great possessions of herds and flocks, more than any who had been before me in Jerusalem. ⁸I also gathered for myself silver and gold and the treasure of kings and of the provinces; I got singers, both men and women, and delights of the flesh, and many concubines.

⁹ So I became great and surpassed all who were before me in Jerusalem; also my wisdom remained with me. ¹⁰Whatever my eyes desired I did not keep from them; I kept my heart from no pleasure, for my heart found pleasure in all my toil, and this was my reward for all my toil. ¹¹Then I considered all that my hands had done and the toil I had spent in doing it, and again, all was vanity and a chasing after wind, and there was nothing to be gained under the sun.

Having found that the sober approach to life produces only grief, Koheleth decides to try the life of pleasure. Speaking in Solomon's voice but with a touch of ironic self-consciousness that the real Solomon may have lacked, "the king" notes that he engaged in heavy drinking and whatever folly went with it (v. 3) for scientific purposes only; his "wisdom" remained in command (v. 9). This experimental tone is new in wisdom literature. As we have seen in Proverbs, earlier sages appealed to the teaching of father and mother, of famous people from the past as well as countless anonymous ancestors, of Wisdom "herself." But Koheleth depends fundamentally on his own experience; that is what he offers to his students.

And from the outset, he cautions them not to be too impressed: "This also was *hevel*, vanity" (v. 2). It is an extraordinary thing that "the Teacher" should talk this way about the experience on which his authority rests. Karl Marx took "doubt everything" as his motto. In the Vietnam War years, college students frequently wore buttons reading, "Question authority." But rarely are the people who vaunt such slogans radical enough. They do not doubt everything; above all, they do not doubt themselves. The authority of their own crowd is never called into question. Maybe Koheleth's words have been granted the supreme authority of inclusion in the canon just because he does not set himself up as someone who has "made it" in the world and on that basis can direct others to success. Instead, he speaks in the unassuming language of truth, with all its contradictions, and trusts us to draw our own conclusions. For this reason he can win the trust of the young, whose experience is so fresh and in some areas slight, yet who are afraid to yield everything to the authority of their elders. He appeals also to the old and to people in desperate straits, whose experience is vast and often bitter, who know things of which "the authorities" have never dreamed. In his quiet irony about himself, Koheleth shows a deep humility and, for all his nay-saying, a strange gentleness. This "king" who does not exalt himself over any of his listeners, however battered and uncertain, may be seen as one partial model within the Old Testament of the "servant" whom the prophet Isaiah describes:

> a bruised reed he will not break,
> and a dimly burning wick he will not quench.
> (Isa. 42:3)

In his humility and gentle teaching, Koheleth is (as some have said) "a schoolmaster leading to Jesus Christ," who comes later in Israel's history as the complete fulfillment of the prophet's words (Matt. 12:20).

"I made great works" (v. 4): "Solomon" recalls the construction of the Temple-palace compound in Jerusalem. Generally in the Bible, "works" worth remembering are those that God has done. Koheleth follows this standard usage (see 3:11; 7:13; 8:17; 11:5). More specifically, God's "works" is a term that often denotes what we call "creation" (Psalms 8:3;

19:1; 104:24; 145:8, 10). It is likely that "Solomon" is here comparing his creation to God's creation of the world. This is so, first, because Israel conceived of the Temple compound as a remnant of Eden. Jewish legend locates the Holy of Holies on the spot where the tree of life once stood. The cherubim that guarded against Adam and Eve's return to Eden (Gen. 3:24) stand guard in the inner sanctuary of the Temple (1 Kings 6:23–28). (The view that the Temple is the "garden of God" is fully developed in the commentary on the Song of Songs which follows.)

The link between Solomon's works and God's is reinforced by the literary structure of the passage. Solomon's catalogue contains seven elements. Each element is described in a rhythmic line consisting of two parts, which is the typical structure of Hebrew poetry. (This structure is less clear in the NRSV, which has rendered the passage as prose.) The following translation (AT) shows the poetic structure of the first two elements: house and vineyard (the staple of every household) and pleasure park.

> I built for myself houses, // I planted for myself vineyards.
> I made for myself gardens and parks, // and I planted in them every kind of fruit tree

The rhythm continues through the other five elements: pools, male and female slaves, herds and flocks, silver and gold, singers and concubines. The sevenfold pattern evokes the seven days of creation, which are also recounted in rhythmic style. Once one has caught the rhythm, Koheleth's sweeping judgment appears even more striking. In the beginning, God pronounced each thing good in itself, and with the addition of humanity, the whole was "very good." But for Koheleth, "all was *hevel* and a chasing after wind" (v. 11).

Of course, rulers of every age typically boast of great accomplishments, and the ancients frequently inscribed their own praise on monuments whose ruins still provide "photo opportunities" for travelers. They strike us as picturesque. How often do we consider the human "vanity"—both absurd illusion and ephemerality—to which those ruins attest? This point did not escape Koheleth, who lived in Jerusalem with the vivid memory of Solomon's magnificent Temple and palace, destroyed by the Babylonians (587 B.C.E.) long before his own day. In their stead stood a small sanctuary and the residences of foreign governors. It seemed that Solomon, the wisest of Israel's kings (1 Kings 3:12) and builder of empire, had been mocked by history, like the imaginary king of Percy Bysshe Shelley's poem *Ozymandias*. Koheleth would have appreciated the irony of his monumental inscription:

"My name is Ozymandias, king of kings,
Look on my works, ye Mighty, and despair!"
Nothing beside remains. Round the decay
Of that colossal wreck, boundless and bare,
The lone and level sands stretch far away.

The historians who composed the history of Israel's kings (in the books of Samuel and Kings) gave Israel's sin as the reason for the fall of Jerusalem and the disappearance of all that Solomon had built. Koheleth's portrayal of Solomon does not refute that analysis, but it suggests an even more radical understanding of the problem of history. Regardless of Israel's moral failures (a subject that Koheleth himself never explores), the kingdom was from the beginning bound to be *hevel*, an ephemerality, just because it was a human enterprise.

Yet within this strongly negative statement is a glimmer of something positive: "my heart found pleasure in all my toil" (v. 10). Good effort is itself a source of pleasure, even if its results disappoint or are fleeting. The pleasure of work is an important theme for Koheleth (see the comment on 2:18–26). Here again we see the radicality of Koheleth's thought. The earlier sages praised work for its predictable results: economic security and freedom from anxiety. Koheleth, who has less confidence in the outcome, assigns greater importance to work itself. He views it not primarily as the necessary means to a good end but as one of the few regular sources of immediate satisfaction available to many people (cf. 2:24). So often the things on which we depend for happiness eventually become occasions for disappointment and grief. Koheleth is beginning to orient us toward the possibilities for joy that the present moment offers.

No Remembrance (Ecclesiastes 2:12–17)

2:12 **So I turned to consider wisdom and madness and folly; for what can the one do who comes after the king? Only what has already been done.** 13 **Then I saw that wisdom excels folly as light excels darkness.**

14 **The wise have eyes in their head,
    but fools walk in darkness.**

Yet I perceived that the same fate befalls all of them. 15 **Then I said to myself, "What happens to the fool will happen to me also; why then have I been so very wise?" And I said to myself that this also is vanity.** 16 **For there is no enduring remembrance of the wise or of fools, seeing that in the days to come all will have been long forgotten. How can the wise die just like fools?** 17 **So I hated life, because what is done under the sun was grievous to me; for all is vanity and a chasing after wind.**

Although Koheleth affirms the value of wisdom (see the comment at
1:12–18), nonetheless the wise have no advantage over fools in the face of
death. Who has not shared Koheleth's outrage at the death of an exceptionally admirable person? Probably most of us have said, to ourselves if
not out loud: "Why did Jones have to die, when that so-and-so Smith is
going along fine?" Koheleth is tormented not only by the inevitability of
death, but also by the certainty that the good deeds of the dead will be forgotten (v. 16; cf. 1:11). To be thus forgotten is the ultimate dread of the
good citizen. Every college and city benefits from the natural desire of
generous people to be remembered for the buildings, parks, and endowed
chairs to which their names are attached. But Koheleth says that to do
good works for the sake of future remembrance is vain. A comment of
novelist Milan Kundera debunks this notion in a sharp tone reminiscent of
Koheleth: "All men commit a double error: they believe that nothing of
what they do will be forgotten, and at the same time all will be forgiven.
The truth is that *everything will be forgotten, but nothing will ever be forgiven*"
(cited by Ellul, *Reason for Being*, 67n).

Death and forgetfulness for all—it is a moment of recognition so bitter
that Koheleth repudiates life altogether: "So I hated life" (v. 17). As we
shall see in the next section, he immediately begins to qualify that total
rejection. Nonetheless, it represents an important station in the journey of
faith, one through which many people must pass and even stay for a time.
The effect of Koheleth's extreme nay-saying is suggested by a teaching of
the fourteenth-century mystic Meister Eckhart: "No cask holds two kinds
of drink at the same time. If the cask is to hold wine, its water must first be
poured out, leaving the cask empty and clean. If you are to have divine joy,
all your creatures [worldly possessions, or attachment to them] must first
be poured out or thrown out" ("Talks of Instruction," in Blakney, *Meister
Eckhart*, 53). We are following Koheleth through an experience of drastic
intellectual and spiritual purgation, which is clearing the channel for joy
to flow.

On Toil (Ecclesiastes 2:18–26)

2:18 **I hated all my toil in which I had toiled under the sun, seeing that I must
leave it to those who come after me** [19]**—and who knows whether they will
be wise or foolish? Yet they will be master of all for which I toiled and used
my wisdom under the sun. This also is vanity.** [20]**So I turned and gave my heart
up to despair concerning all the toil of my labors under the sun,** [21]**because
sometimes one who has toiled with wisdom and knowledge and skill must
leave all to be enjoyed by another who did not toil for it. This also is vanity**

and a great evil. [22] What do mortals get from all the toil and strain with which they toil under the sun? [23] For all their days are full of pain, and their work is a vexation; even at night their minds do not rest. This also is vanity.

[24] There is nothing better for mortals than to eat and drink, and find enjoyment in their toil. This also, I saw, is from the hand of God; [25] for apart from him who can eat or who can have enjoyment? [26] For to the one who pleases him God gives wisdom and knowledge and joy; but to the sinner he gives the work of gathering and heaping, only to give to one who pleases God. This also is vanity and a chasing after wind.

Another vanity, both absurd and ephemeral: Not only are good efforts forgotten, but the material reward for them passes easily from the industrious to their lax and foolish successors. Koheleth looks pityingly on "the sinner" (v. 26), who thinks only of amassing goods. The Hebrew word for "sinner" literally means "one who misses the target." It is striking that in Koheleth's vocabulary, the word designates someone who, though not wicked, has missed the point of the life that God has given. The point—that is, what gives pleasure to God—is nothing more than our own enjoyment of the good things we receive from God's hand.

Thus Koheleth shows the inherent absurdity of a "total-work" culture. Although he is speaking to Hellenistic Jews on-the-rise, his exposé is perfectly suited to modern professional America, where many of us have learned to value ourselves chiefly in terms of how hard we work. In this culture, it is admirable to be continually pressed for time. Even young children maintain crowded schedules of after-school lessons and play dates. Not surprisingly, we devalue those who are not economically productive or preparing to be so: the elderly, the unemployed, parents who stay at home with young children. The most distorted manifestations of total-work culture appear in the "two-thirds world" of the poor nations. In Bogotá, Colombia, six-year-old children haul bricks from the ovens to the brickyard. They play by the ovens as the bricks bake, dropping their toys as soon as the oven door is opened. They never attain adult stature; their legs are permanently bowed by the weight of bricks on their backs. Yet, in a terrible mockery of our first-world mentality, "These kids feel that they accomplish something more by working than the kids who are going to school, producing nothing. They think that they are imitating adults before they understand that they are working" (photographer Jean-Pierre Laffont, quoted in the *New York Times Magazine*, June 9, 1996, p. 128).

Moreover, a total-work culture expects work to provide what in fact it cannot, namely total satisfaction. We want work to answer "the searching/longing of the heart," as the Hebrew of verse 22 poignantly says

(NRSV: "strain"). We overwork, thinking that will give our lives meaning they otherwise lack. But this is to get things backward. Considered in themselves, many if not most forms of work are tedious. Yet in the context of a healthy life—from a biblical perspective, a life ordered by the fear and love of God—any kind of necessary work is enjoyable, even if it is not inherently interesting or "meaningful." This profoundly faithful understanding of work is expressed in George Herbert's poem, which is known to many as a hymn:

> Teach me, my God and King, in all things thee to see,
> and what I do in anything, to do it as for thee.
> All things may of thee partake; nothing can be so mean,
> which with this tincture, "for thy sake," will not grow bright and clean.
> A servant with this clause makes drudgery divine:
> who sweeps a room, as for thy laws, makes that and the action fine.
> This is the famous stone that turneth all to gold;
> that which God doth touch and own cannot for less be told.
>   (Hymn 592, *The Hymnal 1982*)

Verse 24 goes to the heart of Koheleth's thought. The message is not simply "*Carpe diem* (seize the day)," although this was a popular philosophy in the Hellenistic world, with which Koheleth was doubtless familiar. His own advice is related but more complex: namely, "Accept the gift." God is the Author of life itself and of every possible enjoyment. Therefore to refuse the pleasure that comes to us is to refuse honor to the God who is Giver of all. Inevitably, then, "wisdom and knowledge and joy" go together (v. 26), the lot of those who seek God's pleasure precisely by having the humility to receive pleasure from God's hand.

THE PATTERN WOVEN IN TIME
Ecclesiastes 3:1–15

3:1 **For everything there is a season, and a time for every matter under heaven:**
>   2 **a time to be born, and a time to die;**
>   **a time to plant, and a time to pluck up what is planted;**
>   3 **a time to kill, and a time to heal;**
>   **a time to break down, and a time to build up;**
>   4 **a time to weep, and a time to laugh;**
>   **a time to mourn, and a time to dance;**
>   5 **a time to throw away stones, and a time to gather stones together;**

> a time to embrace, and a time to refrain from embracing.
> 6 a time to seek, and a time to lose;
> a time to keep, and a time to throw away;
> 7 a time to tear, and a time to sew;
> a time to keep silence, and a time to speak;
> 8 a time to love, and a time to hate;
> a time for war, and a time for peace.
> 9 What gain have the workers from their toil? 10 I have seen the business that God has given to everyone to be busy with. 11 He has made everything suitable for its time; moreover, he has put a sense of past and future into their minds, yet they cannot find out what God has done from the beginning to the end. 12 I know that there is nothing better for them than to be happy and enjoy themselves as long as they live; 13 moreover, it is God's gift that all should eat and drink and take pleasure in all their toil. 14 I know that whatever God does endures forever; nothing can be added to it, nor anything taken from it; God has done this, so that all should stand in awe before him. 15 That which is, already has been; that which is to be, already is; and God seeks out what has gone by.

Ours is a highly time-conscious culture. The digital watch is the symbol of the age: at any moment, we are able to calculate time down to seconds. But at the same time, we are hard pressed by time. And like any oppressed people, we measure our well-being in terms of how successfully we are evading the oppressor's whip. I often answer the question "How are you?" by stating how I am doing in meeting various *dead*-lines. What Koheleth offers is an alternative view of time, proceeding from the remarkable (to us) assurance that there is in fact an adequate and appropriate time for every necessary element of life.

The poem reduces life to its basic elements. These include the physical and emotional rhythms of our private lives: birth and death, love and hate, killing and healing. Some of the "hard sayings" may and in most cases should be taken figuratively. On killing and healing, fourth-century theologian Gregory of Nyssa offers a perceptive analogy:

> Doctors say that tapeworms . . . are engendered in our intestines by some faulty humour; if they are destroyed by some medicine the patient will be restored to health again. . . . When anger, sucking within, or enervating by resentment the vigor of the soul and the rational powers, generates the parasite of envy, or malice generates some other such evil, the one who perceives that his soul is nourishing a parasite inside him will use in good time the medicine which eliminates diseases (that is, the teaching of the Gospel), so that, when they have been killed, healing may be implanted in the one who was ill. (*Homilies*, 106–107)

Included also are the various activities that constitute social existence: war and peace; the uprooting and planting, breaking down and building up of nations (compare vv. 2–3 with Jer. 1:10); economics ("throwing away stones and gathering stones together" most likely refers to the commercial practice of using stones as counters for goods exchanged).

These various pairs are not free alternatives, "choices" in a primary sense. Rather, they are moments of life that more often than not are thrust upon us and likewise pass away, whether we wish it or not. Here the notion of *hevel*, the fleetingness of all human activity, becomes fully concretized. We cannot determine the times for most of the important things in life, nor even choose "the business . . . to be busy with" (v. 10), for that is a gift from God. Nonetheless, there is a crucial element of choice involved in living well. We must decide whether our posture will be one of acceptance or resistance, whether we will fight to the death the ever-changing rhythms of life, or whether we will dance to them.

The paired experiences Koheleth names are not opposites that cancel each other out and thus render all human activity futile. Rather, his view seems to be that because everything "under the sun" is fleeting, then enjoying ourselves as long as we live (v. 12) is not a matter of good luck but a work of great delicacy and skill—that is, a dance. The poem's orderly cadence reinforces its message that there is a pattern to human experience, just as there is a regular pattern to the events of the nonhuman world (v. 15 echoes the language of 1:4–11). When we learn to discern the pattern, then we see that there is a place for every *essential aspect of life*—not "everything." Note that there is no right time for oppression or wretched suffering, for foolishness or deceit.

Indeed, Koheleth affirms that "[God] has made everything *beautiful* in its time" (v. 11)—a statement so bold that the NRSV modifies it. But the modification mutes what is in fact one of Koheleth's most striking statements of faith. Only because all necessary things are finally God's work can they be pronounced beautiful and complete. It is impossible either to "add to or detract from" the pattern that God has worked in human life (v. 14). Koheleth echoes the book of Deuteronomy (4:2; 13:1) with phrases that there describe the perfection of the great Teaching given on Sinai, which the faithful Jew must heed. The rarity of traditional religious language in this book makes the phrases stand out. Koheleth seems to be pointing to his own notion of faithfulness: namely, striving always to discern the perfect pattern of God's work in our own lives, preparing ourselves to receive the gifts of God, yielding gracefully when familiar gifts are withdrawn and new ones, perhaps unwanted, are given.

The problem, of course, is that the pattern is so often obscure to us. God "has put a sense of past and future" in our minds (v. 11), and perhaps it is just this that keeps us from perceiving what God is doing in time. Our grasping minds continually reach forward and back, driven by the impossible desire to retain what is already fleeing from us—our precious talents and achievements, the people we love—and the equally impossible desire to project the future on the basis of what we have known in the past. It is a profound insight: we have no fruitful relationship to the past, apart from the God "who seeks out what has gone by" (v. 15). Memory devoid of faith is the source of guilt, sadness, sentimentality—all the things that keep us from present joy and openness to the new gifts of God. There is irony here: the pattern that God is working in time is perceptible only to the mind that can stand, at least for a moment, outside time—that is, stand wholly in the "now." We see the perfection of God's work when we stand still before God in awe (v. 14) and trust, resting on the gospel promise that nothing of substance perishes eternally, nothing of value is forgotten by the God who seeks and saves the lost.

Possibly the most profound modern meditation on time is from the Christian poet T. S. Eliot. His *Four Quartets* grapples with the paradox to which Koheleth points, that we who are inevitably moved by the ebb and flow of time can nonetheless glimpse the pattern of God's work, which "endures forever":

> Time past and time future
> Allow but a little consciousness.
> To be conscious is not to be in time
> But only in time can the moment in the rose-garden,
> The moment in the arbour where the rain beat,
> The moment in the draughty church at smokefall
> Be remembered; involved with past and future.
> Only through time time is conquered.
>
> ("Burnt Norton," II)

"Only through time time is conquered." Eliot reminds us that in a fallen world, time does not advance as a series of beautiful moments. Although every necessary thing may have its proper time, that right time is not always found and claimed. For example, careless tending of a marriage may kill love long before "we are parted by death." Eliot's poem complements Koheleth's. Despite all the "right times" that are missed or violated, the life, death, and resurrection of Jesus Christ are for Christians the assurance that God's work in time is at the last brought to perfection in Christ. The changeless God entered fully into time and its vicissitudes. Through time, time is even now being conquered and redeemed for God.

INJUSTICE: FORSAKING OUR CREATUREHOOD
Ecclesiastes 3:16–22

> 3:16 **Moreover I saw under the sun that in the place of justice, wickedness was there, and in the place of righteousness, wickedness was there as well.** [17] **I said in my heart, God will judge the righteous and the wicked, for he has appointed a time for every matter, and for every work.** [18] **I said in my heart with regard to human beings that God is testing them to show that they are but animals.** [19] **For the fate of humans and the fate of animals is the same; as one dies, so dies the other. They all have the same breath, and humans have no advantage over the animals; for all is vanity.** [20] **All go to one place; all are from the dust, and all turn to dust again.** [21] **Who knows whether the human spirit goes upward and the spirit of animals goes downward to the earth?** [22] **So I saw that there is nothing better than that all should enjoy their work, for that is their lot; who can bring them to see what will be after them?**

Here Koheleth is resolutely agnostic about the afterlife; later in the book he will make a stronger statement about the absence of consciousness "in Sheol, to which you are going" (9:10). "Who knows whether the human spirit goes upward . . . ?" Koheleth is probably taking issue with Greek philosophical speculation about the eternality of the soul, which had for the first time opened the way for Jews to hope for life after death (contrast Psalms 6:5; 30:9). In the context of Christian scripture, Koheleth's firm refusal to forecast an afterlife is troublesome. Some readers consider that these statements of Koheleth do not reflect the inspiration of the Holy Spirit that animates the rest of scripture. But it is mistaken to expect every part of scripture to convey the full message of the gospel, as it is equally mistaken for Christians to read Ecclesiastes apart from the gospel affirmations (see, for example, the comment on p. 185 about "gospel promise"). To take offense at what Koheleth does *not* have to teach us is to run the danger of missing the very important message he does convey here, namely, that human beings inescapably share in the fate of all the creatures (v. 19).

The logic of the passage is initially difficult. Koheleth seems to be treating two separate topics: the prevalence of injustice and the mortality of all creatures. But in fact the juxtaposition shows how firm is Koheleth's grasp of the fundamental nature of injustice, which he sees as the greatest evil "under the sun." For injustice is nothing other than my failure to acknowledge this other as a creature of God, like myself. All matters of justice have their root in the fact of creation; for, as the thirteenth-century theologian Thomas Aquinas taught, justice is the debt that one creature owes to another. The Declaration of Independence acknowledges the connection between justice and creation: We are endowed by our Creator with certain inalienable rights. Doing justice is fundamentally a matter of observing with care what God has done in creation. It means respecting the needs and the dignity of each of my fellow creatures, acknowledging that we are more similar than different, for we depend for our existence entirely on God's gracious acts of creation and preservation.

So Koheleth begins his rambling reflection on injustice (a theme to which he returns repeatedly) with the observation that humans are mere animals with respect to death (v. 18). Koheleth's blunt statement should not be heard as mere cynicism. The echo of God's reproof to Adam is clear: "You are dust, and to dust you shall return" (Gen. 3:19; see v. 20 here). Koheleth reminds all "children of Adam" (the Hebrew term for "human beings," appearing in vv. 18, 19, 21) that no self-elevation can deliver us from our physicality; we are as ephemeral (*hevel*, v. 19) as the beasts in the field.

It is crucial that our generation, especially, hear this *as a divine word*, for the very survival of humanity may now depend on our recognizing that we are "at the mercy of the same processes that carry off strong beasts and bring decay to giant trees" (Hall, *Imaging God*, 165). We live in an age when human activity is wantonly destroying countless others of God's creatures. The accelerated rate of species endangerment and destruction for animals is often cited. Even more serious is the destruction of mountains, rivers, seas, and forests—all of which, the Bible attests, give pleasure and praise to God (Psalms 29; 93; 104; 148). Such destruction as we have already wrought is possible only because we have largely forgotten this most basic fact of our existence, our common creaturehood. In light of our present dangerous situation, Koheleth's words acquire fresh poignancy as an expression of what we are coming slowly to see as "the new solidarity of the vulnerable" (Hall): " . . . as one dies, so dies the other" (v. 19). Strip mines, factory and automobile emissions, chemically poisoned rivers and farmlands evidence a mounting hostility against nature in the industrialized nations. It is likely that the cause is a proud but suicidal struggle against that dawning recognition.

Koheleth concludes his initial reflection on injustice and creaturehood in a surprising way: "So I saw that there is nothing better than that all should enjoy their work" (v. 22). How does this speak to the great evil of injustice? The Hebrew word for "work" means more than "toil, labor" (compare 3:13). The same word is used of the work of God's hands, that is, creation (see the comment at 2:1–11). Here it connotes all one's healthful productive activity. Good work—work that does not treat the worker like an automaton but requires thought and affords the opportunity to acquire knowledge and skill—such work is one of the chief means by which we form a realistic and even loving connection with the world. Good work enables us both to grow and to contribute something of genuine value to the world, and thus it tends to curb the temptation to injustice. For unjust acts most often stem from a vague but comprehensive dissatisfaction, a sense that the world owes me something, and I must extract payment however I can. Good work, on the other hand, enhances my sense of how much I have been given; it gives me delight in the abilities I am privileged to have and to use.

The passage marks a transition in Koheleth's book. He has completed his general comments about the nature of the world, the ephemeralities and vanities (*hevel*) that preoccupy us all. Now he will begin to speak in more particular terms about human experience. At this point, Koheleth seeks to lower his audience's sights, weaning them from vain speculation about the unknowable and reorienting them to immediate responsibilities. Koheleth's advice is echoed by the archangel Raphael, speaking to the newly created Adam in John Milton's *Paradise Lost*, that great poetic exploration of what it means to be truly human. To Adam's inquiry concerning the motions of the heavenly bodies, he replies:

> . . . heav'n is for thee too high
> To know what passes there; be lowly wise:
> Think only what concerns thee and thy being;
> Dream not of other worlds. . . .
>
> (8:172–75)

Adam accepts the correction in words that were doubtless inspired by Koheleth:

> . . . to know
> That which before us lies in daily life,
> Is the prime wisdom; what is more, is fume,
> Or emptiness, or fond impertinence,
> And renders us in things that most concern
> Unpracticed, unprepared, and still to seek.
> Therefore from this high pitch let us descend
> A lower flight, and speak of things at hand
> Useful . . .
>
> (8:192–200)

Koheleth rejects the "fume" (*hevel*) of dreaming about a world of which he has been granted no revelation. For the rest of the book, he will "speak of things at hand, useful."

PERVERSIONS OF GOOD WORK
Ecclesiastes 4:1–8

4:1 **Again I saw all the oppressions that are practiced under the sun. Look, the tears of the oppressed—with no one to comfort them! On the side of their oppressors there was power—with no one to comfort them.** 2 **And I thought the dead, who have already died, more fortunate than the living, who are still alive;** 3 **but better than both is the one who has not yet been, and has not seen the evil deeds that are done under the sun.**

4 **Then I saw that all toil and all skill in work come from one person's envy of another. This also is vanity and a chasing after wind.**

5 **Fools fold their hands**
   and consume their own flesh.
6 **Better is a handful with quiet**
   than two handfuls with toil,
   and a chasing after wind.

7 **Again, I saw vanity under the sun:** 8 **the case of solitary individuals, without sons or brothers; yet there is no end to all their toil, and their eyes are never satisfied with riches. "For whom am I toiling," they ask, "and depriving myself of pleasure?" This also is vanity and an unhappy business.**

Having commended the pleasure of productive work in the previous section, Koheleth now speaks of the things that make pleasure in work impossible: oppression, envy, and overwork.

The brief treatment of oppression (4:1–3) is one of Koheleth's most penetrating observations. He is appalled by oppression; it is an evil of such magnitude that, reflecting upon it, he uncharacteristically judges death to be better than life (contrast 9:4–6). But Koheleth does not content himself with a conventional slap at the oppressor. Astonishingly, he makes no distinction between oppressor and oppressed. Slave and slave owner, prisoner and prison guard, battered woman and abusive man—both are to be pitied, for they are caught in the same system, "with no one to comfort them." The phrase would have rung with special poignancy in the ears of Koheleth's audience, for it is an echo of the refrain describing guilty and fallen Jerusalem in the book of Lamentations (1:2, 9, 17, 21). It is not enough to tell the oppressor to stop oppressing; in most cases, oppression does not represent a conscious choice. Rather, mistreatment of others is a way one has learned to survive in a sick family, a sick political system, a sick economy. The real task, for both prayer and pastoral ministry, is to break open the system and show a new way forward for both oppressor and oppressed.

Although Koheleth commends hard work (9:10), he harbors no illusions about why most of us work as hard as we do. A competitive spirit drives us to excel; Koheleth rightly names it "envy" (v. 4). Here it is useful to remember that Koheleth's original audience was probably composed of young men anxious to "make it" in an urban society that was very far from the biblical ideal for community, namely, the kinship-based villages of their ancestors. Koheleth follows the sages of Proverbs in seeing that envy is a pervasive and often destructive element of human life (Prov. 6:34; 14:30; 27:4). In so far as we work for the sake of beating out our neighbor, it is "vanity and a chasing after wind."

But there is an alternative motivation for excellence—one which Koheleth does not mention here, but which is fully consonant with his perspective. Koheleth is the great biblical teacher of humility, and, as Thomas Aquinas taught, humility is nothing other than the patient pursuit of one's own excellence. It is a remarkable insight, which every teacher should hold forth to her students. Striving to do the best *I* can—regardless of what others are able to do—is not a matter of sinful pride. Indeed, it is the very opposite. Even my greatest abilities may be modest by someone else's standards, but using them to the fullest is how I give praise and glory to God and how I sometimes discover with grateful surprise how much God has given me. In my own life, one of the surprising discoveries has been physical strength. As a child I was a miserable athlete; if I ever made contact with a ball, it was by sheer accident. But in my young adulthood I discovered long-distance running, a sport that requires more persistence than skill. And for some years my most effective prayer took place in the time that I ran, as I delighted in the strength that God had supplied to my still-uncoordinated body. "Whatever your hand finds to do, do with all your might" (9:10).

Next Koheleth treats the problem of internal oppression, which we now call workaholism. This passage moves in counterpoint. Work prompted by a competitive urge is vanity (v. 4). Yet one would be a fool not to work (v. 5); here Koheleth seems to be quoting a popular proverb (compare Prov. 6:9–11; 24:30–34). A second proverb (compare Prov. 15:16–17; 16:8; 17:1) makes a different point. Working for more than one needs is also vain (vv. 6–8), for it takes away pleasure and rest (compare 2:23; 5:12).

Koheleth upholds the value of leisure, which is little prized in the modern world. We consider it a mark of professionalism to be able to complain about being over-busy. Moreover, our language reflects our values. We regard work as primary, while the rest of what we do is "time off." But it was the opposite in the ancient world. The Latin word for "business" is *neg-otium*, literally, "not leisure"; the time when one does not have to work is the norm by which other activity is measured.

The difference in these ways of thinking is not merely a matter of temperament, as though they reflected personal laziness or industriousness. Rather, the valuing and devaluing of leisure represent two different ways of thinking about what it means to be human. Ultimately, then, the difference between them is theological. For the leisure that Koheleth values is not just spare time; it is time specifically for pleasure (v. 8), which is always the gift of God (see 2:24–26). Fundamentally, leisure is an *attitude*, a disposition of receptivity toward what God has made and given. "It is not only the occasion but also the capacity for steeping oneself in the whole of creation" (Pieper, *Leisure*, 52). Such receptivity is possible only for the person who is herself whole, or more accurately, who is capable of using time not occupied with work in order to move toward wholeness, coming "to full possession of [one's] faculties, face to face with being as a whole" (ibid., 57).

The incapacity for leisure takes two forms, and with gentle irony Koheleth points to both: idleness (v. 5) and frenetic labor (v. 8). These seeming opposites are in fact related; in different ways they bespeak an inability to enjoy the world that God has made and to express that enjoyment in both work and play. Both idleness and overwork, then, are forms of boredom. A chilling statement of that boredom is found in the private journal of the poet Charles Baudelaire (1821–1867): "One must work, if not from taste then at least from despair. For, to reduce everything to a single truth: work is less boring than pleasure" (cited by Pieper, *Leisure*, 75). Koheleth is alert to the despair that underlies excessive work and rightly judges it "vanity and an unhappy business" (v. 8).

THE WISDOM OF RETICENCE
Ecclesiastes 5:1–7

5:1 **Guard your steps when you go to the house of God; to draw near to listen is better than the sacrifice offered by fools; for they do not know how to keep from doing evil. 2 Never be rash with your mouth, nor let your heart be** quick to utter a word before God, for God is in heaven, and you upon earth; therefore let your words be few.

³ For dreams come with many cares, and a fool's voice with many words.

⁴ When you make a vow to God, do not delay fulfilling it; for he has no pleasure in fools. Fulfill what you vow. ⁵ It is better that you should not vow than that you should vow and not fulfill it. ⁶ Do not let your mouth lead you into sin, and do not say before the messenger that it was a mistake; why should God be angry at your words, and destroy the work of your hands?

⁷ With many dreams come vanities and a multitude of words; but fear God.

Koheleth speaks of the pitfall of conventional religiosity, expressed here in the form of sacrifices and pledged gifts to support the Temple. His tone is ironic throughout, as he strings together quotes from traditional teachings, but with a slight twist of meaning designed to confound the unreflectively pious. Verse 1 echoes Samuel's admonition to Saul, when he offers an unauthorized sacrifice (1 Sam. 15:22): "Listening [or 'obedience'] is better than sacrifice" (v. 1) is. Koheleth uses the familiar saying to poke fun at the "fools" who offer sacrifices without troubling to acquire any religious understanding. His audience would know that Saul was ultimately rejected by God for his failure to listen. Moreover, he adds to the quoted words his own sharp barb, which the NRSV distorts. The Hebrew reads, "For they do not know *how to do evil*"; and this is exactly what Koheleth means. If they are "good," according to the conventional definition of that term) it is simply because they are not even smart enough to be wicked!

The warning about prompt payment of vows (v. 4) is a quote from Deuteronomy 23:21, regarding the payment of vows (of money, goods, some years of one's own life, or even of a child to sanctuary service) made in exchange for some favor from God. However, the present context of the warning implies that God is not impressed by a profusion of religious vows. "God is in heaven"; in Psalm 115:3, the same phrase is spoken as an assurance that God has the power to do as God will—specifically, in bestowing blessing upon Israel. But Koheleth is emphasizing the vast disparity between God and ourselves; can we really know what brings God pleasure? God is too far above us to be impressed with fine words—yet not too distant for presumptuous "fools" to feel God's anger (v. 6). ("The messenger" in verse 6 may refer to the Temple emissary coming to collect an unpaid pledge. However the same word may also mean "angel," and many commentators see here a reference to the angel who presides over the sacrifices, or even the angel of death, coming to collect the backslider.) Therefore it is wise to be reticent in our religious claims. It is noteworthy that Koheleth himself makes no positive statements about what God is like or what God can do or promises to do for us. For Koheleth, God is recognizable only in the gifts that God has already given. Perhaps it is his acute consciousness that everything we have and enjoy comes from God's hand (2:24; 5:19) that makes Koheleth so cautious about ascribing any value to human gifts that supposedly benefit God.

The book of Ecclesiastes has been called "the Song of the Fear of God." The term itself appears numerous times (v. 7; 3:14; 7:18; 8:12–13; 12:13). More significantly, Koheleth's reluctance to speak directly about God suggests that he follows his own advice to "let your words be few" (v. 2). Here he alerts us to one of the chief paradoxes of the spiritual life. The one who feels genuine fear before God may in fact be closer to God than the one who is religiously confident; because the God-fearer has a clearer understanding of who God is: the one "who can destroy both soul and body in hell" (Matt. 10:28). In verse 7, the admonition to fear God bears a crucial connection to the declaration of *hevel*, which in this instance is well translated "vanity"—meaning both unreality and a foolish preoccupation with self. Indeed, "dreams"—that is, fantasies unconnected with reality—stem from self-absorption; Koheleth is thinking of private fantasies unconnected with reality. By contrast, fear of God is the ultimate realism. Yet religiosity is no proof that preoccupation with self has been transcended. Indeed, the opposite is often the case. Very much of what purports to be theology is less concerned with God's glory and truth than with little me and my eternal life. Of the preoccupation with individual salvation that is such a prominent element of modern religion, Jacques Ellul rightly observes: "We always center the matter on ourselves. But we are astonished to find that Jesus did just the opposite. If 'I' is vanity, then the main question is not my salvation, but the turning over of myself to the One who should be everything and in everyone" (*Reason for Being*, 127). Jesus continually refers everything to "the One who sent me" (John 12:44–45). Similarly, it is instructive to note how frequently Koheleth refers to God (thirty-eight times) and how radical is his one positive religious claim: It is God "who makes everything" (11:5).

ECONOMIES OF GRIEF AND JOY
Ecclesiastes 5:8–20

5:8 **If you see in a province the oppression of the poor and the violation of justice and right, do not be amazed at the matter; for the high official is**

watched by a higher, and there are yet higher ones over them. ⁹ But all things considered, this is an advantage for a land: a king for a plowed field.
¹⁰ The lover of money will not be satisfied with money; nor the lover of wealth, with gain. This also is vanity.
¹¹ When goods increase, those who eat them increase; and what gain has their owner but to see them with his eyes?
¹² Sweet is the sleep of laborers, whether they eat little or much; but the surfeit of the rich will not let them sleep.
¹³ There is a grievous ill that I have seen under the sun: riches were kept by their owners to their hurt, ¹⁴ and those riches were lost in a bad venture; though they are parents of children, they have nothing in their hands. ¹⁵ As they came from their mother's womb, so they shall go again, naked as they came; they shall take nothing for their toil, which they may carry away with their hands. ¹⁶ This also is a grievous ill: just as they came, so shall they go; and what gain do they have from toiling for the wind? ¹⁷ Besides, all their days they eat in darkness, in much vexation and sickness and resentment.
¹⁸ This is what I have seen to be good: it is fitting to eat and drink and find enjoyment in all the toil with which one toils under the sun the few days of the life God gives us; for this is our lot. ¹⁹ Likewise all to whom God gives wealth and possessions and whom he enables to enjoy them, and to accept their lot and find enjoyment in their toil—this is the gift of God. ²⁰ For they will scarcely brood over the days of their lives, because God keeps them occupied with the joy of their hearts.

In this section Koheleth lays out the two basic alternatives for organizing economic life in a "free society." The first option, and historically the most common, is hoarding: the rich get as rich as they can and keep their wealth to themselves as long as they can. There is indeed "a time to gather stones together" (3:5), but it does not last forever. Hoarded wealth will one day be lost, if not in one generation then in another; no wealthy family or nation remains so in perpetuity (vv. 13–15). Verse 16 cites another "grievous ill." It is not clear how this differs from the first, but the repeated observation, "just as they came, so shall they go," suggests he is expanding his view beyond the occasional unfortunate incident to the general human condition: "You can't take it with you!" Even wealth retained for a lifetime does not enhance one's stature in any real way. So why spend all your days "eating in darkness"— working long hours after the sun has gone down—and even then chewing resentment with your food (v. 17)? Koheleth may well be offering his students a meditation on a psalm familiar from the Temple liturgy:

> It is in vain that you rise up early
> and go late to rest,

eating the bread of anxious toil;
for [God] gives sleep to his beloved.
(Psalm 127:2)

The alternative to hoarding might be called "appropriate consumption." Koheleth accepts as a fact of life that some people are richer in possessions than others (v. 19). But this in itself is not the gift of God. Blessing lies in being able to *enjoy* possessions, as well as to enjoy the work associated with wealth—including the demanding but joyful work of giving your resources away (see the comment on 11:1). To work for more than you can enjoy—"the surfeit of the rich" (v. 12)—is to guarantee frustration. The rich person is overburdened with dependents (v. 11; compare Prov. 14:20), but they do not provide the comfort of friends. The contrast is sharply drawn between the hoarder's "vexation and sickness and resentment" (v. 17) and the steady joy of the person who accepts life as a fleeting but wonderful gift (v. 18). It is a wonderful insight: Truly relishing God's gifts is time-consuming. If we make that our occupation, rather than the properly subsidiary goal of getting money, then there simply isn't much time for misery (v. 20).

The destructive economy of hoarding is dramatically evidenced in the recent history of the Papago culture that until this century flourished in Mexico and Arizona. The Papago are desert dwellers. They once managed to live well in the harsh habitat of the Sonoran desert, but only by being "intricately respectful of the means of life, surpassingly careful of all the possibilities of survival. . . . The Papago communities were at once austere and generous; giving and sharing were necessarily their first principles" (Berry, *Gift of Good Land*, 51). The people needed each other too much to risk trying to "make it on their own," hoarding without regard for the well-being of their neighbors. There could be no such thing as a personal accumulation of wealth. In the Sonoran desert, whose few scattered springs were all that made human life possible, "power came from toil and could only be stored in other human beings. . . . Having little, they shared all" (Berry, citing Charles Bowden). Thus the Papago created a society of full sufficiency, free of the poverty we have come to take for granted as a by-product of "civilization." But their cultural achievement was destroyed by conformity to the standards of industrialization. Deep wells were drilled into underground aquifers, permitting the introduction of cattle farming on a large scale. Instead of their former sufficiency, born of careful regard for one another and for nature, the Papago now suffer from water shortages, overgrazing, and economic inequity.

Koheleth shows more awareness of the dangers of amassing wealth than any other Old Testament writer. This reflects the fact that in the third century B.C.E., many Jews were eager to participate in the highly aggressive mercantile economy developed by the Ptolemaic rulers in Egypt, whose power extended over Palestine. Koheleth is himself an urbanite, as were his students. Unlike earlier sages, he does not directly advocate care of the land (see Prov. 24:30–34; 27:23–27), the base of the traditional peasant economy. But he upholds the values of cooperation and sharing that are fundamental to virtually all traditional societies, be they in Palestine or the Sonoran desert:

> 4:9 Two are better than one, because they have a good reward for their toil. [10] For if they fall, one will lift up the other; but woe to the one who is alone and falls and does not have another to help. [11] Again, if two lie together, they keep warm; but how can one keep warm alone? [12] And though one might prevail against another, two will withstand one. A threefold cord is not quickly broken. (4:9–12)

Koheleth is no revolutionary (v. 9, see also 10:7, 20). He seems to regard a bureaucratic government as a necessary evil, even if it inevitably means that some get rich at the expense of others (v. 8). But despite his acceptance of social inequities, Koheleth commends cooperation; and that is an effective hedge against capitulation to the ruthless individualism of a hoarding economy.

HUMAN LIMITATIONS
Ecclesiastes 6:10–12

> 6:10 **What has come to be has already been named, and it is known what human beings are, and that they are not able to dispute with those who are stronger. [11] The more words, the more vanity, so how is one the better? [12] For who knows what is good for mortals while they live the few days of their vain life, which they pass like a shadow? For who can tell them what will be after them under the sun?**

This is a hinge passage, marking a shift in Koheleth's thought. The previous chapters have focused on the subject of what constitutes human satisfaction, and specifically what a person can do to guarantee satisfaction. Conversely, they identify the sort of activity that is "vanity and a chasing after wind"; this refrain occurs seven times (a number that in biblical tradition symbolizes wholeness) between 1:14 and 6:9. The verses immediately preceding (6:1–9) are a forceful recapitulation of the key teaching of those chapters, namely, that wealth unaccompanied by enjoyment and rest is "a grievous ill" (v. 2). The rest of the book will treat a different but related subject: the nature of wisdom itself.

The present passage is a strong statement of human finitude, in two senses. First, the range of human experience is limited. "Whatever has come to be has already been named"; the poem in chapter 3 lists virtually all the experiences of positive value. There is indeed, as Koheleth said at the very beginning, "nothing new under the sun" (1:9). Second, human power is limited. We have seen that, with respect to mortality, the human being is like the beasts (3:18–20). It is then the height of folly for this loquacious animal (v. 11) to enter into dispute about ultimate matters with *"the one who is stronger."* (The NRSV translation of v. 10 is misleading; the word is a grammatical singular and clearly refers to God [compare the argument in Job 9].)

This twofold demonstration of finitude argues against the view that human beings can by virtue of their (undeniably great) intellectual power experience a "breakthrough" into a higher realm of existence. In Koheleth's age, no less than in our own, there were those who thought that some human beings can control their destiny by means of advanced knowledge. Scholars of the ancient world call this view "Gnosticism," from the Greek word *gnôsis,* "knowledge." Koheleth subtly mocks such self-aggrandizement with his oft-repeated phrase "under the sun"; the sun was for the Greeks the symbol of enlightenment. Speaking of life under the sun, Koheleth calls attention not to its brightness but to its shadowy quality—that is, to its swift decline. (Compare Psalm 144:4, which, like our passage, describes life as "a shadow" and *hevel.*) The ambiguous Hebrew word *hevel* is used in two senses in the present passage. In verse 11, used in connection with useless speech, it carries the negative connotation of "emptiness." In verse 12, the *hevel*-life is of short duration, but this fact does not lessen its value (contrary to the NRSV "vain"). Indeed, the image of the shadow—the word may also be translated "shade"—might suggest to an audience living in the arid climate of Israel something not only fleeting but also lovely. The poet-librettist Hugo von Hofmannsthal uses the same image to convey a sense of delicate beauty:

> I know but little, yet I have cast a glance
> Into the depths and have recognized this:
> This life is nothing more than shadow-play.

So, lightly let your eyes glance over it;
Then you can bear it. But if you hold it tight,
It crumbles in your fingers.
                    (*Der weisse Fächer* [*The White Fan*])

In verse 12, Koheleth poses a second time the question that he aspired
to answer at the beginning of his search: What is good for humans to do
in their short lives (2:3)? This time the question functions as a disclaimer
of any certain knowledge: Who knows what is good . . . ? The placement
of the disclaimer is important, for as we shall see in the next section,
Koheleth is about to offer a tentative answer in the form of a series of "wise
sayings." It is said that "Angels can fly because they take themselves so
lightly" (G. K. Chesterton). If Koheleth's words have been received into
the canon as divinely inspired, perhaps that is because, difficult though his
sayings are, his touch is invariably light.

FINDING THE BALANCE THAT IS WISDOM
Ecclesiastes 7:1–22

Koheleth sets forth his notion of the good—or at least, "the better"—in
two closely related sections. The first (vv. 1–14) is in its form a traditional
wisdom address (a series of proverbs with a concluding exhortation), but
the content of most of these sayings is far from conventional. The second
section (vv. 15–22) is a personal testimony in Koheleth's characteristic
style.

Relative Goods (Ecclesiastes 7:1–14)

7:1 **A good name is better than precious ointment,**
      and the day of death, than the day of birth.
  2 **It is better to go to the house of mourning**
      than to go to the house of feasting;
      for this is the end of everyone,
      and the living will lay it to heart.
  3 **Sorrow is better than laughter,**
      for by sadness of countenance the heart is made glad.
  4 **The heart of the wise is in the house of mourning;**
      but the heart of fools is in the house of mirth.
  5 **It is better to hear the rebuke of the wise**
      than to hear the song of fools.

6 For like the crackling of thorns under a pot,
   so is the laughter of fools;
   this also is vanity.
7 Surely oppression makes the wise foolish,
   and a bribe corrupts the heart.
8 Better is the end of a thing than its beginning;
   the patient in spirit are better than the proud in spirit.
9 Do not be quick to anger,
   for anger lodges in the bosom of fools.
10 Do not say, "Why were the former days better than these?"
   For it is not from wisdom that you ask this.
11 Wisdom is good as an inheritance,
   an advantage to those who see the sun.
12 For the protection of wisdom is like the protection of money,
   and the advantage of knowledge is that wisdom gives life to the one
   who possesses it.
13 Consider the work of God; who can make straight what he has made
   crooked?
14 In the day of prosperity be joyful, and in the day of adversity
consider, God has made the one as well as the other, so that mortals may
not find out anything that will come after them.

The sages of Proverbs use "better than" statements to point to the complexity of "what is good" (v. 12), that is, the frequency with which one must choose the lesser of two evils, or at least settle for a situation that falls far short of the ideal (see the comment at Prov. 17:1). But Koheleth's proverbial wisdom is even more subversive of simplistic notions of the good. The first six sayings are grouped in three pairs.

7:1–2. The two parts of verse 1 are integrally related, so the comparison in the first half is crucial for understanding the problematic comparison in the second. The problem with perfumed oil is its instability: Though good when fresh, it has a tendency to spoil quickly. So also with a young life. Birth and the beginning of life are almost always attended by joy. "The house of feasting" (v. 2) probably refers to the feast traditionally held when a child was weaned (see Gen. 21:8). But if the delightfulness of the small child does not mature into good character, which Hebrew idiom terms "a name," then the life is ultimately a source of bitterness to self and others. Alphonse Maillot comments: "the day of my death is the day of truth: . . . the day that gives birth to my 'name,' my existence in all its truth. *Death strips away all appearances* . . . " (cited by Ellul, *Reason for Being,* 175n, italics mine). It is for this reason that the deeply religious keep the thought of death steadily in view. In some ancient Eastern monasteries, the skulls of all the dead monks from generations past are piled in a room where any visitor or resident can see them. They are meant as a sobering but not grim reminder that death is not only "the end of everyone" (v. 2); it is also our final responsibility. Arguably, death is our chief responsibility, for which our whole life should prepare us, so we may not be ashamed when all appearances are stripped away. Despite its sadness, a death that fully discloses a soul well-formed is indeed "beautiful in its time" (Eccl. 3:11, AT).

An unforgettable saying of the ancient rabbis has an affinity with Koheleth's sharp statements: "Do not believe in yourself until the day of your death" (*Mishnah Avot*, 2:4).

7:3–4. On occasion the sages of Proverbs remind us of the inevitability of sorrow (14:13; see the comment above). Nevertheless, they stop short of ascribing to it any positive value: "A glad heart makes a cheerful countenance, but by sorrow of heart the spirit is broken" (Prov. 15:13). Koheleth controverts what would seem to be the obvious truth of this saying, though in doing so he contradicts his own repeated commendation of enjoyment. One might suppose that Koheleth frames his words for shock value rather than truth, were it not for the fact that the Gospel of Matthew echoes his words here: "Blessed are those who mourn" (Matt. 5:4). Likewise, Paul teaches that Christians are to be recognized "as sorrowful, yet always rejoicing" (2 Cor. 6:10).

The sorrow that Koheleth commends is not "the foolish sorrow which people make up for themselves" (Luther, *Notes*, 110) but the real trouble that all must face who do not shrink from the challenges of living and loving. Thus he encourages us to endure our difficulties with confidence in the generosity of God the Giver. The blunt saying, void of any reference to extenuating circumstances, is confrontational. It is a strong antidote to the common temptation to believe that disappointment and sorrow are always signs that we should escape from our present situation and responsibilities to something—a different job or marriage or church—that seems to promise more gratification.

Conversely, Koheleth rejects "mirth" as a sign of folly (v. 4). The saying is deeply puzzling, for he uses the same Hebrew word numerous times elsewhere for the enjoyment he commends (2:26; 8:15; 9:7; see also 5:20). So what does Koheleth mean to repudiate here? There is a kind of resolute frivolity that invariably has a hidden link to fear, if not to despair. There is a difference between being cheerful—that enjoyment is the gift of God—and *having* to be cheerful because we are afraid of looking squarely at ourselves and the world and naming what is there, both bad and good. The mourning on which the Gospel of Matthew pronounces a blessing is one essential way of connecting to reality. It is only after we have deeply mourned our disappointments, our losses, and our sins that we are ready to make a new beginning on a secure foundation.

7:5–6. These sayings are in line with those of the traditional sages, who often comment on the value of an apt rebuke or an appropriate disciplinary measure (Prov. 12:1; 13:1, 18; 15:5, 12, 31–32). The comparison of fools' laughter to thorns used for fuel is brilliant. Dried thorns blaze up more quickly than does charcoal, but after a few minutes of noise and brightness, the fire dies away, having yielded no warmth. It is *hevel* in both senses: ephemeral and useless. Moreover, a pun between two homonyms—*sîrîm*, "thorns," and *sîr*, "pot"—makes the verse memorable in Hebrew.

7:7. "Surely oppression makes the wise person foolish [or 'mad']." It is not clear whether the (supposedly) wise are engaged in oppression and thus revealed to be foolish, or whether being victims of oppression drives them out of their senses. Two things argue against the former interpretation. First, it is a truism, a rehearsal of the obvious, and Koheleth does not normally bother with those. More conclusively, the second half of the verse—"a bribe [Hebrew: 'gift'] corrupts the heart"—presents an instance when character is altered because of *another person's* action. It is likely, then, that a parallel situation is envisioned in the first line; it is better translated, "Oppression drives the wise person mad." We may well take this as a caution against a form of romanticization to which our own generation is prone, perhaps more than the ancients. Many of us have experienced little or no real oppression, yet we thrill to stories of extraordinary faith, endurance, and purity of heart as revealed through the horrors of the Nazi Holocaust. The Hollywood film *Schindler's List* has captured the popular imagination and, moreover, served an important educational function to a generation unfamiliar with that recent history. But it is well to remember that countless other stories could be told of good people, even people with some wisdom, whose spirits were shattered or perverted by that nightmare and others like it. Evil must be remembered but never romanticized; every period of great oppression produces some heroism and much more madness among its victims.

7:10. We often remember "the good old days" as better than they were. But even if memory is accurate, valuing the past over the present does not derive from wisdom. The saying is directed against nostalgia, which is essentially a repudiation of the possibility of present joy—and less obviously, a repudiation of present responsibilities. Assuredly, we can and must learn from the past; Koheleth himself sometimes cites "historical" examples (4:13–15; 5:13–14; 9:13–16). But if our relationship with the past is fruitful, then we will not merely regard the present with distaste. Rather, reflection on the good things of the past should encourage and guide us in working on the difficulties we now face. It should heighten our sensitivity to the danger of irreparable loss, both of human insight and of material resources. This danger is especially great in our own age of rapid cultural change—indeed, when many traditional cultures are becoming extinct—and radical transformation of the physical world. Fifty years ago the penetrating religious thinker Simone Weil asserted that renewal would come to us only if we love the past. But loving the past cannot mean wishing ourselves back into it; that is the vanity (absurdity) of nostalgia. Properly cherishing the past means "seeking out what has gone by" (Eccl. 3:15). It means living with the painful awareness that we may even now be destroying things whose value we have forgotten. Thus it means living humbly with our present power and ignorance, mindful that we cannot know all the consequences of our present actions.

7:14. Luther's insight into the wisdom of this saying is unsurpassed:

> That is, prepare yourself in such a way that you are also able to be sorrowful; enjoy the things that are present in such a way that you do not base your confidence on them, as though they were going to last forever. . . . But we should be happy in such a way that we do not immerse ourselves [in present joys], but reserve part of our heart for God, so that with it we can bear the day of adversity. Thus it will happen that the adversities foreseen for us will bother us less. (*Notes,* 120)

Overscrupulosity (Ecclesiastes 7:15–22)

7:15 **In my vain life I have seen everything; there are righteous people who perish in their righteousness, and there are wicked people who prolong their life in their evildoing.** [16] **Do not be too righteous, and do not act too wise; why should you destroy yourself?** [17] **Do not be too wicked, and do not be a fool; why should you die before your time?** [18] **It is good that you should take hold of the one, without letting go of the other; for the one who fears God shall succeed with both.**

[19] **Wisdom gives strength to the wise more than ten rulers that are in a city.**

[20] **Surely there is no one on earth so righteous as to do good without ever sinning.**

[21] **Do not give heed to everything that people say, or you may hear your servant cursing you;** [22] **your heart knows that many times you have yourself cursed others.**

Here Koheleth makes his most direct attack on "orthodox wisdom." Earlier he observed that righteousness and justice are sometimes displaced by wickedness (3:16), but here he pushes that observation further: righteousness is no guarantee of happiness or long life, and wickedness does not necessarily hasten one's death (*contra* Prov. 10:24, 25, 27, etc.). We have already seen that the book of Proverbs as a whole complicates the doctrine of retributional justice—"good comes to the good and punishment to the wicked"—which isolated proverbs may present in a simple way. But never does any previous sage suggest that it is actually possible to be "too righteous," and certainly this advice seems to run contrary to Jesus' blessing on those who "hunger and thirst for righteousness" (Matt. 5:6). Yet there is wisdom here—in my judgment, wisdom that is especially necessary for "church professionals."

It is hard to discern Koheleth's logic from the published translation. In the NRSV verse 16b—"why should you destroy yourself?"—is imprecise. The verb normally means "make oneself desolate, deserted." Two inferences are possible here. One, the overscrupulous person is susceptible to acute discouragement, for "it is impossible in human affairs to act so well that everything comes out right and no more evils remain" (Luther, *Notes*, 27). It is impossible to eradicate even the evil in oneself, and so over-scrupulosity may issue finally in self-hatred. A second inference: Excessive confidence in one's own righteousness leads to isolation from other people, who invariably fail to measure up to the standard expected. Koheleth is then cautioning his students against overrighteous naïveté about themselves (perhaps the most dangerous form of naïveté) and judgmentalism toward others, and at the same time against their own corruption: "Do not be too wicked" (v. 17). In both respects, he alerts them to their own capacity for evil.

It is obviously undesirable that we "take hold of" evildoing (see v. 18) as a positive goal, even in moderation. Nonetheless, we are far less likely to do serious harm or to be undone by wickedness if we recognize that no human life remains untouched by evil, coming from both within and without. Koheleth's advice here has an affinity with the one prayer that Jesus taught his disciples. "Forgive us our trespasses, as we forgive those who trespass against us. Lead us not into temptation, but deliver us from evil." There is an inherent paradox in the prayer, which Koheleth would perhaps appreciate: We acknowledge our propensity for sin and ask that we not be tempted beyond our strength to resist, yet at the same time we seek forgiveness for the sins we regularly commit. Likewise, we pray both to be delivered from the evil actions of others and that we may forgive them for evil committed against us. It is a prayer of both realism and hope—and what other genuine prayer could be offered by those who stand in the midst of this world and look for God's kingdom to come?

The saying in verse 19 sounds like a popular proverb (compare Prov. 20:9); Hellenistic cities, including Jerusalem, were in fact governed by a council of ten leading citizens. Some believe that Koheleth cites it mockingly, but there is no need to draw that conclusion. In the present context, the wisdom that gives strength consists in knowing that our righteousness is not perfect and thus avoiding the moral arrogance that is a common failing of people in positions of public responsibility—especially if they are religious!

The section ends with a bit of practical advice that strikes home with those who have some aspiration to be righteous—and that includes the writer and probably most of the readers of this book. We are generally very interested in what others have to say about us, perhaps because we secretly hope to hear ourselves praised. But Koheleth warns us not to be too interested. Addressing members of the upper class, he mentions the critical talk of servants; we might think of our children, employees, students, parishioners—anyone who is affected by the exercise of our authority and consequently resents our mistakes. It has been aptly observed that people in positions of authority judge themselves by their intentions; others judge them by the outcome of their actions. Koheleth adds the further uncomfortable reminder that our own criticisms of others are frequently ungenerous (v. 22). "Forgive us our sins, as we forgive those who sin against us."

A PERSONAL NOTE: KOHELETH'S LONELINESS
Ecclesiastes 7:23–29

> 7:23 All this I have tested by wisdom; I said, "I will be wise," but it was far from me. 24 That which is, is far off, and deep, very deep; who can find it out? 25 I turned my mind to know and search out and to seek wisdom and the sum of things, and to know that wickedness is folly and that foolishness is madness. 26 I found more bitter than death the woman who is a trap, whose heart is snares and nets, whose hands are fetters; one who pleases God escapes her, but the sinner is taken by her. 27 See, this is what I found, says the Teacher, adding one thing to another to find the sum, 28 which my mind has sought repeatedly, but I have not found. One man among a thousand I found, but a woman among all these I have not found. 29 See, this alone I found, that God made human beings straightforward, but they have devised many schemes.

Evidently the warning in verse 7:16, that too much wisdom leads to desolation and isolation, reflects Koheleth's personal experience. His words here are the most self-revealing in the book, and they show that his own life, devoted to the search for wisdom and "the sum of things," was lonely and to some degree sad. The section is unified by the threefold usage of the Hebrew word *heshbôn*, which is used in two senses: "sum" (vv. 25 and 27) and "schemes" (v. 29). In both instances a good English equivalent might be "scheme" or "design," which likewise can be used in two senses, to designate an overall plan or pattern, or a particular human intention (frequently viewed negatively).

It is telling that in this autobiographical statement, the chief instance of wickedness and folly that comes to Koheleth's mind is an embittering romantic relationship. It has been rightly observed that Koheleth speaks too harshly of "the woman who is a trap" not to have loved at least one woman greatly and, in the end, bitterly. The Hebrew phrasing is unusual: "I turned, I and my heart, to know . . . " (v. 25). As at the beginning (1:13), Koheleth externalizes the activity of his searching heart (the NRSV has translated "mind," for which there is no distinct word in biblical Hebrew). The effect here is striking; we sense his vulnerability to another heart, which proved to be "snares and nets" (v. 26).

The highly personal character of this statement distinguishes it from misogyny. It does not purport to be objective reflection on "how women are." Rather, it is an honest statement of disappointment, which Koheleth still feels keenly. He never found a life partner to share his enjoyment, but he does not disparage that pleasure for others (9:9). Nor did Koheleth fare much better in friendships with men. Human companionship, male or female, is one crucial component of "the whole scheme of things" (v. 25) which he was not able to master.

There is probably some defensiveness in his blaming human perversity (v. 29) rather than his own personality, which was doubtless crusty. But at a deeper level, it seems that Koheleth must after all draw a distinction within the created order between people and animals (contrast 3:18). Humanity is the sole part of creation that can "devise many schemes" (v. 29) and willfully depart from the intention of its Maker. Moreover, Koheleth's experience suggests that moral perverseness is overwhelmingly more common than integrity. We are the only creature who can misuse the gifts we have from God's hand, and the spectacular character of our gifts makes their misuse terrifying. Anthropologist Loren Eiseley comments on the uniqueness of the human mind in terms that Koheleth would deeply appreciate: "Man is not as other creatures . . . without the sense of the holy, without compassion, his brain can become a gray stalking horror, the deviser of Belsen" (cited in Hall, *Imaging God,* 182). Mindful of widespread moral perversion (compare 8:11), Koheleth in the next chapter returns to the concept of fearing God.

AGAINST PRESUMPTION
Ecclesiastes 8:1–9

8:1 **Who is like the wise man?**
   And who knows the interpretation of a thing?
   Wisdom makes one's face shine,
   and the hardness of one's countenance is changed.
2   **Keep the king's command because of your sacred oath.** [3] **Do not be terrified; go from his presence, do not delay when the matter is unpleasant, for he does whatever he pleases.** [4] **For the word of the king is powerful, and who can say to him, "What are you doing?"** [5] **Whoever obeys a command will meet no harm, and the wise mind will know the time and way.** [6] **For every matter has its time and way, although the troubles of mortals lie heavy upon them.** [7] **Indeed, they do not know what is to be, for who can tell them how it will be?** [8] **No one has power over the wind to restrain the wind, or power over the day of death; there is no discharge from the battle, nor does wickedness deliver those who practice it.** [9] **All this I observed, applying my mind to all that is done under the sun, while one person exercises authority over another to the other's hurt.**

In the previous section, Koheleth indicates that wisdom has eluded him completely (7:23), at least in the crucial area of intimate relationships. The reflection comes to a dead end of personal isolation tinged with bitterness. It is instructive to see here how the structure of the book (which may be the work of an editor and not necessarily Koheleth himself) moves beyond that impasse. Koheleth looks beyond his own experience and asks a contemplative question: What is it that we see in that rare person whom we would designate, not just smart, but truly wise? His answer carries the ring of truth: The very face of the wise person has a distinctive quality, gentle and bright. In biblical literature, a shining face denotes more than cheerfulness. The identical phrase appears in the high priest Aaron's blessing: "May the LORD make his face to shine upon you" (Num. 6:25). It recalls also Moses' face, which shone whenever he spoke with God (Exod. 34:29–35; the Hebrew phrase here is somewhat different). A shining face is, then, a sign of God's benevolent presence; it shows forth the light of the Holy Spirit.

The second element of the description is also striking: "The hardness of one's countenance is changed" (v. 1). It is rare to encounter someone in whom a penetrating mind is matched with a mild expression. The shining yet softened face of the wise person suggests a major teaching of the preceding chapter: True wisdom in many cases does not yield "hard data." "Who knows the interpretation of a thing?" The question sounds like a riddle, in which the wise are skilled (Prov. 1:6). In Koheleth's view, the truly wise person is the one who does not even claim to know "what is happening under the sun" (see 8:16–17). Such a person is not likely to gain a large following, for the world respects those who can give the "right" interpretation of events, emotions, words, even people. This is why news commentators are celebrities in our society. But the wise person has the strength to resist the craving for certainty, the humility to reserve judgment and let wheat and weeds grow together until the harvest (Matt. 13:30).

A bright, soft face—I think of an elderly nun whom I was privileged to know in the last few years of her life, one of very few people I have known whom I would confidently describe as "saintly" in the full sense. She had a large and close family that often came to visit her and stay at the convent, although none of them was a Christian. In what was to be one of our last conversations, I asked Sister Mary Monica if it bothered her that none of these people she so dearly loved shared her faith. Her answer surprised me: "Not as much as it probably should." I now realize the gentle refusal to judge or even to worry about the spiritual welfare of these others was a mark of her wisdom and her trust in God. She knew the limits of her own power to influence and did not strain against them. Even more important, she knew the limits to her own understanding. "Who knows the interpretation of a thing?" She did not presume to know how anyone else stood in the eyes of God.

The following verses are likewise a teaching against presumption and overestimating one's own powers. The instruction is apparently directed to a courtier. But the same advice—obey the king's command and be cautious of his power—could easily be applied to the service of the heavenly King. Obedience and caution are key elements in Koheleth's own attitude toward God (see 5:1–7; 12:13–14). Moreover, the language of this passage seems to point toward such an interpretation: the reference to "the oath of God" (v. 2, author's translation), and further, "He does whatever he pleases" (v. 3). The latter echoes the psalmists' affirmation of God's sovereign freedom over heaven and earth (Psalms 115:3; 135:6). On the other hand, the advice to be cautious applies to any situation where "one person exercises *power* over another with the potential for doing harm" (v. 9; on the revised translation, see the comment below).

The effect of the whole passage is to remind us that we are at every moment subject to forces well beyond our control, in heaven and on earth, human forces, but also forces of nature, death, and war—forces that finally only God may control. The word "power" occurs four times (vv. 4, 8a, 8b, and 9; the NRSV has "authority" in v. 9). The purpose is not to induce terror (v. 3) or abject submission but rather to point to the strict limits to personal power that only the fool ignores.

IS THERE ANY JUSTICE?
Ecclesiastes 8:10–17

> 8:10 **Then I saw the wicked buried; they used to go in and out of the holy place, and were praised in the city where they had done such things. This also is vanity. ¹¹ Because sentence against an evil deed is not executed speedily, the human heart is fully set to do evil. ¹² Though sinners do evil a hundred times and prolong their lives, yet I know that it will be well with those who fear God, because they stand in fear before him, ¹³ but it will not be well with the wicked, neither will they prolong their days like a shadow, because they do not stand in fear before God.**
>
> ¹⁴ **There is a vanity that takes place on earth, that there are righteous people who are treated according to the conduct of the wicked, and there are wicked people who are treated according to the conduct of the righteous. I said that this also is vanity. ¹⁵ So I commend enjoyment, for there is nothing better for people under the sun than to eat, and drink, and enjoy themselves, for this will go with them in their toil through the days of life that God gives them under the sun.**
>
> ¹⁶ **When I applied my mind to know wisdom, and to see the business that is done on earth, how one's eyes see sleep neither day nor night, ¹⁷ then I saw all the work of God, that no one can find out what is happening under the sun. However much they may toil in seeking, they will not find it out; even though those who are wise claim to know, they cannot find it out.**

Here Koheleth returns again to the problem of failed justice. The immediate stimulus for his reflection is a sight common enough in any city: a wicked person gets a big funeral and elaborate eulogies (v. 10). Koheleth impatiently observes that it is the delay in divine retribution that encourages the perpetuation of wickedness (v. 11); repentance takes a lot of imagination, because those who commit evil seem to be getting away with it! But Koheleth is troubled also by the question of whether retribution *ever* comes. He seems to affirm the conventional view that eventually the right-eous will be justified and sinners be punished (vv. 12–13). But does he really believe that?

Interpreters are divided on the answer, which depends on their view of what Koheleth means here by *hevel*, repeated three times (vv. 10, 14) as he struggles with the problem. Does it mean "ephemerality" (as so often ear-lier in the book) or "vanity," connoting a moral absurdity? If the former, then Koheleth is contrasting the ephemerality of the wicked person's tri-umph with the eternality of God's justice, slow in coming though it may be. In other words, he contrasts what he *sees* (v. 10) under the sun—the undeserved funeral procession—with what he *knows* (v. 12) to be true, namely, that God is a just judge presiding over all eternity. The other pos-sibility is that Koheleth is making a pronouncement of moral absurdity and cites the conventional view of retributional justice ironically, in order to expose its inadequacies. He has already said that, even if God does judge the righteous and the wicked (3:17), they "all go to one place" (3:20)—along with the animals!

The first of these views is hard to reconcile with Koheleth's assertions in the next section that the same fate comes to both righteous and wicked (9:2), that there is no reward for the dead (9:5). The second view cannot be excluded; irony is certainly one element of Koheleth's rhetoric and may be operative here. But in light of the rest of the book, I believe that a third view of Koheleth's meaning is finally the most satisfactory. Maybe Koheleth is not speaking of *end-time* rewards and punishments at all. The Hebrew can just as easily be translated: "I know that it *is* well with those who fear God, . . . but it *is* not well with the wicked, neither *do* they pro-long. . . . " Koheleth here gives greater emphasis to a theme he has intro-duced earlier, the importance of fearing God; and his comment helps to clarify his earlier terse admonitions. Previously he commended God-fearing precisely as an antidote to rash religious speech (5:7) and over righteousness (7:18). Fearing God is the necessary basis for living modestly in our religiosity; it keeps us from making excessive claims about what God likes and doesn't like, as well as excessive claims about our own righteous-ness before God. Following on those statements, I believe Koheleth now means, not that fearing God guarantees some heavenly reward, but rather that fearing God *already* constitutes the well-being of the righteous. The reward for fearing God is fearing God. "It is well with those who fear God," simply because it is better to be in touch with reality, however painful that may be, than to be lost in the delusions that inevitably beset those who fail to feel that fear. "It is not well with the wicked," who fear nothing but the failure of their own desires and puny powers, and that failure must inevitably come to everyone in this life.

With the concept of the fear of God, Koheleth makes contact with the bedrock of human existence, below the level of contingency, disappointment, and even injustice. That contact enables him to move out of an intellectual impasse, as the rest of the passage and the next section show. Confronted by hypocrisy (v. 10) and frequent failures of justice in this world (vv. 11–12a, 14), with no assurance about the next—how then does the thoughtful person respond? One response, perhaps the most "reasonable" one, is to become cynical. But Koheleth advances another option, one that is less logical but more profound: namely, to attend more seriously to the business of enjoying oneself. Joy is the antidote to the abiding topsy-turviness of the world.

Earlier Koheleth offered the same advice in the context of a warning against overwork (5:18–20). In the present context, the commendation of enjoyment cautions against too much puzzling over the incomprehensible and morally offensive facts of life. In other words, Koheleth warns against the attempt to be overwise (7:16). The order of the passage suggests that taking a firm hold on all the good things that God has given us to enjoy is intellectually freeing. The commendation of joy supersedes Koheleth's earlier resolution to be wise (7:23). Koheleth is at last free *not* to know "what is happening under the sun" (v. 17). Not knowing is itself his deepest insight into "all the work of God." Embracing joy frees him to let God be God, whose trademark is work that exceeds our comprehension. Maybe this also frees him to let humans be truly human, which is the subject of the next section.

The writings of philosopher and theologian Søren Kierkegaard record a similar struggle with hypocrisy and moral absurdity that ends in an enlargement of freedom. One parable, which clearly shows the influence of Ecclesiastes, suggests how the sad disillusionment of youth is at last transformed into gaiety:

> As it befell Parmeniscus in the legend, who in the cave of Trophonius lost the power to laugh, but got it back again on the island of Delos, at the sight of the shapeless block exhibited there as the image of the goddess Leto, so it has befallen me. When I was young, I forgot how to laugh in the cave of Trophonius; when I was older, I opened my eyes and beheld reality, at which I began to laugh, and since then I have not stopped laughing. I saw that the meaning of life was to secure a livelihood, and that its goal was to attain a high position; that love's rich dream was marriage with an heiress; that friendship's blessing was help in financial difficulties; that wisdom was what

the majority assumed it to be; that enthusiasm consisted in making a speech; that it was courage to risk the loss of ten dollars; that kindness consisted in saying, "You are welcome," at the dinner table; that piety consisted in going to communion once a year. This I saw, and I laughed. (*Either/Or*, 1:33)

There is "a time to laugh" (3:4). Like Koheleth, Kierkegaard experiences revulsion against hypocrisy and a foolish human claim to have grasped the infinite: a block of stone set up as deity. Strangely (though it is a strangeness the ancient sage would appreciate), the intensity of the experience enables him to "break through" to laughter that is debunking yet not bitter. Laughter makes it possible for us to make a negative judgment while yet remaining open to the other person, or even to parts of ourselves that we find inadequate and embarrassing. Koheleth's laughter is like the free laughter of children, which is so often provoked by incongruities that their elders merely find irritating. Skeptical yet unembittered laughter is one of the childlike ways that enables us to receive the kingdom of God (Mark 10:15).

TO LIFE!
Ecclesiastes 9:1–12

9:1 **All this I laid to heart, examining it all, how the righteous and the wise and their deeds are in the hand of God; whether it is love or hate one does not know. Everything that confronts them** 2 **is vanity, since the same fate comes to all, to the righteous and the wicked, to the good and the evil, to the clean and the unclean, to those who sacrifice and those who do not sacrifice. As are the good, so are the sinners; those who swear are like those who shun an oath.** 3 **This is an evil in all that happens under the sun, that the same fate comes to everyone. Moreover, the hearts of all are full of evil; madness is in their hearts while they live, and after that they go to the dead.** 4 **But whoever is joined with all the living has hope, for a living dog is better than a dead lion.** 5 **The living know that they will die, but the dead know nothing; they have no more reward, and even the memory of them is lost.** 6 **Their love and their hate and their envy have already perished; never again will they have any share in all that happens under the sun.**

7 **Go, eat your bread with enjoyment, and drink your wine with a merry heart; for God has long ago approved what you do.** 8 **Let your garments always be white; do not let oil be lacking on your head.** 9 **Enjoy life with the wife whom you love, all the days of your vain life that are given you under the sun, because that is your portion in life and in your toil at which you toil under the sun.** 10 **Whatever your hand finds to do, do with your might; for**

there is no work or thought or knowledge or wisdom in Sheol, to which you are going.

[11] **Again, I saw that under the sun the race is not to the swift, nor the battle to the strong, nor bread to the wise, nor riches to the intelligent, nor favor to the skillful; but time and chance happen to them all.** [12] **For no one can anticipate the time of disaster. Like fish taken in a cruel net, and like birds caught in a snare, so mortals are snared at a time of calamity, when it suddenly falls upon them.**

Having said that no one can really know "what is happening under the sun" (8:17), Koheleth now goes on to make what is perhaps the most radically agnostic ("not-knowing") statement in the Bible. Though the righteous and the wise are (like everyone else) in the hand of God, one cannot even know if God regards them with love or hatred! Those harsh words are shocking in the context of the Bible, which in both Testaments assures us of God's enduring love. Koheleth never retracts them, even though he goes on to speak of God's approval (v. 7). The logic here is not that of strict rationality, but rather the more fluid logic of the heart. Even those who believe in God's love do not always feel it. In a time of deep trouble, I once heard myself say, "If God hated me, it is hard to imagine how things could be much worse!" (This was, of course, not the end of the story.) The sixteenth-century mystic and theologian Teresa of Avila was once traveling during a terrible storm, and she nearly drowned in a raging river. As she cried out to God in fear, Jesus appeared to her in a vision and asked, "Why are you afraid, Teresa? Don't you know that you are my friend?" The spunky saint had the wit to ask her Lord the right question in return: "Did you ever wonder why you have so few friends?"

Koheleth maintains that what we do not know "under the sun," we will never know; for everyone alike will die, and "the dead know nothing" (v. 5). This state of things is more than vanity; it is evil (v. 3). Little wonder, then, that personal chaos is the norm; "madness is in their hearts while they live." The only "security" (a better translation than "hope" for the Hebrew word in v. 4) that anchors the living is the knowledge that they will die. Such a view of life could easily engender cynical apathy; we might expect Koheleth's counsel to be: "Don't try anything. Save yourself the grief." But in fact, it is the opposite: Whatever you do, give it all you've got (v. 10), in work but above all in play. The commendation of pleasure here becomes a call to perpetual celebration of life, complete with white garments and perfumed oil (v. 8). White clothing was a great luxury in the ancient Mediterranean world, where water was scarce and people did not wash their clothes very often; it was normally reserved for the most special occasions (see Rev. 3:4, 5; 4:4; 7:9).

How can Koheleth make this move, from stark confrontation with death as the one absolute to energetic investment in life? As so often in this book, the key lies in the notion of *hevel*. "All the days of your *hevel*-life" (v. 9)—if the NRSV is correct and Koheleth really views life as empty ("vain"), then the celebration he calls for could hardly be more than self-indulgence, which is often linked with despair. But if, as I have tried to show, what dominates his thought from beginning to end is the awareness that life is short, then the move makes sense. "Enjoy life . . . all the days of your *fleeting* life," whose beauty is like that of a flower garden; the loveliness is only enhanced by the fact that it is always passing away.

Chaim Potok tells the story of a young Jewish boy, Asher Lev. One day on a walk with his father, he encountered a bird lying on its side by the curb near their home.

> "Is it dead, Papa?" I was six and could not bring myself to look at it.
> "Yes," I heard him say in a sad and distant way.
> "Why did it die?"
> "Everything that lives must die."
> "Everything?"
> "Yes."
> "You too Papa? And Mama?"
> "Yes."
> "And me?"
> "Yes," he said. Then he added in Yiddish, "But may it be only after you live a long and good life, my Asher."
> I could not grasp it. I forced myself to look at the bird. Everything alive would one day be as still as that bird?
> "Why?" I asked.
> "That's the way the Ribbono Shel Olom [Master of the Universe] made His world, Asher."
> "Why?"
> "So life would be precious, Asher. Something that is yours forever is never precious!"
>
> (*My Name Is Asher Lev*, 156)

But even if the call to enjoyment is understandable, still there is a remarkable incautiousness to Koheleth's assurance that "God has long ago approved what you do" (v. 7). How can Koheleth, knowing so well the human propensity for foolishness, give a blanket assurance of God's approval? Such an assurance would indeed be dangerous if addressed to potential arsonists or the religiously self-satisfied. But it is strong medicine for those who have long striven to be righteous and wise (v. 1) and yet remain perpetually anxious. God is pleased by your pleasure in the "ordinary" things of life: enjoying your spouse and your work, even though you have no assurance of results (vv. 11–12). God likes the way you fulfill your responsibilities, even the way you meet your basic necessities, including the necessity of companionship. Such an assurance could be healing for us, who habitually engage in excess. One might think that we who live in a hedonistic society do not need to be told to enjoy ourselves. But perhaps the problem is that we do not *sufficiently* enjoy the means by which we obtain our necessities and the small luxuries that ordinary life affords. Being overworked and underpleasured, we depend on "hard drugs"—consumerism in its various forms—to keep going. Koheleth is pointing us to "sustainable" forms of pleasure: that is, those that are within realistic reach for most people and are not ultimately destructive of ourselves, other people, and our world itself.

This focus on God's approval reflects an aspect of God's love that we do not speak about often enough. The Old Testament no less than the New affirms that God's love is unmerited and unconditional. But if we are not to be disheartened by trouble, then we, like all children, need to know that the One who cares for us also *likes* us. If we are to thrive in our relationship with God, then we must believe that some of what we do brings God pleasure.

"Whatever your hand finds to do, do with your might": Koheleth cannot be celebrating human achievement, which is never certain (see vv. 11–12). Rather, these words should be heard as urging humility (see the comment at 4:1–8) and a realistic appreciation of three limitations that affect all human activity. First is the limitation of time. Work hard now; this is the time for it, while we are under the sun. Though Jesus does not share Koheleth's skepticism about the fate of the dead, he, too, affirms that this world is the place for strenuous work: "We must work the works of him who sent me while it is day; night is coming when no one can work" (John 9:4). Second is the limitation of ability. Jacques Ellul's reading of the passage is perceptive:

> You are to accomplish this work you are about to undertake with *your* might, and nothing else. You must not undertake a task that is too much for you. For instance, you must not count on God to enable you to accomplish some heroic or athletic feat, to break a record or to create a work of art for which you lack the ability. . . . You must know your ability and its limitations. . . . We must learn to grow old, then, and not attempt to overcome the aging process when our strength begins to decline, maintaining we can still do what we did twenty years ago. (*Reason for Being*, 104)

Third is the limitation of chance. When beginning a new endeavor, it is right to pray that God may bring it to a successful conclusion, but there is never any guarantee that I will live to see it. Indeed, if I steadily put my hands, mind, and heart to work, I can be certain that at some unforeseen "time of calamity" (v. 12), I will leave good and important work unfinished. The great teacher of early Judaism, Rabbi Akiba, uttered a memorable saying that echoes this passage: "Everything is given in pledge, and a net is spread over all" (*Pirke Avot* 3:25). Some day we will each have to trust God with the unfinished work we hold most dear.

RECKONING WITH PRIVILEGE
Ecclesiastes 10:16–20

10:16 **Alas for you, O land, when your king is a servant,**
      and your princes feast in the morning!
  17 **Happy are you, O land, when your king is a nobleman,**
      and your princes feast at the proper time—
      for strength, and not for drunkenness!
  18 **Through sloth the roof sinks in,**
      and through indolence the house leaks.
  19 **Feasts are made for laughter;**
      wine gladdens life,
      and money meets every need.
  20 **Do not curse the king, even in your thoughts,**
      or curse the rich, even in your bedroom;
      for a bird of the air may carry your voice,
      or some winged creature tell the matter.

The chapter as a whole is an assortment of sayings which variously illustrate the maxim that "one bungler destroys much good" (9:18). They represent vividly instances of folly and mishap, those common underminers of all that wisdom builds.

Here and several other places in the book, Koheleth reflects on the phenomenon of kingship, a common theme in wisdom literature throughout the ancient Near East. Among the sages, he is the first to explore in any depth the phenomenon of irresponsible rule. Since earlier sages were often members of the court circle, it is not surprising that their perspective on kingship was generally positive. Near Eastern kings were wise "by definition"; it was part of their mythology. Pharaoh was worshiped as a god; his rule was believed to be inspired by Ra, the protector and guide of the universe. Babylonian royal tradition treats wisdom as a divine gift revealed only to the king.

A remnant of the same ideology is operative in early Israelite thought (see Prov. 20:8, 28; 21:1; 25:2, 5). It reaches fullest expression in connection with Solomon, whose wisdom is of legendary proportions: "God gave wisdom to Solomon and very great understanding, and breadth of heart like the sand that is on on the seashore, so that Solomon's wisdom surpassed the wisdom of all the people of the east, and all the wisdom of Egypt. He was wiser than any other person . . . " (1 Kings 4:29–31). Yet the history of Solomon's reign reveals that he did not always act wisely, and David's kingdom was torn apart on that account (1 Kings 11:4–9, 31–33). The rest of the history of the Israelite and Judean monarchy dispenses altogether with the myth of royal wisdom. With rare exceptions, it is a history of futile power brokering and apostasy, ending in exile to the royal court of Babylon (2 Kings 25:27–30).

From then on, Jews had to reckon with foreign potentates. "By me kings reign . . . and nobles, all who govern rightly" (Prov. 8:15–16), personified Wisdom declares. Thus the sages assert that all just government is part of the divinely ordained cosmic order. Koheleth does not espouse their confidence; his enthusiasm for kingship is qualified at best. Very often authority is exercised in damaging ways (5:8; 8:9). A king is something like an elemental force, no more to be restrained than the wind or the day of death (8:8). In these sayings, Koheleth evokes the reckless behavior of unfit rulers, and even their words (could v. 19 be a fragment of a drinking song, or a toast?). Possibly he has in mind Ptolemy IV (238–205) who came to the throne as a teenager. In place of the NRSV's "servant" in verse 16, it is preferable to read "youth/child." This ruler, possibly Koheleth's contemporary, proved to be drunken and debauched. But it is not necessary to assume one particular reference. Koheleth and his audience lived in a time and place that would have made them aware of the vagaries of monarchy. From the time of Alexander's death (323 B.C.E.), Palestine was the site and the subject of regular controversy between the Ptolemaic rulers in Egypt and the rival kingdom of the Seleucids, centered in Syria and Iran. Both kingdoms furnished examples of sudden changes of rulers, in which children and incompetents succeeded to the throne.

Despite his reservations about dynastic rule, Koheleth is no anarchist or revolutionary; generally speaking, "a plowed field"—that is, a settled land—profits from having a king (5:9). In this matter Koheleth is in accord with the New Testament's ratification of temporal authority; political power is given "from above" (John 19:11; compare 1 Tim. 2:2), although those who misuse it are judged accordingly. Whether or not Koheleth himself was born into the upper class, he supports the system of privilege and is repelled by the sight of slaves on horseback and princes on foot (10:5–7; compare Prov. 30:22). Perhaps Koheleth's very awareness that, existentially speaking, we are always at the mercy of unpredictable forces (9:11–12) gives added impetus to the social conservatism that he shares with many sages. He cautions even against framing negative thoughts about the king or the wealthy (10:20)—although he fails to follow his own advice!

Doubtless some of Koheleth's contemporaries would have fiercely resented his quietism (v. 20). Already in the third century there was in Jerusalem a nationalistic faction strongly opposed to Hellenistic rule and culture, although the Maccabean revolt did not break out until some years later (175 B.C.E.). Nonetheless, Koheleth's frank criticisms of those in power may have exercised influence even on the religious thinking of conservatives. In the next generation of sages, Jesus ben Sirach continues the reflection on the use and misuse of power and makes a *theological* statement much stronger than Koheleth's:

> An undisciplined king ruins his people,
> but a city becomes fit to live in through the understanding of its rulers.
> The government of the earth is in the hand of the Lord,
> and over it he will raise up the right leader for the time.
>
> > The Lord overthrows the thrones of rulers,
> > and enthrones the lowly in their place.
> >   (Sir. 10:3–4, 14)

Sirach himself follows Koheleth in affirming the validity of privilege—"One who is honored in poverty, how much more in wealth!" (Sir. 10:31). Yet it is easy to see in his view of God's action a trajectory that culminates in Mary's *Magnificat:*

> > [God] has brought down the powerful from their thrones,
> >   and lifted up the lowly;
> > he has filled the hungry with good things,
> > and sent the rich away empty.
> >   (Luke 1:52–53)

It is ironic—but perhaps it is also the work of the Holy Spirit within Israel's tradition—that Koheleth's incisive yet socially conservative perspective is linked with one of the most revolutionary songs in the Bible.

THE GRACE OF NOT KNOWING
Ecclesiastes 11:1–6

11:1 Send out your bread upon the waters,
          for after many days you will get it back.
  2 Divide your means seven ways, or even eight,
          for you do not know what disaster may happen on earth.
  3 When clouds are full, they empty rain on the earth;
          whether a tree falls to the south or to the north,
          in the place where the tree falls, there it will lie.
  4 Whosoever observes the wind will not sow;
          and whoever regards the clouds will not reap.
  5 Just as you do not know how the breath comes to the bones in the mother's
womb, so you do not know the work of God, who makes everything.
  6 In the morning sow your seed, and at evening do not let your hands be
idle; for you do not know which will prosper, this or that, or whether both
alike will be good.

The theme of all the sayings in this section is "not knowing." This theme
has appeared frequently before (3:21; 6:12; 8:7, 17; 9:1, 12). But here the
element of natural frustration that attends human ignorance has been transcended altogether. This section is about the *grace* of not knowing what lies
ahead, for good and for ill. The grace of not knowing first frees us from the
compulsion to control our situation, to secure our own advantage in everything and kick ourselves—or curse God—when we guess wrong. In this section and the (closely connected) section that follows, Koheleth is preparing
us for the Gospel imperative, " . . . do not worry about your life" (Matt.
6:25; compare Phil. 4:6). Moreover, the grace of not knowing disposes us
also for a second Gospel imperative, the call to service; for, as we shall see,
"grace" in this matter translates into generosity and eagerness for work.

Farmers cannot wait to sow or reap until they are certain the weather
will be favorable (v. 4). Someone building a house in the precious shade of
a tree has no assurance that a windstorm will not one day bring the tree
down onto the house (v. 3). It is a hard lesson of life: in every single enterprise we undertake, we are acting on the basis of data insufficient to guarantee success. That is the bad news. Yet we must put our hands to work.
And the good news is that *some* of what we do "will be good" (v. 6). The
reason is that God works at the same time we do, in cooperation with us
and doubtless at times against our designs and best efforts (see 9:1), and it
is God who "makes [or 'does'] everything" (v. 5).

There is a necessary tension that underlies all human action. We must be energetic and resourceful and yet do our work without anxiety about its results, for "God . . . makes everything." The same mysterious interaction between God's work and ours is suggested in Paul's encouragement to the Christians in Philippi: "work out your own salvation with fear and trembling, for it is God who is at work in you, enabling you both to will and to work for his good pleasure" (Phil. 2:12–13).

Koheleth's statement is radical in the extreme. Directly or indirectly, God's unfathomable work includes the storm that brings down the tree, timely rains but also unseasonable ones and (far more common in Israel) dry spells. Therefore we cannot cleanly separate out the good as coming from God and disasters as nasty accidents. Maybe insurance companies are not entirely wrong to classify floods and lightning storms as "acts of God." God asks Job: "Have you seen the storehouses of the hail, which *I have reserved* for the time of trouble?" (Job 38:23)! Perhaps we could see that our distinctions between "the good" and "the disastrous" are not so meaningful after all, if we could only stretch our minds toward the idea that everything is God's work. But that stretch is too great to maintain for long, and so Koheleth characteristically brings us back to something we can comprehend and enjoy even in difficult circumstances: "it is pleasant for the eyes to see the sun" (v. 7; see the next section).

While the first verse has become proverbial in English, its meaning is in fact much debated among modern interpreters. Many modern interpreters believe that, like the immediately preceding saying (10:20), it offers cautionary advice of a highly practical nature. The image of "sending bread upon the waters" is seen to connote shipping trade. Accordingly, verse 2 is read as advising diversified investment. Yet such prudent advice hardly accords with Koheleth's view that "riches [do not go] to the intelligent" (9:11). Moreover, throwing bread on water is not an effective image for the exercise of business acumen.

The traditional interpretation is probably correct: Koheleth is commending acts of charity. In fact, an Egyptian wisdom text from the same period as Koheleth employs a similar metaphor in this sense: "Do a good deed and throw it in the water; when it dries you will find it" (*Instruction of Onchsheshonqy* 19:10). The image is powerful, although it requires some translation for modern ears. Ancient bread was not made in large loaves, which would sink immediately. What is envisioned is a *pita*, a thin, flat and probably hard disc that will float at least briefly on the current, until it is carried out of sight. The medieval Jewish interpreter Rashi captures the sense well: "Do good, act kindly to the person whom your heart tells you,

'You'll never see him again'—like a person who throws his sustenance upon the surface of the water." The logic is staggering. Not only should you give without certainty of repayment; you should give with the fair certainty of *not* being repaid. Disperse as widely as your means will stretch, "for you do not know what disaster may happen on earth" (v. 2). Our instinct is to hoard in anticipation of scarcity. Koheleth's reasoning is: give now; one day you may not have any more to give. No calamity, not even death itself, can strip us of what we have chosen to give away. Generosity, like joy, thus escapes the judgment of *hevel*.

YOUTH AND AGE
Ecclesiastes 11:7–12:8

In this final section, Koheleth for the first time addresses his youthful audience directly: "Rejoice, young man" (11:9). The two parts of his address, which treat youth and age respectively, are closely connected by common words and images: days and years, light and dark, remembrance and *hevel*. In most of its occurrences in this section the word *hevel* (11:10; 12:8 [three times]) should be translated "fleeting," not (as in the NRSV) "vanity." The latter translation undermines Koheleth's emphasis throughout on making the most of youth, which is precious but transitory. The ambiguity of the Hebrew word asserts itself in 11:8. If "all that comes" refers to "the days of darkness," then indeed the word connotes emptiness ("vanity"). But if the emphasis is on the first half of the verse, then it refers to whatever comes one's way to enjoy and reminds us that even the pleasures of a long life are "fleeting" in comparison to the dark days ahead.

Abiding Sweetness (Ecclesiastes 11:7–10)

11:7 **Light is sweet, and it is pleasant for the eyes to see the sun.**

8 Even those who live many years should rejoice in them all; yet let them remember that the days of darkness will be many. All that comes is vanity.

9 Rejoice, young man, while you are young, and let your heart cheer you in the days of your youth. Follow the inclination of your heart and the desire of your eyes, but know that for all these things God will bring you into judgment.

10 Banish anxiety from your mind, and put away pain from your body; for youth and the dawn of life are vanity.

Koheleth describes two things as "sweet": sleep for the laborer (5:12), and the light of the sun (11:7). Coming from the crusty sage, the simple word is disarming, and especially here at the end, when we know that he has no illusions about all that goes on "under the sun." Nonetheless, sunlight itself is sweet; a deeply personal note sounds here, even though Koheleth has now ceased to speak directly of himself. Koheleth affirms his own experience of steady pleasure (if there is one thing that abounds in Israel, it is sunlight!) in the midst of much just cause for weariness and despair.

Both the "sweet" sayings point to one essential element of humility: namely, the ability to take pleasure in gifts so small that most of the time we scarcely think of them as gifts. Yet without such humility it is impossible to be happy for long. "This is the day that the LORD has made; let us rejoice and be glad in it" (Psalm 118:24); the words belong in our daily routine, along with brushing our teeth and getting some physical exercise. Like muscles, the capacity for joy atrophies if we do not use it regularly. Those who wait for some great occasion for joy and gratitude to God are not likely to recognize it when it happens. But from a biblical perspective, lack of humble gratitude leads to loss far more significant than our own unhappiness. For if we fail to take delight every single day, then God will not be adequately praised—and it is quite possible that resounding praise is the whole reason the world was made in the first place. (This is probably the intended message of Psalms 146–150, where the theme of creation is woven into the great crescendo of praise that rightly forms part of the daily prayer service for orthodox Jews and some Christians.)

Joy is imperative, even into old age, because "the days of darkness will be many" (v. 8). An old woman I knew used to say, in words that (consciously or not) echoed Koheleth: "Well, I will live until I die, and then I'm going to be dead a long time." It was her answer to the myriad small irritations or dangers that constitute so much of the daily experience of the elderly (see 12:5). Thus she refused to let them deprive her of the pleasure of "seeing the sun."

"Even those who live many years should rejoice in them all": We must not overlook the "should"; the elderly are *expected* to rejoice. But it takes courage and humility to rejoice when your powers are failing. It is nearly impossible without the compassionate help of others. Therefore Koheleth indirectly challenges those who are themselves not yet old "to do justice, and to love kindness, and to walk humbly" (Micah 6:8), a challenge as strenuous as any in scripture. His challenge has particular force for our society, where more people are living to extreme old age than ever before in history. Many of us will reach advanced age; probably all of us have some opportunity (if we are open to it) to meet the frail elderly and to be aware of their special needs. The young, the middle-aged, and even the healthy elderly have the responsibility for creating—in our families and churches, in society at large—the conditions that make it possible for the frail to rejoice. We must remember that only those who feel uniquely valued can truly rejoice:

> The glory of youths is their strength,
> and the beauty of the aged is their grey hair.
> (Prov. 20:29)

Many interpreters consider that the warning of judgment (v. 9) is the addition of a moralistic editor seeking to neutralize the shocking advice that the young man should follow his own inclination! Doubtless, Koheleth intended to be shocking. The image of following after heart and eyes resembles the Torah's description of idolatry (Num. 15:39) too closely to be accidental. Idolatry is, from a biblical perspective, the worst of all sins. Not surprisingly, therefore, it was this verse that occasioned the ancient debate among the rabbis about whether Ecclesiastes was in fact a sacred book, and Ben Sirach, the more conventional sage of a later generation, reversed Koheleth's breezy advice (Sir. 5:2). Nonetheless, it is in my view likely that the sober conclusion to the verse also comes from Koheleth. Indeed, the rapid change from sobriety to cheer and *vice versa* is one of the features of his style. Further, the strong contrast between the imperative "know" and the repeated "you do not know" in the preceding section (11:2, 5 [twice]) has the ring of authenticity. Most importantly, the content of the afterthought is consonant with Koheleth's message. He knows we are accountable to God for our actions (3:17; 5:4–7; 8:5–6); that is why the concept of "fearing God" is meaningful—indeed, crucial—to him (see the comments at 5:1–7 and 8:10–17).

The two halves of verse 9 can be seen as complementary; I would translate the conjunction "*and* know that for all these things" (the Hebrew particle can mean either "and" or "but"). The complementarity has two aspects. First, the mention of judgment clarifies the nature of proper enjoyment. It is *responsible* pleasure, not license to exploit others or squander our own bodies and abilities. Such pleasure bespeaks genuine responsiveness to what God has given us. Therefore, it entails daring to believe that "the ways of your heart" are good and ordering your young life by healthy disciplines rather than the physically and emotionally punishing regimes that zealously pious youth sometimes choose (v. 10). Koheleth is a wise and compassionate teacher of the young; no doubt he was effective precisely because he trusted his students and encouraged them to trust themselves. This leads us to see the second aspect of complementarity between the two halves of the verse: Judgment does not cancel out rejoicing but on the contrary makes it imperative. Could it be that this is the chief thing for which we have to answer to God (see Phil. 4:4–5)? Koheleth's repeated observation that "there is nothing better for people under the sun than to . . . enjoy themselves" (3:12; 8:15) is not a counsel of despair but a call to responsibility before the God who is continually *taking us into account*, which is what God's judgment is. Our enjoyment is the right answer to God's abiding (it would not be wrong to say "obsessive") interest in the creatures who bear something like a family resemblance to God. Is not the children's joy the answer that the parent's love most desires?

Remembering the End (Ecclesiastes 12:1–8)

12:1 **Remember your creator in the days of your youth, before the days of trouble come, and the years draw near when you will say, "I have no pleasure in them";** 2 **before the sun and the light and the moon and the stars are darkened and the clouds return with the rain;** 3 **in the day when the guards of the house tremble, and the strong men are bent, and the women who grind cease working because they are few, and those who look through the windows see dimly;** 4 **when the doors on the street are shut, and the sound of the grinding is low, and one rises up at the sound of a bird, and all the daughters of song are brought low;** 5 **when one is afraid of heights, and terrors are in the road; the almond tree blossoms, the grasshopper drags itself along and desire fails; because all must go to their eternal home, and the mourners will go about the streets;** 6 **before the silver cord is snapped, and the golden bowl is broken, and the pitcher is broken at the fountain, and the wheel broken at the cistern,** 7 **and the dust returns to the earth as it was, and the breath returns to God who gave it.** 8 **Vanity of vanities, says the Teacher; all is vanity.**

Ecclesiastes begins with a poem and ends with a poem, and both have the same refrain (1:2; 12:8). However, there is a striking difference in tone. At first Koheleth portrays a static world: nothing new ever happens, and there seems to be no point in trying anything (1:14). But at the end he has moved past resignation and speaks with open urgency in a series of imperatives addressed to the "young man" (11:9): "rejoice . . . let your heart be cheerful . . . follow . . . know . . . banish" (11:9–10) and finally, "Remember."

The element of time is very prominent in this last section. In three verses (11:9–12:1) Koheleth makes six references to the youthfulness of his listener. The idea that youth is the time for pleasure is logical enough. It is less obvious why the young person should be particularly advised, "Remember your creator" (v. 1). Koheleth seems to recognize an important truth about spiritual formation: The different seasons of life are most appropriate for different kinds of spiritual growth. It is unwise to assume that one can ignore God at one stage of life and "catch up" on spiritual work at another. Koheleth's view that youth is the time to come to know God as Creator is highly suggestive. We experience the special grace of God the Creator as the invitation to be at home in the world. Taking our place in the world, not as foreign conquerors but as children of the household coming into responsibility, is the proper spiritual work of youth. Children and young adults serve God the Creator by learning about the world in school and in play, by acquiring the knowledge and skills to do useful and beautiful work. The implication of Koheleth's words is that there is a time when it may no longer be possible to *begin* knowing and worshiping God as your creator. Those who have missed that opportunity may at the end come only to fear God as judge. God the Judge, *separated off from God the Creator*, is a figure of tyranny. That separation is of course false, for God is One (Deut. 6:4). Nonetheless, it comes to dominate and distort the spiritual lives of many people, especially in older age. Their tragedy is that, never having been at home in the world, they become at the end afraid to leave it. And Jesus' parable of the wedding banquet (Matt. 22:1–14) confirms that they are right to fear judgment by the God whose hospitality they earlier declined.

The flip side, then, of remembering our creator is remembering our own mortality. Death is never far from Koheleth's mind; but he never talks about what it might mean to him personally until this final poem, which is an elusive conclusion to a difficult book. While the general message is clear enough—remember *your* death, dear reader—the meaning of almost every image is disputed. Some people see death figured here as an approaching storm, others as a wealthy estate fallen into ruin. One modern commentator sees a fairly literal description of a village halting its normal life to mourn a death. The darkened heavenly bodies are, of course, an exaggeration; but they express the stark individualism of Koheleth's perspective: can anyone really imagine that life goes on when she is gone? Of the several different lines of interpretation proposed by ancient and modern interpreters, by far the most common view is that this is "an allegory of decrepitude," in which the weakening of various body parts is figuratively represented. The guards and strong men (v. 3) are arms and legs (which is which?), the grinding women are the teeth, those looking through darkened windows the eyes; the almond blossoms are white hair. There is less agreement about the rest of the images. Maybe verse 4b points to the tendency of the aged to awaken with the birds—but sadly, they can no longer sing with them. The grasshopper, a burden to itself, may be swollen ankles, a bad back, sexual organs grown impotent, the whole body. Some see further references to body parts in the silver cord, the golden bowl, the pitcher, and the wheel (v. 6): the tongue or the spinal cord, the marrow or the head, the stomach or the heart, the body or the eyeball. Others see more general images of death: a lamp fallen to the floor and its "golden bowl" of oil spilled, the apparatus for drawing water broken. (The word for "cistern" is in fact often used in scripture to denote the grave.)

No single line of interpretation explains everything; nonetheless, this remains one of the most powerful evocations of death ever written. Probably part of the power resides in the fact that the poem suggests multiple metaphors and still resists complete "decoding." Death approaches each of us differently; moreover, what each of us fears or fantasizes about death is different. But in every case there is disruption and loss without parallel. Koheleth draws powerful sketches of normal life brought to a halt. We look for light and water, and there is none. We listen for birdsong, and there is none. Even the hum of the women grinding grain, the sound that came in the evening from every household and signaled a contented and blessed population (Jer. 25:10; Rev. 18:22)—that, too, has fallen silent. We modern readers might create analogous images from our own daily lives in order to personalize the scene of our death as vividly as Koheleth has done for his contemporaries. The last image is timeless and universal: "the dust returns to the dust as it was" (v. 8; compare Gen. 3:19), before our creator breathed it into life. Breath itself is the first source of joy received from God the Giver, and the last to be returned.

THE EPILOGUE
Ecclesiastes 12:9–14

12:9 **Besides being wise, the Teacher also taught the people knowledge, weighing and studying and arranging many proverbs.** [10] **The Teacher sought to find pleasing words, and he wrote words of truth plainly.**

[11] **The sayings of the wise are like goads, and like nails firmly fixed are the collected sayings that are given by one shepherd.** [12] **Of anything beyond these, my child, beware. Of making many books there is no end, and much study is a weariness of the flesh.**

[13] **The end of the matter; all has been heard. Fear God, and keep his commandments; for that is the whole duty of everyone.** [14] **For God will bring every deed into judgment, including every secret thing, whether good or evil.**

Most modern interpreters take these last verses to be an addition by one or more editors seeking to mediate between Koheleth and his audience. Some consider them to be a sort of "character reference": Koheleth was a careful teacher and writer; and he spoke the truth, even if it is sometimes hard to hear. Others think that the last several verses are completely alien to Koheleth's perspective; maybe an "orthodox" editor hoped that people would remember this and nothing else from the book! But in fact the themes of fearing God and God's judgment have been introduced numerous times by Koheleth himself. The epilogue is conceivably from his own hand, as the older commentators traditionally assumed. At the least, it comes from someone who admired Koheleth and shared some of his crustiness and skepticism.

The famous saying in verse 12 may be better translated "Making many books has no purpose." This final contradiction cannot fail to evoke a smile; that view didn't stop Koheleth from having his say "in print"! But on reflection, one sees that Koheleth did not write much after all—less than ten pages in my Bible. No modern academic institution would retain him with a record like that. This is the most direct comment in any biblical book on the value of writing books and studying them. Since that is exactly the enterprise in which this commentary engages its author and readers, it is appropriate to end the present reflection on Ecclesiastes by thinking about what these words mean for us and the wise use of our intellects.

The negative statement is balanced by a positive one: "The words of the wise are like goads, and like nails firmly fixed" (v. 11). The goad carried by a shepherd (v. 11) is sharp and prodding, uncomfortable for sheep reluctant to move forward onto new ground (as they must be continually prodded to do, or they will ruin both the pasture and their own health). But who in our culture has the moral authority and the imagination to make uncomfortable words heard in the public forum? Few teachers or clergy, even fewer politicians. Wendell Berry has identified the chief problem in modern public life as the fact that we have "abandoned discourse as a means of clarifying and explaining and defending and implementing . . . ideas" (*Continuous Harmony*, 92). Everywhere the language of the advertising world has been adopted: in political speeches, sermons, "capital campaigns," drives in schools and churches. Slogans, euphemisms, flattery, and caricatures of the opposition are desirable because they are easily heard and repeated. People may be persuaded to "buy" a candidate or "invest in" a program, but they are not helped to grapple with the sometimes overwhelming complexity of the truth. Certainly such language does not challenge them to grow or make difficult change in their ways of thinking and acting. By contrast, the sayings of the one shepherd are like well-driven nails: few in number and strategically placed to provide firm support. They are (literally) "edifying"; they *build up* the people (v. 9), the community of faith. From the raw materials of human lives and well-chosen words firmly driven home, it is possible to build social structures hospitable to truth. By contrast, our loose talk aims merely at establishing the talker's own power.

The modern university provides good evidence of the saying that making many books is endless, or pointless. "Publish or perish" is the slogan by which the present generation of scholars lives—as though good books can be coerced by institutional pressure rather than emerging organically from the teaching process, as Koheleth's own did. Moreover, the focus on producing new books profoundly affects the quality of study. Scholars and students alike are pressed to keep abreast of all the new arguments, new theories, and new data. Huge quantities of pages must be read; and almost all those pages have been written within the last ten years, or twenty at most. But the sad cost of maintaining a respectable "relevancy" is growing ignorance of and contempt for the past, even among the most highly educated people in our society.

Of course, there is always new data that needs to be taken into account, and the intellectual life quickly becomes stifling if we do not claim the freedom to think differently from our ancestors and our own teachers. No one knew that better than Koheleth himself. Yet it is important to realize that our present conception of the educational process is unprecedented in the history of the world. Innovation has traditionally played a very small role in education. The main job of teachers (and likewise of parents, preachers, and writers) has been to identify and redefine for each new generation the relatively few things that people need to master in order to endure hardship and not lose heart, to live in harmony with one another and their environment, to have true knowledge of God. The work of those who teach—inside and outside the classroom—involves less bold invention than careful tending of the hard-won and easily lost wisdom of the past. It is work that requires humility as its chief virtue, as T. S. Eliot's description of the poet's task suggests:

> And what there is to conquer
> By strength and submission, has already been discovered
> Once or twice, or several times, by men whom one cannot hope
> To emulate—but there is no competition—

> There is only the fight to recover what has been lost
> And found and lost again and again: and now, under conditions
> That seem unpropitious. But perhaps neither gain nor loss.
> For us, there is only the trying. The rest is not our business.
>
> (*Four Quartets*, "East Coker," V)

If it is the teacher's job to recover what has been found and lost over and over, then it is fitting that Koheleth the Teacher's book ends, as the ancient rabbis observed, "with words of *Torah* (Hebrew, 'teaching')," the ancient teaching given to Israel at Sinai: "Fear God, and keep his commandments." The "motivation clause" that follows (v. 13) is better translated in one of two ways: "For that is every person," or "For that is the whole of a person" (the Hebrew does *not* include the word "duty"). The shaping force of a fully human life is fear of God, that lively attention to where the real power in the universe lies which all scripture tries to breed in us. Eliot says, "My end is my beginning." Koheleth takes the grand tour of life and in the end comes up with no genuinely new sources of meaning for human life. For all his genuine sophistication, Koheleth's final wisdom is the same teaching that he learned as a child at home (see Prov. 1:7–8).

Some critics object that these final verses represent a failure of nerve on the part of a later editor trying to make the book look "biblical" by toning down the radicality of Koheleth's message. But in fact, the statement is, like so much else in this book, radical in the true sense. It plunges to the root (Latin, *radix*) of the matter. Keeping God's commandments is an intelligent and faithful response to the cardinal fact that "all is *hevel*" (1:2; 12:8). For the one stable thing "under the sun" is the revelation of God's will for our world. Therefore orienting our lives toward the commandments enables us, "while we are placed among things that are passing away, to hold fast to those that shall endure" (*Book of Common Prayer*, 234).

The Song of Songs

Introduction to the Song of Songs

The task of writing a theological commentary on the Song of Songs is a daunting one. Is it the least "biblical" book in the Bible, or the most? There is in the whole book not a single overt reference to God, to prayer, or to any aspect of Israel's religious practice or tradition. Archaeological discoveries of the past century have revealed a pronounced resemblance between the Song of Songs and the love poetry of ancient Egypt. Some scholars now believe that the biblical poem originated as a popular drinking song, or perhaps a wedding song. Overwhelmingly, modern interpreters read the book as purely secular love poetry, even soft pornography. Yet, taking a longer view, Christians have through the centuries regarded the Song of Songs as one of the most religiously profound—and most difficult!—books of the Bible. Except for Genesis and the Psalms, the Song has generated more commentary than any other book of the Bible. Medieval Christians especially were fascinated by it. By the year 1200, more than one hundred commentaries had been written on the wonders and puzzles of this small book.

The approach taken in this commentary is that the Song of Songs is, in a sense, the most biblical of books. That is to say, the poet is throughout in conversation with other biblical writers. The Song itself is a comparatively late composition. Despite the ascription to Solomon, the linguistic evidence indicates that it is to be dated between the fourth and the second centuries B.C.E. As we shall see, the Song is thick with words and images drawn from earlier books. By means of this "recycled" language, the poet places this love song firmly in the context of God's passionate and troubled relationship with humanity (or, more particularly, with Israel), which is the story the rest of the Bible tells. Far from being a secular composition, the Song is profoundly revelatory. Its unique contribution to the biblical canon is to point to the healing of the deepest wounds in the created order, and even the wounds in God's own heart, made by human sin. Most briefly stated, the Song is about repairing the damage done by the first disobedience in Eden, what Christian tradition calls "the Fall."

But that statement requires some explication. According to the third chapter of Genesis, the consequence of that disobedience was a threefold rupture in the original harmony of creation. In the highly condensed language of myth, Genesis acknowledges that our fallen world is characterized by three fundamental forms of tension or alienation. First is the asymmetry of power between woman and man. Women in ancient Israel would have heard the hard truth in God's warning to Eve: "Your desire shall be for your husband, and he shall rule over you" (Gen. 3:16). The second level of alienation is between humanity and nature, represented in the cursing of the fertile soil (3:17) and the enmity between the snake and the woman (3:15). Third and most terrible, there is now a painful distance between humanity and God. The great mythic symbol of this is the expulsion of Adam and Eve from Eden, the delightful garden where they lived in God's presence and joined in God's evening stroll (3:8; "Eden" means "delight"). From a biblical perspective, the sadness in our world stems from what happened in the Garden of Eden. That mythic exile is mirrored in the most dreadful event of Israel's history, the exile to Babylon following the fall of Jerusalem in 587 B.C.E. Virtually all the books of the Bible bear traces—one might say "scars"—of the great and terrible experience of exile as a result of disobedience to God.

The theological importance of the Song is that it represents the reversal of that primordial exile from Eden. In a word, it returns us to the Garden of God. There, through the imaginative vehicle of poetry, we may experience the healing of painful rupture at all three levels. First, woman and man embrace in the full ecstasy of mutuality. Two people, equally powerful, are lost in admiration of one another—or, more accurately, in admiration they truly find themselves and each other. Second, the natural world rejoices with them. It is alive with birdsong and rampant bloom. The lovers' garden of delight is the very opposite of the harsh world into which Eve and Adam "fell," where snakebite threatens the heel (Gen. 3:15) and thorns and thistles choke the good seed (Gen. 3:18). Third and finally, as I shall try to show, the lover's garden is subtly but consistently represented as the garden of delight that Eden was meant to be, the place where life may be lived fully in the presence of God.

MULTIPLE MEANINGS

Because healing must occur at multiple levels, the language of the Song of Songs plays simultaneously upon several registers. It speaks about human love in language as exuberant, and at the same time delicate, as has ever been written. It speaks also, as the mystics have always seen, about love between the human soul and God. Further, the poem uses language and symbols that elsewhere in the Bible represent the love that obtains between God and Israel. And finally, it evokes in striking images the beautiful earth; more specifically, it evokes the geography and the flora and fauna of Israel. The land is not only the setting for the love encounter; it also becomes an object of love, especially as the perfumed mountains and lush fields of Israel are at times identified with the lovely "topography" of the woman's body.

I have tried to keep my own commentary fluid, following this quicksilver poem as it glides and skips among these several different levels of reference. In my judgment, interpreters of the Song are always in danger of becoming doctrinaire in one of two directions. Modern commentators tend to adhere rigidly to a sexual interpretation, decoding the highly metaphorical language of the Song into a series of physically explicit references. The suggestion that religious experience is part of what the poet had in mind is regarded as foreign, if not hostile, to the Song's celebration of faithful human love. Their ancient and medieval counterparts erred in the other direction. For them, the poem was an allegory, a coded account, of religious experience. So every image had to be decoded: the two breasts that are "more delightful than wine" (1:2) were the Law and the Prophets, the Old Testament and the New Testament, Christ's mercy and truth, and so on.

I have learned from these two mutually exclusive approaches yet differ from them both. I hope to show that the sexual and the religious understandings of the Song are mutually informative, and that each is incomplete without the other. For a holistic understanding of our own humanity suggests that our religious capacity is linked with an awareness of our own sexuality. Fundamental to both is a desire to transcend the confines of the self for the sake of intimacy with the other. Sexual love provides many people with their first experience of ecstasy, which literally means "standing outside oneself." Therefore the experience of healthy sexual desire can help us imagine what it might mean to love God truly—a less "natural" feeling for many of us, especially in our secular society. On the other hand, from what the Bible tells us about God's love we can come to recognize sexual love as an arena for the formation of the soul. Like the love of God, profound love of another person entails devotion of the whole self and steady practice of repentance and forgiveness; it inevitably requires of us suffering and sacrifice. A full reading of the Song of Songs stretches our minds to span categories of experience that our modern intellects too neatly separate.

Yet the Bible itself often allows the two realms of human love and religious experience to interpenetrate. It is telling that the metaphors by which the prophets—who were themselves poets—most commonly characterize God's relations with Israel are those of courtship and marriage, and also adultery, divorce, and difficult reconciliation. That the Old Testament represents God chiefly as angry judge and vicious warrior is a false stereotype. These images are not absent, but they are more than balanced by striking portrayals of God as lover or husband, infatuated with Israel beyond all reason or deserving. God is not too proud to grieve terribly over Israel's unfaithfulness, or to be giddy over her return home. These "undignified" portrayals reveal that Israel's covenant with God, like human marriage (which is also designated by the word "covenant"; see Mal. 2:14), is only secondarily a legal arrangement. Its primary quality is love at the highest pitch of intensity. Of course, the covenant can only really work if love is strong on both sides. The recurrent tragedy of biblical history is that human love and responsiveness to God repeatedly weakens and fails.

The Song of Songs answers that tragic history, stretching all the way back to Eden. What we hear throughout—and only here in the Bible—is mutual love speaking at full strength. Here there is no narrative, only dialogue; no story, only each lover singing the praises of the other. But isn't that the very essence of intense love, that it must offer praise, over and over? Lovers' talk characteristically conveys pleasure and appreciation rather than information: "I love you. . . . You are so beautiful. . . . This is great. . . . Wow!" Talking about love is itself pleasurable. We want to "tell the world"—not boasting, but cherishing, savoring. It is a fact that receives too little attention in our modern culture, which is so obsessed with the physical aspects of love: sexual enjoyment depends even more upon the giving and receiving of genuine praise than it does upon physical consummation. And praise is no less essential to the pleasure of truly loving God. The basic movement of both worship and evangelism is the overflowing of love as praise.

But still a difficulty remains. This exchange between lovers is so intimate—what are we *as the audience* supposed to do with it? Understanding that one of the lovers may be God does not really remove the problem of feeling like an awkward eavesdropper on some very private moments. It must be admitted that, while the Song is the most initially intriguing book in the Bible, claiming its thought for ourselves is very difficult. How does it invite us to share that intimacy, to claim it as one aspect of our own life with God?

CLAIMING INTIMACY

The thing that intrigues and embarrasses us about the Song—precisely the fact that its language is so private—is surely also the key to its unique value. The Song is the strongest possible affirmation of the desire for intimate, harmonious, enduring relationship with the other. The fact that it is found within the canon of scripture suggests that genuine intimacy brings us into contact with the sacred; it is the means through which human life in this world is sanctified. No generation has stood more in need of that affirmation than does the present one. Our world is groaning under the burdens of instantaneous contacts and temporary relationships, high mobility, commitments lightly undertaken and readily set aside. Too many souls are stunted, arrested in permanent adolescence. Could it be that the cultivation of real intimacy is the greatest social and spiritual challenge of our time? As we look to apply the message of the Song to our own lives, I suggest three levels at which its affirmation of the sacred significance of intimacy is required.

First and most obviously, the Song affirms as incomparable the joy of faithful sexual relationship. Thus its message stands over against our society's infatuation with constant newness, even in sexual partners. A sophisticated, urban woman, now married after many years of a "single lifestyle," reflects, "I never realized how lush sex could be, when each of you knows for sure that you are the only one." The images of the Song underscore throughout the lushness of sexual exclusivity: "I come to my garden, my sister, my bride. . . . My dove, my perfect one, is the only one" (5:1; 6:9).

In some social settings the devaluing of devoted sexuality is literally epidemic. In inner cities in North America, in war-ravaged African countries, single-parent homes have become the norm; AIDS is rampant. In my own church, an African American pastor uses the Song of Songs as a basic teaching text for the men in her congregation, asserting: "To us, it speaks an essential evangelical message: 'Cherishing your wife is manly; giving her respect and pleasure—that's cool.' "

Second, the Song affirms that longing for intimacy with God is a necessary desire for a healthy soul. It is part of our modern sickness that even regular churchgoers are not generally conscious of this desire and therefore do not nurture it. There are two kinds of love of God, both of them good. The more common one is the grateful love that we feel in response to our countless experiences of God's mercy, generosity, blessing. This is the love that prompts us to murmur, when things turn out better than we dared hope, "Thank God!" But there is another love that is even more precious. It does not come from anything God has done for us, but simply out of delight in who God is. It arises in us spontaneously because our souls were made for the love of God. One great modern teacher and mystic, Rabbi Abraham Isaac Kook, has suggested that all the rich imagery of the Song of Songs exists precisely for the sake of making vividly real this rare love which does not derive from material benefits. His teaching draws attention to one important aspect of the Song: namely, that the lover's mutual delight is completely nonutilitarian. The Song shows us love in its purest form. This is the only place in the Bible where the love between man and woman is treated without concern for childbearing or the social and political benefits of marriage. Of course, in this world, all love, including the love of God, is inevitably "tainted" by an awareness of practical benefits. Perhaps this is why the Song has no clear story line (despite the attempts of numerous commentators to give it one!). The words of the lovers are not embedded in any narrative; they are in a sense "out of this world." The Song shows us only the essence of love, isolated moments of pure desire and delight in the presence of the other.

So the Song affirms that the desire for loving intimacy both in sexual relationship and in relationship with God is fundamental to our humanity. There is a third kind of love to which its images point, namely love of a beautiful land, the land of Israel. It is a curious feature of the poem that, for all the long descriptive passages, we never get a clear picture of what the lovers look like. (It is noteworthy that they have been almost completely overlooked by painters seeking "biblical subjects.") The only portrait that emerges clearly is of the lush land bursting with spring. We can imagine what this might have meant to an ancient audience. Love of the land of Israel and its centerpoint, Jerusalem, is one of the most prominent elements of biblical thought. The Song of Songs was composed during the Persian or the Hellenistic period (fifth to third century B.C.E.), when many Israelites were scattered in foreign countries, and the rest were reduced to living in vassalage on their own land. In that situation, the Song's indirect affirmation that the land of Israel remains an object of love in God's eyes might well provide encouragement, as well as a focal point for national and religious identity.

But this suggestion about what might have been the Song's original historical setting raises a problem: what religious value can this portrait of a lovely land have for us as modern Christians? If this third kind of intimacy, love of the land, is no less essential to our humanity than sexual and religious love, then how are we to realize it in our lives? I propose that one indispensable function the Song can serve in our age is to remind us that loving attachment to land, both our particular homes and the fragile planet that we share with all other living creatures, is a religious obligation. Indeed, from a biblical perspective, it is our very first obligation to God: "And the LORD

God . . . set [Adam] in the Garden to till it and keep it" (Gen. 2:15, NRSV). In fact, that translation is somewhat misleading. The Hebrew verbs translated "till" and "keep" are not primarily agricultural terms. Rather, they occur most often in the Bible with religious reference. The first means "to work (for), to serve" a master, either human or (often) divine. The second word, "keep," is used most often in reference to observance of God's teaching, keeping God's law. The inference of the Genesis text is that, from the first, limits were attached to human use of the land. This perspective from the Garden suggests that we are not only to *observe* and *preserve* the land; we are also further told that we are to *serve* it, as one aspect of our service to the God who created both us and the land. The notion that land is something to which loving service is due is profoundly challenging to us in the industrial and postindustrial nations, who claim the right to egocentric mastery of the earth. This severe perversion of the biblical message threatens to destroy us and the earth together.

Perhaps the greatest religious value of the Song of Songs for our generation is to make the perspective from the Garden real and compelling. I suggest that the rich natural imagery of the Song is a powerful aid, first in feeling God's own love for the earth, and then in coming to share that love. Such a profound change of attitude can only come through deep prayer, and the Christian and Jewish traditions have always understood that the only way to enter into the Song is to open ourselves in prayer. Conversely, they warn that because the Song treats the things that are most essential for our humanity, failing to understand it brings us into the greatest danger. The Talmud preserves a rabbinic saying that anyone who treats the Song lightly (as a mere drinking song) "forfeits his place in the world to come and will bring evil into the world and *imperil the welfare of all humankind*." (*Tosephta Sanhedrin* 12:10, and *Baba Sanhedrin* 101a; emphasis added). That warning is astonishing; the rabbis are not given to dire threats. Could it be prophetic? The Talmudic rabbis lived centuries before recognition of a global ecological crisis. Nonetheless, they sensed that the Song has power to counter the depraved images of self and world that go back far in our history and have brought us to this present crisis.

> *Just as I have been rewarded for what I have explained, I have also been rewarded*
> *for what I have not explained.*
> —Nahum of Gimzo, *Talmud*

I do not imagine that the comments that follow *explain* the Song of Songs. Indeed, the time I have spent with this book has convinced me that anyone who thinks to explain it has understood neither its nature nor its invitation to us. The Song of Songs is, more than anything else, like a dream transcribed. The scene shifts constantly and without apparent logic; characters appear and disappear abruptly; fragmentary images are left unintegrated. Yet the images, though jumbled together and sometimes bizarre, are not random. Dream images are rooted in a personal and social history, and working with them inevitably leads below the surface of awareness, often revealing surprising connections. So it is with the Song: its images are deeply contextualized. Their roots can be traced into ancient Near Eastern religion, art, literature, and history, and the physical geography of Israel, as well as through many books of the Old Testament. Like our most important dreams, the Song reaches far back in order to say something startlingly new. Therefore it resists simple decoding and invites us instead to ponder, puzzle, draw connections, and push beyond what we thought before. In short, it encourages the vigorous exercise of the religious imagination, while assuming that our imaginations have already had some "training" in biblical tradition.

Finally, of course, the Song is not a dream. It is a poem that imitates the movement of a dream. And so we must learn to read it from poets, not psychoanalysts. The poet Archibald MacLeish points to something essential when he says:

> A poem should be palpable and mute
> As a globed fruit.
> ("Ars Poetica")

MacLeish shows us the way the Song of Songs offers itself to us to be enjoyed. Like a piece of fruit, it asks to be handled, savored, chewed. (The medieval commentators, who had particular appreciation for the Song, said that every word of scripture must be chewed slowly until, like a grain of spice, it yields its full flavor.) At the same time, a poem is in a sense "mute." It should not accost us with a message, forcing its meaning upon us. Such a use of language is not poetry but advertising, political jargon. Rather, as MacLeish goes on to say, a poem should simply "be," in order that it may, by the grace of God, teach us something about our own being.

SOLOMON'S BEST
Song of Songs 1:1

1:1 **The Song of Songs, which is Solomon's.**

Ancient tradition ascribed the Song of Songs to Solomon; the rabbis said he wrote it in his youth, when, as we know, he was highly susceptible to love. Yet the language of the book indicates that it comes from a time many centuries after Solomon, for the Hebrew poet borrows Persian and possibly Greek words. It is likely that the poet was, like the author of Ecclesiastes, a Hellenistic Jew. Furthermore, the modern debate about authorship has raised a new and interesting possibility: a number of scholars now suggest that the author is a woman. They note accurately that female characters and voices are more prominent in the Song than male. Especially, the poem foregrounds the voice and the desire of the woman called "the Shulammite" (see 6:13).

Is it really a woman speaking here, or is this (as some maintain) a man's fantasy about a woman? The question of authorship will probably never receive a definite answer. However, there is good historical reason for thinking that the poem might well be the creation of a woman. It is noteworthy that the Bible frequently associates women with song. One of their (probably unofficial) roles in the Israelite community was to sing songs of victory (Exod. 15:20–21; 1 Sam. 18:6–7) and mourning (2 Chron. 35:25; Jer. 9:17–22). Moreover, professional women singers performed at religious events (Ezra 2:65) and banquets (Eccl. 2:8). Even allowing for vast differences between ancient performers and modern ones, it seems likely that for the latter occasions, at least, they sometimes wrote and sang love songs. Perhaps one of those women went on to compose this far-more-than-ordinary song of love.

Although it is unlikely that Solomon wrote the Song, nonetheless there is a sense in which it may justly be called his. He never appears as a speaking character, yet Solomon—or Solomon's world—figures importantly in the lovers' imaginations, both positively and negatively. The woman imagines herself in the royal court with the lover she calls "the king" (1:4, 12). On the other hand, the man feels pity or contempt for Solomon, the husband of too many wives, when he himself is so happily devoted to one woman (see the comment at 8:11–12). Solomon's identity is also important in less direct ways. He is known in biblical tradition as "a man of peace" (1 Chron. 22:9) par excellence. His name itself—Hebrew *Shlomo*—echoes *shalom*, "peace, well-being." It is because Solomon is "a man of peace" (in contrast to his warrior father David) that he is qualified to build the Temple in Jerusalem. As we shall see, peace emerges as an *explicit* theme in the concluding chapters of the Song.

But it is my contention that the Song more often conveys meaning *implicitly*. Accordingly, I suspect that the most important reason the Song is called "Solomon's" lies precisely in this association with the Temple. Although the Temple in Jerusalem is never mentioned directly, I shall try to show that the cumulative effect of the language and images of the Song is to orient us toward that place of ultimate intimacy with God. Indeed, even the book's unusual title may begin pointing us in that direction. The phrase "the Song of Songs" is (grammatically) a superlative; it means "the best song." No other biblical book makes such a claim with its title; moreover, this particular grammatical formula, "the X of Xs," is rare in Hebrew. It occurs in only a few other phrases—and significantly, almost always in phrases that evoke the ultimacy and uniqueness of God. Israel's God is "God of gods and Lord of lords" (Deut. 10:17) and dwells in "the heaven of heavens" (Psalm 148:4). In fact, one of these superlatives occurs so frequently that we may assume it was a household phrase known to every Israelite: namely, "the Holy of Holies." This was the inner sanctum of the Temple, the room where the ark of the (Sinai) covenant was kept. As Isaiah's great Temple vision (Isaiah 6) shows, the Holy of Holies was conceived as the earthly counterpart of God's heavenly throne room, the place where God's majestic presence was most powerfully felt. The "spiritual voltage" there was so high that it was entered only once a year, on the Day of Atonement, and then by only one person, the high priest.

"The Song of Songs, which is Solomon's"—could this title be phrased specifically to evoke in our minds Solomon's other "superlative achievement," that place of ultimate sanctity and deepest awe? Further, perhaps the title suggests that the Song is one way of entering that holy place— even, the only way. For by the time the Song was accepted as part of the canon of scripture, in the first century of the Common Era (C.E.; the term is used here instead of the older term "A.D."), the Temple in Jerusalem had been destroyed by the Roman army. In other words, the physical focal point for prayer and pilgrimage was gone. Yet a rabbinic story suggests that some ancients believed that the Song of Songs was worthy to replace the Temple as a means of access to God.

We know that in the decades following the destruction of the Temple, the rabbis gave special attention to the questions of which religious books were to be included in the canon of scripture. This was not an academic question but the most fundamental issue of religious survival. Now without their Temple, the Jews would truly become "the people of the Book," taking the scriptures as the chief point of orientation for religious and ethnic identity. It is recorded that the rabbis debated hotly about whether to rank the Song among their holy books. Wasn't it just another bawdy drinking ditty, and maybe the worst of the lot? But the great teacher Rabbi Akiba made the defense speech that settled the matter: "All the Scriptures are holy, but the Song of Songs is the Holy of Holies" (*Mishnah Yadayim*

3:5) Maybe Akiba, himself a profound mystic, meant exactly what he said. Though the visible Temple be destroyed, through the medium of the Song, it is still possible for those who pray to enter the presence of "the King." (See further the comments at 4:1–5:1.)

Note: Since Hebrew distinguishes between the masculine and feminine pronouns "you" and "your," identity of the speaker is sometimes easier in the original text than in English translation. Where it is possible to identify the speaker with certainty, I have done so.

DESIRE AND IMAGINATION
Song of Songs 1:2–2:7

Longing for Love (Song of Songs 1:2–4)

(*Woman*)

1:2 **Let him kiss me with the kisses of his mouth!**
   For your love is better than wine,
 3 **your anointing oils are fragrant,**
   your name is perfume poured out;
   therefore the maidens love you.
 4 **Draw me after you, let us make haste.**
   The king has brought me into his chambers.
   We will exult and rejoice in you;
   we will extol your love more than wine;
   rightly do they love you.

The woman's expression of desire erupts without preface. Her exclamation catapults us into the experience of intense longing that dominates the poem. At first she lets her lover "overhear" her wish ("Let him kiss me . . ."), as though for a moment she does not dare to express her desire directly to him. The prevalence of longing over satisfaction in the poem as a whole is an important factor in its religious interpretation. Many commentators, both Jewish and Christian, have found here expressions of hope for the coming of the Messiah. Sometimes an apparent incongruity in the text provides the impetus for a nonliteral interpretation of this kind.

For example, the ancient rabbis were struck by the apparent superfluity of the phrase "of his mouth." Don't kisses by definition come from the mouth? (Some modern commentators say the contrast is with a supposed ancient Near Eastern practice of nose-kissing, an observation that is hard either to verify or to deny.) The rabbis reason thus: the mouth is the organ of speech as well as kissing. In fact, the phrase particularly recalls the giving of the Torah (God's teaching, or law) at Sinai, where God spoke to Moses "mouth to mouth" (Num. 12:8). Therefore they see the woman here as a figure for the people Israel. Whatever Moses taught the people, they forgot. So they say to Moses, "If only God would speak to us again, and 'kiss us with the kisses of his mouth,' speak even more intimately than before, that his Torah might be set in our hearts!" Moses replies that this will happen only in the age to come, that is, when the Messiah has come.

This style of Jewish interpretation, which dates back to the first century, opens the way for Christian commentators, to whom the Song speaks of the mystical marriage between Jesus Christ and the church (see Eph. 5:28–32). According to one medieval Christian reading, the bride Israel received the kiss for which she longed in the Incarnation, when at last the Divine Lover became fully and physically present to Israel.

If the woman is at first shy, she quickly grows confident, turning to her lover with a statement that is even more direct than the translation shows: "your *lovemaking* is better than wine." The Hebrew word (*dôdîm*) connotes physicality. The language of these first few lines is highly sensuous, rapidly evoking three senses: touch, taste, and smell. These three senses will guide us through the rest of the song—a fact that is noteworthy, for everywhere else in the Bible hearing and sight predominate. Even the lover's name is here more associated with scent than with sound. "Perfume poured out"— an ancient audience would immediately imagine a banquet scene, where cones of ointment placed on the heads of the guests gradually melted and filled the air with scent. They might also think of the perfumed oil with which the high priest was anointed (Psalm 133:2), and also the kings of Israel. Indeed, the title "messiah" means "anointed one." So here, too, we can see how messianic hopes take root in the Song.

This unusual emphasis on the inseparably related senses of taste and smell obviously refers to the full engagement of these senses in intimate physical lovemaking. But less obviously, they are also important for certain kinds of religious experience. Taste and smell are the senses associated with sacrifice. The odor of incense ascending to heaven was a sign of prayer; eating the meat of the sacrificial animal was a sign of fellowship with God and with fellow worshipers. The engagement of these senses is not wholly lost even in modern worship. I think of the pungent taste of communion wine breaking the night's fast, the odor of candlewax lingering in a small stone chapel, the sweet scent of Easter lilies filling a pitch-black chapel before the Vigil begins, a silent proclamation that sadness is turned to joy.

The sense of smell is peculiarly connected with the deep memory. In an instant a scent penetrates to the core of our being, stirring thoughts and feelings long forgotten, beliefs and commitments now set aside. Sights and sounds often distract us, but a memorable scent makes us genuinely reflective. Maybe it is for the sake of remembrance that the poem's first images evoke intense smells: wine and perfumed oils. Moreover, the words of the poem make a commitment to remember: "We will *keep in remembrance* (NRSV: extol) your lovemaking" (v. 4). The Old Testament throughout calls for us to remember what God done, the acts of mercy and redemption performed for the sake of love (e.g., Deut. 7:18; 8:2; 1 Chron. 16:12). Already in a few lines, the Song is pointing beyond the immediate, stretching our imaginations forward and backward in time. This love poem is surely something very different from "soft pornography."

To ears attuned to biblical idiom, another phrase stands out and points beyond a literal interpretation: "We will exult and rejoice in you" (v. 4). First, the diction is too elevated for ordinary love language. Further, if "you" is the man, then who is "we"? The best answer to the puzzle is that the whole phrase is a quotation from the religious tradition. Specifically, this is the language of public worship. The identical phrase occurs twice, in both cases referring to corporate celebration of what God has done: "This is the day that the LORD has made; let us rejoice and be glad in *him* [or, 'in *it*']" (Psalm 118:24, compare Isa. 25:9). The use of this phrase suggests, then, an "evangelical" dimension to the Song. This celebration of love is intensely personal yet also, paradoxically, a public event, in which this woman gladly shares with "the maidens" (v. 3) her rejoicing in "the king."

The Woman Introduces Herself (Song of Songs 1:5–8)

(*Woman*)
1:5 I am black and beautiful,
    O daughters of Jerusalem,
    like the tents of Kedar,
    like the curtains of Solomon.
 6 Do not gaze at me because I am dark,
    because the sun has gazed on me.
    My mother's sons were angry with me;
    they made me keeper of the vineyards,
    but my own vineyard I have not kept!
 7 Tell me, you whom my soul loves,
    where you pasture your flock,

> where you make it lie down at noon;
> for why should I be like one who is veiled
> beside the flocks of your companions?

(Man)

> 8 If you do not know,
> O fairest among women,
> follow the tracks of the flock,
> and pasture your kids
> beside the shepherds' tents.

The woman's proud assertion that she is "black *and* beautiful" (v. 5) has been brought into modern usage by the African American community. In that context, as well as in the biblical text, the assertion is an answer to disdain—or, at the very least, it corrects a misconception. The disdain the woman anticipates (v. 6) is not ethnically motivated; there is no indication anywhere in the Song that she is not herself a "daughter of Jerusalem." Rather, it is a matter of social class. Whereas in our society a good tan may advertise that one has enough money for vacations at the beach, in the ancient world it marked a person as a peasant. The wealthy could afford to stay indoors, while hired laborers worked in the fields. But the woman here chooses images that prove darkness to be part of her allure. She is black like the goats' hair tents of the Kedarites, a nomadic Arabian tribe famed for their power and splendor (Isa. 21:16–17). She is beautiful as Solomon's curtains. Significantly, the only curtain described in the Bible is indeed Solomon's. It hung in the Temple before the Holy of Holies, woven of fine linen with blue, purple, and crimson threads, embroidered with cherubim (2 Chron. 3:14). These are the glories to which the woman is to be compared.

Verse 6 introduces the theme of opposition, threat, and punishment that recurs throughout the Song. The woman has been forced to tend her brothers' vineyards at the expense of her own. It is unlikely that she means "my own vineyard" literally. Israelite women did not generally own land, and furthermore, "vineyard" is elsewhere in the Song a figurative term for the woman in her desirability (see 8:12). The woman, then, complains that she has not had time to make *herself* desirable for her lover.

The vineyard is a common biblical metaphor for one particular object of desire: namely Israel, God's special planting in the holy land (Psalm 80:8; compare Exod. 15:17). Sometimes the vineyard is a source of bitter disappointment to God. In language close to that of the Song, Isaiah sings "for my beloved my love-song concerning his vineyard" (Isa. 5:1), which repaid careful tending with a yield of scrub grapes. Hosea compares Israel to a luxuriant vine whose fruits were shamefully offered to foreign gods (Hos. 10:1). Against this background, recurrent emphasis on care of this vineyard and proper disposition of its fruits (2:15; 6:11; 7:12; 8:12) suggests that at one level the Song is reversing the painful history the prophets recount.

The medieval Christian commentator Gregory the Great interprets this passage at a different level. He produces a spiritual interpretation that speaks to every age. Gregory argues that the brothers' vineyards stand for worldly affairs. The woman is here the awakened soul, who now sees how much time "she" has wasted on things that did not matter: "My vineyard, that is, my soul, my life, my mind, I have neglected to care for: for while I was absorbed outside myself in the business of worldly affairs, I failed to keep watch over things within" (cited in Denys Turner, *Eros and Allegory*, 243). Is there any of us, however mature in the spiritual life, who does not waste time on things that do not make us more desirable to God?

Again she turns to her lover. The somewhat contrived way that she addresses him—"you whom *my soul loves*"—appears four more times in the Song (see the comment at 3:1–4). Therefore it is surely meant to make an impression on the hearer. Here the Song's language for the first time echoes strongly other biblical love language, namely the commandment to "*love* the LORD your God with all your heart, and with all *your soul*, and with all your might" (Deut. 6:5). The suggestion that anyone is supposed to catch an echo like this, let alone make something of it, may seem strange to modern readers. That is because we are far from the sensibilities of an oral culture such as ancient Israel, where few people had books (more accurately, scrolls). Most literature, including religious texts, circulated orally. Read aloud and repeated, it became engrained in the public memory. Sadly, the best analogy for many of us is television advertisements, which are so familiar that anyone can make reference to them by quoting just a few words.

The fact that this beloved-of-the-soul is a shepherd further reinforces his identification with God. The Old Testament, like the New, frequently portrays God as the Good Shepherd. Verse 7 makes a specific verbal connection with the most extended of these Old Testament passages, from the prophet Ezekiel: "I myself will be shepherd of my sheep, and *I will make them lie down*, says the Lord GOD" (Ezek. 34:15; see also the same verb in Psalm 23:2). At the same time, the poet seems to be playing with the theme of love between a human shepherd boy and girl, which has engaged many lyric poets from ancient times up to the nineteenth century. The shepherd couple is appealing because they are supposedly untainted by the artificiality of city life. Something of this contrast between city and country folk may be present here as well. The challenge to "the daughters of Jerusalem" already suggests what will become more evident as the poem develops: The city is a place of tension and even suffering for the lovers.

The woman may already feel some anxiety when she asks, "Tell me . . . where you pasture your flock." The reason she gives here—"for why should I be like one who is veiled . . . ?"—is obscure. Is she afraid of being taken for a prostitute? In fact, that is exactly how the city guards will treat her when she goes out at night to seek her lover (5:7–8). Many ancient versions reflect another reading, in which two Hebrew letters are transposed to read "one who loses her way." This emendation accords better with the lover's reply (v. 8) and also with Israel's long history of losing her way to God.

Echoing Praise (Song of Songs 1:9–17)

(*Man*)
> 1:9 I compare you, my love [Hebrew "*ra'yatî*"],
> to a mare among Pharaoh's chariots.
> 10 Your cheeks are comely with ornaments,
> your neck with strings of jewels.
> 11 We will make you ornaments of gold,
> studded with silver.

(*Woman*)
> 12 While the king was on his couch,
> my nard gave forth its fragrance.
> 13 My beloved [Hebrew, *dôdî*] is to me a bag of myrrh
> that lies between my breasts.
> 14 My beloved is to me a cluster of henna blossoms
> in the vineyards of En-gedi.

(*Man*)
> 15 Ah, you are beautiful, my love;
> ah, you are beautiful;
> your eyes are doves.

(*Woman*)
> 16 Ah, you are beautiful, my beloved,
> truly lovely.
> Our couch is green;

¹⁷ **the beams of our house are cedar,
our rafters are pine.**

The lovers engage in a dialogue of mutual admiration. They seem to be engaged in something like a poetic competition, as each one strives to find an image that captures the delightfulness of the other. Then the competition is resolved when the same words of praise—"Ah, you are beautiful!" (vv. 15–16)—are spoken first by the man and then by the woman. The echo expresses the full reciprocity of their love relationship. But their expressions are not quite identical. Each calls the other by a distinctive term of endearment. These are not adequately rendered by the NRSV translation, "my love" and "my beloved"—as though they used active and passive forms of the same word. She calls him *dôdî*, "my darling, my lover." He most often calls her "my comrade/friend" (*ra'yatî*), a term that implies a relationship of equality, an erotic friendship (compare the French *petite amie*, "sweetheart," which is literally, "little friend").

It is important to observe that nowhere in the Song is there a hint of male condescension to "the weaker sex." The woman appears in the man's eyes always as a figure of beauty; but he frequently, as here, chooses images that emphasize her strength, her powerful and even daunting (see 6:5, 10) attractiveness. The comparison to "a mare among Pharaoh's chariots" (v. 9) is among the strangest of these compliments. The poet seems to be referring to a well-known incident of ancient military history, when an enemy general sent a mare in heat running into the stallions that drew Pharaoh's chariots. The inference here seems to be: "You drive men wild!" We might guess that the image was as easy for the original audience to understand as the phrase "like Grant took Richmond" (to characterize a particularly forceful movement) is to us.

The man then takes up a gentler image: "Your eyes are doves" (v. 15). The ancients used doves as a symbol of loveplay; similarly, we speak of lovers "billing and cooing." But the modern reader is likely to miss the fact that there is a mythic dimension here that adds strength to the image. Doves were the messenger birds of the powerful love goddess Ishtar (the Eastern counterpart to the Greek Aphrodite). The Israelite poet may have seen art objects and even (in foreign travels) temples decorated with the goddess's doves. Nevertheless the poet shows no fear of the pagan associations, for the image appears several times in the Song (2:14; 4:1; 5:2, 12; 6:9). Rather, as great religious artists often do, she adapts old symbols to new contexts. Here the goddess's doves are transmuted into animated human eyes that convey messages of love.

The woman, for her part, imagines the "house" that the lovers share. (In fact, the woman is still living with her mother; see 8:2.) She envisions them lying in great groves of standing evergreens. It is no local Lover's Lane to which she refers. Evergreen forests were found, not immediately around ancient Jerusalem, but in the mountains of the Lebanon ridge far to the north. Here again, the poet may be evoking images of the divine from pagan myth, which represents the gods making love on mountain peaks (e.g., the Greek gods Zeus and Hera on Mount Ida) or among cypress (another likely translation for the tree named in v. 17b) and cedar. As the poet may well have known, cypress and cedar figure in the "sacred marriage rite," an erotic ceremony enacted by the Mesopotamian king and the priestess of Ishtar in order to ensure fertility. But cedar and cypress are memorable also within Israel's own tradition. Specifically, they appear in the lengthy descriptions of Solomon's buildings, such as "the House of the Forest of the Lebanon" and especially the Temple (1 Kings 6:15–18; 7:2–3, 7), which was lined floor-to-ceiling in fragrant woods from the northern forests. The woman's language blurs the distinction between indoors and outdoors (e.g., "our couch is green" v. 16). So also does the language and imagery associated with the Temple. On the one hand, it is "the house" par excellence in biblical tradition, the place where God's name dwells (1 Kings 8:48). On the other hand, the symbolism of the Temple strongly suggests that it was conceived as a place of great *natural* beauty, a forest or garden (see the comment at 4:8–15). The lovers' evergreen house evokes that dual aspect of the Temple.

Brief as they are, the images in this passage—eyes as doves and house as forest—serve two functions. First, they elevate the experience of human lovers to the level of the divine. Such elevation is not necessarily either blasphemous or idolatrous (although this is a danger of which lovers should be aware). Human love always pushes toward transcendence. Profound delight in the other person whose soul seems to complete mine moves me some distance out of the self-absorption that seems to be the natural human condition. This movement of self-transcendence is the thing that makes sexual love the least inadequate metaphor and model for the love that we may hope to feel for God, the love that the saints and martyrs *do* feel. Therefore images such as those in this passage may serve a second function. Just because they do hint at divinity, they may push us to imagine and aspire to a love that is wholly transcendent, directed toward the One who is wholly Other than ourselves, whose very being is Perfection, who nonetheless desires to be loved by us.

The Flowering of Love (Song of Songs 2:1–13)

2:1 I am a rose [*havatselet*] of Sharon,
　　 a lily [*shôshannah*] of the valleys.
　2 As a lily among brambles,
　　 so is my love among maidens.

　3 As an apple tree among the trees of the wood,
　　 so is my beloved among young men.
　　 With great delight I sat in his shadow,
　　 and his fruit was sweet to my taste.
　4 He brought me to the banqueting house,
　　 and his intention toward me was love.
　5 Sustain me with raisins,
　　 refresh me with apples;
　　 for I am faint with love.
　6 O that his left hand were under my head,
　　 and that his right hand embraced me!
　7 I adjure you, O daughters of Jerusalem,
　　 by the gazelles or the wild does:
　　 do not stir up or awaken love until it is ready!

　8 The voice of my beloved!
　　 Look, he comes,
　　 leaping upon the mountains,
　　 bounding over the hills.
　9 My beloved is like a gazelle
　　 or a young stag.
　　 Look, here he stands
　　 behind our wall,
　　 gazing in at the windows,
　　 looking through the lattice.
　10 My beloved speaks and says to me:
　　 "Arise, my love, my fair one,
　　 and come away;
　11 for now the winter is past,
　　 the rain is over and gone.
　12 The flowers appear on the earth;
　　 the time of singing has come,
　　 and the voice of the turtledove
　　 is heard in our land.
　13 The fig tree puts forth its figs,

> **and the vines are in blossom;**
> **they give forth fragrance.**
> **Arise, my love, my fair one,**
> **and come away."**

Although "rose of Sharon" and "lily-of-the-valley" are familiar names, there is no firm agreement among scholars on the correct botanical identification of the two wildflowers named here. What is certain, however, and probably more important to our poet, is their symbolic significance within biblical tradition. The same two flowers appear in the Prophets, and specifically in Hosea and Isaiah, the prophetic books of which the poet of the Song seems most mindful. There they appear as symbols of Zion's beauty, restored after a time of alienation from God and devastation by enemies. Isaiah says the wilderness shall "blossom like the *havatselet*" (Isa. 35:2), translated here as "rose." Hosea represents God as saying:

> I will *love* them *generously.* . . .
> I will be like the *dew* to *Israel;*
> he shall *blossom* like the *lily* [*shôshannah*]. . . .
> They shall again *sit* (or, "*return* to sit") *in his* [God's] *shadow* . . .
> and *blossom* like the *vine,*
> and his *remembrance* (i.e., "fragrance") shall be like the *wine* of *Lebanon.*
> (Hos. 14:4, 5, 7 [in Hebrew 14:5, 6, 8], AT)

Virtually every term (noted in italics) in Hosea's lyrical description of restored Israel finds an echo in the Song, many of them in the present passage. Hosea's message is that Israel's fertility comes solely from its God, and not from the Canaanite fertility gods after whom its people "whored." To underscore the point, God, Israel's true lover, makes bold to take over the language and imagery of the fertility cults: "*I* am like an evergreen cypress [a Canaanite sacred symbol]; *from me* comes your fruit" (Hos. 14:9; see the comment on Song 1:16–17). Could it be that God's promise of "generous love," so fervently expressed in the final chapter of Hosea, is fulfilled here, when the woman sits "with great delight *in his shadow*" (see. Hos. 14:7; Hebrews 8)?

The profusion of flowers which is such a prominent feature of the Song also supports the view that the Song represents the culmination of Hosea's and Isaiah's visions of Israel restored. For both prophets, the blooming of Israel's semi-arid landscape is a sign (or a metaphor, a poetic image) of the people Israel restored to faithful covenant relationship with their God. Probably the Song's portrayal of a land in fragrant bloom, the lovers themselves as flowers, is likewise to be seen as a theological statement, and not just a sort of ancient verbal Valentine. There is an Edenic quality to the description of the blooming land, here and throughout the Song. The lovers imagine the land of Israel in its fullest bloom, but beyond that they imagine an exotic landscape, fragrant with the scents of distant lands (see 4:13–14). This super-naturalistic picture, which exceeds the bounty of any one place on earth, may be seen as an imaginative return to paradise, the Garden of God. In other words, the Song accomplishes the full reversal of the cursing of the fertile soil after the first human disobedience, when it is condemned to bring forth thorns and thistles (Gen. 3:18). Thus the fertile soil (Hebrew, *adamah*) from which the human (Hebrew, *adam*) was taken, symbolically bears the "offspring's" ugly produce. But now "the winter is past" (v. 13), the long season when love between humanity and God, Israel and God, was cold. In view of the preceding section, in which the lovers exchange equal praises, the Edenic landscape also signals a restoration of the relationship between man and woman, which since the Fall has been damaged by blame and an asymmetry of power (Gen. 3:12, 16; see further the comment at 7:10).

Each lover asserts the singularity of the other (vv. 2–3), a theme that is of great importance in this book (see 5:9; 6:9; 8:11–12). Singularity is an important theme in Israelite theology, which continually stresses the uniqueness both of Israel's God and of God's choice of Israel. The woman is "a lily among brambles" or (traditionally) "a rose among thorns," a phrase that has entered English colloquial speech. It has also entered the Christian theological tradition. Medieval Christians celebrated the Virgin Mary as a rose in folk hymns (e.g., "Lo, How a Rose E'er Blooming"). As we can see, they were drawing upon an imaginative tradition, already in their time many centuries old, that salvation blossoms forth among the "thorns" of human sinfulness and grief. Applying the image to the Virgin, medieval commentators identified the thorns variously as gossiping tongues aimed at a pregnant teenager, unbelieving Judeans who rejected their own Messiah, or the mother's own agony at the crucifixion.

"As an apple tree . . . ": There is much debate about the proper identification of the tree with which the man is compared. In favor of the traditional translation is the association of apples with love and sexual potency in ancient Mesopotamian texts. This association has long continued in popular lore. Its faint echo is heard even in the (relatively) modern song: "Don't Sit under the Apple Tree with Anyone Else but Me." Against this translation is the botanical objection that the apple may not be native to Israel. At any rate, wild apples are acid, not sweet. The apricot has been suggested as a substitute. The scientific issue remains uncertain, but the suggestion makes good poetic sense. A sun-ripened apricot is a sensual delight, being rich in color, scent, taste, and even touch, as it almost literally melts in the mouth ("his fruit was sweet to my *palate*," v. 3).

The banqueting house (literally, "house of wine," v. 4) is a figurative expression here; she imagines a private meeting place, not a public drinking house. The NRSV translation of the next line is dubious, as it involves emending the sense of a well-known noun; the most obvious reading is, "his *banner over* me is love." The latter reading is fully intelligible as a poetic image, especially in light of the similar image in Psalm 20:5: "In the name of our God [may we] set up our banners." In both cases, the banner signifies a disposition of special regard and protection for the one over whom it flies, as well as vindication in the face of opposition. Moreover, the image as it appears in the psalm anticipates a military victory. This is apt, for we have already seen that the Shulammite's brothers are domineering if not hostile, and they are not her only opponents! (The image of the banner is picked up again in 6:4, 10.)

The NRSV translation implies that verse 6 is an unfulfilled wish, but the Hebrew can more readily be read as a statement of fact: "His left hand is under my head." The couple is already embracing, and therefore she is happily "weak/faint with love." The address to the "daughters of Jerusalem" (v. 7) is therefore not genuine dialogue. The Jerusalemite women play throughout the Song a role similar to that of the chorus in Greek drama. They are not central characters; indeed, they have no personality at all. Nevertheless, they provide another vantage point for viewing the actions of and relations among the main characters. They are the audience within the poem to whom the female lover regularly turns, in her imagination if not in reality, to explain or defend herself. Thus they serve as a foil to bring her thoughts and feelings to articulation.

We have seen that the poet does not hesitate to reuse pagan images and language (see the comment at 1:9–17). The formulation of verse 6 may owe something to the language of the ancient Mesopotamian fertility cult. A line in a hymn celebrating the sacred marriage of the fertility gods Dumuzi and Inanna reads bluntly:

> Your right hand you have placed on my vulva,
> Your left stroked my head.
> (Kramer, *Sacred Marriage Rite*, 105)

Despite similarity in rhythm and content, there is a pronounced difference in tone from the Song. With all its exuberant sensuality, the biblical text is nonetheless comparatively modest. If the "marriage" in the Song is ever physically consummated, we are told that only indirectly (5:1). Maybe the reason for the difference is this: in contrast to the fertility cult, the Song has no "practical" interest in sexual intercourse. Here fertility is not at issue. No mention is ever made of children, which is elsewhere in the Bible treated as the most important outcome of human love. With respect to the symbolical importance of sex, biblical religion sets itself firmly against the pagan notion that human intercourse (or divine-human intercourse, ritually enacted) magically insures the fertility of the soil. Love in the Song is not a means to an end. All that is to be gained from love is the delight of intimacy itself. This "nonutilitarian" view of love applies equally to the relationship between woman and man and that between Israel and its God. As Hosea makes clear, God is not a fertility god who can be ritually manipulated into granting favors. "He" is a passionate lover who will settle for nothing less than Israel's faithful love. If the echo with the pagan rite is deliberate, then the Song may be seen as both parody and refutation of its distortion of love.

In strange and formal language reminiscent of soothsayers (v. 7), the woman calls on the daughters of Jerusalem to take an oath. Both the formulaic saying and its later repetitions at 3:5 and 8:4 draw attention to the seriousness of the admonition not to "stir up love" (on this warning, see further at 3:5). The form of the oath is without parallel in the Bible. Here animals are named where one might expect to find the name of God! Some commentators argue that the substitution is deliberately irreverent, or at least it shows how secular is the lovers' perspective; the presence of God in the world of love never enters their mind. Yet similar oaths occur—a thousand years after the Song—in the early poems of Mohammed, the Prophet of Islam (seventh century C.E.). Certainly these poems express serious religious intent, yet in them even God swears oaths that invoke powerful animals:

> By the chargers as they snort,
> And those who with their hooves strike sparks of fire,
> And those who dash forth in the early morning.
>
> (*Qur'an*, Sura 100)

The meaning of such oaths is obscure, in the *Qur'an* as in the Song. However, there are indications that the poet of the Song has composed the oath carefully, choosing animals to suit this particular context. Wild deer are images of freedom, beauty, strength, and also unapproachability. These qualities qualified them to serve as the sacred animals of Astarte, the Canaanite love goddess. Moreover, the book of Proverbs indicates that for Israelites, too, the "lovely deer" was a common image for sexual attractiveness (see Prov. 5:19).

A more subtle reason for the choice of these animals may lie in their

Hebrew names, all of which lend themselves to complex wordplay. First, the word *tsvî*, "gazelle," has a homonym, identically spelled, which means "beauty." In this sense, it is frequently applied to Israel, "the land of beauty" (Dan. 11:16, 41)—or "the land of the gazelle—and more particularly to the Temple Mount of Jerusalem (Dan. 11:45). Furthermore, both animal names bear a resemblance to divine titles. The first term, *tsva'ot* ("gazelles") is an unusual plural form of *tsvî* (one would expect *tsva'îm*). Very likely the poet has altered it in order to produce a form that is identical with the word for "(heavenly) hosts," as in the common title *Adonai Tsva'ot*, "Lord of Hosts." The second phrase, *'aylot hassadeh* ("wild does"), has nearly the same consonants as the title El Shaddai, sometimes rendered as "God Almighty" (Gen. 17:1, etc.).

In later times, pious Jews avoided swearing by the divine name and substituted meaningless phrases; modern believers may continue this practice (often unconsciously) but using a phrase such as "by gosh and by golly." Maybe we see the origin of this practice here in the woman's oath, but the words she substitutes are not wholly meaningless. Rather, it seems likely that the poet's supple mind is playing with these several associations, linking deer to the freedom and the beauty of both man and woman, and further to the land of Israel, and further yet even to divinity.

It is intriguing that the fifteenth-century Spanish Christian mystic John of the Cross saw an image of God in the representation of the male lover as a leaping deer (vv. 8–9; see also 2:17; 8:14). Although he would not have understood the Hebrew wordplay, he recognizes here a true picture of the way the faithful often experience God's presence—or absence. In his *Spiritual Canticle*, a dream poem deeply influenced by the Song of Songs, he meditates on "the swiftness with which he shows and then hides himself. He usually visits devout souls in order to gladden and liven them, and then leaves them in order to try, humble, and teach them" (*Collected Works*, 484).

SEEKING, FINDING
Song of Songs 3:1–5

(*Woman*)

3:1   **Upon my bed at night**
     I sought him whom my soul loves;
     I sought him, but found him not;
     I called him, but he gave no answer.
  2 **"I will arise now and go about the city,**
     in the streets and in the squares;

I will seek him whom my soul loves."
I sought him, but found him not.
3 The sentinels found me,
as they went about in the city.
"Have you seen him whom my soul loves?"
4 Scarcely had I passed them,
when I found him whom my soul loves.
I held him, and would not let him go
until I brought him into my mother's house,
and into the chamber of her that conceived me.
5 I adjure you, O daughters of Jerusalem,
by the gazelles or the wild does:
do not stir up or awaken love until it is ready!

Most lovers know the experience of longing in the night, when even a routine absence of the beloved may seem intolerable. Although there is no indication of a rupture between these lovers, eagerness turns to anxiety as the woman twice says, "I sought him, but found him not." The most striking feature of her speech is how she describes the one she seeks: "him whom my soul loves." This is not how people ordinarily report missing persons to the police (v. 3). Moreover, the awkward phrase is repeated here four times (vv. 1, 2, 3, 4; see also 1:7); obviously it is not just a slip of the tongue. In fact, it seems to be a deliberate and insistent echo of another biblical passsage, the one that Jesus named as "first of all" the commandments: "You shall *love* the LORD your God with all your heart, and with all your *soul*, and with all your might" (Deut. 6:5; Mark 12:28–30).

That repeated echo of the weightiest verse in the Old Testament confirms—in my judgment, beyond reasonable doubt—that at one level of the poet's meaning, the one who is loved and sought after so intently is God. The poet's original hearers would make this association in the present passage more easily than we do, because they were familiar with biblical idiom. And as the biblical writers recount Israel's history with God, they highlight the theme of seeking and finding—or perhaps, not finding. In some instances, "seek" (*biqesh*) is a technical term for making oracular inquiry (Exod. 33:7). More generally, it denotes the desire for genuine life that should draw Israel to her God. In Moses' final address to the Israelites, which anticipates their disobedience and exile from the land of Israel, he offers them this assurance of return: "From [a foreign land] you will seek (*biqesh*) the LORD your God, and you will find him if you search after him with all your heart and *soul*" (Deut. 4:29; see also Jer. 29:13). Yet often Israel refuses to seek her God (Isa. 9:13; 31:1) and perversely runs after what Hosea calls "her lovers," that is, foreign idols. But that search is doomed to futility. In language that closely resembles the woman's sad complaint here, the prophet warns: "She [Israel] shall seek them, but shall not find them" (Hos. 2:7; see the comment on 2:1–13 for other close connections between Hosea and the Song). In an especially poignant passage, an exilic prophet shows us God's anguish at Israel's religious failure:

> I was ready to be sought out
> by those who did not ask,
> to be found by those who did not seek me.
> I said, "Here I am, here I am!"
> to a nation that did not call on my name.
> (Isa. 65:1)

The woman's account of her anxious search should be heard against the background of these prophetic promises, complaints, warnings. If at one level of interpretation the woman in the Song represents the people Israel, then it seems that one thing we must understand from this passage is that God is not "an easy catch." At this moment, even though it seems that the woman's desire is properly focused on her true lover, "the one whom [her] soul loves" is not ready to be found. But, as John of the Cross perceived (see the previous section), God's elusiveness may itself serve to test and strengthen spiritual love. And, as we shall see in chapter 5, the woman's love, even though properly focused on her true lover, is not yet wholly constant. Many human lovers have learned from difficult experience that the very fear of losing the one who seems to have turned away may itself purify our desire and make it durable (see 8:6). Often maturity comes only when we "wake up" to the anxious but ultimately life-giving discovery that this love has become indispensable to us.

The initial phrase—"*Upon my bed at night* I sought him "—also points to a nonliteral interpretation for the theme of seeking and finding. Certainly an unmarried Israelite woman living with her mother could not realistically seek and expect to find her lover in her bed! But in biblical idiom, the bed signifies more than sleep and lovemaking. It is also a place of prayer, where God is sought, intently and sometimes in great anxiety, and revelations are granted (Psalm 4:5; 6:6 [Heb. 7]; 22:2 [Heb. 3]; 119:62; 149:5; Job 33:15; compare Hos. 7:14).

Part of the witness of the Song, then, is that God is not always ready to be found. But if frustration is a necessary part of our search for God, that does not make it any easier to bear. Teresa of Avila (1515–1582), the great Spanish mystic and monastic reformer, speaks with remarkable candor about the frustration that even a saint feels in seeking after God. She complains that a busy mother superior has too little time for contemplation—and when she finds it, God often seems to be hiding. Thus she forcefully confronts "His Majesty": "How is this compatible with Your mercy? How can the love You bear me allow this? I believe, Lord, that if it were possible for me to hide from You as it is for You to hide from me, that the love You have for me would not suffer it; but You are with me and see me always! Don't tolerate this, my Lord! I implore You to see that it is injurious to one who loves You so much" (*The Book of Her Life* 37.8, in *The Collected Works of St. Teresa of Avila*, 1:255). For boldness in love, Teresa is a match for the woman in the Song. And maybe it was from the Song that "the Madre" learned her boldness. For her, as for her friend John of the Cross (see the previous section), this was the most important book of the Bible. Teresa's *Meditations on the Song of Songs* remain to this day one of most engaging interpretations ever written.

A seemingly futile search, and then suddenly—there he is! The picture of the woman grabbing her lover and pulling him through the streets to her mother's house is humorous, and distinctly countercultural. An unmarried women was expected to stay at home, in what was commonly called "the father's house," until a suitable mate was found *for* her, by her parents or perhaps by her older brothers (see Song 8:8). The alternate expression, "mother's house" (v. 4) occurs only twice in the Bible, here and in the book of Ruth (1:8). Significantly, these are the two books that most consistently represent the world through women's eyes. The mother is in fact the only parent mentioned in the Song. Moreover, she is mentioned seven times, a number which in biblical symbolism signifies completeness. In a composition as sophisticated as this one, we should infer that the poet is spotlighting the mother in a deliberate way.

In what connections does she appear here? First, the mother is represented as the source of nurturance (6:9), identity (1:6; 3:11), of life itself (8:1, 2, 5). We know that after the exile, with the end of the monarchy and Israel's political independence, the home became crucial for maintaining national and even religious identity. Probably most education took place in the home, and in this the mother played a central role (Prov. 1:8). The poet of the Song underscores the powerful presence of women in Israelite society and consciousness. If, as is likely, the poet is a Hellenistic Jew (see the introduction), then the Song may be deliberately countering the Greek philosophers' negative treatment of women. They argued in cool rational terms that women were of a different species than men, and distinctly inferior. (The gradual influence of these Greek ideas upon Jews may be detected in the apostle Paul's dictum that women should be silent in church [1 Cor. 14:34]). By contrast, the Song of Songs upholds the position set forth in the first chapter of the Bible, that women and men are equally created in the image of God (see Gen. 1:27).

Bringing her man into her mother's bedchamber seems overly bold even for the most determined young woman. But the emphatic expression "to the house of my *mother*, to the chamber of *her that conceived me*" (v. 4) makes sense when we recognize that the poem's unusual focus on the mother may reflect more than social circumstance. Probably it has a symbolic dimension as well. In both Testaments, a major city (2 Sam. 20:19) or a nation (Ezek. 16:3) is imaged as "mother"—again, the source of nurturance and identity. Most importantly, this image characterizes Jerusalem (Gal. 4:26) and the nation Israel (Isa. 50:1; 54:1; Hos. 2:2, 5 [Heb. 4, 7]). That seems to be one aspect of its meaning in the Song. The best evidence for that is the fact that the italicized words in verse 4 seem to be quoted from the prophet Hosea, upon whose words, as we have seen, the poet has dwelt deeply. Thus Hosea denounces Israel's infidelity: "For their *mother* has played the whore, *she who conceived them* has acted shamefully" (2:5; Heb. 7). It is probable that with this echo the poet of the Song intends to reverse that old and shameful image. Once the "mother"—the nation, and especially, in the eyes of the prophets, its leaders—sinned, and as a result all her children suffered exile and enduring national shame. Now the lover is coming into the mother's house, and even her private chamber. Could this suggest the Temple itself, the "house" of Mother Israel, the place of greatest intimacy? As we shall see, in chapter 4 there is an abundance of phrases which, to ears attuned to biblical idiom, strongly suggest that the poet's imagination is ultimately directed toward the Temple. With hints such as this one, that do not quite make sense at the literal level, we are being challenged to develop our own poetic imagination and follow the poet "on pilgrimage."

Concluding the section (v. 5) is the second occurrence of the strange oath addressed to the daughters of Jerusalem. We have previously considered its odd form (see the comment at 2:7); now it is time to consider the possible meaning of the prohibition, "Do not stir up or awaken love until it is ready!" The wording is ambiguous in Hebrew as in English. On the one hand, the woman may intend to prohibit *disturbance*. She pleads to be left alone with her lover until love is sated. That meaning is self-evident and requires no further comment.

But a second and nearly opposite meaning is also possible. The woman may be warning against the untimely *stimulation* of love. In that case, she who is experienced in happy love is offering advice to the Jerusalem women and to us: "Wait for love, do not rush it." She is warning against the temptation to court the passion of love. Falling in love with love is common for the young and easy enough at any age. Our culture romanticizes—in movies and television, popular songs and novels—the fiery passion of love, to which we fall helpless victim. Even the love of God may be romanticized, and so a small industry thrives on producing soupy religious greeting cards and worship music that mimics popular love songs.

Although the Song is certainly not afraid of passion, it exposes that sentimental view of love as an illusion. Genuine love does not just happen to us. The woman's repeated phrase—"the one whom *my soul loves*"—alerts us to the truth: love is soul-work, of the most demanding kind. Cultivating a true love relationship, with a person or with God, calls forth sustained effort from the core of our being. Therefore the soul must be prepared, even trained, to love well, just as the body must be trained for rigorous physical action. Faithful sexual love, like the love of God, requires that we learn habits of self-examination and repentance, that we acquire a capacity for self-sacrifice and forgiveness. The stories of David and Bathsheba (2 Samuel 11) and Amnon and Tamar (2 Samuel 13) are strong reminders within the Bible that where love is merely passion, and not the action of a well-prepared soul, the consequences are often disastrous.

"Do not stir up or awaken love until it is ready!" Our secular society gives the contrary advice, urging every unattached (or unsatisfied) person to be on the lookout for sexual love and offering countless tips on how to kindle its flame. In reaction, the church worries about how to contain the worse effects of raging passion. Virtually every modern church, whether liberal or conservative, is centrally occupied with "sexuality issues": infidelity, pederasty, harassment, the legitimacy of homosexual relations and premarital sex. The church needs to be concerned with these matters. But would not our spiritual vision be clearer, and our proclamation of the gospel be more persuasive, if we gave more attention to the bedrock ethical issue to which the woman's words directs us: How do we make our souls ready for love? How does the passion of love enter into character and become stabilized as a habitual disposition of loving? What can the church do to foster the soul-work that "let[s] love be genuine" (Rom. 12:9)? Imagine what a change would occur in the household of God if those questions were established at the heart of our common life, and all of us—youths and adults, single and married, seekers after human love partners and seekers after God—were committed to finding answers and living them out together.

UP FROM THE WILDERNESS
Song of Songs 3:6

3:6 **What is that coming up from the wilderness,**
like a column of smoke,
perfumed with myrrh and frankincense,
with all the fragrant powders of the merchant?

The NRSV treats this verse as the introduction to a section that continues through verse 11. According to this arrangement, the answer to the question posed here is given in verse 7: "Look, it is the litter of Solomon!" The problem with this interpretation is that the question does not read (in Hebrew), "*What* is *that* . . . ?" Rather, it is unambiguously "*Who* is *this* (a feminine singular pronoun) . . . ?" A person, not a thing, is in view, and specifically a female. Therefore the following description of Solomon's litter (or bed) does not fit as an answer to the question, and it seems best to regard verse 6 as standing on its own. This is a rhetorical question that receives no answer and thus leaves suspended in the mind of the hearer one of the most haunting images of the Song.

Who speaks here is uncertain: perhaps the women of the royal harem? They pose the similar question in 6:10 and are mentioned in the passage immediately following here. However, in the kaleidescope of images that is the Song, it is not necessary or even possible to determine the speaker and the exact setting for each. The important thing is the image itself: a lovely woman coming up from the wilderness (see also 8:5).

Yet that picture does not seem to fit here. The rest of the poem locates the lovers in the streets and houses of Jerusalem and its immediately surrounding fields. When they are in the natural world, it is in garden or a forest (1:17), not the desert wilderness. But, as often happens in this dream-poem with its odd juxtapositions, the misfit is itself a clue to interpretation. A piece that stands out oddly in its immediate context prods us to think associatively, not in a narrow literal way. It jogs our memory and sends us back to the biblical story to find the appropriate context for seeing its meaning.

"Who is this coming up from the wilderness . . . ?"—the question resounds deeply with the biblical tradition of Israel entering into the Promised Land after forty years in the wilderness. The Song of Songs is one of the latest books of the biblical canon. Moreover, in the order of the Jewish Bible (which differs from that of the NRSV), it is placed near the end. Both chronologically and literarily, then, our poet's question follows upon hundreds of references to Israel's wilderness journey in the Torah and Prophets. There can be doubt about the identity of this "female." This is the bride Israel. The wilderness is remembered as a place of testing, grumbling, and death for Israel. But it is also remembered as the place where Israel "honeymooned" with God:

> I remember the devotion of your youth,
> your love as a bride,
> how you followed me in the wilderness,
> in a land not sown.
>   (Jer. 2:2; see also Hos. 2:14–15)

In the Song, the bride is redolent with myrrh and frankincense. Yet here is another piece that doesn't fit. Ancient women wore perfume made of myrrh (Esth. 2:12), but frankincense was not a cosmetic. It was reserved for sacred use, to accompany sacrificial offerings and make a "pleasing odor to the LORD" (Lev. 6:15, etc.). It seems, then, that the poet is picturing Israel as itself a sacrificial offering to its God. That implication is reinforced by the fact that the verb "come up" also has strong associations with sacrifice. The offering burnt on the altar "comes up" to God. But the associations are even more complex. The same verb also regularly designates the journey of the pilgrim ascending to the Jerusalem Temple, on the crest of the Judean Hills on the edge of the wilderness: "Rise, let us *come up* to Zion, to the Lord our God" (Jer. 31:6; see also Psalm 122:4). The woman who is "coming up" thus appears in a dual aspect, as both the one who offers sacrifice to God and the perfumed offering itself.

If that is the idea behind this passage, what can it possibly mean to us? Temple worship and sacrificial offerings seem to us primitive, far removed from any modern "enlightened" understanding of worship. Yet perhaps the distance is less than it seems. Modern liturgies of bread and wine may incorporate the words of the apostle Paul: "I appeal to you . . . to present your bodies as a living sacrifice, holy and acceptable to God, which is your spiritual worship" (Rom. 12:1). Paul is, of course, speaking figuratively, as the term "spiritual worship" signals. Paul means that God wants lives wholly offered up to God's service, not perfumed corpses on an altar. The Song is likewise speaking figuratively, evoking the scents of sacrifice—myrrh and frankincense—to image Israel's self-offering to God.

So Paul's words help us to understand this haunting image of the Song. (He may even have had it specifically in mind, as it was in his day a prominent religious text.) But the Song also enables us to see something that goes beyond what Paul tells us. Namely this: when we come before God in true worship, God sees us, not as dutiful, but rather as beautiful, even irresistible, like a bride perfumed for her husband. It is almost too bold to say: when we worship God truly, God's desire for us grows (see also the comment at 6:13–7:13). But that is the revelation which the Song discloses to us. The Song's unique contribution to the canon lies in the fact that it is the only sustained expression of happy love that comes to us as "the Word of the Lord." After countless passages that express God's anguished love, the Song assures us that God the gracious Lover may still look at the world, at Israel, at the church, at our souls—and catch "his" breath at the beauty of the bride.

DESIRE SATISFIED
Song of Songs 4:1–5:1

Beauty and Strength (Song of Songs 4:1–7)

(*Man*)

4:1 How beautiful you are, my love,
how very beautiful.
Your eyes are doves
behind your veil.
Your hair is like a flock of goats,
moving down the slopes of Gilead.

2 Your teeth are like a flock of shorn ewes
that have come up from the washing,
all of which bear twins,
and not one among them is bereaved.

3 Your lips are like a crimson thread,
and your mouth is lovely.
Your cheeks are like halves of a pomegranate
behind your veil.

4 Your neck is like the tower of David,
built in courses;
on it hang a thousand bucklers,
all of them shields of warriors.

5 Your two breasts are like two fawns,
twins of a gazelle,
that feed among the lilies.

6 Until the day breathes
and the shadows flee,
I will hasten to the mountain of myrrh
and the hill of frankincense.

7 You are altogether beautiful, my love;
there is no flaw in you.

This is the only example in the Bible of a poetic form whose technical name is *wasf* (Arabic, "description"). It is a highly imagistic description of various parts of the lover's body, female or male. Ecstasy fires the poet's imagination to draw comparisons that would seem farfetched to the ordinary mind. The form has a long history in the poetry of the Near East, beginning in ancient Egypt a thousand years before the Song was composed and continuing in modern Arabic poetry. It was popular also among European poets until Shakespeare effectively ended the tradition with his parody:

> My mistress' eyes are nothing like the sun;
> Coral is far more red than her lips' red;
> If snow be white, why then her breasts are dun;
> If hairs be wires, black wires grow on her head.
>   (Sonnet 130)

Although some scholars also read the present poem as a parody, such a reading sets it at odds with the genuine admiration that the rest of the Song clearly expresses. I assume that the poem is a serious statement of admiration, foreign though its style is to us. Initially, it seems that the strangest thing about the descriptive poem is that when we finish reading it, we have no idea what the woman looks like. But in fact, this is not unusual for love poetry and is one of the things that distinguishes it from pornography. The woman's body is not a sex object. That is, it is not viewed from the uninvolved, objectivizing perspective that characterizes pornography. On the contrary, the poet is completely involved with his subject, and we see her only as he sees her. Despite its overt physicality, there is a kind of modesty about the poem. What is described are not the woman's breasts, but rather the associations they evoke in her lover's mind. Moreover, her body is not viewed in isolation, as in a magazine centerfold. Pornography sees the body—or body parts—and nothing else. But here the woman's body becomes a focal point for viewing the whole world of the lovers in its natural, geographic, and even historical dimensions. In a remarkably condensed series of images, this poem invites imaginative and loving engagement with the world of which the Bible speaks.

The poem treats seven aspects of her appearance, moving gradually downward from eyes to breasts. The number seven symbolizes completeness or perfection (see the comment at 2:1–13). Thus the form of the poem implies what the last line makes explicit: "All of you is beautiful, my friend." The similes at first seem startling, laughable, even ugly:

cheeks like pomegranates, teeth like sheep (v. 2)?! These should not be taken as comprehensive statements of similarity. A good set of teeth resembles a flock of sheep only on the points of whiteness and relative uniformity of appearance. Throughout the Song, the poetic images work the same way, usually highlighting only one point of similarity and emphasizing it all the more by the very *unlikeness* of the things compared on other points. The poet sketches a series of small scenes, each one made vivid through the unexpected comparison, which is invariably dynamic, suggesting animation, color, strength. "Your hair is like a flock of goats *churning/surging* down the slopes of Gilead" (v. 1). The verb implies vigorous action: black curls or waves, like dark-haired goats, tumbling thick and loose.

One thing that sets the Song apart from most modern love poetry is the frequent appearance of specific geographic references. In modern Western culture, poems tend to be individualized statements. Like many of their authors and readers, they do not belong to any particular place or claim a share in its history. But the poet of the Song sets the "hair scene" specifically in the Gilead, east of the Jordan River. The topography of this undulating mountain region may recommend it to the poetic imagination. Then again, there is a pleasing alliteration between "Gilead" and the verb *galshû* ("surge"]. But the most important effect of mentioning Gilead is that it evokes a series of associations with the foundational period of Israel's history. Here the tribes of Reuben, Gad, and Manasseh settled at the end of the wilderness wandering. At Gilead, God first brought deliverance to Israel through Saul (1 Samuel 13), which led to his anointing as king. Later, possession of the region became a bone of contention between the kings of Israel and Damascus (see Song 7:4). Is an assertion of Israelite identity and power implied here, as the poet's vision extends to the old boundaries of the Solomonic Empire and confidently "incorporates" Gilead into the body of the beloved?

The poem culminates in the sixth and seventh elements of comparison: neck like the tower of David and breasts like fawns (vv. 4–5), images of power and beauty respectively. Neither the Bible nor excavation has revealed a tower built by King David (the so-called Tower of David that stands in modern Jerusalem is only a few hundred years old). Probably what lies behind the image is not an actual building but rather David's reputation as the warrior par excellence of Israel's history. It is one of several images that suggest that the woman's strength is formidable (see 1:9; 6:5; 6:10). But the association with David carries a further connotation: this strength is given, and its exercise blessed, by God.

The last of the seven images is the most arresting: breasts like fawns feeding among lilies. The simile is highly sensuous yet, like all the Song's images, not fully explicit. Some interpreters miss this point and speculate on the angle of viewing whereby breasts resemble fawns, on whether the "lilies" in which the "fawns" nestle is the woman's hair or the man's? This is being too literal. The motif of fawns with stylized lilies is a standard one in ancient Near Eastern art, as fawns were sacred to Ishtar (Astarte), the goddess of love. Even a reader unaware of that association sees here an image of exquisite beauty, a loveliness that hardly belongs to this world. Anyone privileged to see this stands still, scarcely breathes—who would disturb fawns grazing among lilies?

There is a further difficulty with attempts to read the Song's metaphorical language as a series of sexually explicit references. For that approach obscures the one portrait that does emerge clearly from the Song. We never really "see" the lovers. But we do see, with increasing clarity, an exceptionally beautiful and fruitful land, bursting with life, for the lovers share it with sheep and goats, gazelles and foxes, lions and leopards. The Song may be altogether the most "ecological" book in the Bible, if we understand ecology as a recognition that each creature on this planet is inescapably bound to a particular place, dependent on the fruitful soil, and connected through an infinitely complex network of relations with every other creature of God. What the Song may contribute to our ecological education is the further recognition that it is love that animates our world and holds us all in life.

Reflection on beauty brings resolve: "I will hurry to the mountain of myrrh and the hill of frankincense." These cannot be literal places, as the plants do not grow in Israel (see Jer. 6:20). Rather they belong to the imaginary landscape evoked by the woman's body, with which myrrh and frankincense are particularly associated (3:6; 4:13–14; 5:1, 5). As we have seen, both these strongly scented spices play important roles in Temple ritual. Myrrh was the primary ingredient in the "holy anointing oil" that was liberally applied to the Temple building, its furnishing and vessels, and the priests. Frankincense was mixed with the grain offering presented by every Israelite, so the burnt offering would raise "a pleasing odor to the LORD" (Lev. 2:2). It is clear then, that the woman's personal "scent" is in fact the perfume of the Temple. The lover hastens like an eager pilgrim to the spice mountains, an image that beautifully evokes both the curves of a female body and the Holy Mount in Jerusalem, where the strong odors of myrrh and frankincense call to remembrance the people Israel's intimacy with their God.

The Song of Lebanon (Song of Songs 4:8–15)

(Man)

4:8 Come with me from Lebanon, my bride;
    come with me from Lebanon.
    Depart from the peak of Amana,
    from the peak of Senir and Hermon,
    from the dens of lions,
    from the mountains of leopards.

9 You have ravished my heart, my sister, my bride,
    you have ravished my heart with a glance of your eyes,
    with one jewel of your necklace.
10 How sweet is your love, my sister, my bride!
    how much better is your love than wine,
    and the fragrance of your oils than any spice!
11 Your lips distill nectar, my bride;
    honey and milk are under your tongue;
    the scent of your garments is like the scent of Lebanon.
12 A garden locked is my sister, my bride,
    a garden locked, a fountain sealed.
13 Your channel is an orchard of pomegranates
    with all choicest fruits,
    henna with nard,
14 nard and saffron, calamus and cinnamon,
    with all trees of frankincense,
    myrrh and aloes,
    with all chief spices—
15 a garden fountain, a well of living water,
    and flowing streams from Lebanon.

We are now at the midpoint of the Song. There are good reasons to think that this section has been carefully composed to serve as the center of gravity for the whole book. The most obvious indication of the importance of this section is that here, for the first time, the man addresses the woman as "my bride." That term occurs six times in this and the following section (4:8, 9, 10, 11, 12; 5:1). Accordingly, many regard this as a marriage scene, and the language achieves a peak of sensual and emotional intensity. But there are other, less obvious indicators that the poet has constructed this section also to evoke a quality of profound mystery and wonder, and that the language suggests intense religious as well as sexual experience.

Two elements in particular call for theological interpretation of the passage. First, the poet's practice of creating echoes with other books of the Bible is especially pronounced here. This is the most "resonant" part of the Song; virtually every line sounds an echo from another biblical text. Especially notable are many connections with the Prophets and psalms, and also the description of Solomon's Temple (1 Kings 6–7). The difficulty of this passage—arguably, the most difficult in the whole book—lies precisely in the abundance of scriptural allusions and the consequent density of theological meaning. Second, the image of the garden reaches its fullest development here. At the theological level of interpretation, the Song as a whole represents a return to the Garden of God, Eden, the place where humanity once enjoyed full intimacy with God. These two aspects of the poet's technique here are in fact related. For in the imagination of ancient Israel, the Temple *is* the Garden of God (see below), and this Song aims to draw us into the experience of ultimate intimacy that is the reward of the pilgrim, the devoted lover of God.

As is often the case with the Song, the best clue to theological meaning is a piece that does not fit the immediate context or seems out of place altogether in an ordinary love song. The present passage begins with such an odd-fitting piece, namely, the mention of Lebanon and the great cedar-covered mountain peaks far to the north of Jerusalem, where the main action of the Song takes place. The Lebanon region is not only mentioned but emphasized. It is named four times in this so-called "Song of Lebanon" (vv. 8, 11, and 15) and a total of seven times in the whole book (see also 3:9; 5:15; 7:4 [Heb. 5]). To the biblical writers, the number seven symbolized perfection; with this subtle literary device, our poet focuses attention on something of particular importance.

We hear the name "Lebanon" and perhaps think of a war-torn country. But an ancient audience would have heard and imagined something completely different. First, in this context, they would probably hear an echo between two nearly identical words. The Hebrew pronunciation *Levanon* recalls the word *levonah*, "frankincense," which appeared two verses before (4:6). So "the hill of *levonah*" that is the woman's body evokes the legendary mountain region of *Levanon* (4:8). Ancient mythology, which would have been known to our poet, identified these 10,000-foot peaks as "the cedar mountain, abode of the gods, throne-seat of Ishtar" (Epic of Gilgamesh). The association with the goddess of love and her ferocious feline "pets" (v. 8) might have appealed to the poet's imagination. But probably for every Israelite, the first association that "Lebanon" brought to mind was the Temple in Jerusalem. Solomon imported cedar logs in vast quantities to build the Temple and his adjacent palace, as well as other buildings in the royal

compound. We may guess that he valued the cedars of Lebanon as much for
their aura of divine mystery as for their practical use. So the small hilltop of
Judah called Zion becomes a new "cedar mountain," a divine abode that
supersedes that of the ancient gods. The connection between Lebanon and
Jerusalem apparently entered into Israel's religious imagination. "Lebanon"
became a code word for Jerusalem's glory as God's dwelling place. After the
destruction of Solomon's Temple by the Babylonians, an anonymous prophet
(known to modern readers as "Third Isaiah") promises devastated Jerusalem:
"The glory of Lebanon shall come to you" (Isa. 60:13). No Israelite could
miss the meaning: God will restore the Temple to its former glory!

Among all the prophets, this "Third Isaiah" (the author of Isaiah 56–66)
is the one to whom the poet of the Song owes the greatest imaginative and
theological debt, and that debt is especially evident in this "marriage
scene." Earlier prophets—Hosea, Jeremiah, Ezekiel—spoke of Israel as a
bride, but one who had gone astray. But Third Isaiah gives that bridal
image a wholly positive cast. Thus he (?) frames God's powerful assurance
of love for the shattered city:

> You shall no more be termed Forsaken,
> and your land shall no more be termed Desolate,
> but you shall be called My-Delight-Is-in-Her,
> and your land Married ,
> for the LORD delights in you,
> and your land shall be married.
> For as a young man marries a young woman,
> so shall your Builder marry you,
> and as the bridegroom rejoices over the bride,
> so shall your God rejoice over you.
>
> (Isa. 62:4–5, AT)

It is probable that the Song of Songs was inspired by Third Isaiah's
vision of Jerusalem as the bride in whom God delights, and that the Song
is at one level a highly imaginative amplification of that image. If that is so,
then there is a genuinely prophetic dimension to the Song of Songs and
especially to this marriage scene. The poet dares to set forth a vision that
runs counter to the evident facts of history. For in the period when the
Song was composed (fifth to third century B.C.E.), Israel was a vassal state,
subject to a series of foreign (Persian and Greek) rulers who were often
harsh and hostile to Israel's God. Although the Temple in Jerusalem was
rebuilt, it fell far short of its former glory. Against that background, the
poet takes up the prophetic task of celebrating God's enduring passion for

"the bride." The external threat to love is real; as we have seen, opposition to love is one of the recurrent themes of the Song. Nonetheless, the Song is important testimony to Israel's faith that God continues to long for intimacy with Israel, and that God's longing will ultimately be satisfied.

Although there is much in the Song that pushes us to *look beyond* what is obvious, that is no warrant for *ignoring* the obvious fact that the image of the bride may also be used to speak of sexual love. Even so, the term "sister-bride" is not quite literal, for sibling marriages were outlawed in Israel (see Lev. 18:9). The point of the endearment, used also in Sumerian and Egyptian love poetry, is to suggest total affinity between the lovers. It denotes a profound recognition of kinship, such as the first human lover expressed: "This *at last* is bone of my bones and flesh of my flesh!" (Gen. 2:23). Adam's expression captures the feeling of finding true love. When we find the one who is "fit for [us]" (Gen. 2:18, 20) , we feel that we have waited all our lives for nothing but this—"at last!" The Song likewise expresses that feeling of long delay. The special endearment "my sister, my bride" is held back until now, halfway through the Song. Then the man repeats it several times in quick succession (4:9, 10, 12; 5:1; compare 5:2) as he revels in the joy of full identification with another human being.

The image of the bride, and the Song of Lebanon altogether, is like one of those pictures whose content shifts before your eyes: is it a vase or two faces, an old woman or a young one? Looking closely, we see at one moment a human love scene, and a lover who is both luscious and chaste ("a garden locked," v. 12). Then we blink, and now we see the special intimacy between God and Israel, which reaches its high point in Temple worship. Neither finally succeeds the other as the *one* correct interpretation; but the mind continually oscillates between the two. It happens in nearly every line: "honey and milk are under your tongue" (v. 11). The words speak of sweet, nourishing, comforting words and kisses. But can anyone familiar with biblical idiom miss the echo of the description of Israel as "a land flowing with milk and honey" (Deut. 31:20; Jer. 11:5), the rich land that is God's betrothal gift to his chosen people?

The picture of the bride as a locked garden (vv. 12–15) is, like all imagery in the Song, both sensual and delicate. It is noteworthy that there is in the entire Song no clear genital reference, although the present translation obscures this fact. "Your *channel* is an orchard of pomegranates" (v. 13)—one modern interpreter explains this as the vaginal canal, ending in the pomegranate-shaped cervix! But the Hebrew word rendered "channel" is in fact a plural noun, meaning something like "extensions, limbs." Probably a better rendering of the whole line is: "Your limbs are a *paradise* of pomegranates." (The Hebrew word *pardes*, "orchard," derives from the Persian word *pairidaeza*, a sumptuous garden, of royalty or gods.) Although the image resists decoding into an anatomically specific reference, it suits a young female body. Pomegranates are firm, highly colored, intensely delicious. Moreover, because of their many seeds, they were a popular symbol of fertility and life.

At the same time, the description of the locked garden can be seen as a highly imaginative but nonetheless surprisingly precise description of the Temple as the biblical writers represent it. First, as the lengthy description of the Temple (1 Kings 6–7) shows, the Temple is designed as a garden. Ideologically, it is a second Eden (legend has it that the Temple was built on the spot where the Garden of Eden once stood). The cedar-paneled walls were carved "all around about" with palm trees, open flowers, and cherubim (1 Kings 6:29). Before the Holy of Holies stood ten golden lampstands shaped like flowers (1 Kings 7:49). In the forecourt were two great bronze pillars (1 Kings 7:18–19, 42), each a stylized tree of life surmounted by a lily-shaped capital. Nearby was the huge bronze basin, also shaped like a lily (1 Kings 7:26). Small washbasins rested on stands decorated with cherubim, lions, and palm trees (1 Kings 7:36). Pomegranates, cedar, lions, lilies, and palm trees—all these are features of the "paradise" that is both the lovers' landscape and the woman herself. The language of the Song leads us into the "locked garden" of the Temple precinct, where true lovers of God may dwell in peace (see Psalms 15; 23; 84).

An especially striking point of connection with the description in the Song of Lebanon is the fact that the Temple court itself was "a paradise of pomegranates." A latticework of two hundred bronze pomegranates hung on each of the two great pillars that stood in the forecourt, where they glittered in the strong sunlight. We may imagine that Israel saw in those pomegranates a promise of life. The biblical account of the destruction of the Temple ends with the painful note: the Babylonian army carried them off as scrap metal (2 Kings 25:17). Perhaps the poet of the Song is now answering that old history of destruction and death by painting "a paradise of pomegranates," a picture of glowing life in the Garden of God.

One more detail of the Song of Lebanon compels the careful reader to draw a connection between the lovers' garden and the Temple, namely, the emphasis on abundant waters (v. 15). The well-watered garden described here is lush almost beyond the imagining of any Israelite. In their semi-arid land, ancient householders were fortunate if they could sustain a few irrigated plants, the proverbial vine and fig tree. But the biblical writers know of one place where waters flow freely, and that it is the

Temple. For the psalmists, Jerusalem is where the River of Life flows (Psalms 36:8; 46:4), for God is "the Watersource of Life" (Psalm 36:9 [in Hebrew v. 10]). They are speaking in the language of lovers, not mapmakers. For in "reality," Jerusalem is watered by one small spring and uncertain rainfall. Nonetheless, the poet of the Song understands the language of love and draws upon it. Notably, the poet describes the water sources with three phrases—"a garden *spring*, a well of *living* [*running*] *water*, and *flowing streams* from Lebanon"—each of which appears elsewhere in reference to God and also to the holy mountain of Jerusalem. God is the sole "source of *living water*" (Jer. 2:13), who enables Israel to draw water from "*springs* of salvation" (Isa. 12:3) and makes Jerusalem itself—to a pilgrim's eyes—a place of abundant *springs* (Psalms 84:6; 87:7). *Lebanon's* "cold *flowing streams*" are a symbol of the constancy that Israel should (but does not) show to God (Jer. 18:14–15).

I hope I have shown that in this Song of Lebanon, echoes of the love language associated with the land of Israel and its centerpoint, Jerusalem and the Temple, are too many to ignore. But that does not solve the modern reader's problem: why should we care? The Temple was long ago destroyed. Moreover, the whole idea of sacred places, a holy land or city or building, is to most of us remote, if not hopelessly antiquated. The Song seeks to draw us into the experience of the pilgrim, the one who returns to the Garden of God to enjoy life as it was meant to be. A theological reading of the Song must reckon with the honest recognition that this not an experience that most modern Westerners readily appreciate.

The best starting point for theological appreciation is to look behind the Temple building itself to the spiritual reality for which it stands. The Song points to the possibility of intimate encounter with God in this world. More than that, it attests that such encounter is necessary for a truly human life in this world (every Israelite was commanded to make pilgrimage to the Temple each year, once or several times). The Incarnation of God in Jesus Christ affirms the same spiritual reality. Indeed, as the Gospel of John shows, there is a sense in which the body of Jesus *is* the Temple (John 2:21; see also Luke 23:45). That is, Jesus' body represents the physical presence of God in this world. It represents both the approachability and the vulnerability of God—for are not both these things implied in the notion that intimate encounter with God is possible in this world?

The Song's gift to the church is to enable us to deepen our experience of God's presence in our world. I would suggest that in this present generation, the ecological crisis reveals how desperately we stand in need of receiving that gift and putting it to use in our service of the world. The

Song itself is a "locked garden" (v. 12) that can be entered only by prayer. We might pray as we read the Song that it may awaken in us a pilgrim spirit, an ability to perceive that we who live on this earth are standing on holy ground, sanctified by God's abiding presence. Meditating on the Song might give us eyes to see that this "pale blue dot," the planet Earth, is in fact nothing other than the Garden of God, where God invites us into delighted encounter, which God has charged and privileged us "to serve and to keep" (Gen. 2:15).

The Invitation (Song of Songs 4:16–5:1)

(**Woman**)

4:16 Awake, O north wind,
and come, O south wind!
Blow upon my garden
that its fragrance may be wafted abroad.
Let my beloved come to his garden,
and eat its choicest fruits.

(**Man**)

5:1 I come to my garden, my sister, my bride;
I gather my myrrh with my spice,
I eat my honeycomb with my honey,
I drink my wine with my milk.

Eat, friends, drink,
and be drunk with love.

Here for the first time the woman speaks with assurance and authority. Perhaps her newfound assurance is a result of being recognized and honored as the "sister-bride" (see the previous comment). This command to the winds is a remarkable assertion of personal power. Elsewhere in the Bible, this is something done only by God (Exod. 14:21; Ezek. 37:9; Mark 4:41)! She concludes with an indirect invitation to her lover to enter the "locked garden" (4:12). From the beginning the Song portrays the woman as "proprietor" of herself. In figurative language, she is (or wishes to be) keeper of her own vineyard (1:6). Here she lays claim to the garden, to which, on her own authority, she grants him access and even shared ownership: "my garden" becomes "his garden" (v. 16). If the passage be understood in the context of sexual love, this is a marked contrast to the standard biblical practice of a father (or brother) giving—or selling!—the young woman in marriage. As a kind of sexual property, she belongs to the father's household until she enters a new "father's house"—namely, that of her husband. As we have already seen, the Song of Songs pays little heed to such conventional arrangements. This is itself an important consideration for its interpreters (see below).

The man eagerly accepts the offered share in the garden, as indicated by the ninefold repetition of the personal pronoun "my" (5:1). We may imagine a pause before he responds in 5:1, although I read this verse as concluding the literary unit, which spans the chapter division. Some lapse of time may be implied by the grammatical form of the Hebrew verbs. They are "perfect" forms, which normally designate completed action. The sense may be better conveyed in English by a past-tense translation: "I have come . . . , I have gathered . . . , I have eaten . . . , I have drunk. . . . " It seems that admiration and longing are turned—however briefly—into full satisfaction. Therefore many interpret this as a statement that the couple's marriage has been sexually consummated.

There are, however, serious problems with that interpretation. It is hard to reconcile a marriage here with the following verses (5:2–8), which portray the woman in bed alone behind a bolted door, while her lover calls to her plaintively. Further, in the final chapter the woman's siblings (presumably her brothers) are still debating about what to do "on the day that she is spoken for" (8:8). In another place, the woman herself admits that a public demonstration of affection would be frowned upon (8:1–2). These passages indicate that, unless the time sequence of the Song is completely random, the endearment "my sister, my bride" here does not indicate that a legal marriage has taken place.

This, then, raises the vexed question of whether the Song (contrary to the rest of the Bible) condones sexual intercourse outside marriage. It must be admitted that the Song is ambiguous on this matter. This ambiguity is itself remarkable, in light of the stringent controls set upon sexual behavior in ancient Israel, and especially the high premium placed on female virginity at the time of marriage (see Deut. 22:13–21). Reinforcing social norms for sexual morality is emphatically not this poem's concern. Its interest lies elsewhere: namely, in the essential *quality* of love that is worthy of such exuberant celebration. What the Song does make unmistakably clear is that this love is an intimacy characterized by mutual devotion, and equally, mutual admiration. The lovers belong fully and exclusively to one another: "My beloved is mine, and I am his" (2:16; compare 6:3; 7:10). Yet their union involves no loss of self; it is complementary, not symbiotic. Virtually every speech of both the man and the woman expresses frank admiration for the powers, as well as the beauty, of the other.

This strong affirmation of mutually respectful sexual love would have been a bold social statement in the Hellenistic world (i.e., the extension of Greek culture following on Alexander the Great's military conquests) in which the Song may well have been composed. Some Jewish writings from that period show the influence of the Greek view that women were a "second species," distinct from and inferior to males. The philosophers do not wax eloquent over marriage as a meeting of two minds or souls. Rather, they see the union of woman and man as an arrangement of convenience, whose primary purposes are to contain lust and provide for the care of children. Significantly, the canon of the Old Testament does not include Jewish writings that reflect these views, representing women as the weaker and morally inferior sex. On the contrary, the view that the Song not only expresses but celebrates is fully in accordance with the first two chapters of Genesis, where human beings are created equally in the image and likeness of God (1:26). Man and woman are full partners (2:18), "one flesh" (2:24).

The fact that the Song is generally uninterested in reinforcing sexual norms (bridal virginity) or deliberately flaunts them (male "ownership" of a woman's sexuality) is important for interpretation. It may be a subtle way of redirecting our attention to another level of experience altogether. The man's murmur of satisfaction may be sexual, but it should also be heard as expressing a moment in the spiritual life—one moment, not a settled disposition. The dominant tone of the Song, in the speeches of the man as well as the woman, remains one of longing or happy anticipation. But it is important also that here in the heart of the Song, however briefly, every desire is fully satisfied. Indeed, this confirms the interpretation of the preceding Song of Lebanon (4:8–15) as pointing to the Temple. For the biblical writers, Solomon's Temple is the place of consummate satisfaction, out of all the world the spot where it is possible to experience the height of pleasure in the love relationship between God and humanity.

"I have eaten . . . , I have drunk"—the poet's words evoke the experience of the pilgrim. For the Temple was a place of feasting, more like a picnic ground than a modern church. People worshiped outside; and "worship" meant eating. Pilgrims offered an animal for sacrifice and made festive meals from its flesh, shared with family and friends. These were great events, as most people could afford to eat meat only a few times a year. Moreover, these thanksgiving meals were eaten at God's house, in God's gracious presence. They forecast the great banquet on the day when God "swallows up death forever" (Isa. 25:6–9; the echo of this passage at Song 1:4 suggests that the poet has the important prophetic promise in mind). Myrrh, spice, honey, wine, and milk—these evoke the holy sensuality of

Temple worship, with its rich smells and tastes, and also the sensuous delight of dwelling in the "land flowing with milk and honey," enriched by all the gifts of the Divine Lover (Hos. 2:8).

The final line sounds like it comes from a popular drinking song. The speaker and the audience cannot be certainly identified. Since the couple seems to be alone, this may be an anonymous narrative voice addressing them—although that does not occur elsewhere in the Song. Or maybe the couple is speaking here, with the expansiveness natural to lovers, to an imaginary assembly of wedding guests. Or, assuming a Temple scene, the pilgrim is inviting others to share in the "love feast" (what the church would later call an "*agape* meal") of the sacrificial offering.

However, the French mystical theologian Francis de Sales (1567–1622) offers the most spiritually rich—and also daring!—interpretation. He compares eating and drinking to meditation and contemplative prayer, respectively. Meditation, like eating, requires effort: we must chew the Word, "turning [our] spiritual meat hither and thither between the teeth of consideration, to bruise, break, and digest it." Contemplation, by comparison, is effortless as well as pleasurable, like drinking—and the Song advises us to get good and drunk! So, Sales concludes, the nourishing work of meditation is necessary. Nonetheless, we must dare to get drunk, that is, "to contemplate so frequently and so ardently as to be quite out of self, to be wholly in God. O holy and sacred inebriation, which . . . does not dull or besot us, but *angelicizes* and in a sort deifies us, putting us out of ourselves . . . to raise us above ourselves and range us with angels, so that we may live more in God than in ourselves, being attentive to and occupied in seeing his beauty and being united to his goodness by love!" (*Treatise*, 6:6, p. 250).

TESTIMONY TO THE WOMEN OF JERUSALEM
Song of Songs 5:2–6:3

Frustrated Love (Song of Songs 5:2–8)

(**Woman**)
5:2 I slept, but my heart was awake.
Listen! my beloved is knocking.
"Open to me, my sister, my love,
my dove, my perfect one;
for my head is wet with dew,
my locks with the drops of the night."

3 I had put off my garment;
  how could I put it on again?
  I had bathed my feet;
  how could I soil them?
4 My beloved thrust his hand into the opening,
  and my inmost being yearned for him.
5 I arose to open to my beloved,
  and my hands dripped with myrrh,
  my fingers with liquid myrrh,
  upon the handles of the bolt.
6 I opened to my beloved,
  but my beloved had turned and was gone.
  My soul failed me when he spoke.
  I sought him, but did not find him;
  I called him, but he gave no answer.
7 Making their rounds in the city
  the sentinels found me;
  they beat me, they wounded me,
  they took away my mantle,
  those sentinels of the walls.
8 I adjure you, O daughters of Jerusalem,
  if you find my beloved,
  tell him this:
  I am faint with love.

Rather than narrating an ordered sequence of events, the Song shows us particular moments in the life of love, viewed from inside the relationship. Experience of both human love and spiritual love demonstrates that in neither case is there a smooth progression "from strength to strength" (Psalm 84:7). Even the closest relationship evidences a fluctuating rhythm between union ("one flesh," Gen. 2:24) and separateness, intimacy and distance, full satisfaction and frustration of desire. We have just seen the lovers enjoying the fullest intimacy (4:16–5:1). By contrast, this section shows the kind of missed connection that is sadly familiar to all lovers, yet always finally inexplicable.

The NRSV translation renders the first line of verse 2 in the past tense, presumably to suggest that the scene is a flashback to a time before the lovers were intimate. But the Hebrew suggests that is not the case. The verbs here are present participles, which have the effect of rendering the scene vividly immediate to both speaker and hearer. The woman, whom her lover previously described as "a garden locked" (4:12), is now literally locked—behind a door that excludes even him! So he discovers when he puts his hand through the keyhole (the wooden keys of antiquity were large) and is unable to slip the bolt. He speaks only one line, a plea for admittance which is both loving and plaintive. As before, in happier times (5:1), he names her repeatedly as "his": "my sister, my love, my dove, my perfect one." Yet now it seems too much trouble for her to get up and open the door—almost incredibly, in light of the intense longing she everywhere else expresses. Why does she refuse until it is too late, and he has gone away? Perhaps she is teasing him and carries it a little too far. Or maybe she is simply not in the mood for love. The Bible is relentlessly honest in exposing the vacillations of the human heart!

We might also imagine that it is the Divine Lover who "stands at the door knocking" (Rev. 3:20). Understood at this level, the woman's failed response is a graphic representation of the spiritual condition that is traditionally known as torpor, spiritual sluggishness. (The passage in Revelation is addressed to the lukewarm, self-satisfied, lackadaisical church in Laodicea—a textbook case of torpor!) God makes an advance toward us when we do not expect it, seeking admittance to our hearts. But so often we are unwilling to lose any sleep or get our feet dirty (v. 3) when God approaches. Torpor is not a condition that affects only those who are lukewarm toward God. It is a recurrent problem with which all who seek to grow in genuine love of God must struggle. Moreover, as the structure of the Song suggests, a period of torpor often follows times of deep spiritual satisfaction. When that happens, the memory of the intimacy we enjoyed with God makes our present failure to respond all the more painful to us—and maybe to God, too!

Some modern commentators see a transparent reference to sexual foreplay in the phrase, "My beloved thrust his hand into the opening" (v. 4). Such an interpretation would seem to be reinforced by the following line, which in Hebrew is extremely graphic: "And *my guts heaved/churned* [*me'aî hamû*] for him." What initially appears to be a surprisingly indelicate sexual reference is in fact a quote from the prophet Jeremiah. Those words are unforgettable. Just because they are unforgettable, it is probable that the poet of the Song expects us to remember them in their original context. They are part of God's lament over the loss of "Ephraim," a pet name for the Northern Kingdom of Israel, destroyed by the Assyrians in 722 B.C.E.:

> Is Ephraim my dear son—
> a dandled child?
> As often as I speak against him,
> surely I remember him still.
> Therefore do my guts heave/churn [*hamû me'aî*] for him;
> Surely I will have mercy upon him, says the LORD.
>
> (Jer. 31:20, AT)

When God says, "my guts churn for [Israel]," it is a message of hope and assurance for exiles, despite the apparent evidence that they have been abandoned in punishment for their sin. Later the same phrase recurs, now in a bold prophetic reproach to God, when redemption is too long delayed: "Where is 'the churning of your guts' [for Israel]?!" (Isa. 63:15). It seems, then, that the remarkable expression of God's "visceral" attachment to the people Israel has become an established figure of prophetic speech. An astonishing transformation occurs here when this woman repeats those words. Assuming that she is a symbol for Israel, we may now hear the words as something like a message of hope *for God*, an assurance that Israel reciprocates God's visceral attachment! There may be a further reflection of prophetic speech in the woman's lament: "The very life (soul) went out of me when he spoke" (v. 6b, AT). The prophets' repeated message is that God has spoken and Israel refuses to respond. Considered now in retrospect, the lover's plaintive words evoke in the woman a sense of both connection and loss that reaches to the core of her being. We might say, "I almost died." Looking back, the pain of having heard and yet not responded to the one we most love is almost unbearable.

Another memorable figure of speech has religious as well as erotic overtones: As she throws back the bolt, her hands "drip with myrrh." The myrrh on the door handles could come either from her hands or from his (see also 1:13 and 5:13, where myrrh is associated with the man's body). Imported myrrh was enjoyed by royalty and the very rich, as a perfume for body oil (Esth. 2:12), clothing (Psalm 45:8), and bed linens (Prov. 7:17). But expensive perfume does not fit the budget of young peasant lovers. As before, they may be imagining themselves as royalty. But probably the numerous references to myrrh throughout the poem point to the realm of religious experience. As we have seen, myrrh is the distinctive scent of holiness, the chief ingredient in the "holy anointing oil" with which the priests and the sanctuary itself were anointed (Exod. 30:22–33). This, then, smells like an encounter with the Divine Lover.

Too late—he is gone! There follows a second search (compare 3:1–4), this one unsuccessful, and worse. The beating by the sentinels is the fiercest instance of the opposition that is a recurrent theme in the Song. It is not clear why the city guards suddenly turn on her so viciously (contrast 3:1). Maybe they are enraged by her defiance of convention. A young woman going about the city in the middle of the night is acting dangerously like a prostitute. And that is how they treat her, stripping off her outer clothing (cf. Ezek. 23:26–27), in flagrant abuse of their authority. It sounds like too many modern news stories, when those who regard themselves as guardians of conventional morality—police, military officers, church leaders—perpetrate physical and even sexual abuse upon those whom they consider to be "out of bounds."

The hostile reaction of the city guards may also serve a symbolic function. The city is for these lovers always a place of opposition, separation, and suffering. It contrasts with the garden, which is a place of satisfaction and union. Here in the Song, city and garden are not primarily different geographic locations. Rather, they are two poles of experience, but the two poles cannot finally be separated. Garden and city represent the two faces of Jerusalem as it appears in the Bible, positive and negative respectively. Positively, Jerusalem is celebrated by the psalmists and some prophets as the place for intimate encounter between God and humanity. This is the garden. Yet the Holy City has another aspect. Ezekiel calls it "the city of blood" (Ezek. 22:2; 24:6, 9); Jesus calls it the killer of prophets (Matt. 23:37). For them, Jerusalem symbolizes holiness, and at the same time it represents the powers that seek to destroy what is holy and true. Here in the Song, "those sentinels of the walls" stand for Jerusalem in its vicious aspect. Perhaps the poet remembers the psalmist's unhappy vision of the city:

> I see violence and strife in the city.
> Day and night they go around it on its walls,
> and iniquity and trouble are within it.
> (Psalm 55:9–10)

The woman's own tone is now deeply plaintive: "I am faint with love" (v. 8). She said this once before (2:5), but then the words were spoken coyly, in the sweet languor of her lover's embrace. Now they bespeak real suffering, a result of the woman's own failure and her lover's silent departure, the futility of her search and the hostility she encountered. Yet there is such a thing as health-giving lovesickness. If the woman's desire formerly fluctuated (v. 3), now it is strong and pure. This is clear from the next section, which includes her fullest description of this most desirable lover (5:10–16). Paradoxically, then, the declaration of lovesickness is at the same time a declaration of her soul's strength. It bespeaks the wise anguish of someone who now knows what it means to lose what matters *absolutely*. The third-century Christian commentator Origen understands that she speaks as someone whose soul has been struck by God's "health-bestowing wounds":

If there is anyone anywhere who has at some time burned with this faithful love of the Word of God . . . so that [one] yearns and longs for Him by day and night, can speak of nought but Him, would hear of nought but Him, can think of nothing else, and is disposed to no desire nor longing nor yet hope, except for Him alone—if such there be, that soul then says in truth: "I have been wounded by charity." (*Song of Songs*, 198)

A Unique Lover (Song of Songs 5:9–6:3)

(*Daughters of Jerusalem*)

5:9 What is your beloved more than another beloved,
     O fairest among women?
     What is your beloved more than another beloved,
     that you thus adjure us?

(*Woman*)

10 My beloved is all radiant and ruddy,
   distinguished among ten thousand.
11 His head is the finest gold;
   his locks are wavy, black as a raven.
12 His eyes are like doves
   beside springs of water,
   bathed in milk,
   fitly set.
13 His cheeks are like beds of spices,
   yielding fragrance.
   His lips are lilies,
   distilling liquid myrrh.
14 His arms are rounded gold,
   set with jewels.
   His body is ivory work,
   encrusted with sapphires.
15 His legs are alabaster columns,
   set upon bases of gold.
   His appearance is like Lebanon,
   choice as the cedars.
16 His speech is most sweet,
   and he is altogether desirable.
   This is my beloved and this is my friend,
   O daughters of Jerusalem.

(*Daughters of Jerusalem*)

6:1 Where has your beloved gone,

O fairest among women?
Which way has your beloved turned,
that we may seek him with you?

(*Woman*)
2 My beloved has gone down to his garden,
   to the beds of spices,
   to pasture his flock in the gardens,
   and to gather lilies.
3 I am my beloved's and my beloved is mine;
   he pastures his flock among the lilies.

After the Shulammite enlists the help of the daughters of Jerusalem (5:8), there follows something like a conversation. This is the only time in the Song that the Jerusalem women shows any "personality." Their question—What is so special about this so-called "beloved"?—carries more than a hint of skepticism. Moreover, the compliment to the woman's beauty (v. 9) is probably insincere; we know from the beginning that they are scornful of her sun-darkened skin (see 1:5–6). But the woman is "faint with love" and therefore oblivious to skepticism. All she thinks of is her lover's beauty, which she praises in the form of a *wasf* (a descriptive poem; see the comment on 4:1–7). It is noteworthy that the metaphorical poem does not really serve its ostensible purpose in the "story line": to enable the women to help her find her lover. No one could pick a man out of a crowd on the basis of this description, but telling them *what he looks like* is not the point. Rather, she uses metaphors to communicates *how she feels about him*.

Her poem blends images from the natural world with what sounds like the description of a piece of statuary. The images of the *wasf* should not be interpreted with too much anatomical precision. "His cheeks are like beds of spices" (v. 13): Some interpreters see a reference to a beard, thick and curly like bedding plants. More likely, it means that he smells good, with his own distinctive fragrance. "His 'body' (?) is ivory work encrusted with sapphires [or lapis lazuli]" (v. 14): Perhaps this evokes blue veins or dark hair against pale skin (some say the uncertain Hebrew word denotes the erect male member), but probably it is a more general statement: he is rarely beautiful.

Yet the physicality of the statue image is in fact a daring move on the poet's part, though not for its anatomical specificity. As is well known, biblical law prohibited the creation of "graven images" (Exod. 20:4) of God. As far as we know, Israel, unlike its neighbors, did not practice the art of fine sculpting at all, for fear of trespassing on what came to be known as the "image prohibition." What is, then, most striking about this *wasf* is that it is a kind of verbal statue, executed in precious materials, analogous to the statues that were commonly erected to honor Mesopotamian and Egyptian gods and (semi-deified) kings. They, too, were made of gold, lapis lazuli, marble, and alabaster. The Bible parodies such statues in the "great statue" of King Nebuchadnezzar's dream (Dan. 2:31), and our poet may be playing with that story. In the king's dream, as in the present poem, the first feature noted is "a head of fine gold" (2:32). But the strong legs and feet of this beloved, made of alabaster and gold, contrast (deliberately?) with that idol's fragile feet of mixed iron and clay, which proved to be its downfall. The poet may also have had in mind works of pagan religious art. About 450 B.C.E., the Greek sculptor Phidias created colossal (thirty-nine-foot) composite statues—wood, gold, ivory, and precious stones—of Olympian Zeus and Athena Parthenos. They were famed throughout the Mediterranean world as the most perfect representations of divinity ever made by human hands. The similarities between Phidias's work and the present poem suggest that this piece of "verbal statuary" is consciously rivaling and correcting that claim. A poetic description such as this one is as close as Israel can come to physical representation of divinity. Israel's theology has an inherent reserve that distinguishes it from pagan religious thought. Israel's scriptures everywhere testify to the nature and will of God. Yet they do not directly "show" God. That is something God alone can do.

It is intriguing to note a difference between this *wasf* and the similar poems that celebrate the woman's beauty (4:1–7; 7:1–9). The man's poems of praise regularly conclude with his own resolve to enjoy the pleasures of the lover's beautiful body (4:6; 5:1; 7:8). It is, one might say, "self-interested praise." But that move does not occur here. Rather, she involves herself only to the extent of declaring him to be "my darling [*dôdî*] and . . . my friend." With complete lack of self-consciousness, she sums up in an almost objective testimony: "All of him is delights!" For all her enthusiasm, she practices a kind of reserve, testifying to his loveliness and yet not claiming to take possession of it herself. There is an inherent modesty to her speech; she claims nothing but a special place in his affection. On the other hand, she happily anticipates the pleasure he will take in "his garden" (6:2)—that is, herself. It would be a mistake to see this as a woman's hesitancy to seek her own sexual pleasure; nowhere does the Song of Songs enforce that stereotype. Instead, the fact that the woman does not venture to lay hold of the man's body reinforces the suggestion that this *wasf* may, at one level, be seen as pointing to the Divine Lover. She is practicing the kind of reserve characteristic of the best of Israel's theology, which is at the same time both modest and daring. Israel modestly refrains from laying possessive claim to God's exquisite beauty, yet dares to imagine that we humans might be a source of pleasure for God.

By now the skepticism of the daughters of Jerusalem is wholly swept aside; they are ready to join the search for this gorgeous lover (6:1). Formerly the woman appealed to them as her advocates (5:8). But sensing that they have now become rivals, she quickly clarifies the situation with the lovely line that captures most succinctly (only four words in Hebrew) the mutuality and exclusiveness of this relationship: "I am my lover's and he is mine" (6:3). The words express not clutching possessiveness but full belonging, one to the other. The words can also be translated more actively: "I am *for* my lover, and my lover is *for* me!" That translation implies each lover's commitment to advance the well-being of the other. In modern Israel, the Hebrew words are cast in gold and silver and worn as pendants and rings. Young lovers think of this, quite rightly, as the biblical love slogan; wearing it, they anchor their own fresh experience in the tradition. But the tradition that underlies the slogan is longer even than many of them know. It stretches all the way back to Mount Sinai, where another statement of total mutual commitment was made: "I will be your God and you will be my people" (Lev. 26:12; compare Exod. 6:7; Ezek. 36:28; 37:27).

The ancient rabbis catch that echo between the covenant made at Sinai and the commitment that these lovers embrace. They read the present passage as Israel's praise of her God, and they develop that interpretation with wonderful imagination. The following story is told by Rabbi Akiba, who regarded the Song of Songs as supreme among all the books of scripture (see the comment at 1:1). All the nations of the world came to Israel to ask the question posed by the daughters of Jerusalem: "What is so special about your 'beloved,' your God, that you are ready even to suffer and die for him?" (Akiba himself died a martyr at Roman hands in the Second Jewish Revolt, 135 C.E.) Thus the nations try to seduce Israel away from their God: "You are attractive and strong, come intermingle with us." Israel can hardly believe they are so obtuse: "Do you know Him? We will tell you just a little bit of his praise. 'My beloved is all radiant and ruddy . . . ' (Song 5:10)." After hearing the song of praise, the nations, like the daughters of Jerusalem, are eager to join Israel in seeking God (5:9). But Israel forestalls them: "You have no part in him. No, 'I am my beloved's and he is mine' (6:3)."

This story enables us to understand why Akiba made his famous declaration, "All the Scriptures are holy, but the Song of Songs is the Holy of

Holies!" In his reading, the Song reveals the depth dimension of all the scriptures. The Bible as a whole is a love story. It tells the long history of a relationship which, however flawed from the human side, is nonetheless powerful enough to sustain God's people even through persecution and martyrdom. But the power of that relationship is not available to those who seek God casually, as one among many attractive options. No, "I am my beloved's and he is mine." Only those who commit themselves fully are vindicated in faith—even, like Akiba himself, on the other side of death.

FORMIDABLE BEAUTY
Song of Songs 6:4–10

(Man)

6:4 You are beautiful as Tirzah, my love,
comely as Jerusalem,
terrible as an army with banners.

5 Turn away your eyes from me,
for they overwhelm me!
Your hair is like a flock of goats,
moving down the slopes of Gilead.

6 Your teeth are like a flock of ewes,
that have come up from the washing;
all of them bear twins,
and not one among them is bereaved.

7 Your cheeks are like halves of a pomegranate
behind your veil.

8 There are sixty queens and eighty concubines,
and maidens without number.

9 My dove, my perfect one, is the only one,
the darling of her mother,
flawless to her that bore her.
The maidens saw her and called her happy;
the queens and concubines also,
and they praised her.

10 "Who is this that looks forth like the dawn,
fair as the moon, bright as the sun,
terrible as an army with banners?"

The poem begins with similes comparing the woman to the capital cities of the Northern and Southern Kingdoms of Israel and Judah. Tirzah was the first capital of the Northern Kingdom, following the division of the united kingdom of David and Solomon. Its name, which means "desirable, pleasing," is well suited to a lovely woman. Indeed, Tirzah sometimes appears as a woman's name (Num. 26:33); it might be rendered, "Desirée." Yet even if the name is suitable, it is an odd thing to compare a woman to a city. (Cities are often personified as women in the Bible, but the reverse is unparalleled elsewhere.) No one in our culture could say, "You are laid out as symmetrically as Washington, D.C.," and expect the compliment to be well received. The fact that this poet does make such a comparison is another important indicator that the Song is something more than ordinary love poetry. Israel's history and spiritual geography are embedded in the Song too deeply to be ignored.

"Comely as Jerusalem"—the adjective "comely" is uncommon in Hebrew, yet it occurs five times in the Song of Songs, which suggests that the poet uses it with deliberate effect. Indeed, the Bible shows a very interesting pattern of usage for this word. Half of its eight occurrences outside the Song refer to Jerusalem and the Temple, where holiness and prayer are "comely" (e.g., Psalm 93:5). Thus the word reinforces the link between the woman and the Holy City that has been building throughout the poem.

More puzzling is the connection between the woman and Tirzah. Why should the Northern capital, Jerusalem's rival and sometimes her enemy, be mentioned at all in a work that focuses on and exalts the Southern capital? The effect of the dual comparison is that the woman reunites in herself the two kingdoms that together make up the people and the land of Israel. She is, in her lovely person, a symbol of peace and unity, a symbol at once both political and spiritual. As we shall see in the next section (6:13–7:13), the theme of peace is central to the identity of this woman, who ultimately declares herself "as one who finds peace" (8:14). Modern readers should be wary of an over-spiritualized notion of peace. The political dimensions of the poet's vision should not be dismissed as irrelevant to its theological message. All the biblical writers recognized something that modern Western Christians tend to forget: Religious and political realities are inextricably bound together. God's blessing of peace is not a wholly inward experience. It is experienced also in the body politic, which in ancient Israel was not distinct from the faith community.

The assertion of unity appears again in verse 9. The Hebrew word order makes this emphasis even more clear than the NRSV translation suggests: "*One* is she, my dove, my perfect (one). *One* is she to her mother" (v. 9, AT). We might guess that the intended meaning is something like this: "Mother Israel" (see the comment at 3:1–5) knows the essential integrity of her offspring. But it would have been hard for the poet's contemporaries to relate this vision of peace and unity to the political realities they knew. Assuming that the Song dates from the Persian or the Hellenistic period, it had been well over five hundred years since there had been any unified people Israel. Both kingdoms had by now lost their political independence, the ten Northern tribes had been nearly obliterated, and many of the Southerners were living in permanent exile in Babylon and Egypt. Yet in the face of these disheartening facts, this poet says, in effect, "I have a dream," a dream of God's people appearing again, in beauty and in strength, as one people.

The theological question for us is: Is this poet speaking to one historical situation, now long past, or may we also draw inspiration from this expression of longing for unity? Listening to the Song, might we begin to dream our own impossible dream of a church that is truly "one, holy, catholic, and universal"? We have long accepted as permanent, divisions between rich and poor, Protestants and Catholics, Eastern and Western churches, liberals and conservatives, evangelicals and workers for social justice. "Where there is no vision, a people runs amok" (Prov. 29:18, AT). Inspired by this poet's vision of unity, we may pray that the church at last overcome the divisions that shame us and badly mute our witness to the God who is One (Deut. 6:4).

The final verse of this section is the most arresting image of the woman's power in the entire Song. The translation "terrible" (vv. 4, 10) carries the wrong inference. The Hebrew word (*'ayummah*) implies a presence that is compellingly attractive and yet also daunting. The French expression "*Formidable!*" captures the intended ambiguity perfectly. In English, we might say she is literally "terrific." The image here may owe something to graphic representations of the goddess Ishtar, who is often portrayed surrounded by sun, moon, and stars (v. 10). Ishtar was worshiped as the patroness of war as well as love. (The combination of sex and violence was as compelling for ancients as it is for us.) Her Canaanite counterpart Astarte was worshiped in Israel even by Solomon, as the biblical historians note disapprovingly (1 Kings 11:33). It seems that some Judeans continued to worship her, as "the queen of heaven" (Jer. 44:17–19, 25), up to the time of the Babylonian exile. Perhaps the poet is intentionally creating a positive counter-type to that ancient goddess of love and war with this larger-than-life figure of a woman who combines sex appeal with *peace*.

It is intriguing to compare this luminous image with that of the prophet-poet known as the "Third Isaiah." He represents Israel, restored from exile, as a marriageable woman, highly desirable to her God (Isa.

62:4; see the comment at 4:8–15). Moreover, part of "her" allure is associated with light:

> Arise, shine, for your light has come,
> and the glory of the LORD has risen upon you . . .
> Nations shall go to your light,
> and kings to the brightness of your rising.
> Look up, look around and see:
> all of them are gathered, they come to you!
> Your sons from afar are coming,
> and your daughters carried, nursing.
>
> (Isa. 60:1–4, AT)

Isaiah's vision is explicitly evangelical; God's light is what draws the nations, as well as the returning Israelites. Could there be an implicit evangelical element in the Song's portrait of a woman who is beautiful enough to attract, daunting enough to compel respect, and exclusively devoted to a Lover who is himself "radiant . . . , distinguished among ten thousand" (Song 5:10)?

THE DANCING SHULAMMITE
Song of Songs 6:13–7:13

(*Crowd*)
   6:13 **Return, return, O Shulammite!**
       Return, return, that we may look upon you.

(*One of the Crowd? Woman? Man?*)
       Why should you look upon the Shulammite,
       as upon a dance before two armies?

(*Crowd or Man*)
   7:1 **How graceful are your feet in sandals,**
       O queenly maiden!
       Your rounded thighs are like jewels,
       the work of a master hand.
     2 **Your navel is a rounded bowl**
       that never lacks mixed wine.
       Your belly is a heap of wheat,
       encircled with lilies.
     3 **Your two breasts are like two fawns,**

twins of a gazelle.
4 Your neck is like an ivory tower.
Your eyes are pools in Heshbon,
by the gate of Bath-rabbim.
Your nose is like a tower of Lebanon,
overlooking Damascus.
5 Your head crowns you like Carmel,
and your flowing locks are like purple;
a king is held captive in the tresses.

(Man)

6 How fair and pleasant you are,
O loved one, delectable maiden!
7 You are stately as a palm tree,
and your breasts are like its clusters.
8 I say I will climb the palm tree
and lay hold of its branches.
O may your breasts be like clusters of the vine,
and the scent of your breath like apples,
9 and your kisses like the best wine

(Woman)

that goes down smoothly,
gliding over lips and teeth.*
10 I am my beloved's,
and his desire is for me.
11 Come, my beloved,
let us go forth into the fields,
and lodge in the villages;
12 let us go out early to the vineyards,
and see whether the vines have budded,
whether the grape blossoms have opened
and the pomegranates are in bloom.
There I will give you my love.
13 The mandrakes give forth fragrance,
and over our doors are all choice fruits,
new as well as old,
which I have laid up for you,
O my beloved.

*See below for a re-translation of verse 9b–c.

Verse 6:13 is altogether a puzzle. Does it conclude the preceding verses, or
mark the opening of a new section, or is it an isolated fragment? "Return"—

from where and *to* where? Who is speaking here, and to whom? Several possibilities may be noted. It seems that a crowd is calling the woman out to perform (6:13a). She then replies teasingly, "Why would you want to watch me?" Or perhaps it is her lover who asks, "Why should you look . . . ," maybe implying that they can scarcely appreciate what they see. Or maybe a member of the crowd calls out, in effect saying, "What's the big deal?" I am treating 6:13 as an introduction to the following *wasf* (a descriptive poem, 7:1–5). The description may be spoken by the man, or perhaps by one of the crowd. In this context, it seems to describe the woman as a dancer, although the only mention of dance is in 6:13. While the *wasf* never specifies that her body is in motion, the fact that it begins with her beautiful feet (the other *wasfs* begin with the head) creates that impression.

The fact that it is so difficult to reconstruct the scene behind the words here should be taken seriously; evidently the poet's interest does not lie primarily in the action. What is certain and striking about this passage is the words themselves. Specifically, several words in this poem seem to be of particular importance for our understanding of the identity of this woman, here for the first and only time called "the Shulammite." By following the associations they evoke and the echoes they create with other biblical texts, we may penetrate more deeply into the poet's intention.

The term "the Shulammite" is never explained in the Song, nor does it appear elsewhere in the Bible. It sounds like a word derived from a place name: compare "the Shunammite woman" from the town of Shunem (2 Kings 4:8–37). Sometimes such a geographic designation attains almost the status of a nickname, for example, "Mary, called Magdalen" (Luke 8:2), after her town of Magdala. The difficulty, however, is that there is no known place called Shulam/Shulem, from which the name might be derived, nor is anyone else in the Bible called by this name. Probably it is an original coinage, and anyone who has persevered thus far through the Song knows that the poet's imagination is not confined to the kind of reality reported by maps. Our task as readers and interpreters is to exercise our own imaginations in drawing fruitful inferences from the hints we are given. Three suggestions are offered here.

First, as many commentators have seen, the most likely geographic association is with Jerusalem, otherwise known as Salem (Gen. 14:18; Psalm 76:2), *Shalem* in Hebrew. In other words, the poet is confirming the identification of the woman with Jerusalem. Here, toward the end of a book that never says anything quite directly, we have an almost-but-not-quite-explicit statement that one of the things we are to see in this portrait of a lovely and beloved woman is the city that itself is the focus of so much love, human as well as divine. Thus the psalmist calls Jerusalem "the joy of the whole earth" (Psalm 48:2) and blesses those who love her (Psalm 122:6). The idea that we are meant to see Jerusalem here is reinforced by the otherwise enigmatic comparison of the Shulammite to "a dance before two armies" (or "two [armed] camps"). Although the words themselves seem clear, the meaning is highly uncertain. A reasonable guess is that this refers to Jerusalem's geographical and political position "between the two camps" of the Northern and the Southern Kingdoms. Somewhat like Washington, D.C., it was located near the border between North and South, yet belonged originally to neither (the original "Salem" was a Canaanite city). Possibly that is the reason that David, an astute politician, chose it as his capital. Although the unification of Israel and Judah dissolved immediately after Solomon's death, the romance of Jerusalem as capital of a united people never entirely faded.

Second, the coinage Shulammite has the root letters *sh-l-m*, which immediately connote to a Hebrew speaker the notion of *shalom*, "peace, well-being." The same root letters appear in the Hebrew name *Yerûsha-layim* (Jerusalem), which probably means "foundation of peace." Thus this verse reinforces the suggestion above (see the comments on 6:10 and 8:10), that there is an important association between this woman and peace. The Shulammite is the counterpart to Solomon (Hebrew *Shlomo*, again from the same root), "the man of peace" (see the comment at 1:1)—but without his checkered history! The biblical historian shows that Solomon's religious infidelities were the cause of the dissolution of the united kingdom (1 Kings 11:31–33). By contrast, the Shulammite embodies a peace that binds together the whole people and land of Israel. At another level, countless readers through the millennia have seen in her (quite rightly) a figure of the soul at peace with her God.

These two lines of interpretation leave one problem yet unaddressed. The connection with Jerusalem/*Shalem*, the city of *shalom*, would be more obvious if the woman were called "the Shalemmite." Why does the poet adopt this variation? Perhaps because the poet is simultaneously pointing to another set of associations. So I offer a third suggestion to supplement the other two. As noted above, "the Shulammite" closely resembles—and may be intended to evoke—another geographic nickname, "the Shunammite," a person from the village of Shunem in the Jezreel Valley. In fact, there are two "Shunammite women" in the Old Testament. The first one, who has no other name, has a remarkable story (2 Kings 4:8–37). A wealthy woman, she regularly offers hospitality to the prophet Elijah and even builds a rooftop annex for his private use. She is childless; in return for her kindness, he promises that she will "embrace a son," though her husband is old. A son is born, and a few years pass. One morning the boy sickens, and by noon he is dead in his mother's lap. She rides to the prophet and demands that he call the boy back from death—which he does! The Shunammite woman's story is an especially dramatic instance of God's power and grace, giving life against the odds and restoring it against all odds. The poet may well have seen her story as a type for the history of Jerusalem after the exile, when "her" children were restored, against all odds, from living death. So the identities of *Shalem*/Jerusalem and Elijah's Shunammite woman are folded together in the term "the Shulammite."

The poet's imagination may also extend to the second Shunammite woman, Abishag (1 Kings 1–2), the last consort of David. She figures in the story as a beautiful political pawn. When David dies, his sons fight and kill one another over the question of who will marry Abishag and succeed to the throne (1 Kings 2:13–23). Abishag the Shunammite is *the accompaniment to royal power*, and also to some extent its victim. By contrast, the Shulammite embodies power. Ultimately, with her lover the "king" (7:5; see also 1:4, 12), she calls into question royal pretensions to power (8:11–12). Thus she represents *the incorporation and integrity of power*—in a woman, in a united people, in a soul unified in its devotion to one "Beloved" (vv. 10–13).

In light of this study of the Shulammite's identity, it is possible to make some suggestion about another key word, the charge "Return!" Repeated here four times, the word (*shûvî*) rings in our ears; we are meant to ponder it and its associations. The verb occurs in this particular form (the feminine singular imperative) only a few other times in the Bible. Therefore a mind steeped in the language of the Bible—as was the poet's own, and "she" assumes the same in her audience—hears echoes of the other places of its occurrence. What comes to mind first is Jeremiah 31, a passage that we already know is in the poet's mind. Immediately following the stunning assurance of God's visceral longing for Israel—"my guts churn for him" (see the comment at 5:2–8)—Jeremiah appeals to the prostrate and scattered people. Significantly, Israel is here imaged as a young and beloved woman. Twice she is called to "return":

> Return (*shûvî*), O virgin Israel,
> return to these your cities.
> (Jer. 31:21)

The same moving appeal to return is spoken by the poet of the book of Psalms—strikingly, in an address to his/her own soul (the word *nefesh*, "soul," is always feminine gender in Hebrew and therefore can be addressed as a female):

> I love the LORD, for he has heard
> my voice, my supplications. . . .
> Return (*shûvî*), O my soul, to your rest,
> for the LORD has been generous to you.
>   (Psalm 116:1, 7, AT)

It is crucial to note that in both cases, the call, "Return!" is based upon the prior assurance and demonstration of God's love. Israel called back to her land, the soul called back to contented rest in God—it is appropriate to hear both these echoing behind the call to the Shulammite in this consummate song of love.

The descriptive poem that follows (7:1–9a) is almost like two pictures superimposed one upon another, which combine but never fully blend. We are looking through loving eyes at both the Shulammite's body and the land of Israel. It is notable that, for all the apparently detailed descriptions of the lovers, and especially the woman, no clear impression of their physical appearance emerges. I can conjure up in my mind a picture of Helen of Troy, but not of the Shulammite. The history of religious art confirms the fact that this biblical beauty does not sit for portraits. There are countless Bathshebas and Ruths and Judiths, but the Shulammite is almost entirely absent. (Two modern painters, Marc Chagall and Salvador Dali, have painted her, but both artists' work is characteristically abstract or highly symbolical. Therefore they might be seen as the exceptions that prove the rule.) By contrast, what does emerge with clarity is a picture of the land of Israel at its peak of productivity. The poet seems to range through the country, looking at wheat fields in the northern Jezreel Valley, vineyards in the central hill country, date palms in the southern and eastern deserts. It is an imperial view, taking in also the surrounding lands with which Solomon entered into commercial relations. Damascus and Heshbon were wealthy cities strategically located on the King's Highway, the major route from Western Asia to the Red Sea. Carmel points to the Phoenician coast, the center of the famous "purple industry." Dye was extracted from the shells of mussels found only along this coastline. Since it took eight thousand shells to produce one gram of dye, purple was in ancient times exclusively the color of royalty. The Shulammite's purple hair may sound grotesque to us, but the poet means that she is "a natural aristocrat," who captures "a king" in her glowing dark hair.

Just because the images of the woman are intertwined with and even submerged in those of the land, they should not be interpreted with too much anatomical specificity. Much ink has been spilled over her navel brimming with mixed wine. Navels are not normally noted for holding liquid; is this a euphemism for the pudenda and its intoxicating liquor? Again, commentators puzzle over the picture of a belly rounded like wheat and edged with lilies: Is she fat? pregnant? Is she wearing a fancy girdle, or are "lilies" a reference to the erotic zone? Rather than isolating individual elements in this way, it is better to let the several images create a whole picture in our minds. The Hebrew of 7:2 is more beautiful than the translation shows: "Your navel is a cup of the moon"; presumably the roundness of the full moon is envisioned here. In combination with the heap of threshed and winnowed wheat, one might imagine a golden harvest moon and a field gleaming in its light. The overall impression is one of lush fertility in a dry land where vegetation can never be taken for granted. Therefore the Bible represents it as the chief tangible sign of God's blessing: "The LORD will give what is good, and our land will yield its increase" (Psalm 85:12). Lilies (v. 2) crown the idealized picture of woman and land, and that detail is especially intriguing. Ordinary wheat fields might be hedged by thorns to keep out cattle and prevent the harvested wheat from blowing; lilies would hardly serve the same purpose. But their function is evocative, not practical. The fertile zone of the woman's body produces wine and wheat, which were the central elements of Temple sacrifice. Is it more than coincidence that her fields are edged with lilies, which as we have seen, figure so prominently in the ornamentation of the Temple, the earthly Garden of God (see the comment at 4:8–5:1)?

In verse 9, the woman suddenly interrupts her lover and finishes his speech. The NRSV translation misses this and alters the text so the verse reads like continuous speech of the man. But intertwining speech is part of the play of love. An accurate translation of the Hebrew text of verse 9 is as follows

> Man: and your *palate* like the best wine . . .
> Woman: . . . that flows smoothly for my lover (*dôdî*),
>   gliding over the lips of sleepers.

The word *dôdî*, "my lover," the woman's distinctive term of endearment for her lover, marks the last two lines as her speech. Entering into his fantasy about her kisses, she invites him to share the blissful rest of lovers.

Now that she has the floor, she takes full advantage and holds it for most of the rest of the Song. Some of the woman's most memorable and important statements occur in these final moments of the Song. For the last time she repeats the formula for their mutual devotion (see also 2:16; 6:3), but this third time with a change. "I am my beloved's, *and his desire is for me*" (v. 10). The variation in the formula focuses our attention on the word "desire" (*teshûqah*), which stands out also because it is a rare word, occurring in only two other places in the Bible (Gen. 3:16; 4:7). Those earlier occurrences are crucial for understanding the present passage and the meaning of the Song altogether. They return us to the Garden of Eden, on which we know the poet has meditated profoundly. The word appears first and unforgettably in God's speech to Eve and Adam, after they have eaten from the forbidden tree. God is now telling what life will be like in a world drastically altered by human disobedience. To "the woman" God says: "For your man is your desire—but he will rule over you!" (Gen. 3:16, AT). The human beings have suddenly "fallen" from paradise into the world as we know it, and this fearful sentence points to one of the most grievous ills of our world: the unequal power relation between woman and man that has been a feature of nearly every society from biblical times to the present. It is a striking instance of the realism of the Bible. The pull of both emotional and physical desire—both are included in the term *teshûqah*—holds many women in situations that are demeaning, abusive, even deadly. (It is well to remember that in the ancient world, sex was dangerous for women. Many if not most women died of illnesses related to childbirth.)

Against this background, the Shulammite's exultant statement that the man's desire is *for her* expresses more than personal pride. The statement is literally "radical"; it probes the roots (Latin, *radices*) of God's intention for human beings. She proclaims that the ancient distortion is now corrected; the original symmetry that obtained between woman and man is restored. In the creation account itself, there is no hint of the woman's subordination. Male and female are equally "in the image of God" (Gen. 1:27); the woman is "a helper as [the man's] partner" (2:20). "Helper" does not imply lesser status; on the contrary, the term is used of God (Deut. 33:7; Psalm 115:9, 10, 11, etc.). Therefore this scene in a blooming garden (vv. 11–13) returns humanity to conditions that obtained, however briefly, in Eden. Woman and man meet in full equality of power and desire. She gives him her love freely (v. 12), without fear of penalty.

The Shulammite's proclamation also implies that the primeval rupture has been repaired at another level, namely in the relationship between humanity and God. The background for this reading is the second appearance of the word *teshûqah*, in the story of Cain and Abel. God sees Cain's deadly anger toward his brother and warns him: "Sin is a lurking beast at the door; its desire [*teshûqah*] is for you, yet you may rule over him!" (Gen. 4:7, AT). The mythical language should not mislead us; the Bible is unblinkingly realistic about the nature of sin. "Sin" is not just a fancy word for human weakness; it is a real power, a spiritual force at work in this post-Edenic world. As probably most of us have felt at some time, sin does not just wait for us to stumble into it. Sometimes it seems to be active in seeking us out, eager to prey on our weaknesses (see 1 Peter 5:8). Over against this strong warning of sin's "desire" for us, the Shulammite's declaration can be read as stating that the desire of the Divine Lover is also directed toward us. This is the good news: however eagerly sin lurks to catch us, God seeks us even more ardently. To the extent that we can receive and respond to God's burning desire for us, we shall indeed achieve mastery over sin.

This is an astonishing truth, which the Bible repeats over and over, straining to overcome our incredulity. God, who gives us everything, at the same time desires us wholly. Augustine states the paradox sharply in his comment on the story of Jesus and the Samaritan woman at the well: "He asks for a drink, and he promises a drink. He is in need as one who is going to receive; and he is rich as one who is going to satisfy. 'If you knew,' he says, 'the gift of God' (John 4:10)" (*Tractates on the Gospel of John* 15.12, p. 85).

It is so hard to believe that God could be bound to us in the genuine need that love creates. Can it really be so, that the "King is held captive in the tresses" (v. 9)? Nothing else but God's intense, unslaking desire for humanity makes sense of the biblical story, from the calling of Abraham to the Incarnation of God in Christ, even to Jesus' death nailed to a cross. John of the Cross, the Spanish mystic whose poems and prayers were inspired by the Song, offers a wonderful image to guide our meditation on this wonder: "It is indeed credible that a bird of lowly flight can capture the royal eagle of the heights [Deut. 32:11], if this eagle descends with the desire of being captured" (John of the Cross, *The Spiritual Canticle*, stanza 31.8, p. 598).

THE STRENGTH OF LOVE
Song of Songs 8:6–14

The Seal (8:6–7)

(*Woman*)
> 8:6 Set me as a seal upon your heart,
>   as a seal upon your arm;
>   for love is strong as death,
>   passion [jealousy] fierce as the grave.
>   Its flashes are flashes of fire,
>   a raging flame.

⁷ **Many waters cannot quench love,**
neither can floods drown it.
If one offered for love
all the wealth of one's house,
it would be utterly scorned.

These are the most famous lines in the poem, which often appear in wedding services. Many commentators think that they properly form the conclusion to the Song, and that the following verses are a collection of fragments that have been tacked on. If this view is correct (and it may be), then certainly the Song would conclude on a crescendo. This is the one "objective" statement about the supreme value of love. Whereas the rest of the Song is largely composed of the lovers' personal speeches to one another, the tone here is magisterial, the claim sweeping. Love is not only uniquely precious; it is also powerful to stand against the threats of chaos and annihilation, frequently represented in biblical poetry by the image of "mighty waters" (Psalms 77:16–19; 69:1–2, 14–15; Isa. 8:7–8; 43:2; Hab. 3:15, etc.) As I shall try to show, these lines function equally well as a theological statement and a declaration about human love.

"Set me as a seal": In the ancient world, people often wore personal seals on cords around the neck or the arm. Physical proximity to the lover is part of what the woman seeks, but the seal image suggests much more. The seal mark was a personal signature, affixed to letters, business contracts, and legal documents. Therefore the seal was identified with a person's commitments and integrity; it marked one's word as binding (see Gen. 38:18–26). Similarly, the woman wants to be wholly identified with her lover's intentions and commitments. Set as a seal, she becomes a visible sign of who this lover is, and what he stands for.

The poet-theologian may have in mind a remarkable image from the prophet Jeremiah. God wears Israel's anointed ruler like a seal ring. Dramatically, when the people go into exile, that ring, signaling God's commitment to them, is torn off (Jer. 22:24)! "Set me as a seal"—the inference may be that now it is time for God to put on a new signet (see also Hag. 2:23), a new sign of commitment. I have suggested that the woman may be seen variously as a figure for the unified people of Israel, for Jerusalem, for the lush earth, for the soul intimately bound to God. What the seal image contributes to our understanding is that each of these can serve as a "stamp" of God's identity, a verification of God's loving intention toward the world. There is always a public dimension to intimacy with God. Paradoxically, when our intense personal longing is answered and we are drawn into the inner circle of God's trust, then we may be "set as a seal" and bear public witness out of the most profound intimacy.

"For love is strong as death": Seals were worn as protective amulets, engraved with sacred words (Prov. 6:20–22) or (in pagan cultures) pictures of deities. Could this image of the seal suggest that love itself stands as a kind of protection against what we most fear from death—that our identity will be obliterated, that all we are and try to do finally counts for nothing? Note: the biblical text does not claim that love is stronger than death. All lovers will die. Nonetheless, it affirms that love and death are more *alike* than (as we often think) polar opposites. What can we learn about love by considering how it resembles death?

Love is the one thing in this life that *may*—if we let it—consume us as fully as death *will* one day consume us. Death consumes us even against our will, but we must yield to love. But for those who do yield, love consumes like fire; it is "a raging flame." A literal rendering of the Hebrew reads: "a flame *of the LORD*." Hebrew writers sometimes use the divine name as an intensifying term. The comparable English idiom (though drawn from the opposite end of the spiritual spectrum) would be "a hell of a flame." So the NRSV translation suggests: "a raging flame." Yet our poet's habits and the image itself suggest there is here a deliberate echo of the religious tradition. Israel knows God as "a consuming fire" (Deut. 4:24; Heb. 12:29; see also Isa. 31:9; Zech. 2:5). Love and death, love and flame of God—together these comparisons may help us to see that love, which comes to us as a gift from God, is not undone by death. Rather, love is the best preparation for what Christians have traditionally called a holy death.

How can that be? Because love teaches us to give of ourselves, ever more deeply, to God and neighbor. It enables us to give in costly ways, yet at the same time joyfully. To the extent that we give ourselves up in love, we are protected against the fear of death, which otherwise enslaves every human being (Heb. 2:15). It is a simple truth, but hard to hold fast: Those who have already been consumed by love can never be annihilated. "It is no longer I who live, but Christ who lives in me" (Gal. 2:20). A fifteenth-century Christian prayer (used in a modern hymn) takes exactly this imagery of love and fire to express the work of God's love in the human soul:

> Come down, O Love divine, seek thou this soul of mine,
> and visit it with thine own ardor glowing. . . .
> O let it freely burn, till earthly passions turn
> to dust and ashes in its heat consuming;
> and let thy glorious light shine ever on my sight,
> and clothe me round, the while my path illumining.
> (Hymn 516, *The Hymnal 1982*)

The Song of Songs enables us to glimpse the likeness between love and death. This in turn helps us understand why Christians have traditionally prayed not to die "suddenly and unprepared" (The Great Litany, *Book of Common Prayer*, 149). Viewed from a Christian perspective, death, for all its sadness, is nonetheless an opportunity. Death is our chance finally to give ourselves wholly to God and thus be drawn fully into the *life* of God. Yet using that opportunity well is difficult. It requires careful preparation, in most cases years of training in love. The good news of both the New Testament and the Old is that, contrary to what our culture tells us, death does not defeat what love has built. Rather love's work will be brought to completion when at last we stand fully before God, "in [whose] presence there is fullness of joy" (Psalm 16:11).

"*Passion* [is] fierce as the grave": The Hebrew word *qin'ah* is more accurately translated "jealousy." It refers to the kind of love that gives a single focus to all desire and likewise demands a singular response from the loved one. But this word creates a problem for us who live in a psychologically attuned age. We are well aware that jealousy is often a neurotic expression of desire. The biblical writers know this too, and they consistently render a negative judgment on human jealousy; it is "rot to the bones" (Prov. 14:30)! Yet the present verse seems to view jealousy positively; it is associated with love as the most valuable, as well as the strongest, of passions. How can that be?

There is only one context in which the biblical writers ascribe positive value to jealousy. The passion of jealousy is good—indeed, necessary—when it rises to defend the unique love that obtains between God and Israel. The psalmist cries out to God: "Jealousy for your house has consumed me" (Psalm 69:9 [in Hebrew 69:10], AT, and John 2:17; see also Psalm 119:139). In imagery that is strikingly close to our passage, Moses declares to Israel: "For the LORD your God is a consuming fire, a jealous God" (Deut. 4:24). The same two ideas—fire and divine jealousy—are associated in Deuteronomy 32:21–24, which shares with our passage the unusual word here translated "flashes." These echoes strongly suggest that the poet intends to leave us here, at the end of the Song, with a powerful reminder of God's burning emotion. So often in the past the prophets *threatened* Israel with God's enraged jealousy (Jeremiah 2; Hosea 2, 4–5), when "she" had run promiscuously after other gods. Now, in this poem of mutually devoted love, jealousy in all its fierceness, "a flame of the LORD," is a sign of *promise*. With this image, the poet may be intentionally drawing upon the words of the prophet Zechariah, proclaimed to the exiles in Babylon: "Thus says the LORD of Hosts, I am jealous for Jerusalem and for Zion, with a great jealousy" (Zech. 1:14, AT; cf. 8:2). The city and its Temple will be rebuilt as a home for the returnees, and then "I will be for her, says the LORD, a wall of fire round about" (Zech. 2:5 [in Hebrew 2:9], AT).

Who Is in Charge Here? (Song of Songs 8:8–12)

(*Brothers*)
> 8:8 We have a little sister,
> and she has no breasts.
> What shall we do for our sister,
> on the day that she is spoken for?
> 9 If she is a wall,
> we will build upon her a battlement of silver;
> but if she is a door,
> we will enclose her with boards of cedar.

(*Woman*)
> 10 I was a wall,
> and my breasts were like towers;
> then I was in his eyes
> as one who finds peace.

(*Man or Woman*)
> 11 Solomon had a vineyard at Baal-hamon;
> he entrusted the vineyard to keepers;
> each one was to bring for its fruit a thousand pieces of silver.
> 12 My vineyard, my very own, is for myself;
> you, O Solomon, may have the thousand,
> and the keepers of the fruit two hundred!

It may be that the theory noted above is correct, and verses 6–7 are intended to conclude the Song (see the preceding comment). The remaining verses cannot be assembled into a coherent final scene. Nonetheless, one structural feature indicates that they are not wholly random. A number of the elements from the first chapter recur here in verses 8–14: the domineering brothers, Solomon, "my vineyard" and the vineyard keepers, the man's companions. This suggests that there may have been a deliberate attempt to create a framing structure for the Song as a whole. However, in its present form the Song does not come to a rousing—or even particularly satisfying—conclusion. It simply stops, and that itself may be significant for our understanding of the realities to which it points (see the following remarks on vv. 13–14).

Suddenly and for the first time, we hear what seems to be the voice of the brothers. They set themselves up as supervisors of their younger sister's sexual behavior, and what is more, as proprietors of her person. It was customary in Israel for father and brothers to establish a woman in an honorable marriage (see Genesis 24). When the sad necessity arose, her brothers might avenge a woman's violated honor (Genesis 34; 2 Samuel 13). But contrary to custom, the Song represents a world where women are competent in sexual matters. As we have seen, this young woman looks only to her mother for guidance (see the comment on 3:1–5). In that context, the brothers' speculation about how they will "handle" their sister is presumptuous and deluded, and she treats it as such.

The brothers envision two alternatives. On the one hand, she may be a solid city wall, presumably safe against intruders. The "wall," if such she proves to be, will be crowned with silver to honor its resistance. They are using a well-known metaphor for self-control:

> A city breached—no [defense] wall;
> [So] a person whose spirit has no restraint.
> (Prov. 25:28, AT)

But it is possible also that with this image of the wall the brothers are giving themselves away. Could they be unconsciously identifying themselves as "those keepers of the walls" (5:7) who earlier beat up the young woman for her unconventional behavior?

On the other hand, she may be a door. An ancient city would have a wooden door in its defense wall, but of course it could be readily opened from inside the city. Apparently this is what the brothers fear, so they utter a dire threat if their sister proves to be a door: literally, "We will *lay siege to her* with planks of cedar." Her own brothers will attack in righteous indignation if she has admitted "the enemy."

In response, the confident young woman picks up their image but uses it to counter their presumption. Indeed she is a wall, possessed of both strength and personal restraint. Moreover, contrary to her big brothers' condescending view, she is fully mature, her breasts well-formed, "like towers" (v. 10). But, as she implies, a strong city need not pursue an isolationist policy. She is able both to defend herself and, as we know, to admit the *one* whom she chooses. Through her discretion in this matter she "finds peace" for her lover and herself. Her brothers may be ready to go to war, but she asserts herself as a city that actively makes peace. With this subtle use of poetic imagery she defuses the common image of male sexual advance as conquest, an image which is still current in our day. We have not yet learned as much as we could from the Shulammite!

At another level, the metaphor of a city at peace may be seen as an oblique reference to the name Jerusalem, which is popularly interpreted as "foundation of peace" (see the comment at 6:13). In light of all the ways in which the poet seems to be drawing a connection between that city and this figure of a woman, probably we are meant to hear in this speech the voice of the figure that other biblical poets name, more than two dozen times, "Daughter/Fair Maiden Zion" (*Bat Zion*, Psalm 9:14; Isa. 37:22; Jer. 6:23) or "my daughter-people" (Jer. 6:26). The prophets and psalmists evoke her often with anguished affection. But here the poet's pleasure is unmistakable as that beloved figure, now grown up into strength, asserts that she is ready to receive in peace those who come to worship the Divine Lover.

The speaker in verses 11–12 may be either the man or the woman. Although the point is the same in either case, I am inclined to see this as the man's retort, corresponding to the woman's, to those who misconceive and misuse love. Solomon is the butt of his jibe. We know of no real place named Baal-hamon, but the name itself makes the desired point. It means "master/husband of a multitude" or alternately, "owner of a lot [of wealth]." The Song throughout emphasizes the unique value of "the one" (8:9; see also 2:3; 5:10). Therefore this name mocks Solomon as the poor rich man, whose silver and gold are only a foil to show up the superior wealth of love. Though master of many cities and lands, Solomon oppressed his own people and thus destroyed the empire (1 Kings 12:4). Moreover, our poet imagines that the husband of "a thousand" wives and concubines (1 Kings 11:3) had to give a share to "the keepers of the fruit": the harem guards! Thus the Shulammite's lover returns us to a theme that often occupies the sages of Proverbs: Wisdom and real happiness lie in shunning too much wealth, too many lovers, and treasuring what is "my very own."

The Final Exchange (Song of Songs 8:13–14)

(Man)
> 13 **O you who dwell in the gardens,**
> **my companions are listening for your voice;**
> **let me hear it.**

(Woman)
> 14 **Make haste, my beloved,**
> **and be like a gazelle**

or a young stag
upon the mountains of spices!

The Song ends, as it began, in the middle of things. Has anything happened? Yes, something. She who once tended the vineyards of others, neglecting her own, now "dwells in gardens." He asks for a word—but the answer that comes is disconcerting: "Flee!" (The NRSV's "Make haste" is incorrect.) Probably she is calling him to flee "the companions" and come alone to her "mountains of spices" (see also 2:17; 4:6). But we cannot be sure; maybe she is telling him to flee away, that the garden is not yet wholly safe for love. This is the understanding of an early rabbinic commentary on the Song, in which Israel begs God to flee the unclean world, yet "in time of tribulation, when we pray before You, be like a roe . . . , which when it flees looks behind itself. So do You look upon us."

How different is the effect of that cry—"Flee!"—from the ending we expect in a love story: "and they lived happily ever after." Fairy tales end with a picture of static happiness; we are not encouraged to think what more might have happened to Sleeping Beauty and the Prince. Who can imagine them struggling to grow together, experiencing pain as well as joy, anger and disappointment, as all real-life lovers do? The Bible, by contrast, is relentlessly realistic, if also wildly hopeful. The Song does not end with the lovers sitting together in the garden. They are still in motion, still straining with desire, still hoping for something that is not yet given: a word, a moment of presence. The Song ends on a note of separation, uncertainty, anticipation of their next meeting. It is a realistic picture of young love. And is it not also a true picture of our life with God? For the answer to that, we must appeal to the experience of those who are closest to God, the biblical writers and the saints throughout history who have left us their common testimony: God never fully satisfies us in this world but instead continually stretches our desire toward heaven. Not satisfaction but the expansion and purification of holy desire is the surest sign of God's presence with us. So the art of the spiritual life is the art of learning to live with longing, with the eager expectation that God's presence will be felt yet again in our hearts, in our midst, and always in new ways.

Works Cited

Augustine. *Tractates on the Gospel of John, 11–27.* Translated by J. W. Rettig. *The Fathers of the Church, A New Translation.* Washington, D.C.: Catholic University of America Press, 1988.

Bernard of Clairvaux. *On the Song of Songs.* Vols. 1–4. Translated by K. Walsh and I. Edmonds. Kalamazoo, Mich.: Cistercian Publications, 1971–1980.

Berry, Wendell. *A Continuous Harmony: Essays Cultural and Agricultural.* New York: Harcourt Brace Jovanovich, 1972.

————. *The Gift of Good Land: Further Essays Cultural and Agricultural.* New York: North Point Press, 1981.

————. *The Unsettling of America.* San Francisco: Sierra Club Books, 1977.

Blakney, Raymond Bernard. *Meister Eckhart: A Modern Translation.* New York: Harper & Row, 1941.

Book of Common Prayer, The (Episcopal Church U.S.A.). New York: Church Hymnal Corporation, 1979.

Buber, Martin. *Israel: An Echo of Eternity.* New York: Farrar, Straus & Giroux, 1969.

Camp, Claudia V. *Wisdom and the Feminine in the Book of Proverbs.* Sheffield: Almond Press and JSOT Press, 1985.

Cassian, John. *Conferences.* Translated by Colm Luibheid. Classics of Western Spirituality. New York: Paulist Press, 1985.

Chesterton, G. K. *St. Francis of Assisi.* New York: G. H. Doran, 1924.

Cohen, A. *Proverbs.* Hindhead, Surrey: Soncino Press, 1945.

Donne, John. *Sermons.* 10 volumes. Edited by George Potter and Evelyn Simpson. Berkeley, Calif.: University of California Press, 1953–62.

Eliot, T. S. *The Complete Poems and Plays, 1909–1950.* New York: Harcourt, Brace & Co., 1952.

Ellul, Jacques. *Reason for Being: A Meditation on Ecclesiastes.* Grand Rapids: Wm. B. Eerdmans Publishing Co., 1990.

Gordis, Robert. *Koheleth—The Man and His World: A Study of Ecclesiastes.* New York: Schocken Books, 1968.

Gregory of Nyssa. *Homilies on Ecclesiastes: An English Version with Supporting Studies.* Proceedings of the Seventh International Colloquium on Gregory of Nyssa. Edited by Stuart G. Hall. Berlin and New York: Walter de Gruyter, 1993.

Hall, Douglas John. *Imaging God: Dominion as Stewardship.* Grand Rapids: Wm. B. Eerdmans Publishing Co.; New York: Friendship Press, 1986.

Hengel, Martin. *Judaism and Hellenism.* Philadelphia: Fortress Press, 1974 (German original, 1973).

Hofmannsthal, Hugo von. *Der weisse Fächer. Ein Zwischenspiel.* Leipzig, 1907.

Hölldobler, Bert, and Edward O. Wilson. *Journey to the Ants: A Story of Scientific Exploration.* Cambridge, Mass.: Harvard University Press, Belknap Press, 1994.

Hymnal 1982, The. New York: Church Pension Fund, 1985.

John of the Cross. *The Collected Works of St. John of the Cross.* Translated by K. Kavanaugh and O. Rodriguez. Washington, D.C.: ICS Publications, 1991.

Kierkegaard, Søren. *Either/Or.* Garden City, N.Y.: Doubleday & Co., 1959.

Kramer, Samuel. *The Sacred Marriage Rite: Aspects of Faith, Myth, and Ritual in Ancient Sumer.* Bloomington: Indiana University Press, 1969.

Lane, Belden. *Landscapes of the Sacred: Geography and Narrative in American Spirituality.* New York/Mahwah, N.J.: Paulist Press, 1988.

Lash, Nicholas. "Ministry of the Word, or Comedy and Philology." *New Blackfriars* 68 (1987): 472–83.

Leopold, Aldo. *A Sand County Almanac: With Essays on Conservation from Round River.* New York: Ballantine Books, 1966.

Lewis, C. S. *A Preface to Paradise Lost.* London: Oxford University Press, 1942.

Luther, Martin. *Notes on Ecclesiastes.* Translated by Jaroslav Pelikan. *Luther's Works,* vol. 15. St. Louis: Concordia Publishing House, 1972.

McFague, Sallie. *The Body of God: An Ecological Theology.* Minneapolis: Fortress Press, 1993.

McKane, William. *Proverbs: A New Approach.* Old Testament Library. Philadelphia: Westminster Press, 1970.

Miller, Alice. *For Your Own Good: Hidden Cruelty in Child-Rearing and the Roots of Violence.* New York: Farrar, Straus & Giroux, 1983.

Milosz, Czeslaw. *The Witness of Poetry.* Cambridge, Mass.: Harvard University Press, 1983.

Miskotte, Kornelis H. *When the Gods Are Silent.* London: William Collins Sons & Co., 1967 (Dutch original, 1956).

Newsom, Carol A. "Woman and the Discourse of Patriarchal Wisdom: A Study of Proverbs 1–9." In *Gender and Difference in Ancient Israel,* edited by Peggy Day, 142–60. Minneapolis: Fortress Press, 1989.

Origen, *The Song of Songs: Commentary and Homilies,* translated by R. P. Lawson. Westminster, Md.: Newman Press, 1957.

Perdue, Leo G. *Wisdom and Creation: The Theology of Wisdom Literature.* Nashville: Abingdon Press, 1994.

Pieper, Josef. *The Four Cardinal Virtues: Prudence, Justice, Fortitude, Temperance.* Notre Dame: University of Notre Dame Press, 1966.

———. *Leisure, the Basis of Culture.* New York: Pantheon Books, 1952.

Plato, *The Laws,* in *The Works of Plato* (vol. 5), translated by George Burges. London: Henry G. Bohn, 1852.

Potok, Chaim. *My Name Is Asher Lev.* New York: Alfred Knopf, 1972.

Pritchard, James B. *Ancient Near Eastern Texts Relating to the Old Testament.* Princeton, N.J.: Princeton University Press, 1978. Excerpts reprinted by permission of Princeton University Press.

Sales, Francis de. *Treatise on the Love of God,* trans. H. B. Mackey. Westminster, Md.: Newman Press, 1953.

Schumacher, E. F. *A Guide for the Perplexed.* New York: Harper & Row, 1977.

———. *Small Is Beautiful: Economics As If People Mattered.* New York: Harper & Row, 1973.

Sherrard, Philip. *Human Image, World Image: The Death and Resurrection of Sacred Cosmology.* Ipswich: Golgonooza Press, 1992.

Smith, George Adam. *Modern Criticism and the Preaching of the Old Testament.* New York: A. C. Armstrong & Son, 1902.

Stafford, William S. *Disordered Loves: Healing the Seven Deadly Sins.* Cambridge, Mass.: Cowley Publications, 1994.

Teresa of Avila. *The Collected Works of St. Teresa of Avila.* 2 vols. Translated by K. Kavanaugh and O. Rodriguez. Washington, D.C.: Institute of Carmelite Studies, 1976.

Turner, Denys. *Eros and Allegory: Medieval Exegesis of the Song of Songs.* Kalamazoo, Mich.: Cistercian Publications, 1995.

Visotzky, Burton L. *The Midrash on Proverbs*. New Haven: Yale University Press, 1992.

Waal, Esther de. *Seeking God: The Way of St. Benedict*. Collegeville, Minn.: Liturgical Press, 1984.

Westermann, Claus. *Roots of Wisdom: The Oldest Proverbs of Israel and Other Peoples*. Louisville, Ky.: Westminster John Knox Press, 1995.

Wiesel, Elie. *Four Hasidic Masters and Their Struggle against Melancholy*. Notre Dame, Ind.: University of Notre Dame Press, 1978.

For Further Reading

Arminjon, Blaise. *The Cantata of Love: A Verse by Verse Reading of the Song of Songs*. San Francisco: Ignatius Press, 1988.

Bernard of Clairvaux. *On the Song of Songs*. Vols. 1–4. Translated by K. Walsh and I. Edmonds. Kalamazoo, Mich.: Cistercian Publications, 1971–1980.

Clements, Ronald E. *Wisdom in Theology*. Grand Rapids: Wm. B. Eerdmans Publishing Co., 1992.

Cohen, A. *Proverbs*. Hindhead, Surrey: Soncino Press, 1945.

Ellul, Jacques. *Reason for Being: A Meditation on Ecclesiastes*. Grand Rapids: Wm. B. Eerdmans Publishing Co., 1990.

McKenzie, Alyce M. *Preaching Proverbs: Wisdom for the Pulpit*. Louisville, Ky.: Westminster John Knox Press, 1996.

Murphy, Roland. *The Song of Songs*. Hermeneia series. Minneapolis: Fortress Press, 1990.

Perdue, Leo G. *Wisdom and Creation: The Theology of Wisdom Literature*. Nashville: Abingdon Press, 1994.

Pieper, Josef. *The Four Cardinal Virtues*. Notre Dame, Ind.: University of Notre Dame Press, 1965.

Pritchard, James B. *Ancient Near Eastern Texts Relating to the Old Testament*. Princeton, N. J.: Princeton University Press, 1978.

Westermann, Claus. *Roots of Wisdom: The Oldest Proverbs of Israel and Other Peoples*. Louisville, Ky.: Westminster John Knox Press, 1995.

Note: The following abbreviations are used in this book: AT, Author's Translation; B.C.E., Before the Common Era (=B.C.); and C.E., Common Era (=A.D.)